*John Quincy
Adams*

John Quincy
ADAMS

HIS THEORY AND IDEAS

GEORGE A. LIPSKY

Foreword by Allan Nevins

THOMAS Y. CROWELL COMPANY, *New York*

Foreword

It has been usual for Americans, like Britons, to value high character in public men rather more than high intellectual attainments. History has proved it a sound attitude, for the qualities of character exhibited by Washington, Jackson, Lincoln, Lee, Cleveland, and Wilson have been more useful to their countrymen than any display of intellectual subtlety or brilliance could have been. Sagacity and judgment we need in our national leaders; but any mental endowments beyond this are of less worth to the state than integrity, courage, coolness, and magnanimity. So at any rate most Americans would say, prizing nobleness of mind more than depth of mind. Perhaps because of this general attitude the country, while recognizing the greatness of John Quincy Adams, has been more inclined to think of him as a great personality than a great intellect.

Adams made many mistakes and met many failures, but his eminence in character and spirit has been evident to all who read the history of the first half of the nineteenth century. No more intrepid, conscientious, and laborious public servant, no more honorable, earnest, and devoted leader, ever sat in the White House or lifted his voice in Congress. When, entering the Senate in Jefferson's Administration, he displayed an independence which excited antagonism on all sides of the chamber, the young man realized that he would need exceptional fortitude. "The qualities of mind most peculiarly called for," he wrote in his diary, "are firmness, perseverance, patience, coolness, and forbearance." These qualities he proceeded to exhibit, for they were inborn. He was irritable, tactless, aggressive, and humorless; but he was also an unshakable battler for principle, a man whose high pride lifted him above all pettiness, a patriot who thought of no interest but his country's, a leader of inflexible scruple.

We like to think of Adams's independence in supporting some of Jefferson's principal measures at a time when his New England friends and the Federalist Party which his father had led were exhausting the vocabulary of abuse against the President. We applaud his courage in helping report the Embargo Bill when the trading States, headed by Massachusetts, were sure it would result in their ruin. We admire the dogged tenacity with which, when made Secretary of State, he forced the Spanish envoy to sign a treaty which carried momentous benefits to the United States, and the pertinacious vigor with which he carried it through a Senate which Clay had tried to align against it. We may find his purity at times a little chilling, and his scorn of political arts more than a little unworldly. Nevertheless, we cannot but laud his firmness, as President, in rejecting all demagogic maneuvers, his Roman integrity in refusing to use appointments for political ends, and his tenacity in sticking to his own view of the tariff and internal improvements without regard to popular prejudices.

The most heroic chapters of his life remain to be written—almost as heroic as any in our annals. At the age of sixty-three he accepted election to the House of Representatives. Never did a man of his years more assiduously court toils and battles. He grew palsied, infirm of sight and hearing, subject to sudden bodily spasms; his irritability, sharpness of tongue, and combativeness increased. But though he made few friends and cohorts of enemies, his honesty, his unflinching candor, his grasp and force in handling public questions gave him a greater influence than ever before. His eloquence, struggling up through choked throat and cracked voice, hushed and awed his audience. His intervention in 1839 to bring about the organization of the chaotic House and the orderly election of a Speaker was a signal manifestation of moral power. His struggle to maintain the right of petition, and destroy the infamous gag-rule which slavery men North and South temporarily fastened upon Congress, was one of our great historic battles for principle. It was a singlehanded contest, for the overwhelming weight of the House, the press, and popular feeling seemed against him; but in the end he won, and won because his cause was right. His unwearied industry, meanwhile, gave us not only admirable state papers, but a journal which by common consent is the most valuable record of its kind ever written by an American.

But without abating our admiration for the character of John Quincy Adams, we ought to comprehend his intellectual distinction as well. As a thinker and writer, as a theorist on politics, society, and economics, he holds a high place among the early leaders of the republic. This is the neglected aspect of the man's greatness to which George A. Lipsky calls our attention in this admirably thorough analysis. It would be invidious to compare him with other thinkers of the early era; with his father, with Madison, with Gallatin, Webster, or Calhoun. But like these men, he had an incisive talent for abstract theorizing and its practical applications. He was one of our greatest nationalists, his doctrines rooted both in an intense pride in America's position among nations, and a deep fear that sectionalism might bring the republic to ruin. He had strong convictions as to democracy and its role in the modern world. He held views upon the part the government should play in adjusting, guiding, and elevating American life which belonged much more to the age of Franklin D. Roosevelt than to that of Andrew Jackson. He had ideas upon the internal development of the nation, upon commerce, upon international relations, and upon the place of the fine arts, which are well worth examining. Mr. Lipsky's book offers an illuminating introduction to this body of thought and to the mind behind it.

The author modestly says that it is only an introduction, and that more studies will be needed. That we shall have more studies is certain. It is to be wished that the publication of John Quincy Adams's *Writings,* interrupted when half finished, could be completed; it is to be hoped that within a few years Adams's papers will be thrown open to all scholars. Meanwhile Mr. Lipsky's excellent work, packed with nutriment, should have a wide reading. It proves, if proof were needed, that in John Quincy Adams we have one of the really great thinkers of American political history.

ALLAN NEVINS

Preface

Only recently has serious work been undertaken to reveal the significance of John Quincy Adams in the early history of the Republic. Before the work has been completed, the fullest justification will have been provided for the view that Adams should be placed in the very first rank of the statesmen and thinkers of our early history. No longer should it be possible to relegate him to the obscurity of a footnote or a passing reference, as he generally has been in general histories.

That we should have lived beyond the time of the centennial of his death without an adequate, full-length biographical treatment of the Sixth President appears to this writer to be a critical commentary on the vigor and perspicacity of American historical scholarship. The gigantic proportions of the task warrant no hesitation on the part of scholars to undertake it. Its very magnitude is a gauge of its importance. With special reference to the magnitude of the task, great assistance could be rendered by living members of the Adams family through a decision to release those papers at the Massachusetts Historical Society, now kept from the free inquiry of scholars under the terms of a trust.

In the preparation of the present study I have been aided by the stimulating comments and suggestions of a host of friends too numerous to mention individually. In particular, I wish to indicate my gratitude to a former colleague, Professor Robert C. L. Scott of Williams College, for having first brought to my attention the neglect from which Adams has suffered. The late Professor Raymond G. Gettell provided objective appraisal that constituted an invaluable contribution to whatever may be the merit of this study. Similar forthright and constructive comments from my present colleague, Professor Charles Aikin, were of great assistance. For whatever weaknesses it may have, they can take no responsibility, there being inescapable limits to the capacity of the best advice to remove weaknesses that are patent to all except the author himself. I wish also to express my deep appreciation to Dr. Allan Nevins for his Foreword and for the time he gave so graciously to his reading of the manuscript. His suggestions have served very materially to improve the original product. Finally, Dr. Helen Rosenberg, who undertook the gruelling task of typing the manuscript through several stages of development, has more than earned my most heartfelt thanks.

GEORGE A. LIPSKY

Contents

Foreword	v
Preface	ix

PART ONE
The Context

1.	His Scope and Stature	3
2.	Life and Career: A Survey	7

PART TWO
The Man

3.	An Adams Personality: The World Viewed from on High	49
4.	The Adams Mind: Man and the Universe	65

PART THREE
Men, Society, and Change

5.	Social Origins and Social Solidarity	87
6.	The Political and Economic Hierarchy	104
7.	Race: Slavery, the Vice of the American System	121
8.	Social Change: Evolution and Revolution	128

PART FOUR
The Political Cosmos

 9.   Government: An Instrument of God   139
10.   Government and the Moral Law   163
11.   The Institutionalizing of Political Power   192

PART FIVE
The United States: Man's Greatest Political Accomplishment

12.   The Constitution and the Union   209
13.   The Institutions of American Government   233
14.   Adams's Politics   256

PART SIX
The United States, John Quincy Adams, and International Politics

15.   The World of Nations   275
16.   Adams, a New-World Diplomat   281
17.   Adams and the Major Powers   292
18.   Major Adamsian Concepts in International Politics   299

PART SEVEN
Conclusion

19.   A Summing Up   327

Bibliography   334
Index   341

PART ONE

The Context

1

His Scope and Stature

Have finished the reading of Cerisier's 'Tableau de l'Histoire des Provinces Unies.' It gives a general idea of their history, but it is an unfinished work, written in haste, and requires much labour of the file to give it the perfection of which it is susceptible.
—MEMOIRS, *March 8, 1795*

The Sixth President of the United States, one of the most significant Americans in the period from the inception of the Republic to the threshold of the Civil War, has been unfortunately neglected by his contemporaries and his posterity.[1] The biographical studies of John Quincy Adams, for the most part, are inadequate, the majority of them having been influenced by political bias. The recently published, magnificent study of Adams as Secretary of State by Samuel Flagg Bemis is in a class apart.

Many reasons justify an exposition of his political ideology. His career has implications for an amazingly long period in the life of the American Republic. The breadth of his culture was great enough to comprehend not only the intellectual quality of his own day but also the whole intellectual tradition of Western civilization. John Quincy Adams, moreover, was a product of the eighteenth century and manifests in tremendous scope many of the intellectual trends and traditions of that century, both in his acceptance and in his rejection of

[1] As Allan Nevins has written in agreement, "It was one of the remarkable Adams line—the late Brooks Adams—who wrote that 'John Quincy Adams appears to me to be the most interesting and suggestive personage of the early nineteenth century.'" Allan Nevins (ed.), *The Diary of John Quincy Adams, 1794–1845* (New York: Longmans, Green, 1928), "Introduction," p. xi, quoted from Chapter I, by Brooks Adams, *in* Henry Adams, *The Degradation of the Democratic Dogma* (New York: Macmillan, 1931), p. 13.

those trends and traditions.   Furthermore, in the particular synthesis of his political thought there was much of importance not only for his own day but also for the mid-twentieth century.

It is important to analyze his political and social values in view of his unique personal and intellectual integrity.   John Quincy Adams's devotion to consistency and honesty in political and intellectual matters was always remarked by his more candid and objective contemporaries.   Despite his being for the greater part of his life a holder of political office, whether appointive or elective, he was remarkably capable of preserving his basic attitudes unscathed by the exigencies of the immediate political situation.   Much can be learned, therefore, of the persistent political tenets and philosophy of John Quincy Adams; and they may be systematized and brought into order, even though they must be gathered from a vast number of writings produced in the course of sixty years of public life.   As Bennett Champ Clark has pointed out, despite the very serious and compelling reasons for studying both the life and the intellectual system of this man, the monumental nature of his published writings has discouraged others from engaging in the work.[2]   However that may be, industrious selection can produce a comprehension of his general political and social values.

On first approach it might be presumed that John Quincy Adams presented to the world no systematic political philosophy.   This conclusion results from the absence of any single statement of his philosophy.   But closer study forces the conclusion that there was a body of ideas consistent within and among themselves; there was a system that, in fact, had its roots in his intellectual background and was an understandable, even though unusual, manifestation in its own day. As Brooks Adams asserts, "John Quincy Adams was not only a complex man, who stood at least a generation ahead of his time [in his theory of the purpose and function of government], but he was a scientist of the first force." [3]   He evolved a conception of life, God, and the universe into which his whole policy and his attitude on all the problems of his political life may be neatly fitted.   The erosion of time changed its configuration but not its basic quality.

[2] Bennett Champ Clark, *John Quincy Adams* (Boston: Little, Brown, 1932), pp. 11–12.
[3] Henry Adams, *The Degradation of the Democratic Dogma,* "Introduction" by Brooks Adams, p. 8.

The Adams philosophy must be gathered from a monumental fund of sources. Collected letters and writings, gigantic memoirs, the *Annals of Congress, The Register of Debates,* the *Congressional Globe,* many speeches made during the course of a long lifetime, State Papers of the Sixth President, dispatches and official letters as Secretary of State, inadequate biographies, commentaries (eulogistic and opprobious) of contemporaries, and the history of his time must be inspected and studied in the gathering of the materials that contain the political philosophy of this prodigious worker. Materials in such array present problems to anyone who would attempt their critical evaluation and exposition. Since their mass is almost boundless, the suspicion always remains that there may exist an unperused letter which might produce a qualification of a generalization that, in the light of what is otherwise known, seems sound. The refuge of one beset by such fears is the knowledge that Mr. Adams was a man singularly aware of his principles and consistent in his loyalty to them. If one lacks assurance regarding a definitive conclusion, at least he may feel confident that he may approach a true estimate of Adams's philosophy.[4] Moreover, the implicit nature of the materials cautions the investigator to seek those materials that are more explicit in setting forth ideas. It is important to avoid the dangers of assumption where the allusions are too general. It is important to avoid facile deductions where the context offers little assistance. Where, of course, the entire trend of an historical maneuver or event is known, then it is valid to assess John Quincy Adams's known role in connection with it. A most important rule demands that the definitions that the subject himself would have assigned be kept in mind.

Considerations of validity and final worth demand concern with long-range political values. Such factors demand, furthermore, the avoidance of conclusions presented in the heat of political battle; for John Quincy Adams, despite his discipline, could not disengage himself entirely from the singular heat of the political passions of his

[4] For all that, it would be an invaluable assistance were the trustees of the letters of John Quincy Adams written following the year 1823 moved to release them to the enquiries of the world. As the centennial of his death has been reached, it seems improbable that any sound personal or family reasons could exist to warrant the retention of these letters in the trust following its termination in 1955.

day. Moreover, he was his father's son.[5] Those considerations will also entail refusal to accent unduly John Quincy Adams's description of correct policy or the domestic and international situation at any particular time except where the relevance to a larger concept or idea is obvious.

Attention must be constantly directed to the tradition into which John Quincy Adams was born and of which he became a part. From this assessment of the conditioning factors his private and public values will be better understood. Perhaps the most extraordinary factor in his life was the influence of his parents, particularly his mother. The whole intellectual tradition of the 18th century was his. His schools were both Harvard and European institutions. New England had set him in the mold of that "Puritanism, connected as that term of reproach is, with some associations, calculated to lessen our respect for one of the noblest manifestations of our nature . . ." but which, in the words of Edward Everett, had, in the middle of the 18th century, "laid aside much of its sternness and intolerance and begun to reconcile itself with the milder charities of life. . . ."[6] This tradition and this environment, together with the events of his life, were the significant influences in producing the man whose system of values is the subject of this treatise.

[5] Cf., Everett Somerville Brown (ed.), *The Missouri Compromise and Presidential Politics, 1820–1825. From the letters of William Plumer, Junior, Representative from New Hampshire* (St. Louis: Missouri Historical Society, 1926), S. Hale to William Plumer, Jr., Keine, N. H., January 27, 1823, p. 83: "Mr. Adams [John Quincy] gains ground daily in the consideration of his fellow citizens. His reply to Clay was pithy, that to Smyth overwhelming. Could he stop here, he will have done himself much good by writing. I fear he will be led too far, and that his enemies have a plan to irritate and entangle him. Did not the meeting between him and Smyth result as the latter wished and intended? When old John was at the bar, his antagonists used to put him in a passion and thus gain an easy victory. . . ."

[6] Edward Everett, *A Eulogy on the Life and Character of John Quincy Adams* (Boston: Dutton and Wentworth, 1848), p. 11.

2

Life and Career: A Survey

*Existence itself, and duration, are incomprehensible things. . . .
Matter undergoes perpetual mutation, but is never destroyed;
why not the same of mind?*

—MEMOIRS, *March 2, 1828*

The perspective necessary to an understanding of Adams's system of
ideas can be developed only through an understanding and knowledge of the major events of his life and career. He was born in the
North Parish of Braintree, Massachusetts, on the 11th of July, 1767,
the son of John and Abigail Adams.[1] Among his earliest memories
was the sight of warfare and revolutionary struggle. With his mother
he watched the British attack upon Bunker Hill. Those experiences
of the terrors and rigors of war, as well as others, accounted for his
prejudice against Britain, his pride in the accomplishments of the
Revolution, and his satisfaction in the glories of the American Republic.

In February, 1778, at the age of eleven, he accompanied his father
on a brief diplomatic mission to France. In June, 1779 they left on
a second mission to Europe, John Adams having been commissioned
to negotiate a treaty of peace with Great Britain. It was on this latter
voyage that the young John Quincy began his diary, which he maintained with minor intermissions until a few years before his death.
In the *Memoirs* he revealed his early application to matters of a
more serious concern than those with which a young man, even in
his day, would usually be occupied.

In Europe he resumed his study of the ancient and modern lan-

[1] Josiah Quincy, *Memoir of the Life of John Quincy Adams* (Boston: Crosby,
Nichols, Lee and Company, 1860), p. 1.

guages, which had been interrupted by his return to America, linguistic studies that were to continue throughout his life and which prepared him remarkably for his future career as a diplomatist and statesman.

Very soon John Adams was sent as minister to Holland, and John Quincy left the schools of Paris and entered those of Amsterdam. Later he attended the University of Leyden. His European trips, occasioning a desultory attendance at schools, produced an unusual quality in his education; it was broad and cosmopolitan but acquired an order and a system only by virtue of his precocious intelligence and diligent application to scholarship under the guidance of a unique father.

Among the great opportunities that came to him during this period of his residence in Europe was his removal to St. Petersburg in July, 1781, as the fourteen-year-old private secretary to Francis Dana, newly appointed American representative in Russia. In addition to performing the duties connected with the legation, he continued his linguistic studies in Russia until September of 1782, when he left the Russian capital for Sweden to spend the winter.

In the following spring he traveled extensively in Sweden, visited Denmark and Germany, met his father at the Hague and went with him to Paris. The letters written while he was on this journey were truly remarkable for a youth of this age.[2] They show a deep interest in economic and political matters, an interest which might lead one to compare him with Justinian as a youth who had never been young. His education reminds one of the unusual education and training of John Stuart Mill, as in Paris John Quincy witnessed the signing of the treaty of peace between Great Britain and the colonies and entered into intellectual intercourse with "Franklin, Jefferson, Jay, Barclay, Hartley, and the Abbé Mably."

After spending a few months in England, he returned to study in Paris until May, 1785, when he returned to America. His family remained in Europe, for John Adams was the newly appointed minister in London. After a period of tutorial preparation, in March, 1786,

---

[2] Letter to Abigail Adams, the Hague, July 23, 1783, Worthington C. Ford, *The Writings of John Quincy Adams* (New York: Macmillan, 1913–1917), I, 9. (Hereafter this source will be designated *Writings*.) A letter previously written to his father indicates the precocity of his interests. To John Adams, St. Petersburg, August 21, 1781, *ibid.*, pp. 4–5.

John Quincy entered Harvard University, joining the junior class. His academic record and performance were of such a high order as to procure for him the honor of second place at commencement and the opportunity to deliver a speech on the *Importance of Public Faith to the Well-Being of a Community*. It is noteworthy that he determined to leave Europe and return to America as an act of self-discipline and as a means of escaping European influences unfriendly to his continued consciousness of being an American.[3] After graduation he followed in the path of his father and studied law, spending the next three years, from 1787 to 1790, in the Newburyport office of Theophilus Parsons, later chief justice of Massachusetts. His diary for a portion of this period, published under the title *Life in a New England Town, 1787–1788,* is illuminating from many standpoints. It reveals the reading he was doing at the time, his social habits and inclinations, and many interesting facts concerning New England social life, politics, and religious activities. It is interesting to discover young John Quincy recovering from an early, and perhaps singular, bout with alcohol.[4]

This was a period of rapid and conscious formulation of basic political concepts in his mind. He indicated, for example, a definite opinion concerning the work which had just been accomplished at the Philadelphia Convention:

If the Constitution be adopted it will be a grand point gained in favour of the aristocratic party. There are to be no titles of nobility; but there will be great distinctions and these distinctions will soon be hereditary.[5]

He indicated his willingness to take his chances "under any government whatever" but claimed that it was hard to give up the known for the unknown.[6] The future, of course, worked a great change in

---

[3] His nationalism will be discussed below, but it is interesting to note the following from a letter of this period: "America appears to hasten toward perfection in the fine arts, and any country would boast of a Belknap as an historian, a Dwight as a poet, and a West as a painter." To John Adams, Cambridge, May 21, 1786, *Writings,* I, 23.

[4] John Quincy Adams, *Life in a New England Town:* 1787, 1788. *Diary of John Quincy Adams* (Boston: Little, Brown, 1903), September 30, 1787, p. 41: "Although I had not last night been guilty of excess so far as to be intoxicated, yet I had not sufficiently consulted what my feelings would be this day to be entirely prudent." See also entry for 1st October 1787.

[5] Adams, *Life in a New England Town,* October 12, 1787, p. 46.

[6] *Loc. cit.*

his political temper. With regard to the work of the Convention, he soon had occasion to change his mind. In this instance he revealed his father's great influence upon his thinking. He read his father's defense of the Constitution.[7] His reaction was a change of attitude toward the projected Constitution:

The paper also contains an extract from the concluding letter of the third volume in defence of the American Constitution, which speaks very favourably of the system proposed by the Federal Convention. I did not expect it, and I am glad to find I was mistaken, since it appears probable the plan will be adopted.[8]

The same period betrayed the possibility of an emotional weakness, possibly in the form of an acute anxiety complex, accompanied by insomnia and incapacity for application to the pursuit of learning in the books that he enjoyed so much. The cause may very likely be found in his too conscientious attention to study, necessarily interrupted at times by the call of social obligations and the temptations of lengthy conversations upon political and other matters which so frequently engage the attention of young men. These interruptions, combined with the view of the congenital Puritan that the moment lost may never be regained, served to produce an emotional conflict between the inescapable demands of living and the Olympian intellectual ambitions of a youth of great precocity.[9] The basic discipline of his nature won out, however, against this conflict. The pattern of his personality became clear. Its major aspect was the completely intractable respect he rendered his political conscience during the course of the public life that was very soon initiated in earnest.

In 1790 he was admitted to the bar and at once opened an office in Boston. From the beginning he betrayed rather less than the utmost enthusiasm for the practice of law. While he was in Newburyport, he had been at pains to note a general and popular antipathy

[7] Adams, *Life in a New England Town,* p. 106, note 1, referring to John Adams, *Works,* VI, 219, 220.

[8] *Ibid.,* March 5, 1788, p. 106.

[9] *Ibid.,* September 20, October 1, and October 14, 1788, pp. 167–168. That for September 20th as follows: "I did not sleep a wink the whole night. My nerves are in a very disagreeable state of irritation. . . . I retired early, and went to bed, but could get no sleep. After laying [sic] about three hours, I got up and went over to Dr. Swett, and requested him to supply me with an opiate, which he did; it gradually composed my nerves, and gave me a few hours of sleep," p. 167.

for the legal profession in New England. The exceeding scantiness of his practice served the useful purpose of giving him an opportunity to contemplate the pleasures and significance of a life of public service. More important for the realization of the political ambitions that, as his father's son, he was bound to entertain, he devoted such leisure as he gained from the paucity of clients to the writing and publication of several polemical essays on popular subjects of the day that brought him to the attention of the people and the national Administration, the latter so often, in consequence of the popular storms raging over the French Revolution, in need of popular support.[10] The publicity and acclaim that he thus received resulted in his appointment by Washington as Minister Resident to the Netherlands and his unanimous confirmation by the Senate in that post in June 1794.

From his new post at the Hague, where he arrived in November of 1794, he had a fine opportunity to observe the dynamic European scene. Very shortly after his arrival, Holland was occupied by the French under General Pichegru, and the tide of ideas and physical change emanating from Paris swept over the Low Countries. From this vantage point in Holland Adams was able to continue his development as a diplomatist-observer, a development that he had begun so auspiciously on his trip back from St. Petersburg to the Hague in 1783, during which he had reported at length to his father concerning commercial opportunities and political conditions in Scandinavia.[11] He now kept in close touch with other members of the American diplomatic fraternity in Europe and sent back exhaustively able reports on an infinite variety of subjects to his superiors in Washington.[12] During his residence in Holland he had his best

[10] Letters of "Publicola" (pseud.), published between June 8, 1791, and July 27, 1791, in the *Columbian Centinel,* an attack upon the principles of Thomas Paine and the French Revolution. Letters of "Menander" (pseud.), published December 19, 1792, in the *Columbian Centinel,* a discourse on the right of disobedience. Letters of "Marcellus" (pseud.), published between April 24, 1793, and May 11, 1793, a discourse upon the proper course of the United States in Europe, generally in support of neutrality, remarked by President Washington with especial favor. Letters of "Columbus" (pseud.), published between November 30, 1793, and December 14, 1793, in the *Columbian Centinel,* written as an attack upon the career in the United States of Citizen Genêt and in support of the Administration's neutrality policy. *Writings,* Vol. I.

[11] To John Adams, Gothenberg, February 1, 1783, *Writings,* I, 7, n.

[12] The content of these materials will be considered in the text that follows, as they serve as the source of many of the political ideas of John Quincy Adams.

opportunity to scrutinize social change in the guise of revolution. His letters and diary of this period are filled with reactions to the French Revolution and remarks on the propriety of the attitudes of American public figures and parties toward that great cataclysm.

During this period he made two trips to London, once between October, 1795, and June, 1796, to exchange the ratifications of the Jay treaty, and again the following June, 1797. During the latter visit, on the 26th of July, he was married to Louisa Catherine Johnson, daughter of Mr. Johnson, the American consul, who, although with his family long resident in London, came originally from Maryland.

In November of the same year Mr. and Mrs. Adams went to Berlin, to which court he had been appointed Minister of the United States. He had taken the post despite his own doubts concerning the wisdom and correctness of accepting such an appointment from his father's Administration.[13] The main purpose of his mission in Berlin was the renewal of a treaty of amity and commerce. This treaty was signed by Adams and the Prussian Ministers on July 11, 1799. He notified his government immediately of his willingness to return home, and meantime he occupied himself with a trip through Silesia during which he described his impressions in letters to his brother, Thomas Boylston Adams. His observations in this form were later published, without his authorization, in both the United States and Great Britain.[14] This publication afforded him some considerable embarrassment, for, according to his habit, John Quincy Adams discussed with candor the personalities he encountered. The letters are of considerable interest and importance for their effective description of the Silesian scene and discussion of Silesian industry. His observations of the times covered more than mere provinces, however, and in Berlin, as at the Hague, letters and memoirs were filled with analyses of the current political landscape in Europe and the relations of the United States to these events. They were essays revealing his basic political judgment, philosophy, and values.

In early 1801, by one of the last of his father's political acts, he was recalled from Berlin to the United States, to avoid embarrassing the impending Jefferson Administration, and perhaps also to dramatize

---

[13] Quincy, *op. cit.*, pp. 17–18.

[14] *Ibid.*, p. 20. William H. Seward, *Life and Public Services of John Quincy Adams* (New York and Auburn: Miller, Orton and Mulligan, 1856), p. 72.

the cleavage between the politics of the elder Adams and Jefferson.[15] And thus, on September 4th, John Quincy Adams found himself again in the United States, saved by his long sojourn abroad from the immediate effects of political animosities at home, with his political fortunes in large measure still to be made, and freer to act for having been away. No Adams of that generation could remain long out of public office, and the next year the erstwhile diplomat was a member of the Senate of Massachusetts. In his first legislative experience he revealed without delay the independence and consistency of principle that his later public career would make so clearly known to his countrymen.[16] Most important, he was beginning to betray his lack of accord with both the principles and the practices of the Federalist Party. Despite the suspicions of the various factions, however, in February, 1803, he was elected by the Massachusetts House of Representatives to the Senate of the United States, worsting Timothy Pickering in the contest. He thereby acquired a long-time political opponent with whom his relations progressively deteriorated as Mr. Adams found himself ever less capable of accepting the foreign policy and political tenets of the major New England party.[17]

His career in the Senate was notable on many scores. During the course of his single abbreviated term his bond of sympathy with the Federalists was lost, but he did not lose entirely the sentiment of antipathy that he shared with his father for the politics and most of the philosophy of the Jeffersonian Administration. His disagreement with Jefferson began earlier, as for instances in a letter to his father in 1797 where he noted with some surprise and irony an announcement by Mr. Jefferson that he (Jefferson) possessed a high regard for the "Union." [18] A letter of the same year to his mother deplored Jefferson's letter to an Italian, Mazzei, published in Florence and Paris, charging the Adams Administration with unnatural subservience to Britain and with the purpose of erecting a monarchy in the United States.[19] John Quincy belittled the obstacles to the suc-

[15] John T. Morse, Jr., *John Quincy Adams* (Boston and Cambridge: Houghton, Mifflin, 1895), pp. 24–25.

[16] Seward, *op. cit.,* p. 83.

[17] Quincy, *op. cit.,* p. 28. Morse, *op. cit.,* p. 30. Clark, *op. cit.,* pp. 69–70.

[18] To John Adams, The Hague, April 30, 1797, *Writings,* II, 160.

[19] To Abigail Adams, London, July 29, 1797, *ibid.,* II, 194. John Quincy Adams, *Parties in the United States* (New York: Greenberg, 1941), p. 21.

cess of Jefferson's Administration, holding that its inception came at a time of adjusted relations abroad. He held that Mr. Jefferson, not naturally an economizer, was thus enabled to gain a reputation for being one, while at the same time charging his predecessor with wasteful extravagance in meeting what Adams called the far greater problems of the previous Administration. Jefferson's reputation for economy, thus earned, was the foundation of his fame as a reformer, whereas "he in truth reformed nothing." In point of fact, Adams held, and in this opinion he revealed his nationalism, Jefferson's economies were effected at the sacrifice of the navy and were wasteful of "national safety, of national honour, of national glory," thereby leading "directly to that counteraction which imminently endangered the Union itself."[20] While Mr. Adams was supping at the President's board, he was quite capable of penning stringent diatribes in his diary, questioning the President's veracity and rectitude.[21] Nevertheless he entered the Republican camp. Despite his antipathy for much that Jefferson stood for, John Quincy Adams parted company with the Federalist Party, never again to be associated with it, and by degrees joined the ranks of supporters of the Virginia Presidents. In his view the Federalist Party had become the reposi-

[20] Adams, *Parties in the United States,* pp. 33–34, 44, where he points out that the Peace of Amiens rescued Mr. Jefferson from embarrassment.

[21] Clark, *op. cit.,* p. 10. Contradictory testimony of his regard for Jefferson may be gained from later letters and diary entries, viz., "But enough of the Abbé de Pradt, whom I ought in justice to thank for the opportunity now offered me of recalling myself to your recollection, and of assuring you of the respect and veneration which I entertain for your character." To Thomas Jefferson, Washington, October 11, 1817, *Writings,* VI, 219. *Memoirs of John Quincy Adams,* comprising portions of his diary from 1795 to 1848. Edited by Charles Francis Adams (Philadelphia: J. B. Lippincott, 1874–1877), January 11, 1831, VIII, 270. (Hereafter cited as *Memoirs.*) He recorded that Mr. Jefferson had become a free-thinker and irreligious under the influence of William Small, with "loose morals necessarily following." His "duties to his neighbor were under no stronger guarantee than the laws of the land and the opinion of the world"; *ibid.,* January 12, 1831, pp. 207–208. At this point he finds in Jefferson's *Memoirs,* combined with his patriotism, respect for liberty and human rights, and his deep understanding, a "perpetual watchfulness of public opinion . . . infidel philosophy and epicurean morals . . . burning ambition . . . deep duplicity . . . perfidy worthy of Tiberius Caesar or Louis the Eleventh of France." There is in this reaction to Jefferson, deriving from John Quincy's irritation over his father's defeat, that was not entirely mollified by the sweetening of relations between the Second and Third Presidents in their declining years, much that is basic to the political philosophy of John Quincy Adams. These implications will be discussed below.

tory of sectional influence, a "Tory" party, with the pro-British historical connotation of that appellation working in Mr. Jefferson's interest. In 1799 he disclosed that he was willing to leave the Federalist Party should it become divided over the issue of war.[22] Upon his return from Europe his loose attachment to the Party was noted. His reaction to the affair of the *Chesapeake* and the *Leopard* was violently nationalistic; he approved Jefferson's policy in this crisis.[23] From this time forward, he held that Federalists were abandoning their principles and that there was a discrepancy between "the glaring absurdity and hypocrisy of their professed veneration for the policy of Washington" and their "actions which were aiming a fatal blow at the Union. . . ."[24] The latter allusion is to an alleged project for aiding the British "in a war upon the Union," which Adams writes that he had known of for some time as a project for testing the strength of the Union and the national government.[25] The Federalist Party, he believed, had come to such a condition as to be unable to act except as a "faction."[26] Their great mistake lay, he claimed, in their seeing the interests of party as separate from the interests of the nation.[27] These were the opinions which came to final development during his term in the United States Senate.

The policies that he supported and assisted in formulating in that body, in consequence, were shaped by his new political orientation. But the mistake should never be made of assuming that John Quincy Adams hewed consistently to any particular party line. "Few of our great statesmen have had an individuality as marked; perhaps no other has combined so many anfractuosities, humors, and prejudices with so much ability, liberality, and high rectitude of character."[28] As one biographer describes this quality, "Since parties were first organized in this Republic no American has ever approached him in

[22] To William Vans Murray, Berlin, December 10, 1799, *Writings*, II, 444.

[23] In a resolution drafted by Adams and unanimously adopted by a town meeting held in Faneuil Hall, July 16, 1807. In a Motion of October 28, 1807, *Annals of Congress*, 10th Cong., 1st sess., I, 19. In a Motion on Impressments, November 25, 1807, *ibid.*, p. 38. Quoted in *Writings*, III, 161–163.

[24] To William Plumer, St. Petersburg, October 6, 1810, *Writings*, III, 508.

[25] To Abigail Adams, St. Petersburg, June 30, 1811, *ibid.*, IV, 127.

[26] To William Eustis, St. Petersburg, August 24, 1811, *ibid.*, pp. 190–191.

[27] To William Eustis, Little Boston, Ealing, January 13, 1817, *ibid.*, VI, 138. To Alexander Hill Everett, Washington, November 23, 1817, *ibid.*, p. 261.

[28] Nevins, *op. cit.*, p. xi.

persistent freedom of thought, speech, and action." [29] It is not surprising, therefore, to find Adams agreeing to the right of the Executive to engage with France for the transfer of sovereignty over Louisiana to the United States, and at the same time insisting that the Constitution conferred no right upon Congress to grant to the Executive the power to set up a provisional government in the newly acquired territory.[30] Adams attempted to supply the constitutional deficiency by introducing a proposal for an amendment to the Constitution.[31] Another situation arose which found Adams this time on the side of the Federalists and of Timothy Pickering. This situation concerned the impeachment of Judge John Pickering of New Hampshire. The judge was admittedly unfit for high judicial office; both sides to the controversy admitted this point. The point in controversy was as to the appropriateness of the impeachment proceedings in such a case. The Republicans contended that impeachment and conviction thereunder need not necessarily involve a charge of criminality and might be based upon a mere showing of unfitness. This Republican view would have enabled that party, as a matter of policy, to make a concerted attack upon the Federalist judiciary which had been built up by previous Administrations. The Federalists, on the other hand, were determined that "nothing less than high crimes and misdemeanors" should warrant conviction, which should be based upon an ordinary legal trial. In support of his view that a trial of an impeachment should be subject to ordinary judicial safeguards, and to prevent any individual's acting as both accuser and judge in such a case, Adams submitted a motion on impeachments providing, as follows:

Resolved, That any senator of the United States, having previously acted and voted as a member of the House of Representatives, on a

[29] Morse, *op. cit.*, p. 35. Mr. Adams had not been forty-eight hours in the Massachusetts Senate before he irritated his Federalist colleagues by proposing that the Republicans be permitted "to enjoy a proportional representation in the Council." *Ibid.*, p. 29.

[30] This stand by Adams later gave him some embarrassment during the presidential campaign in 1823. General Alexander Smyth in a campaign for re-election charged before his Virginia constituents that Adams's record in this matter demonstrated his unfriendly attitude toward Louisiana. Adams answered in a letter To the Freeholders of Washington, Wythe, Grayson, Russell, Tazewell, Lee and Scott Counties, Virginia, *Writings*, VII, 335–354.

[31] "Amendment to the Constitution," November 25, 1803, *ibid.*, III, 20–21.

question of impeachment, is thereby disqualified to sit and act, *in the same case,* as a member of the Senate, sitting as a court of impeachment.[32]

In this case, therefore, Mr. Adams stood with the Federalist minority.

The trial of Judge Pickering was but the beginning of a more determined attack upon the Federalist judiciary. The culmination was the impeachment and trial of Samuel Chase, Associate Justice of the Supreme Court of the United States. Chase was admittedly an indiscreet, partisan Federalist, who, after achieving his high judicial office, had continued partisan political activity. From the bench itself he had been guilty of slanders upon the Executive, attacks upon democracy, and stringent criticisms of Federal laws that his oath required him to enforce. The trial of Chase was a *cause célèbre;* Adams voted "Not Guilty" on the question, and he was joined by Federalists and many Republicans in a wide defection from the ranks of their own party.

The continued skirmishing with Great Britain concerning the respective rights of the two countries, the British being at war with Napoleon and the United States attempting to maintain neutrality, was the cause of the final break between Mr. Adams and the Federalists. Mr. Adams was bitter in his denunciation of British policy with respect to neutrals, based upon Orders-in-Council. His choler became extreme when the British man-of-war *Leopard* fired upon the American frigate *Chesapeake* off the Virginia Capes, after the American vessel had refused to be searched. The Federalists, meanwhile, opposed the Administration's adoption of any forceful policy to meet the British aggressions. Federalist leaders, in any event jaundiced in their view of Jeffersonian democracy, considered Great Britain the great barrier against the pernicious doctrines of the French Revolution and the great preserver of the European balance.[33] Mr. Adams considered the Federalist policy unpatriotic,

---

[32] "Motion on Impeachment," January 4, 1804, *ibid.,* III, 25. *Ibid.,* III, 25, n. 1. *Senate Journal,* 8th Cong., 1st Sess., p. 122. Clark, *op. cit.,* p. 85.

[33] It is interesting to note that J. Q. Adams had as early as 1798 rejected the Federalist view, as expressed by Timothy Pickering then Secretary of State, that "Britain appears to be the only bulwark against the universal domination of France by sea, as well as by land." Secretary of State (Pickering) to John Quincy Adams, Philadelphia, March 17, 1798, *Writings,* II, 240–241, n. 2. This view was indirectly, if not directly, rejected in a letter of John Quincy Adams of

anti-Union, and sectional. Thereupon, following the proposal by President Jefferson on December 18, 1807, calling for an embargo, Mr. Adams parted company with every other Federalist in the Senate and voted in the affirmative. Commercial New England, at least the Federalist elements, held this action to be traitorous. Very shortly after this, the Massachusetts legislature, many months before the election would ordinarily have been scheduled, elected Mr. James Lloyd to succeed Mr. Adams by a vote of 269 to 240, the latter receiving the full Republican vote.[34] The solid Federalist vote against him was at once an insult to Mr. Adams and a revelation of the metamorphosis in his political associations. Since the legislature had at the time of the election passed resolutions instructing the Massachusetts Senators to oppose the Jefferson Administration, Mr. Adams, being of no disposition to continue to represent a body the confidence of which he had lost, resigned his seat on June 8, 1808.[35] In his letter of resignation, in effect a denial of the intrinsic right of the legislature to issue instructions, he intimated that resignation was forced upon him, since the resolutions upheld principles with which he could not in keeping with conscience concur.

Thereupon, in the midst of allegations that he had changed parties out of ambition and desire for public office, Mr. Adams turned with greater vigor to the literary pursuits that he enjoyed perhaps above all others. He had since 1805 been the Boylston Professor of Rhetoric and Belles Lettres at Harvard, having rejected a friendly suggestion that he become a candidate for the Presidency of that university following the death of President Willard in 1804. During his Senatorial career he had devoted his free time to the duties connected with this position. He continued his lectures until July of 1809, but, while attending the Supreme Court at the time of Mr. Madison's inauguration in March of that year, he had accepted an appointment to head a permanent American diplomatic mission to Russia. Although the Senate did not confirm the appointment at first, deeming

---

about this time in which he supported ardently the policy of neutrality. To John Adams, Berlin, January 31, 1798, *ibid.*, p. 251.

[34] Seward, *op. cit.*, pp. 89–90. Clark, *op. cit.*, p. 104. Morse and Quincy give the figure for Mr. Adams as 230, Morse, *op. cit.*, p. 57. Quincy, *op. cit.*, p. 40.

[35] To the Honorable Senate and House of Representatives of the Commonwealth of Massachusetts, Boston, June 8, 1808, *Writings*, III, 237–238.

it inexpedient to establish such a mission at the time, under the prompting of another message from Mr. Madison dated June 26, 1809, Mr. Adams was confirmed; on August 5 he left his home in Boston for Europe.

Adams reached St. Petersburg October 23, 1809, after a dangerously stormy and lengthy voyage during which he was stopped by British naval patrols and had opportunities to observe the hardships that the blockade of Europe was working upon American ships. Upon his arrival in St. Petersburg, he immediately established amicable relations with the Imperial Chancellor, Count Romanzoff, and the Emperor Alexander. From the vantage point of that imperial city, the new American Minister with all his customary and congenital diligence was able to survey the dynamic European scene and to render invaluable reports to his government at home through James Monroe, the Secretary of State during the greater part of Madison's Administration. Letters to his brother likewise were the repositories of his acute observations and judgments of the scene:

When we were last in Europe a sort of republican or democratic spirit was prevalent, not only in the official pretensions and varying constitutions of France, but in the political and literary character of the times. It is scarcely conceivable what a change in this respect has taken place. There is not a republic left in Europe. The very name of the people is everywhere buried in oblivion. In England the great concerns upon which all the passions of the country concentrate themselves, are intrigues and cabals of princes and ministers to supplant one another, and the prices of seats at the playhouse. In France and the rest of Europe king-making and king-breaking, orders of chivalry and dissolutions of marriage, blanchisseuses, princesses, and Jacobin grubs bursting into butterfly princes, dukes, and counts, conscriptions and contributions, famine grinding the people into soldiers, soldiers sprouting into sultans, fifty or sixty upstarts wallowing in more than Asiatic luxury, and an iron harrow tearing up the bowels of the nations. This is the present history of the times.[36]

From St. Petersburg, in the process of keeping abreast of the political situation, he kept up a correspondence with other American official representatives in Europe.

[36] To Thomas Boylston Adams, St. Petersburg, February 14, 1810, *ibid.*, III, 397–398.

It was while he was in Russia that he met Madame de Staël; indeed, of all prominent Americans of his generation his acquaintanceships and relations with men and women of many lands were perhaps the most universal and catholic. The noted Frenchwoman, a bitter opponent of Napoleon, greatly stimulated him with the vivacity and volatility, if not the logic, of her mind. But his anti-British prejudices found it difficult to accept her comment that Britain was a "moral nation." [37] He had previously developed doubt concerning the noted Frenchwoman when earlier, at a time when his passions concerning the threat of the doctrines of the French Revolution had been more aroused, he had found her in concert with Paine, Madame Roland, and Benjamin Constant laboring "to wind up the drunkenness of a club or a tavern into a frenzy." [38]

From vast Russia he observed the apogée of Napoleonic power and the dreadful *débacle* of the Grand Army in the rigorous early winter of 1812. At that time he quickly saw that the tide had turned against Napoleon, so long "an instrument of divine wrath to scourge mankind." [39] He later felt competent to deride the genius of Napoleon for its blunders in 1812: for allowing the Turks to make peace with the Russians, the Swedes under one of his own generals to assist his enemies; and for moving on Moscow in September. He concluded, however, that it might be possible for the Emperor to maintain himself in France.[40]

His bitterness against British policy was by no means assuaged during this period, for American-British relations were degenerating until they culminated in the War of 1812. In letters to his government, wherein it might be anticipated he would convey his most serious judgments, he maintained that Britain must undergo more than a change of men, but rather a change of political system "before any rational hopes . . . [could] be entertained." [41] There were, indeed, other observations by John Quincy Adams which indicated

[37] To John Adams, St. Petersburg, March 22, 1813, *Writings,* IV, 451.

[38] To John Adams, London, September 11, 1797, *ibid.,* II, 201.

[39] To Abigail Adams, St. Petersburg, November 30, 1812, *ibid.,* IV, 413.

[40] To the Secretary of State (Monroe), St. Petersburg, February 2, 1813, *ibid.,* IV, 431–432.

[41] To the Secretary of State (Robert Smith), St. Petersburg, March 30, 1810, *ibid.,* III, 414.

some admiration for Britain and the British. But the above example serves to indicate the nature of many of his opinions at this stage of his life concerning that nation and people. In relation to domestic politics, he held that the Federalist Party had allowed itself to be duped by a British faction and that to revive their party strength they must retrace many steps.[42] At the same time he credited our policy of neutrality with carrying us through the most critical period in the world's history, a result that would have been impossible to us as "an *appendage* either to Britain or France."[43] The alternative would have been for the United States to become a humble dependency of one or the other in case of war between the two, a satellite held either in contempt or compassion. Instead, America was the envy of all Europe; this had been accomplished by avoiding both sides: "The fatal friendship of England, and the grinding oppressions of France, ascend in secret or in open curses and execrations to Heaven from every corner of Europe."[44] He was particularly enraged over the policy of impressment as practiced by the British, which he held to give "the lie to every pretence of freedom in their constitution."[45]

A significant event during Mr. Adams's residence in Russia was President Madison's offer of a place on the supreme judicial bench. It was known that he found it very difficult with the limited means at his disposal to maintain his mission in the style he considered essential to the prestige of the United States. The President's nomination of Mr. Adams and the Senate's unanimous confirmation of the nomination to fill the vacancy created by the death of Justice Cushing would have afforded him an opportunity to escape the financial burdens which he found so onerous. He nevertheless declined the appointment on the ground that he had had little judicial experience,

[42] To John Adams, St. Petersburg, September 2, 1810, *ibid.*, p. 481.

[43] To John Pope, St. Petersburg, September 10, 1810, *ibid.*, III, 502. If such sentiments were more widely known to his posterity, it is easy to see how John Quincy Adams might become, on this and other grounds, the darling of modern isolationists. Despite his long European experience, he remained the rather puritanical republican, suspicious of Europe's decadence and proud of the quality of his own people. There are, of course, qualifications embodied in other pronouncements which must be measured against such statements as this one.

[44] *Loc. cit.*

[45] To Abigail Adams, St. Petersburg, February 18, 1813, *ibid.*, IV, 436.

had been for a long time away from the bar, and had been engaged in pursuits of a quite divergent nature.[46]   In a letter to his brother he had declared he would find it difficult, should he be appointed to succeed Cushing, to give up his character of "political partisan," as would have been necessary for a member of the bench.[47]   Although he might be impartial as a judge in dealing with his countrymen as an "umpire in their controversies," he was not confident that they could be sufficiently impartial toward him "to make them fit to be judged by [him]." [48]   He revealed that he had an "aversion to a judicial office." [49]   He further explained his declining a judicial office on the ground that he had neither the energy nor the influence to reform the "moral and legal code of [his] country," although he could discern defects in the system.[50]

John Quincy Adams in his *Memoirs* and letters left surprisingly few observations on social conditions in Russia.   He did perform his duty to report political conditions to Washington, as when he noted a new manifesto embodying a constitution of the "Council of the Russian Empire," variously reported to be merely a means of getting rid of certain ministers, a modification of the autocracy, a new system with new freedoms, or an imitation of France.[51]   But descriptions in the *Memoirs* of the total Russian scene are almost entirely lacking.

In early 1814 he was called upon to leave Russia for the last time, on a mission of importance to his country.   He left on the 28th of April in 1814 on a journey which took him finally to Ghent, Belgium, where he arrived on June 24th.   There, on June 30, 1814, he met with his colleagues on the commission recently appointed to negotiate a treaty of peace with Great Britain.   James A. Bayard and Albert Gallatin, Secretary of the Treasury, had arrived in St. Petersburg on July 21, 1813, as members of a mission including Mr. Adams to negotiate a peace through the proferred mediation of the Tsar. The British government rejected the mediation but soon informally

---

[46] To the President of the United States (James Madison), St. Petersburg, June 3, 1811, *Writings*, IV, 95.

[47] To Thomas Boylston Adams, St. Petersburg, April 10, 1811, *ibid.*, pp. 47–48.

[48] To John Adams, St. Petersburg, July 21, 1811, *ibid.*, p. 145.

[49] *Loc. cit.*

[50] To John Adams, St. Petersburg, June 12, 1812, *ibid.*, IV, 353.

[51] To the Secretary of State (Robert Smith), St. Petersburg, January 31, 1810, *ibid.*, III, 392.

let it be known that they would be willing to negotiate directly. After a long and dreary stay in St. Petersburg, Bayard and Gallatin in January 1814 departed for Amsterdam. Meantime new instructions and commissions arrived from the United States. Two new commissioners, Henry Clay and Jonathan Russell, Minister to Sweden, were added to the American peace mission. The British Commission, consisting of Lord Gambier, Henry Goulburn, and William Adams, arrived in Ghent on August 7th. Thereupon the long negotiations, which so often came near to failure, were undertaken to be terminated with the signing of a treaty on December 14, 1814, with formal ratifications exchanged on January 8, 1815.

The wrangling between the two commissions was matched by the wrangling within the American commission, which had had its beginning as early as the period of Gallatin's and Bayard's stay in St. Petersburg. Mr. Adams then had objected to Gallatin's sending his secretary to London to seek a direct communication from the British government. Clearly demonstrating his irritable and difficult personality, he had accused Bayard of fostering bad relations between himself and Gallatin. These feelings colored the discussions of the commission in Ghent.

Mr. Adams had felt humiliation rankling in his nationalistic heart during the month or more of waiting until the arrival of the British commissioners. He suspected that the "masters of the world" expected to receive the abject submission of the United States, which, being impossible to the "temper" of the Americans, would make the reconciling of American and British claims most difficult.[52] He became irritated and distressed that the English tactics and proposals at Ghent seemed to offer only the alternatives of a hard war or a disgraceful peace.[53] A conversation with the British commissioner, Mr. Goulburn, showed a deep British jealousy of the growing population and territorial expansion of the United States, and, more serious, a desire to stand in the way of her progress and growth.[54] Adams was moved to anguish at the news of the destruction of Washington, which he held to be contrary to all the rules of warfare and worse

[52] To John Adams, Ghent, July 7, 1814, *ibid.*, V, 57.
[53] To William Harrison Crawford, Ghent, August 29, 1814, *ibid.*, p. 105.
[54] To the Secretary of State (James Monroe), Ghent, September 5, 1814, *ibid.*, pp. 119–120.

than the worst excesses of the French Revolution. He explained that this was the consequence of the fact that our war with Britain was in reality a civil war, always "more cruel and unrelenting" than other wars.[55] He lamented the fact that we were being left to face the "colossal power of Britain" alone, for the cause we were supporting was in reality the cause of the whole of Europe.[56] The aggressions of British sea power against the rights of neutrals on the high seas were attacks upon the fundamental rights of all nations. His observations indicated to him that the course of events left Britain in unimpaired control of the seas, and France, although not seriously weakened by her defeat, was "humiliated" and dissatisfied with the settlement being made for Europe. In consequence he could see nothing permanent in the peace.[57]

The major matters of contention between the two commissions at Ghent also had sectional implications. The controversies over methods of settlement and the attitudes of the commissioners with regard to the principles involved were the fuel of future political controversies along sectional lines. The British desired to negotiate on the basis of the principle of *uti posseditis,* the Americans, not feeling in any sense vanquished, determined that the basis must be the *status quo ante bellum.* The British, being in the full flush of their new victories and predominance in Europe and contemplating new victories in campaigns against the United States, quite naturally did not assume a conciliatory attitude. The accomplishment of the United States commissioners in negotiating a favorable peace is all the more remarkable. The Marquis of Wellesley in the House of Lords declared that "in his opinion the American Commissioners had shown the most astonishing superiority over the British, during the whole of the correspondence." [58] A dispute arose over the fishing privileges which had been enjoyed by the New England fishing industry in northeastern waters by virtue of the treaty of 1783. Mr. Adams, deeming this to be the question of major importance, desired to bring the commission's major pressure to bear on this point. The westerner, Henry Clay, was fired to resistance by the British demand

---

[55] To Louisa Catherine Adams (Mrs. John Quincy Adams), Ghent, October 7, 1814, *Writings,* VI, 153–154.

[56] To Levett Harris, Ghent, November 15, 1814, *ibid.,* V, 187.

[57] To Abigail Adams, Ghent, November 23, 1814, *ibid.,* V, 208.

[58] Quoted in Seward, *op. cit.,* p. 103.

for continued navigation rights on the Mississippi and right of access to Mississippi navigation from any part of their northern dominions. Mr. Gallatin was the architect of the final compromise which gave the Mississippi rights to the British in exchange for the fisheries. The American commission refused with firmness the British demand that the United States refrain from maintaining naval forces in the Great Lakes and fortifying their shores. Mr. Adams, in particular, rejected the British proposal of a neutral zone between the United States and Canada comprising a vast stretch of territory, including the present states of Wisconsin, Michigan, Illinois, and much of Indiana and Ohio to be used as a home for Indian allies of Great Britain.

It was Mr. Adams's doctrine that the size of the territorial settlement of Americans "must correspond with their increasing numbers." He contended that the rate of population growth was greater than any before observed in human history.[59] It was ridiculous for Britain to expect her swarming progeny engaged in the work of creating a "powerful empire" in the wilderness to be restrained from carrying on this work of civilization by treaty stipulations that consigned large areas to the use of a "few scattered hordes of savages" numbering no more than the population of an average city. This attitude was in keeping with Mr. Adams's system and doctrines, which will be considered at greater length in succeeding pages. As a nationalistic American, he believed in his country's expansion, and he revealed this quality of his mind on few occasions more strikingly than during the Ghent negotiations. Americans could not be deprived of their "natural right" to the use of lands taken from the aborigines. Vast territories could not be left to the use of a "few hundred savages."[60] At the same time he rejected the British charge that the government of the United States had adopted a policy of "perpetual encroachment upon the Indians under the pretence of purchases," on the ground that it is the duty of a people "to settle, cultivate, and improve their territory."[61] And thus Mr. Adams performed his duties as a diplomat with nationalist fervor.

[59] *Answer to the British Commissioners,* draft by John Quincy Adams, Ghent, August 24, 1814, *Writings,* V, 98–99.

[60] *Memoirs,* September 1, 1814, III, 27–28,

[61] *Ibid.,* September 25, 1814, pp. 41–42.

Following the successful conclusion of the negotiations at Ghent, Mr. Adams went to Paris where he arrived on February 3rd.   Mr. Crawford, American Minister, presented the American Commissioners to Louis XVIII.   Adams entered into relationship, as was his natural habit and inclination, with persons of political importance and intellectual prominence.   He saw Lafayette, Count Marbois, and frequented the brilliant salon of Madame de Staël.   At this time he witnessed the hasty departure of Louis XVIII from his capital on March 20th and the arrival of Napoleon on the same day and had an opportunity to observe the transfer of the fickle popular favor.

He remarked the appearance that France gave of a united nation of twenty-six million contending with "one highway robber" on the day before Napoleon's appearance in Paris, but he preferred to rely on the indications of private conversations that Buonaparte would enter Paris as unopposed as he had entered Lyons.[62]   Observing the transformation overnight of the name of the *Journal des Débats* to the *Journal de l'Empire,* he derived further support for his conclusions in this particular instance and his general convictions concerning the stability of popular support.[63]   He wrote that, having observed the loss of popular favor by the Bourbons as the returned exile approached Paris, he believed the people's loyalty to Napoleon would be no more stable.[64]

At this time the American diplomat revealed in a letter to his mother his persistent interest in the world of politics and social change and his amazingly acute analytical and observational powers. He analyzed the forces that had been at work against Louis XVIII in terms that are little, if any, improved upon by modern historians: Louis XVIII could not win the loyalty of the old army men of the Empire.   The 2,000,000 purchasers of national property, the former properties held under feudal tenure, were alarmed by the acts of public ministers of the Bourbons, the editorial pronouncements of official journals, and the indiscreet discourses of royal princes, even though Louis had confirmed the purchasers in possession by proclamation and constitutional safeguard.   The result was that these properties had been reduced to one-quarter of their former value.

[62] To Abigail Adams, Paris, March 19, 1815, *Writings,* V, 292.

[63] To John Adams, Paris, March 21, 1815, *ibid.,* p. 296.

[64] To John Adams, Paris, April 24, 1815, *ibid.,* V, 308.

The population had further taken alarm at, or become angered in reaction to, the old nobility's claim to rejuvenated feudal privileges, the priesthood's demands for "tythes," the Bourbon government's exclusion of revolutionary figures from appointment to office, the removal of many of them from office, the restoration of old academies, the dissolution of the National Institute, and a series of arbitrary acts in dealings with individuals.[65]   Adams doubted that the Bourbons could be re-established on the basis of the policy they had pursued and the claims they had made prior to the Emperor's return.[66] Despite the mistakes of Louis's regime, it had been on the whole "mild and moderate" and the support of the National Guard in Paris alone might have prevailed against Napoleon's forces, but only if the former had had popular support, and that support had not been forthcoming.   The main reason for lack of such popular approval was that the people, already made suspicious by injudicious governmental action, were linked to the army only through the old army men, the chief men in each locality, who were loyal to Napoleon.[67] Thus Adams showed his deep concern with French and general European affairs, a concern which, of course, persisted after his departure for London, where he arrived on May 25, 1815, to become American Minister to the Court of St. James.

The mission to Britain found Adams at the pinnacle of his foreign service.   No extraordinary achievements marked his tenure, although he initiated conversations that resulted in the Rush-Bagot Agreement of 1818, an Agreement to dispense with armaments on the Great Lakes underlying the present demilitarized frontier between the United States and Canada; and his importunings concerning impressment, the northern fisheries, and the other matters of controversy between the two governments served to keep these issues alive in the minds of British statesmen.

In his role as an observer he was distressed by the presence of returned Bourbons and foreign troops in France.   He wrote on one occasion that the need was for another Joan of Arc.[68]   The old practice of placing *"Les Rois Faineants"* in convents needed reviving,

[65] To Abigail Adams, Paris, April 22, 1815, *ibid.*, V, 301–302.
[66] To John Adams, Paris, April 24, 1815, *ibid.*, p. 308.
[67] To Abigail Adams, Paris, April 22, 1815, *ibid.*, pp. 300–301.
[68] To John Adams, Boston House, Ealing (his British residence), October 9, 1815, *ibid.*, V, 411.

since the Bourbons could both people a convent and bring to it a character and capacity more suitable to such an environment than to the "thrones to which they have been nailed by the royal hammer-smiths of social order and religion." A foreign soldiery, furthermore, could not create a durable foundation for such a system.[69]

During this period there was little diminution in his Anglophobia. Even though he ranked his part in the Peace of Ghent as one of his greatest accomplishments, he confided to one correspondent his belief that that Peace had established little more than a truce.[70] A similar frame of mind evoked a response to Lord Castlereagh which disavowed any intention of claiming for the "diplomatic relations between the United States and Britain" any status of greater permanency than inhered in relations between the two powers and other countries.[71] Such reservations concerning British-American relations appeared in his mind at the time when he was noting, with displeasure, Castlereagh's boast that everything at Vienna had been arranged to Britain's satisfaction, a time in which Britain had achieved a sort of European domination greater in effect than Russia's domination as a land power that he had noted in early 1814.[72] There was similar discomfort in his report from Paris to the Secretary of State wherein he concluded that in a future war Britain would have no maritime rival in Europe or elsewhere. "Whatever the state of things may be in time of peace she has but to raise her arm to interdict the ocean to every European state." He foresaw that, having achieved her will on the oceans, Britain would permit her navy to decline and seek increased strength in her army.[73]

Directing his attention to the domestic condition of Britain, he found that it presented the peculiar spectacle of a "free government," yet a government striving to rebuild and preserve an endangered social order in South America upon the "ruins of colonial, feudal,

[69] To John Adams, Boston House, Ealing, December 16, 1815, *Writings*, p. 447.
[70] To Joseph Hall, Boston House, Ealing, September 9, 1815, *ibid.*, p. 372.
[71] To Lord Castlereagh (no place of writing noted), January 22, 1816, *ibid.*, V, 474.
[72] To John Adams, Paris, April 24, 1815, *ibid.*, p. 306. To George Washington Campbell, State Department, Washington, June 28, 1818, *ibid.*, VI, 375.
[73] To the Secretary of State (James Monroe), Paris, February 23, 1815, *ibid.*, V, 282–283: Britain would recognize that future struggles would be determined primarily on land, but she would not abandon her policy of blockades. To meet that contingency the United States, Adams contended, should adopt a policy of navy building. Such a policy would discourage continued impressment.

jesuitical, and papal institutions." [74]   There was an incompatibility, he charged, between the universal nature of Britain's hegemony and ambitions and her internal situation:

Yet all this availeth them nothing owing to the depreciation of the necessaries of life.   They are perishing by plethora, staggering under a political apoplexy.[75]

There had been no occasion to change this judgment when Mr. Adams was called home to assume the office of Secretary of State in the new Monroe Administration.

He arrived in New York on August 7, 1817, on his last return to the United States from Europe.   By September he was prepared to enter upon his new duties.   His tenure in the State Department came during a most significant period in the relations of the United States with other nations.   He brought as high a natural endowment and training to the office as the United States of the times could have produced. He had his limitations, but they were limitations of temperament rather than of talent, and it is unquestionable that he always erred on the side of zeal rather than timidity or indecision.

Adams maintained as Secretary of State the standard of diplomatic performance that he had achieved in his own service abroad, and he insisted upon that standard in his subordinates.   He held that young diplomats should not remain so long abroad "in a public capacity at the courts of Europe" in the "air of those regions so unfriendly to American constitutions" that they were forced to return to be rejuvenated "by the wholesome republican atmosphere of their own country."   That had been the policy of previous Administrations and would continue to be the policy of Mr. Monroe.[76]   His diplomatic instructions to American diplomats concerning their duties were masterpieces.   American representatives must report concerning all that was of immediate concern and importance to the relations of the countries of assignment not only with the United States but also with Europe and the rest of the world.   It was their duty to describe any

[74] To the Secretary of State (James Monroe), London, September 30, 1815, *ibid.*, V, 395.
[75] To William Plumer, Little Boston, Ealing, February 27, 1816, *ibid.*, p. 519. Yet it should not be assumed that Adams was unrelenting in his strictures upon Britain.   See letter to Alexander Hill Everett, Washington, September 28, 1817, *ibid.*, VI, 203–204.
[76] To Christopher Hughes, Washington, June 22, 1818, *ibid.*, VI, 357.

particular characteristics of the Administrations and those in power, the relations of the latter with their subordinates, the qualities of those next in line of succession to office, the names of those principally in attendance around the seats of power. Washington was to be informed of the nature and names of those in opposition to the government of the country; the effect of opposition upon political fortunes; the nature of the activities of fellow diplomats, whose good will and confidence might be won by blandishments of personality; the substance of all information that the sagacity of the representative could make available. For his part, the Secretary of State promised to answer all communications.[77]

The quality of the diplomatic dispatches that issued from the State Department over the signature of John Quincy Adams was well illustrated by a momentous state paper, a letter of instructions to George William Erving, American Minister to Spain, that set forth at great length the conditions justifying General Jackson's actions in Florida.[78] In masterful, dramatic language, albeit more flamboyant than is common today, the Secretary presented the American case and resisted the Spanish claims. He admitted to others that it had been necessary to stretch argument to the limit in the situation, but he was convinced that it was better to err on the side of vigor. Whatever may have been the error of zeal manifested by the note, the ability that it revealed caused Thomas Jefferson to speak of it as "among the ablest compositions [he had] ever seen, both as to logic and style . . ." and to suggest that it should be thoroughly circulated and publicized in Europe as an illustration of the level of American statecraft.[79] A letter of instructions to Hugh Nelson, a successor to Erving at Madrid,[80] evidenced a similar mastery of the techniques and details of diplomacy, but the letter to Irving was "possibly the greatest state paper ever penned by its author." [81]

[77] To Christopher Hughes, Washington, June 22, 1818, *Writings*, VI, 357–358. To Alexander Hill Everett, State Department, Washington, August 10, 1818, *ibid.*, pp. 427–428.

[78] To George William Erving, State Department, Washington, November 28, 1818, *ibid.*, pp. 474–502.

[79] From Jefferson to President Monroe, January 18, 1819, *ibid.*, VI, 502, n. 1.

[80] To Hugh Nelson, State Department, Washington, April 28, 1823, *ibid.*, VII, 369–421.

[81] Clark, *op. cit.*, p. 147.

Fully conscious of the importance of international relations to the nation's welfare and mindful of the financial rigors of his position at St. Petersburg, Adams took occasion to deplore the *"inexorable economy . . . in regard to the expenses of foreign intercourse"* so frequently demanded by the Congress.[82] He feared the effect of "parsimony" upon the diplomatic service.[83] In these matters, as in many other spheres of governmental action, Mr. Adams was not one to minimize the role of government, nor to take a niggardly stand with regard to the amounts of money government should spend in order to accomplish its purposes adequately.

In his diplomatic dealings, Adams was conscious of his own disposition to harshness and irritability. His colleagues in the government were likewise aware of ths quality in the Secretary of State. He wrote thus of the Spanish Minister: "I have seen slippery diplomatists, more than one; but Onis is the first man I have met with who made it a point of honor to pass for more of a swindler than he was." [84] This stricture revealed the complete assurance the Secretary had that defect of character and manner was always on the side of his opponent in negotiation, and that high rectitude of principle was always in his own possession. His occasional consciousness of this tendency to undue severity was revealed on one occasion when he called upon the President to strike out whatever may appear "unnecessarily harsh" in a draft he had prepared of a note to be sent to the British Minister, Canning.[85] It then comes as rather an amusing surprise to find Mr. Adams claiming that "The Government of the United States [acting through Mr. Adams], by a forbearance perhaps unexampled in human history, has patiently waited for your [the Spanish Minister's] arrival [with news of the ratification of the Florida treaty by the Spanish king], always ready to give in candor, and sincerity, every explanation that could with any propriety be demanded." [86] In fact, the President and members of the Cabinet council were constantly called upon to modify the severity of the

---

[82] To Richard Rush, Washington, May 29, 1818, *Writings,* VI, 339.

[83] To William Plumer, Washington, July 6, 1818, *ibid.,* p. 382.

[84] To Charles Jared Ingersoll, Washington, August 7, 1821, *ibid.,* VII, 167.

[85] To the President, James Monroe, Washington, August 3, 1821, *ibid.,* p. 165.

[86] To Don Francisco Dionisio Vives, Spanish Minister, State Department, Washington, D. C., May 8, 1820, *ibid.,* p. 23.

Secretary's language.[87]　William Crawford, Secretary of the Treasury, obviously under the stress of ambition to succeed Mr. Monroe to the Presidency, for which office Mr. Adams was likewise a natural candidate, was no doubt expressing the occasional temper of the Cabinet when he complained of constantly having to tone down the "asperities" of the State Department's official notes.[88]　This quality of Adams's temperament gave ammunition to other political opponents.　General Alexander Smyth in a printed handbill soliciting the suffrages of his constituents in Virginia contended that " 'pernicious passions [warped Adams's] judgment and [did] not leave [his] mind in a proper state to decide on the interest of a nation and to adopt an enlarged and liberal system of policy.' " [89]

Many decisions of Mr. Adams as Secretary of State later became the foundations of political animadversions against which he was constrained to defend himself.　For example, in 1836, it was charged in the House of Representatives by Representative Waddy Thompson that Mr. Adams had ceded Texas to Mexico by agreeing to the location of the boundary along the Sabine River as part of the price of the Spanish agreement to the treaty on Florida.　Adams in his diary of a later year pointed out that the Sabine had been preferred by President Monroe to the "Rio del Norte," for the President had thought that the further extension of our territory would weaken our defense position.[90]　On the earlier occasion, however, his answer to the charge consisted of a reference to a diary entry of the time of the treaty negotiation, the diary reference revealing that the treaty provision with respect to the boundary had been submitted to General Jackson, the source of Thompson's information, who had agreed to it.[91]　Living a full and constructive life, Adams was faced naturally

[87] See the words in brackets struck out by the President or the Cabinet council in the notes To Hyde De Neuville, French Minister, State Department, Washington, July 28, 1821, *Writings*, VII, 137–160.　To Hyde De Neuville, State Department, Washington, February 22, 1822, *ibid.*, p. 212.　And To Don Joaquin De Anduaga, Spanish Minister, State Department, Washington, April 15, 1822, *ibid.*, pp. 222, 224.

[88] From William Crawford to Albert Gallatin, May 13, 1822, *ibid.*, p. 317.

[89] Quoted in Adams's letter To the Freeholders of Washington, Wythe, Grayson, Russell, Tazewell, Lee and Scott Counties, Virginia, *ibid.*, VI, 388.　See page 16, note 30, *supra.*

[90] *Memoirs*, March 29, 1843, XI, 348.

[91] Dorothie Bobbé, *Mr. and Mrs. John Quincy Adams* (New York: Minton, Balch & Co., 1930), pp. 259–260.　When Jackson was presented with the evi-

by much opposition to his career, but no one could deny that he possessed the weapons with which to strike back and often silence his enemies.

Despite the volatility of Adams's temperament, it is but just to point out that intrinsically United States foreign policy was restrained and cautious during his incumbency as Secretary of State. There is plausibility in his contentions to the Spanish Minister that the United States had been reasonable in seeking a concerted recognition of "Buenos Ayres" only after it was inevitable for Spain herself to render recognition and under conditions that would make such a move beneficial to all the powers concerned. The policy of the United States, particularly in supporting concerted action, should have convinced Spain of the Administration's "moderation and discretion." [92] United States policy, formulated and implemented by Adams with respect to Latin America, in great measure was based upon his view of the political system that he saw dominant in Europe. In one of his didactic letters of instructions to an American diplomat, in this case Henry Middleton, appointed to Russia, he analyzed that system: His view was that the contemporary political system of Europe, based on the treaties of Vienna, Paris, and Aix-la-Chappelle, had the purpose of eliminating the influence of the French Revolution. The core of the system was a compact among the five major powers designed to eliminate the paramountcy of one of their number, swayed by revolution, through a concert of their numbers. His judgment was astute in assessing the limitations of the system:

Whether they perceived in its full extent, considered in its true colors, or provided by judicious arrangements for the revolutionary temper of the weapons by which they had so long been assailed, and from which they

---

dence of the diary, he fell into a rage, remarking, "Sir, that diary comes up on all occasions—one would think that its pages were as immutable as the laws of the Medes and the Persians! Sir, that diary will be the death of me!" The charge against Adams on this score carries over into more contemporary writings. See Clark, *op. cit.*, p. 9: "He sincerely loved the Union, yet it was his trade of our right to Texas as part of the consideration in the purchase of Florida which laid the foundation for the question of Texan annexation with its attendant bitterness, and thus did much to bring about the Civil War."

[92] To Don Francisco Dionisio Vives, State Department, Washington, May 8, 1820, *Writings*, VII, 25–26; of course, there was no gainsaying Washington's preference for Latin American independence; but the preference made United States "moderation" more notable.

had so severely suffered, is a question now in a course of solution. Their great anxiety appears to have been to guard themselves against the other.[93]

In the same letter the Secretary of State with the finesse of the seasoned diplomat contended that the American political system precluded the adherence of the United States to the "Holy Alliance," the great principles of which American policy could more adequately support in a status of detached neutrality than according to the principles of the European system. He declared it to be better for the "repose" of Europe as well as of America for the systems of the two to be kept as "separate and distinct" as possible.[94]

Adams's paramount role in the formulation of the Monroe Doctrine has long been recognized. In January, 1819, he put it down as a line of policy that the United States should take the lead in recognizing South American independence, persuading England to act in support of the principle, but letting her know that America would act independently.[95] The first direct and explicit hint of the Doctrine was contained in a statement of July 17, 1823, by Adams to Baron Tuyl, the Russian Minister, that the United States would contest the establishment of any Russian foothold on this continent and, further, that she considered the American continents no longer subject to colonization.[96] He considered another communication with Baron Tuyl as an opportunity to affirm basic American political principles, which the United States should not impose on Europe or elsewhere and which she expected Europe to respect by abstention from imposing European principles and force on the American Hemisphere.[97] Adams never doubted that he was the architect of the Doctrine, and three years before his death we find him asserting that belief to George Bancroft.[98]

The major events and problems of foreign affairs during the Adams tenure of the State Department were of a momentous nature and his handling of them in large measure reveals his political system. The question of major importance, one of long standing, concerned the

[93] To Henry Middleton, State Department, Washington, July 5, 1820, *Writings*, VII, 46–47.

[94] *Ibid.*, p. 50.

[95] *Memoirs*, January 2, 1819, IV, 207.

[96] Morse, *op. cit.*, p. 132.

[97] *Memoirs*, November 21, 1823, VI, 194.

[98] *Ibid.*, December 6, 1845, XII, 218.

controversy with Spain over the western boundary of Louisiana, placed by the United States along the Rio Grande, and the possession of the Floridas. The problem was complicated by General Jackson's invasion of Spanish territory in Florida and his storming of Pensacola in retaliation for depradations of Seminole and Creek Indians across the borders of Georgia and Alabama. The Secretary of State stood almost alone in the cabinet in support of General Jackson.[99] He warned the French Minister not to assume that the President would disavow the American commander.[100] He held that the action taken had been *"defensive,"* neither an act of war nor in volation of the Constitution,[101] that the taking of Pensacola was in anticipation of a threat from the Spanish governor to drive Jackson out of the province that he had entered in pursuance of his orders.[102] Taking the stand that it was preferable to err on the side of vigor, he cited chapter and verse from Martens on International Law in support of his stand. He opposed a paragraph in a proposed article by the Attorney General prepared for the *National Intelligencer* declaring the President's view to be that he was without power to order Jackson to take Pensacola.[103] The execution during the course of the expedition of two British subjects following a court martial at which they had been charged with inciting the Indians to war and supplying them with arms did not brighten the picture and served thoroughly to arouse the British whose relations with Spain had to be considered in connection with the negotiations.

Another interfering factor was the difficulty over Amelia Island off the northeast coast of Florida. The island had been occupied by a band of filibusterers, under the leadership of one McGregor, avowedly an agent of the rebel government of Buenos Aires. The real purpose of the expedition was to use the island as a base for the conquest of Florida, which in turn would be sold to the United States. The United States was forced to occupy the island and expel the adventurers. Despite Spain's desire for its return, American forces

99 *Ibid.*, July 15, 1818, IV, 108.
100 *Ibid.*, July 7, 1818, p. 102.
101 *Ibid.*, July 17, 1818, p. 111.
102 *Ibid.*, July 19, 1818, p. 113.
103 *Ibid.*, July 21, 1818, IV, 114. This stand on the part of Adams, vindicating Jackson at a critical juncture of his career when many people were ranged against the volatile general, is interesting in the light of the bitter enmity that later developed between the two men.

remained there, following the course suggested by Calhoun and Adams, but making no easier the larger negotiations in which the Secretary was involved.

At this time there was much agitation in the United States for the recognition of the revolting provinces of Spain in South America. Many factions for political and strategic reasons were attempting to produce an abandonment of the United States' neutral position before the time was ripe for the taking of this step. Although Mr. Adams opposed premature recognition, he refused, on the other hand, to withhold recognition as a *quid pro quo* for the making of the Florida treaty upon terms favorable to the United States. When the Spanish government through Hyde de Neuville sought to extract such an agreement, he was informed that the Government of the United States would offer no pledge in return for a treaty.[104]

The prolonged negotiations were brought to an end when the treaty was signed by Adams and the Spanish representative on February 22, 1819. Mr. Adams closed the day "with ejaculations of fervent gratitude to the Giver of all good."[105] Although his satisfaction was later marred by the discovery that, undoubtedly with the cognizance of the Spanish Minister, certain large land grants of the Spanish King had not been technically annulled as he had thought, the treaty was finally brought into force after a long-delayed ratification by the Spanish. This diplomatic accomplishment remained in his mind as one of his greatest achievements.

Turning to events of more personal moment during Adams's incumbency in the Department of State, it is necessary to observe that much of the second term of James Monroe was occupied by the struggle of the contenders within the Administration for strategic advantage in the contest for the succession to the Presidency. Adams's disdain for seeming to desire the office, an essential quality of his character and the source of much chagrin to his supporters, could only partially conceal his ambition, for his very reiteration of his disinterestedness belied his unconcern. Pointing out the sufficiency of other candidates who had not the delicacy of restrained ambition he proposed to manifest, he proclaimed such delicacy natural to his disposition. With self-righteous smugness he asked, "Do

[104] *Memoirs*, December 28, 1818, IV, 199–200.
[105] *Ibid.*, February 22, 1819, p. 274.

they call it aristocratic hauteur and learned arrogancy? Why, so be it, my worthy friends and approved good masters. It is not then cringing servility, nor insatiate importunity." [106] He could so far preserve this character as to call upon Robert Walsh, Jr., the editor, to avoid Adams partisanship and to do his "duty as a public journalist," independently and disinterestedly.[107]

The years in the White House, which he achieved despite his professed lack of desire for the office, brought Adams less satisfaction than achievement of such eminence might have brought to others, or to him under different circumstances. In his mind, it was proper to seek the office only "upon the foundation of public service." [108] It was a disappointment to him that the vote through which he received the election did not reflect complete public confidence in his record. He had considered himself to have more at stake than all the other candidates in the election; he believed that the election constituted more of a popular test of his past service than any other candidate's. Despite the fact that he called upon himself for the kind of spirit that could endure defeat as well as victory, he could not dissemble his fears and doubt.[109] And the course of the Administration did not reduce his fears. He noted the mortifying majority against him, particularly mortifying to the patriot in his own country.[110] When he failed to achieve a second election, he submitted with resignation, heartened that the sun of his "country [shone] unclouded," although the "sun of [his] political life [was setting] in the deepest gloom." [111] He plunged into the work that he always relied upon to suspend "the pains of disappointment." [112]

He was correct in assuming the prosperity of his country, which makes even more singular his failure to be re-elected.

The story of Mr. Adams's Administration will detain the historian, and even the biographer, only a very short time. Not an event occurred during those four years which appears of any especial moment. Our

---

[106] To Louisa Catherine Adams (Mrs. Adams), Washington, October 7, 1822, *Writings,* VII, 315–316.
[107] To Louisa Catherine Adams, Washington, September 29, 1822, *ibid.,* p. 309.
[108] *Memoirs,* May 2, 1820, V, 90.
[109] *Ibid.,* May 9, 1824, VI, 323–324.
[110] *Ibid.,* March 13, 1828, VII, 474.
[111] *Ibid.,* December 3, 1828, VIII, 78.
[112] *Ibid.,* December 31, 1828, p. 88.

foreign relations were all pacific; and no grave crisis or great issue was developed in domestic affairs. It was a period of tranquillity in which the nation advanced rapidly in prosperity.[113]

It was the kind of prosperity of which he could write in such glowing terms in his *Report on Manufactures,* submitted to the House of Representatives by Adams as chairman of the Committee of Manufactures on May 23, 1832,[114] a prosperity the fostering of which he considered his highest presidential duty.

Nevertheless, for all the prosperity of the Administration the major events of the period, 1825–29, were related to the campaign leading to the presidential election of 1828. The Adams Administration had been inaugurated under the cloud of a charge by the Jackson forces, subscribed to by the General, that Clay had supported Adams against Jackson as a part of a deal whereby Adams promised in return to appoint Clay Secretary of State. Some time before the election, Adams had been informed that rumors were circulating that there had been some understanding between the Secretary of State and Clay concerning the Presidency, rumors which Adams was at pains to deny.[115] Such charges, in addition to pressure from the Calhounites in the form of advice that it would be dangerous to appoint Clay Secretary of State because of the threat of a Jackson opposition on that ground, were not enough to deter Adams, as a rigid man of principle, from his course. The charge persisted in its adverse effect on Adams's political fortunes, persisted to disturb him to the very closing years of his life, when he was forced to listen to speeches in the House of Representatives reviving the old story.[116] Such matters as these were not, however, in the mainstream of human affairs, nor the deciding factors in the unfolding of the history of the times. The Adams Administration came to a close in "an upheaval"; "Adams, Clay, Federalism, the Virginia Dynasty, the Secretarial Succession, were brushed aside by the rush of the cheering masses bearing their hero to the White House."[117] Adams, for the time being, appeared

[113] Morse, *op. cit.,* p. 194.

[114] *Register of Debates* 22nd Cong., 1st sess., III, 3090–3091. See *Register of Debates,* appendix, 22nd Cong., 1st sess., III, 83–92.

[115] *Memoirs,* November 30, 1822, VI, 113–114.

[116] *Ibid.,* April 23, 1844, XII, 16 and April 30, 1844, XII, 21.

[117] Claude G. Bowers, *The Party Battles of the Jackson Period* (Boston and New York: Houghton, Mifflin, 1922), p. 34.

to be a symbol of an era which had spent itself; a revolution thus retired him for two years of bitter reflection, which saw "indecision and instability" in the beginning of the Jackson Administration, as well as the tendency to "feed the cormorant appetite for place." [118] He commented acidly on the role of Martin Van Buren who had sold New York to both Crawford and Jackson, playing "over again the game of Aaron Burr in 1800," and just as likely to reap the "reward of treachery." [119] He remarked with relish Mr. Vance of Ohio's wish that military government might collapse in the United States just as Jackson's friends, observing the disturbances in Britain, were praying for the collapse of military administration in England.[120] Adams charged that a claim by Jackson that his (Jackson's) actions in Florida had been consequent upon a collusive arrangement with Monroe was an effort to quiet his own conscience, aware of its ingratitude to Adams, an effort "as rotten as his own heart" and "in direct violation of the Constitution and of all its conservative principles." [121]

It was in this temper that John Quincy Adams, disregarding the sentiments and advice of family and friends, entered the most glorious period of his career. In September, 1830, he was approached to determine whether or not he would accept election to the House of Representatives from the Plymouth district. He declared that he had no desire to be elected a member of Congress and would not consent to announce himself as a candidate. He said that, if he were chosen, circumstances of a public and private nature would determine whether or not he would accept.[122] To announce that he would accept would be to ask for votes,[123] which he would not do, since he had never solicited the vote of any person in his own behalf for a public office and never would do so.[124] In view of the unfortunate two-term precedent, he pointed out that it was inevitable that ex-Presidents should generally survive by some time the termination of their terms of office. Their election to Congress would in no wise

[118] *Memoirs,* March 14, 1829, VIII, 113.
[119] *Ibid.,* June 8, 1829, p. 154.
[120] *Ibid.,* December 26, 1830, pp. 256–257 and December 29, 1830, p. 257.
[121] *Ibid.,* August 30, 1831, pp. 404–405.
[122] *Ibid.,* September 18, 1830, VIII, 239–240.
[123] *Ibid.,* September 25, 1830, p. 241.
[124] *Ibid.,* August 27, 1831, p. 404.

be a "derogatory descent."[125]   In fact, an ex-President could not be degraded by serving as a selectman in his home town.[126]   He pointed out that, if he had rejected the election, he would have been charged with arrogance or would have been ridiculed.[127]   Despite his seeming wish not to be elected, in order that he might spend an old age of leisure in avoidance of the political struggle, he recorded that his election "as President of the United States [had not been] half so gratifying to [his] inmost soul."[128]

Mr. Adams as a member of Congress faithfully and outstandingly performed his duties.   He sometimes remarked the habitual absence from the chamber of some of his colleagues, paid from the public treasury as if they had been present fulfilling their obligations twelve hours a day.[129]   Only the most severe illness could keep him at home; he worried over being late at the House; the heaviest work of committee would not deter him; and he rarely allowed the pleas of his age and physical deterioration to discourage him from the most conscientious effort.   Although his interests and the public business might push him to the end of his endurance, every impulse of his nature drove him from day to day into the struggle and into controversies that discretion would have avoided.   Determining to demonstrate his principle that a legislator must learn to take the buffeting of the political world without flinching,[130] he set out to manifest that industry and frugality, that patience and persevering effort, through which he had early concluded he might win honor in the world.[131]   Many years of "incessant active intercourse with the world [had] made political movement to [him] as much a necessary of life as atmospheric air."[132]   And thus he plunged into the fray, which was gathering force as the major crisis of the Republic approached.

The major problems, both foreign and domestic, confronting the United States while Adams was a representative in the House, as he

[125] *Memoirs,* November 7, 1830, pp. 245–246.
[126] *Ibid.,* September 18, 1830, pp. 239–240.
[127] *Ibid.,* November 7, 1830, pp. 245–246.
[128] *Ibid.,* November 7, 1830, VIII, 247.
[129] *Ibid.,* March 21, 1844, XI, 538.
[130] To John Spear Smith, Washington, September 26, 1817, *Writings,* VI, 193.
[131] Adams, *Life in a New England Town,* Letter to Abigail Adams, Newburyport, December 23, 1787, p. 74.
[132] *Memoirs,* March 23, 1841, X, 451.

was until the very day of his death on February 23, 1848, were modified or warped in their solution by the increasing problem of slavery.
His views concerning that institution will be dealt with below, but
it should be pointed out that John Quincy Adams, while always anti-
slavery, represented in his transition of thought from his first to his
last years in the House a change that was marked at large in the
country during the same period. In the first session of the twenty-
second Congress he presented fifteen petitions from the Society of
Friends in Pennsylvania calling for the abolition of slavery and for
the abolition of the slave trade.[133] He made clear his disagreement
with the purposes of the petitions, adding "that the most salutary
medicines, unduly administered, were the most deadly of poisons."
Ten years later he accepted resentfully but without denial the contentions in a speech by Wise of Virginia that he characterized as
follows: "Abolition, abolition, abolition was the unvarying cry; and
he represented me as a fiend, the inspirer and leader of all abolition." [134] Shortly after he noted in his diary the numerous threats
of lynching and assassination that he was continuously receiving from
the South and concluded that this was a fair index of the state of
morality of communities in which slavery existed.[135] Finally he
described his greatest affliction as the abandonment by his country
of the basic political and social principles to which she owed her
existence, the irreparable ruin of these principles "under the tran-
scendent power of slavery and the slave-representation.[136]

Closely related to the factor of slavery, in fact having its origin
in the national division deriving from it, was the fight for the unob-
structed right of petition limited at this time by the "gag" imposed
by the dominant Southern representation, a fight led by John Quincy
Adams to his everlasting honor.[137] The struggle began when the
slave-representation decided to introduce a resolution to be em-

[133] *Register of Debates*, 22nd Cong., 1st sess., II, December 12, 1831, pp.
1425–1426. *Memoirs*, December 12, 1831, VIII, 434.

[134] *Memoirs*, June 14, 1841, X, 479.

[135] *Ibid.*, May 21, 1842, XI, 159.

[136] *Ibid.*, May 29, 1844, XII, 37.

[137] "He was cordially disliked and disturbed by Garrison and Birney, the
chiefs of the Abolitionist sect, a feeling he returned in Scriptural measure, heaped
up, pressed down, running over, yet by his fearless, singlehanded fight for the
right of petition he did more to advance their cause than both of them combined."
Clark, *op. cit.*, p. 9.

bodied in the rules of the House, reading "that no petitions relating to slavery or the trade in slaves in any State, district, or Territory of the United States shall be read, printed, committed, or in any manner acted upon by the House." [138]   Adams precipitated the conflict by refusing to answer when his name was called on the question except to declare that the Southern tactic was unconstitutional as a violation of the right of petition of his constituents and the people of the United States, as well as of his right to freedom of speech in the House. The struggle continued through the vicissitudes and drama of many parliamentary battles with Adams in the vanguard and taking the brunt of the wrath of the slave-representation, until the day arrived on which he could note a thrilling victory against the architects of the "gag." [139]

Other issues which related closely to the issue of slavery were, of course, the tariff and the annexation of Texas.   Adams took his natural stand on the issues at stake.   To Jackson's assertion in a message that, since imposts placed an unwarranted burden upon the South, there should be a reduction of the tariffs in the interest of equity, except upon goods necessary to the safety of the nation in time of war, he (Adams) retorted that the President was giving way to the pressure embodied in the Ordinance of Secession and Nullification of the convention in South Carolina, thus canceling out the good effects of Jackson's Proclamation in answer to the South Carolinians.[140]   His stand on the annexation of Texas, a serious qualification of his expansionist nationalism, was likewise a product of his anti-slavery, typically Northeastern view.   He denied the validity of the conclusion of a report that represented Texans as struggling for liberty.   He said that they were really struggling for slavery.[141]   With greater vigor he later maintained that, beginning with Jackson, the deepest treachery had marked the project for Mexico's dismemberment and the perpetuation of slavery in Texas.[142]   Clearly indicating his view that the slavery factor was central, he contended that he would vote

[138] *Memoirs*, December 21, 1837, IX, 454: There were other forms, all directed toward the same purpose.

[139] "Blessed, forever blessed, be the name of God!," *ibid.*, December 3, 1844, XII, 116.

[140] Minority report of John Quincy Adams and Lewis Condit, Committee of Manufactures, *Register of Debates*, appendix, 22nd Cong., 2nd sess., II, 53.

[141] *Memoirs*, December 24, 1836, IX, 333.

[142] *Ibid.*, June 18, 1844, XII, 69.   *Ibid.*, April 8, 1844, p. 6.

for the annexation of Texas, if slavery could be abolished there and, in the interest of consistency, if Mexico would consent.[143]

The Bank question was not so clearly related to slavery; in fact, it was related to the other pressing issue of the day, the struggle between the masses, who were becoming politically and intellectually enfranchised, and the interests, an issue that was muddied rather than cleared by the struggle over slavery. Mr. Adams's stand was what his intellectual and social background and his current development demanded. He early became alarmed over the turn the public mind was taking on the matter of the Bank. On his way to Washington early in his career in the House, anticipating a struggle over that institution, he stopped in Philadelphia to see Nicholas Biddle and to divest himself of his certificates of stock in order to leave himself morally free to take his stand without fear of charges of ulterior interest.[144] Later he criticized the "base persecution of N. Biddle and the bank directors." [145] He early had a practical opportunity to champion the cause of the Bank, when he offered a resolution accepted by the House limiting the scope of an investigation, by a special committee of which he was a member, of the Bank's records and operations at its headquarters in Philadelphia.[146] As a member of the committee he later submitted a minority report that served as a general apology for the Bank and laudatory exposition of the principles that underlay it,[147] which he submitted for the consideration of the House on May 14, 1832.[148]

It should not be assumed that he was in unrelenting opposition to all Administrations that followed his own. In the French crisis, precipitated by the refusal of the French Chamber to appropriate money to pay the indemnity for losses by American vessels incurred during the Napoleonic wars according to the stipulations of the treaty of July, 1831, Adams parted company with his Whig colleagues in Congress and excoriated them for their failure to support the

[143] *Ibid.*, January 25, 1845, XII, 152.

[144] *Ibid.*, November 9, 1831, VIII, 425.

[145] *Ibid.*, December 26, 1833, IX, 61.

[146] *Register of Debates*, 22nd Cong., 1st sess., II, March 14, 1832, p. 2160; he later had occasion to protest that the committee had violated its instructions. *Ibid.*, April 30, 1832, pp. 2662, 2663.

[147] Minority Report on the Bank of the United States, *Register of Debates*, appendix, 22nd Cong., 1st sess., III, 54–73.

[148] *Register of Debates*, 22nd Cong., 1st sess., III, 3036.

President in a time of national crisis.[149] In a speech on January 22, 1836, Adams rose to answer Webster on the French crisis in a speech which he later claimed "demolished" his opponent, "drove him from the field, and whipped him and his party into the rank and file of the nation in the quarrel with the French King." [150] His capacity for rising above party strife is indicated in the *Memoirs,* wherein he noted the victory of Jackson in the negotiations with France that had resulted in the appropriation of the indemnity by the French Chamber, even though coupled with a French demand for explanations, and objectively stated that this victory would sweep away the political opposition, the members of which had been more blundering than the Administration and had forgotten that "the interest of the country was involved." [151] In his speech Adams affirmed his readiness to believe that the Executive could be relied upon to make proper use of the $3,000,000 that the House had appropriated, and he denied that such a belief could be charged up to "man worship." [152]

John Quincy Adams, of course, is always accounted a Whig, and with some reason, but the label is subject to qualification. He remained all his life more than most others of his day independent of any strict party line. And so it might be anticipated of any man who could remark, in connection with his struggle over the right of petition,[153] "That I have eternal right on my side, is certain." Such a man would not budge before the whiplash of the party struggle. He had called for a new party alignment to counteract the divisive results of the "progress of this [Jackson's] administration," and he anticipated that Mr. Clay would take the lead.[154] He had seen the importance of uniting the Antimasonic Party with the National Republicans, in order to forestall the alignment of the former with the forces of Jackson.[155] But the diary comment that "The Whig party, as they call themselves, is splitting up into a thousand fragments," rendered almost a decade later, is not that of a man who has completely identified himself with that party.[156] Nor is the attention

---

[149] See Bowers, *op. cit.,* pp. 386–422, for a full discussion of the crisis.

[150] Summary of the Year, following entry of December 31, 1836, *Memoirs,* IX, 339.

[151] *Ibid.,* May 26, 1835, IX, 238.

[152] *Register of Debates,* 24th Cong., 1st sess., II, January 22, 1836, p. 2272.

[153] *Memoirs,* December 28, 1841, XI, 45.

[154] *Ibid.,* January 24, 1830, VIII, 180.

[155] *Ibid.,* January 13, 1834, IX, 75.

[156] *Ibid.,* November 5, 1841, XI, 28.

paid by Adams in the diary to a visit by General Gaines, who said he had come to see again the only President of the United States he had ever seen, all the others being Presidents of a party, the reaction of a congenital party stalwart.[157]   He had always supported the goals of the Antimasonic Party from the time he had remarked the disappearance and death of the Antimason Morgan in New York,[158] but he described that party on one occasion as a product of "restless and turbulent spirits," always prepared "to quarrel," and "the germs of the Jacobin clubs," that spirit which had produced a great host of societies and a new one "beating the drum and blowing the trumpet for a holy Sabbath." [159]

On only one occasion did Adams, with relenting spirit, bask in the sunshine of party or popular adulation. This occasion was his triumphal tour from his home in Massachusetts to Cincinnati to give a speech at the dedication of the observatory there on the invitation of the Cincinnati Astronomical Society.[160]   In his early life he had dwelt upon the inexplicable quality of human nature and prayed that he might learn to put his trust in it before he advanced upon the political stage.[161]   During this trip, which greatly to his surprise produced an avalanche of popular acclaim, he in some measure relaxed and took joy in it, but it was short-lived, for as the trip was drawing to its end he found in the plaudits of the people

empty honors showered upon me ostensibly by the people as I pass along, but embracing only part of the people, and carrying with it no solid permanent opinion. They bring to my heart no feeling of pride, to mind no new or useful truth.[162]

Thus without any final reason for a transformation of his fundamental attitudes toward men, John Quincy Adams came to the day of his death, February 23, 1843, in the Capitol building where he had been stricken, to the last true to his sense of duty.

[157] *Ibid.,* January 1, 1842, p. 48.
[158] *Ibid.,* October 25, 1827, VII, 345.
[159] *Ibid.,* January 21, 1844, XI, 491.
[160] *Ibid.,* October 24 to November 23, 1843, XI, 410–441.
[161] Adams, *Life in a New England Town,* November 23, 1787, p. 65.
[162] *Memoirs,* November 21, 1843, XI, 439: note his reference to "part of the people," for the conviction is implicit in the Adams philosophy that principle and truth should have an appeal to all the minds of rational men, not merely some of them. Of course, John Quincy Adams was capable, in the tradition of his day, of unequivocal conviction that he was the vehicle of principle and truth.

PART TWO

The Man

3

An Adams Personality: The World Viewed from on High

The question comes with yearly aggravation upon my conscience, what have I done with the seventy-four years that I have been indulged with the blessing of life?
—MEMOIRS, *July 11, 1841*

John Quincy Adams's quality as a human being has a direct and obvious relation to his political and social thinking. The reactions of his contemporaries to his personality are, of course, important to the rendering of a sound critical judgment, but those reactions are so inextricably bound together with political passions, the immediate prejudices of the day, and the effect of party or sectional loyalties that it is worth while to seek another source of appraisal. Adams's own writings are a profitable source of information about his personality and nature. They in high degree reveal why it was Brooks Adams's fervent wish that his grandfather might live again in another light, understood for his ambitions, his purposes, and his failures, and not remain merely a "martyr to his belief in God, education, and science."[1] Thus may be revealed those "anfractuosities, humors, and prejudices" that no doubt have in considerable measure prevented his posterity from viewing him with the interest and admiration that his stature and contributions merit.[2]

The failure of those who have followed properly to evaluate him is the more difficult to understand when the eulogies of his fellow countrymen at the time of his death are read, and it is recognized how

[1] Henry Adams, *The Degradation of the Democratic Dogma*, p. xiii.
[2] Nevins (ed.), *The Diary of John Quincy Adams, 1794–1845*, p. xi.

49

widely they cut across sectional and party lines.[3] Not the least of these came from Mr. Holmes of North Carolina, a fellow-member of the House representing that part of the country where in many quarters the name of John Quincy Adams had long been an abomination by reason of his stand on slavery and related issues.[4] A most confirmed political opponent, Senator T. H. Benton of Missouri, with whom Adams had been in controversy on an issue exceedingly close to his heart, internal improvement and the public lands, rose in the Senate at the time of Adams's death to do him honor and pay him the last respects of that body.[5] It would have been well for the record had sentiments then expressed forever put to rest the "intrigue, hatred, and slander" that had surrounded him and through which he had "pursued his undeviating course in the serene consciousness of high motives." [6]

The very consciousness of high rectitude and motive that he never lost may be a major reason for a forgetful posterity, which would have preferred more common human weaknesses. The consistency with which he maintained his standards of industry, frugality, patience, and perseverance which he early established as guides to success understandably could make enemies of those who disliked appearing at a disadvantage in relation to such standards. A man who could impose upon himself the keeping of a "letter-book, a diary [of the size of the *Memoirs*], a book of receipts and expenses . . . without intermission . . . [as] the rule of duty of every man who can

[3] See *Token of a Nation's Sorrow,* Addresses in the Congress of the United States (Washington: J. and G. S. Gideon, 1848).

[4] *Ibid.,* p. 15. The following reference suggests a change in attitude toward him among members of the House. A reading of the *Congressional Globe* will indicate a change in the language of the reporter, particularly after 1844 when it became common to refer to him as the "venerable" member and to note that the members crowded about him eager to catch what he said in his feeble and failing voice: "There he sat, with his interested eye upon every thing that passed, the picturesque and rare old man; unapproachable by all others in the unity of his character and in the thousand-fold anxieties which centered upon him. No human being ever entered this Hall without turning habitually and with heartfelt deference first to him, and few ever left it without passing as they went to pour out their blessings upon that spirit of consecration to the country which brought and which kept him here." *Ibid.,* p. 18, from the speech of Mr. McDowell of Virginia.

[5] John Quincy Adams, *Poems of Religion and Society* (Auburn and Buffalo: Miller, Orton and Mulligan, 1848), introductory essay, "The Character of Mr. Adams," pp. 12–14.

[6] Nevins, *op. cit.,* p. XV.

read and write" might well be a man of the kind of grim determination that repels those of inferior discipline.[7] Had more of his closest contemporaries known that there was also in him a faculty of critical self-analysis, albeit combined with much self-assurance, he would have suffered less at the hands of his critics.[8] He was occasionally aware of the severity of his judgment of the performance of others. His account of small experiences betrayed this awareness, as when through a negligence, which he admitted he would have found inexcusable in another, he mistook the hour of the morning upon rising and did not get himself and his family off on time upon their journey to Washington after their arrival in New York from Europe.

He seldom was unwilling to see his judgments embodied in public action or decision. Some measure of this quality may be seen in his attitude in the expulsion case of Senator John Smith, accused by indictment of a grand jury of involvement in the remarkable plots of Aaron Burr. Adams objected to Smith's request for counsel and judicial proceedings, and for the establishment of facts in an ordinary legal way. The action of the legislature prior to projected expulsion was, he said, necessarily *ex parte*, with the proper guide "a sound discretion, what the Constitution requires and what every man's experience in private life teaches him the value of." [9] He deemed Senator Smith sufficiently protected and was willing to decide the case on his (Adams's) own discretion guided by his sense of right and wrong. At this early date the precedents were not clearly established, but he was not deflected from his opinion by the attitudes of others, such as Senator Pope, who expressed surprise at Adams's view of the proceedings, which Pope held to be in substance an avoidance of equity and justice.[10] Adams denied that the basis of the committee report which he was defending was mere suspicion, and claimed that, far from being too suspicious, he had probably always been guilty of an "excess of confidence in the political integrity of other men." [11]

[7] *Memoirs,* July 20, 1834, IX, 159.

[8] *Ibid.*, December 4, 1803, I, 276: "Pride and self-conceit and presumption lie so deep in my natural character, that, when their deformity betrays them, they run through all the changes of Proteus, to disguise themselves to my own heart."

[9] *Annals of Congress,* 10th Cong., 1st sess., I, January 7, 1808, pp. 66–67, 73–74.

[10] *Ibid.*, January 20, 1808, p. 94.

[11] *Ibid.*, April 9, 1808, pp. 317–321.

He viewed the moral and intellectual quality of others from unassailable heights whereon he felt himself for the most part secure despite occasional lapses of self-analysis. Forgetting his own youthful unscathed experience in Europe, he noted the preparation of one T. P. Barton for a journey to Europe, which he considered the journey of a young man just fit to be ruined by such an experience.[12] An even more remarkable example of this quality of mind was provided when he decided that in the future, as a rule of operation, when President Monroe, his chief, was considering a proposition or subject that did not merit adoption or consideration he should, rather than expend effort in opposition, "leave absurdity to die a natural death."[13] Or, when he discovered Silesian engravers pretending to superiority over British craftsmen, he recorded, no doubt with himself in mind, that "mediocrity can never forbear carping at talents superior to itself."[14] His opinions and judgments were quickly formed, often extreme in statement, and firmly held; some of his capacity for extreme statement may be discerned in his charge to the Secretary of State that the Smithsonian fund should not be dissipated "to feed the hunger or fatten the leaden idleness of mountebank projectors, and shallow and worthless pretenders to science."[15]

His associates who wished him well hoped that he would guard against being led too far by his irritations. Others believed that he should adjust himself more completely to the tempers and dispositions of those with whom he associated, that he should develop manners more accommodating, and "a readiness to yield small points, that he . . . [might] carry great ones."[16] Although he might on occasion indicate an awareness of defects in his personality, for the most part he plunged unrelentingly forward. He was adamant in his conflict with Clay over the disposition of the papers of the American peace mission at Ghent.[17] His political enmities were in an

[12] *Memoirs*, April 7, 1821, V, 340.

[13] *Ibid.*, November 2, 1819, IV, 429.

[14] John Quincy Adams, *Letters on Silesia* (London: J. Budd, 1804), p. 66.

[15] 25th Cong., 3rd sess., H. Doc. 11, Executive, "Letter from John Quincy Adams to the Secretary of State, John Forsyth, Esq.," Quincy, October 11, 1838, p. 7.

[16] Brown, *The Missouri Compromises and Presidential Politics, 1820–1825*, Letter to William Plumer, Sr. from William Plumer, Jr., Washington, D. C., December 3, 1821, p. 64.

[17] *Memoirs*, December 31, 1814, III, 138.

amazing degree lasting and personal enmities. The politics of his day were often the politics of undisciplined passions, and it is true that John Quincy Adams suffered severely at the hands of the political opposition, but there is much reason to believe that his spirit was particularly vulnerable, that he sometimes took with unbecoming irritation normal political opposition. He saw all the political world against him. In 1840 he recorded in the *Memoirs* that he felt that he had been exceedingly restrained in having submitted without retort to "the foulest and basest aspersions" upon himself and his father in a campaign led by Jackson who began with denunciations in his first inaugural address, a campaign supplemented by the assaults of the "old Hamiltonian federalist," particularly in his native state of Massachusetts.[18] Later he noted that speech by New Hampshire's Edmund Burke was symbolic of the Democracy of that state and impregnated with the spirit of slavery, malignant in its partisanship and its "oozing out of personal venom against me."[19] On another occasion he affirmed that of all men living none had used baser means of attacking his reputation and character than the Secretary of the Navy, David Henshaw.[20] Adams displayed infinite willingness to use invective against those who attacked him because he claimed to have exposed their evil purposes.[21] A statement in the *Memoirs,* remarkable for the range of personalities it covered, records all the devices that men had used to stand in his way, "base and dirty tricks to thwart [his] progress in life and destroy [his] character," and the men thus guilty run an amazing sweep to include Harrison Gray Otis, Parsons, Pickering, Bayard, Clay, Russell, Crawford, Calhoun, Jackson, Webster, John Davis, Giles, and Randolph.[22]

His air of public superiority must often have been more than enough to incite his colleagues to anger, for he could with great facility vary his weapons, substituting self-righteous indulgence for scorn and sarcasm. He mght publicly congratulate himself that it was unnecessary to reply to the Chairman of the Committee of Ways

[18] *Ibid.,* August 13, 1840, X, 347.
[19] *Ibid.,* March 16, 1844, XI, 533.
[20] *Ibid.,* December 14, 1843, XI, 448.
[21] *Ibid.,* February 11, 1843, p. 316: "In the House, Gwinn, of Mississippi, disgorged his swindler spleen upon me for exposing his knavery and that of his Governor, McNutt."
[22] *Ibid.,* November 23, 1835, IX, 263.

and Means in the same tone that the Chairman had used.[23] Or, gaining a laugh from his hearers at the expense of another who in white-
hot anger stared at him as if to subdue him into silence, he relished
the opportunity to note that he (Adams) "looked at him occasionally
in the face with cool indifference, and went on." [24] The records of
Congressional debates are dramatic with undertones of his legislative
personality as he is recorded as "exultingly" reading to the House a
"very delectable letter" of Mr. Wise of Virginia with reminders that
attention should be kept sharpened to enjoy the "sweetest part." [25]

The political opposition bitterly attacked him, as when General
Smyth of Virginia declared his passions made him unfit to hold an
office of high responsibility.[26] He was accused in the most explicit
manner and vicious innuendo of corruption, viz., in making "constructive journies" for which he charged the government, or for doing
political favors at the taxpaper's expense in return for votes.[27] His
greatest accomplishments were disparaged by political enemies in
terms that inevitably embittered his nature.[28] Despite his relative
and ostensible disinterestedness, he was accused of having an over-
wrought desire for office and the emoluments thereof and charged
with having no regard for others.[29] As a matter of fact, highly sensi-
tive to such accusations, he took refuge in "reserved, cold, austere,
and forbidding manners," the reputation of a "gloomy misanthropist"
or "unsocial savage," and he was not so much without the means of
reforming himself as without a desire to do so, since, by his nature,
this was the front with which he must meet the world's criticism.[30]
He asserted that he had never been and would never be a man
popular with the people, that he was unqualified by nature, his train-

[23] *Register of Debates*, 22nd Cong., 1st sess., III, 3290–3291.

[24] *Memoirs*, May 2, 1838, IX, 521–522.

[25] *Congressional Globe*, 27th Cong., 2nd sess., January 22, 1842, p. 163.

[26] To the Freeholders of Washington, Wythe, Grayson, Russell, Tazewell, Lee
and Scott Counties, Virginia, *Writings*, VII, 338.

[27] Anon., *Plain Matters of Fact, Undenied and Undeniable* (Richmond, 1828),
from the *Richmond Enquirer*, pp. 1–57.

[28] Anon., *The Treaty of Ghent and the Fisheries, or the Diplomatic Talents of
John Quincy Adams Candidly Examined* (Boston: J. H. A. Frost, 1824), p. 3:
"Who has not heard of the triumphant result of the negotiations of Ghent? Who
does not know that the glory of the triumph is claimed by John Quincy Adams?
He is the intellectual giant who prostrated with ease the sophistry, and the arguments; the arts, schemes and strategems of a superannuated admiral and two
more diplomatic machines."

[29] *Congressional Globe*, 24th Cong., 1st sess., appendix, p. 709.

[30] *Memoirs*, June 4, 1819, IV, 388.

ing, and his experience for the role of the "courtier," and was just as little desirous of being flattered by others.[31]   In fact, although his reactions show interest in the good will of the people, it is true that his concern was never enough to bring him to deviate from the course he had chosen, however unpopular it might be.

No consideration of personal interest deterred him from riding against the center of the enemy's line in the fight for the causes that he had determined to support.   Hurling the charge of dictatorial methods at others in debate, it was natural that he should meet the same charge from the opposition, which could easily dramatize his intransigeance in such terms.   However much such qualities of persistence earned popularity in some sectors, they were not the political qualities that would earn general acclaim.   Few of his opponents doubted his abilities, his vast knowledge, and his integrity, but the manifestation of these qualities in Mr. Adams's case produced respect more often than popularity.   It comes as no surprise, then, to discover him at the beginning of his career in the House charging himself to remember for the sake of his peace of mind the lesson of experience, that strong attachments to persons or things should be avoided.[32]   He attempted to insulate himself from the importunities of others and their praise, which he often interpreted as flattery, and would have preferred to view ostensible "professions of veneration" more with contempt than otherwise.[33]   He chose rather to find superiority in withstanding the masses as a test of character, accepting the chance of being abandoned by all the world "sustained only by an overruling consciousness of rectitude." [34]

This granite quality of character could not crowd out a sympathetic awareness of misery.   During the journey through Silesia he was quick to observe the miserable quality of the villages through which he passed inhabited by a poor and miserable population of beggars, and ironically he pressed himself to do justice to the land by admitting that he did see some comfortable and attractive houses of the nobility.[35]   Feeling a deep concern for man's physical well being, he opposed the abandonment of the pillory as a punishment for felony,

[31] To Louisa Catherine Adams, August 11, 1821, Washington, D. C., *Writings*, VII, 170.

[32] *Memoirs*, July 19, 1831, VIII, 382.

[33] *Ibid.*, October 19, 1841, XI, 27.

[34] *Ibid.*, December 22, 1833, IX, 58.

[35] Adams, *Letters on Silesia*, p. 3.

since it operated on the moral sense of man rather than upon his physical nature. Punishments acting upon the latter he would soften.[36] Declaring military law always harsh, he held that Congress must protect the lowly from the harsh penalties of such law imposed by military or naval administrators. He, therefore, opposed a bill that proposed to grant power to a board of naval officers to draw up rules and regulations for the governance of the navy that should be the law of the land in appropriate cases unless Congress by positive action disallowed them. He found such a grant of legislative authority particularly abhorrent because it granted the power to impose the death penalty.[37] This quality of sympathy for the lowly was shown on another occasion when, as President, he refused to sanction the death penalty imposed on a soldier during peace time on the ground that such a penalty was too severe except in time of war.[38] Without treating broadly his doctrinal view of the institution of slavery at this point, we may with relevance here indicate the revulsion that he felt at the "hideous reality of the slave ascendancy." [39] The institution violated the principle of man's natural liberty as he understood it, and it offered to him a theme for great eloquence. Nor was his interest only in the abstract institution of slavery, for individual cases of hardship among slaves reached his heart. It was revolting to him that slaveowners, depending upon what suited their interests, could look upon their slaves as both subjects and chattels.[40] He looked with disdain upon the "slave-scourging republicanism" of the slavocracy.[41] In the closing years of his life, he saw this force turning Texas, while Texans were toasting glory, from a land of freemen into a land of slaves.[42] In the assiduous opposition to all that he held evil there was a high order of courage of which the whole of his life was the evidence.

Adams stands out as a man whose most earnest determination was to pursue and support principles to which in reason he could sub-

[36] *Congressional Globe*, 25th Cong., 3rd sess., February 23, 1839, p. 202.

[37] *Ibid.*, 27th Cong., 2nd sess., May 17, 1842, p. 510.

[38] *Memoirs*, June 13, 1825, VII, 29.

[39] *Ibid.*, June 12, 1843, XI, 381.

[40] John Quincy Adams, *Argument before the Supreme Court of the United States in the Case of the United States, Appellants, v. Cinque, and others, Africans* [15 Peters 518] (New York: S. W. Benedict, 1841), p. 17.

[41] *Memoirs*, July 5, 1819, IV, 398.

[42] *Ibid.*, June 6, 1838, X, 11–12.

scribe, but, remarkable as this struggle was, it would be an error to assume that he had little personal ambition. He was no ascetic moralist; he also felt the promptings of desire for success and place:

> I want the seals of power and place,
>   The ensigns of command,
> Charged by the people's unbought grace
>   To rule my native land.
> Nor crown, nor sceptre would I ask
>   But from my country's will,
> By day, by night, to ply the task
>   Her cup of bliss to fill.[43]

At forty-five, when he was the diplomatic representative of the United States in St. Petersburg, he expressed fear that he had allowed a major portion of his life to slip by without distinction and regretted that qualities of weakness and "indolence"—of all things—should frustrate his achieving the goals he sought. Thenceforth, he determined, his resolutions must be fulfilled.[44] Seven years before, a very young Senator acquitting himself with distinction if not to the entire satisfaction of the party of his original affiliation, he gloomily saw the decline of his political prospects.[45] On another occasion as a young politician, he expressed his fear that faction and party would make it impossible for him to remain true to his principles without sacrificing all opportunity for advancement.[46] In fact throughout his life he expressed fears that his life was being wasted and that it would not be marked by history. For example, when the State Secretaryship placed upon his shoulders such a great burden of work, he apprehended that the desultory accomplishment of the day to day business of the Department would result in his being able to leave behind him in the office no evidence of having occupied it.[47] He feared not only that life might pass him by but also that his own principles might stand in the way of accomplishment.

One finds more than a trace of regret that these principles precluded his caballing and canvassing to procure advantage in the

[43] Adams, *Poems of Religion and Society,* "The Wants of Man," stanza XXII, p. 22.
[44] *Memoirs,* July 11, 1812, II, 387.
[45] *Ibid.,* December 31, 1805, I, 380.
[46] *Ibid.,* December 31, 1803, I, 283.
[47] *Ibid.,* April 26, 1819, IV, 352.

struggle for office, even though he put on a brave face and prepared himself for "unwilling retirement" rather than use the political methods he had rejected.[48]   While ostensibly rejecting the political methods of the day for his own use, at the same time he anticipated with concern that Secretary Crawford's rivalry in the struggle for the Presidency, which took the form of opposition on all occasions, might have the effect Crawford desired.[49]   Adams noted also that rumors concerning his *own* political actions were circulated by his enemies to discredit him.   There was, for example, the report that as Secretary of State he had refused to see Bassett, a House committee chairman.   The existence of this rumor was a warning, he wrote, that he had "watchful enemies at the Capitol" whose intrigues he must overcome in his progress toward higher success.[50]   With respect to the project he formulated as Secretary of State for regulating the relative rights of belligerents and neutrals in time of war, a project that was to mark a great change in the laws of war, there is no doubt that he was sincerely interested in improving the condition of mankind. Nor is there any doubt that he looked upon such projects as means of adding increased honor to his name for having proposed them.[51] When he was apprised that the Antimasonic forces were considering the prospect of nominating him for a second term in the Presidency, he professed to Seward that he desired neither the nomination nor the office, yet he affirmed that he would not reject a convention nomination, should it be offered.[52]

His ambitions to achieve place were matched by his ambitions to achieve solid accomplishments that would be remembered by a grateful posterity.   It was with deep distrust that he concluded that the Jackson Administration was destroying everything of which he had planted the germ.   He feared that the opposition he received from others would endanger the recognition that he hoped the future would give him.   This opposition varied in direct proportion to the extent of obligation to him, and he assessed "demerits" in keeping with the degree of opposition.   Of all his enemies, Jackson earned the most "demerits."   Adams felt that Crawford, next to Jackson, most owed him gratitude, rather than political opposition. Although Calhoun's obligation was least of all, Adams noted that he was guilty of duplicity in seeking the Presidency in 1824, of mendacious dealings with Jackson in the same year, and, after March 4, 1829, of heartless neglect of social amenities out of fear of Jackson.[53] This distress caused Adams briefly to entertain the thought of seeking complete retirement after the Presidency. Upon being asked to attend a dinner being given for Clay by the latter's friends shortly before Clay's departure from Washington and immediately following the end of the Adams Administration, Adams asked to be excused, since he proposed to retire to the same degree "as a nun taking the veil."[54] But it was not many months thereafter that he was in the thick of the political battle again, and, moreover, exhorting his legislative colleagues to keep in mind their posterity and subscribe to the *Register of Debates*.[55]

For the most part, however, as Brooks Adams made clear, although "the President" until the end of his life never lost his ambition to implant his principles in American society, he came to have little hope of success. His apprehension was that he would die leaving little more than goals beyond the power of his abilities to accomplish, and tenets and principles too refined for the time in which he had lived.[56] In moments of extreme anguish he was capable of contending that in a long life he could remember almost no instance of success attending any of his projects.[57] He determined to leave to his son's good judgment the disposition of many volumes of materials and "multitudes of fragments—trash inexpressible, which I pray to God may never be exposed" to be collected into a memoir of his life then to be passed on to a worthy grandson and thence on to future generations. This was in the hope that it would gain the admiration of those who followed him, but the *Memoirs* indicate little optimism that this goal would be achieved. Despite his prodigious literary production, the world's judgment being even before his death neither

[53] *Ibid.*, January 4, 1831, VIII, 275; one sentence in this illuminating reference indicates both his ambition and his egocentrism: "I walk between burning ploughshares; let me be mindful where I place my foot."

[54] *Ibid.*, March 6, 1829, p. 107.

[55] *Register of Debates,* 22nd Cong., 1st sess., III, June 16, 1832, pp. 3602–3603.

[56] *Memoirs*, December 28, 1839, X, 177.

[57] *Ibid.*, August 9, 1833, IX, 14.

"just nor kind," he concluded that mankind would judge him and know him not:

> Oh God!—Horatio, what a wounded name
> Things standing thus unknown shall live behind me.[58]

It was not with pleasure but with some reason and confidence that he wrote that his old age promised to witness his being forsaken by men, his only consolation a great assurance of rectitude.[59]

Adams deserved the recognition that he sought on the score of general intellectual ability and integrity. His whole career attests to his ability. In moments of crisis, even his inveterate enemies, in recognition of his capacity, were accustomed to turn to him. At one time he was called upon to resolve a nearly hopeless snarl at the opening of a session in the House of Representatives. Two separate delegations from New Jersey demanded recognition. The clerk of the House refused to render decisions necessary to the organization of the House until one of the two delegations had been recognized. The House by acclaim turned to Adams to preside over the sessions, wherein his great prestige and incisive mind assisted in the resolution of the difficulties.[60] In the words of William Plumer, Jr., Adams's "talents" and "knowledge" were "universally acknowledged" even though he might be wanting in "*popular* talents." [61] Often his abilities won for him victory over assailants who were constrained thereby to run from the field of political battle. One such occasion was described by Rep. J. R. Underwood of Kentucky, a slaveholder, in a speech opposing an attempt to censure Adams for submitting a petition recommending the dissolution of the Union. Underwood described a previous occasion when such a censure of the redoubtable representative from Massachusetts had been attempted because he asked whether petitions from free Negroes or slaves could be received

[58] Letter to Charles W. Upham, Washington, February 2, 1837, as quoted in Edward H. Tatum, Jr. (ed.), "Ten Unpublished Letters of John Quincy Adams, 1796–1837," *The Huntington Library Quarterly*, IV, No. 3 (April, 1941), pp. 369–388.

[59] *Memoirs*, December 22, 1833, IX, 58.

[60] *Ibid.*, December 3, 1839, X, 143, *passim*. *Congressional Globe*, 26th Cong., 1st sess., pp. 20, 21.

[61] Brown, *op. cit.*, letter to Salma Hale from William Plumer, Jr., Washington, D. C., April 5, 1820, p. 47.

under the rules of the House: "After the gentleman had effectually 'used' up his assailants—after their missiles had rebounded from the mighty shield of the ex-President, and inflicted ghastly wounds on those who sent them—when there was no charge left, upon which to base a censure, except that he had given 'color to an idea,' we got clear of the whole affair by laying it on the table, never to be taken up again." [62]   Those who contended with him in the political arena could never sincerely question his abilities.

Adams was almost as much a product of Europe as of America. His capacious mind had absorbed tastes and ideas unusual in Americans of his generation.   His mind was intricate, in many ways ahead of its time, not only in the arts, but also in science, his knowledge of which was remarkable.

The integrity that was so characteristic of Adams had as one of its major components a strong, almost crushing, sense of duty, an almost medieval sense of community deriving through Locke and Hooker from the Middle Ages, although that of Locke had been greatly modified by a new stress upon the individual.   It might have been considered crushing to another, but Adams prayed for more hours in the day during which he might pour out his energies.[63]   The sense of duty that he felt was part of a duty to society imposed on each generation to contribute to succeeding generations in payment of a debt to its predecessors; this duty, not being payable directly, is owed to the whole order of generations.[64]   He was impressed by the glories of generations "passed away," and asked himself what the duties were that had devolved upon his own.[65]   In this higher type of social duty, man, adding the obligations of justice, fidelity to others, and industry in providing for mutual assistance to the "duties of self-preservation," must exchange the surplus of his own production for "an equivalent supply to his own wants" from others, and the greater

[62] *Congressional Globe*, 27th Cong., 2nd sess., appendix, p. 234.

[63] Quoted in Quincy, *Memoir of the Life of John Quincy Adams*, pp. 52–53: "If the day was forty-eight hours, instead of twenty-four, I could employ them all, if I had but eyes and hands to read and write."

[64] "Letters to my children," *Memoirs*, II, 10–11.

[65] Adams, *An Oration Delivered before the Inhabitants of the Town of Newburyport, at their request, on The Sixty-first Anniversary of the Declaration of Independence, July 4, 1837* (Newburyport: Charles Whipple, 1837), p. 13. Hereafter cited as Adams, *Newburyport Oration, 1837*.

his fulfillment of these obligations the more will his time be absorbed by hard work and the end of his existence achieved.[66] Under a driving sense of his obligation to society, Adams worked often far beyond the normal capacity of his body, but, despite that, he was oppressed by a sense of failure, which he thought was a product of "passions, indolence, weakness, and infirmity." [67] His own sense of failure in a life marked by more than adequate distinction indicated that he charged himself with a far higher standard of performance than he imposed upon his children who were merely admonished to take their part in extending the blessings of existence to others in return for their enjoyment of those blessings.[68] He felt a pre-eminent mission, not always articulated, but implicit in his projects and his performances.

His passive attitude in the struggle for political place, which forbade him to seek office, assumed that when he was chosen either by an electorate or by the constitutional authorities to occupy a position or to perform a mission he had a duty to accept the mandate despite the opposition of his own inclinations or judgment. It was as if he assumed that the arm of right destiny or divine wisdom had made the selection, and his duty was to heed the wishes of the "public sense" or authority. Under the influence of such ideas, he accepted the appointment to St. Petersburg and other offices during his long career. His decision as to right and wrong once made, no threat to life or health or political advantage could deter him from his defense of the former and his attack upon the latter. His effective, although not direct, legislative support of the abolitionist cause by means of his championship of the right of petition and his diatribes against slavery, at a time when, through the conjuncture of political forces, the advantages were on the other side, thoroughly illustrates this principle. His association with the Antimasonic forces, a party often ridiculed by potent political forces, illustrated his principle of the duty publicly to oppose what his reason rejected. The index references to Adams's participation in the controversies of the House of Representatives compared to the index references to the statements of his colleagues are ample illustration of this.

[66] Adams, *Newburyport Oration, 1837*, p. 13.
[67] *Memoirs*, July 11, 1812, II, 387.
[68] "Letters to my children," *ibid.*, p. 9.

His great activity in the House may be accounted for by another principle of Adams directly bearing upon his sense of duty. He refused to go to New York to make a speech because he considered it wrong to be away from the House a single day.[69] He would not agree to give a speech commemorating the second centennial of his native town of Braintree, since it would take him away from his work at the House of Representatives.[70] Imposing upon himself an arduous legislative burden, he resented the habitual absence of many other members of the House. In a reference just short of comic, we find Adams fretting beneath his habitually composed exterior against waste of precious time as he sat in the two-hour silence of a Quaker meeting, his mind rambling "from this world to the next." [71] There was, in addition to his sense of obligation to institutions and his simple feeling of a duty to avoid wasting time, at least a professed will to do simple deeds of goodness, for he claimed to believe, in the manner of the Emperor Titus, that a day is lost without the accomplishment of a good deed.[72] On a higher level, his deeply felt duty to science was exemplified in the great efforts he devoted to his *Report on Weights and Measures* to the Congress [73] and in the views expressed in his oration delivered on the occasion of the dedication of an astronomical observatory in Cincinnati.[74] This devotion to causes was often dramatically, although sincerely, expressed, and nowhere more completely than when as an old man he devoted much time to preparing his argument in United States *v.* Cinque for presentation before the Supreme Court and later for publication, pressed on by

[69] Quincy, *op. cit.,* p. 263.

[70] *Memoirs,* October 29, 1839, X, 141.

[71] *Ibid.,* March 25, 1821, V, 335.

[72] *Ibid.,* June 29, 1820, p. 162.

[73] *Report of the Secretary of State upon Weights and Measures,* 16th Cong., 2nd sess., H. Doc. 109 (Washington, 1821), hereafter cited as Adams, *Report on Weights and Measures.* This was a monumental report also printed as S. Doc. 119, prepared by Adams in obedience to a Resolution of the Senate of the third of March, 1817. Not only did he do a vast amount of research in preparing it, but the results of much original experimentation went into it. Its quality earned a delayed, but nevertheless genuine, recognition from other students of the subject both at home and abroad. One of the tragedies of his later life was his view that selfishness, greed, and competition in rapidly expanding America were making science and education the tools of evil. See Henry Adams, *op. cit.,* p. 85.

[74] See John Quincy Adams, *An Oration, Delivered before the Cincinnati Astronomical Society on the Occasion of Laying the Corner Stone of an Astronomical Observatory* (Cincinnati: Shepard and Co., 1843), hereafter cited as Adams, *Cincinnati Oration.*

his interest in the cause of the miserable Africans and determination to "die upon the breach." [75]

The views of Adams held by other politicians, especially those in strong opposition, are exceedingly illuminating and perhaps a better guide to an understanding of his personality than any others. Surely the impressions of his enemies are distilled, and where they convey praise we may assume that candor demanded a recognition of ability and integrity. No appraisal would be more valuable than that of Martin Van Buren, a political opponent of high quality from whom fairness might be expected. He was a political partisan who accepted party strife and parties as Adams never did theoretically. Van Buren could consequently rise above partisanship, for he accepted it as part of the political process; whereas Adams, immersed in rigid principle, could not attain the objectivity of the avowed politician.

Van Buren understood Adams's "want of popularity," as the politician inevitably would.[76] But he praised the New Englander for his incorruptibility, his support of the Embargo, his stand on the War of 1812, his successes as a diplomat and Secretary of State.[77] Adams's constitutional interpretations and, especially, his rejection of "party distinctions" could gain no support from the successor to Jackson, who likewise disagreed with his support of internal improvements and his independence of the will of his constituents.[78] The praise was fulsome when the occasion demanded it, however. For example, consider Van Buren's comments on Adams's support of the project to give power to Jackson to enforce an indemnity against the French: ". . . no liberal mind can fail to admire the spirit and indomitable firmness with which he maintained opinions which he, doubtless, conscientiously believed to be right although they were not always in harmony with those of the House. On more than one of these occasions he presented a full-length portrait of the 'old man eloquent' not often exhibited to that body." [79]

[75] *Memoirs,* March 29, 1841, X, 453–454.
[76] John C. Fitzpatrick, "The Autobiography of Martin Van Buren," *Annual Report of the American Historical Association,* Vol. II for the year 1918 (Washington: Government Printing Office, 1920), p. 157.
[77] *Ibid.,* p. 192.
[78] *Ibid.,* pp. 192–195.
[79] *Ibid.,* p. 271.

4

The Adams Mind: Man and the Universe

I suggested to him the establishment of an astronomical observatory, with a salary for an astronomer and assistant, for nightly observations and periodical publication; then annual courses of lectures upon the natural, moral, and political sciences; and, above all, no jobbing—no sinecures—no monkish stalls for lazy idlers.

—MEMOIRS, *June 24, 1838*

The outer layer having been viewed, it is possible to go deeper to inspect the mind and its qualities. To enter more deeply into the mind of Adams, as revealed in his writings, his public pronouncements, and his actions, it is necessary to keep many cautions in view. It is necessary to weigh perhaps contradictory judgments to determine what the long-range judgment was or what emerged as the common denominator. It is necessary to view his thinking from the standpoint of the chronology of his life. And it is necessary to consider to what degree Adams was influenced by the audience to which he spoke. The task of analyzing the quality of a man's mind is an infinitely difficult undertaking, especially since, no matter how articulate he was, there always remains the irreducible unknown in the human personality, the true quality of which may never be communicated to others. With these inescapable limitations fully in view we may proceed.

Although being fully and almost determinedly American, Adams was a cosmopolitan in education. He had moved easily in European society from childhood and had acquired tastes strange to his father and to most of his own generation at home. All evidence indicates that he was very much at home in the lavish environment of a European court, as when, for example, he was entertained in 1809 at a sumptuous dinner by Count Romanzoff, the Chancellor of the Russian Empire. At the same time, however, Adams's republican turn of mind caused him to remember the "mutability of human fortunes" as he noted that the former owner of the house had been the Marquis de Vérac, who had represented pre-revolutionary Bourbon France.[1] And yet, for all his European experience, he remained the strict American puritan and republican. His education was varied and comprehensive, drawn from many sources and broad experiences, and aided by an insatiable love of learning that is well illustrated by his references to his studies while he was employed in the office of Theophilus Parsons at Newburyport. The drive for education never ceased; the *Memoirs* are filled with reflections upon his reading. On one occasion he charged the proponent of a system of universal education with the weaknesses of a visionary; [2] yet his greatest praise of Frederick the Great was reserved for that man in his role as an educator of his people.[3] Among his greatest interests was the increase and diffusion of human knowledge. He berated the failure of the American people to understand the importance of promoting scientific education "as a principle of political action," and he decried the tendency of the slavocracy to oppose all public support for the "progress of the mind." [4]

It is perhaps true that the mind of John Quincy Adams was, as Morse states, less unique than the very distinguished character and personality of which it was a part,[5] but there will be few to gainsay the contention that within its field of operation it was a powerful mind. In many respects it did operate within a system natural to its own day. He found the world about him confined and controlled by a paramount law of nature, superior to the regulations of humans, a law which the logical mind could discern and apply to every situation.[6] For example, he rejected the demand, pressed on the Wash-

[1] *Memoirs,* October 28, 1809, II, 49.

[2] *Ibid.,* December 7, 1826, VII, 200.

[3] Quincy, *op. cit.,* pp. 21–22.

[4] *Memoirs,* November 24, 1843, XI, 441.

[5] Morse, *John Quincy Adams,* p. 232.

[6] III "Marcellus," *Writings,* I, 146: Mr. Adams could, as might be expected, use the concept very conveniently to justify the course that he had chosen.

ington Administration, that the United States support France, in the struggle with Britain, as contrary to a discovered "universal" law that no treaty could oblige one nation to assist another in the perpetration of folly and injustice.[7] Since the natural law concept by its very nature provided a source of justifications for *a priori* conclusions, it would be surprising to discover that Adams had not, unconsciously, used it as such. The result, however, of this combination of principle and natural law was in his case a particularly rigid adherence to the course that he deemed right. He might be the dupe of his own system, but within the system had been compounded a code. If he felt himself incapable on significant occasions of following the dictates of any party and at the same time obeying the requirements of his own principles, the principles won the day, even though adherence to them might destroy popular support and leave him to the solitude of his "own reflections." [8] "Eternal truths" existed, but, more than that, they had a direct relevance to the lives of men.[9]

Although on many occasions he fought vigorously to implant his view of the natural order of things in the solution of problems, other occasions found him quiescent and waiting for the implications of principles to be felt without his assistance. Such was the rule he lived by in the contest for public office. For the most part he found no alternative to nonaction; his principles would make their own force known or he would not be elected. *"Detur digniari* is the inscription upon the prize and the choice of ten millions of people by their delegated agents must award it." [10] In this philosophical scheme the United States occupied a unique position, for it was the first nation in history to announce foundation principles embedded in the "law of nature." [11] No state, of course, could embody an undeviating adherence to natural laws, but Adams could go so far as

[7] *Ibid.*, pp. 144–145.

[8] *Memoirs,* December 31, 1804, I, 282–283.

[9] *Ibid.,* February 11, 1820, IV, 524–525: With respect to the debate on the Missouri question, he remarked, "Oh, if but one man could arise with a genius capable of comprehending, a heart capable of supporting, and an utterance capable of communicating those eternal truths that belong to this question. . . ."

[10] "The MacBeth Policy," *Writings,* VII, 360–361: "If chance will have me king, why chance may crown me." And yet Adams was not really awaiting the decision of chance; he was waiting for the force of principle to be expressed through him.

[11] John Quincy Adams, *An Oration Addressed to the Citizens of the Town of Quincy on the Fourth of July, 1831* Boston: (Richardson, Lord & Holbrook, 1831), hereafter cited as Adams, *Quincy Oration, 1831.*

to justify and support violation of the municipal laws of a state in the event they came too sharply into collision with the "ties of nature." [12]

In Adams's system natural law was always closely interwoven with his religious principles, and, to the extent that the latter were assailed by doubts, the whole structure was weakened.[13] His defeat for a second term in the White House probably created his first major doubts concerning God and the purposes of life, although his life shows that he never could fully admit those doubts.[14] He experienced doubts concerning the religious foundation of his philosophical system, but this fact does not mitigate the contention that Adams adhered with singular rigidity to the precepts that he found in a body of natural law. Nor is there a contradiction of the original contention in pointing out that on occasion he could specifically sanction departure from principle, although the departure was explained within the terms of natural law. On the occasion of the acquisition of Louisiana he held that, although the consent of the inhabitants should have been gained, it would have been impracticable to try to obtain it prior to the treaty and "theoretic principles of government" had to be modified to meet the "situations of human events and human concerns." [15] The treaty-making power had been used constitutionally in acquiring the territory; a plebiscite might have denied the result of the treaty. But the United States could not be relieved of the obligation to procure the consent of the inhabitants after the treaty.

And as nothing but necessity can justify even a momentary departure from those principles which we hold as the most sacred laws of nature and of nations [he adds later "of God"], so nothing can justify extending the departure beyond the bounds of necessity. From the instant when that [necessity] ceases the principle returns in all its force, and every further violation of it is error and crime.[16]

[12] *Memoirs,* August 30, 1816, III, 439. In this reference Adams justified action assisting the escape of a prisoner on the ground that the imprisonment was a violation of natural law. However, despite the view he took of slavery as an outrageous violation of natural law, his sense of the practicable opposed extralegal attempts to destroy it.

[13] *Ibid.,* March 19, 1843, XI, 341: "I have at all times been a sincere believer in the existence of a Supreme Creator of the world, of an immortal principle within myself. . . . I entertain involuntary and agonizing doubts. . . ."

[14] Henry Adams, *op. cit.,* pp. 9–11.

[15] "Notes on Speech on Motion," *Writings,* III, 28–29.

[16] *Loc. cit.*

Therefore the law of nature itself, in the final analysis, determines the extent of deviation that necessity may occasion from its precepts. Man must recognize the necessities of situations; "abstract truths" must be modified in the face of surrounding dangers.[17] He once wrote in the *Memoirs,* moreover, that principles should be adhered to strongly only to the degree of their importance and of the importance of the results deriving from their application.[18] However, there existed principles by reference to which man might judge the importance and validity of results. With the qualifying judgments taken fully into account, it remains true that Adams kept with unique determination to his basic principles.

The great body of compelling laws that governed Adams's universe was the special manifestation of a faculty with which man was peculiarly endowed, the divine gift of reason. So endowed, man was "little lower than the angels," inherently capable of progress, and possessed of the "advantages of individual discovery." [19] Adams put particular stress upon that quality of reason that deals with abstraction and theory, for, despite his great admiration for the educational work of Frederick the Great, he observed with distress that Frederick's educational system overstressed practical things and neglected the fact that theory was the source of understanding of the uses of the common things in life.[20] Adams had a great faith in the power of "the light of reason" and the "incomprehensible energies of the human intellect" to discover and reveal truth, however much these powers might be obstructed by ecclesiastical and political power.[21]

Reason could be brought to bear upon a situation to produce governing principles. Whereas perverted reason, a tainted source of "moral principle," might conclude that human rights should be dis-

[17] To George William Erving, State Department, Washington, D. C., *ibid.,* November 28, 1818, VI, 498: He justified Jackson's stern methods against the Indians in Florida on the ground that that by the law of nations ferocity begets ferocity. *Memoirs,* March 29, 1820, V, 47–48: He agreed that fraud and artifice were justifiable in war.

[18] *Memoirs,* December 22, 1833, IX, 58.

[19] John Quincy Adams, *Lectures on Rhetoric and Oratory,* "Inaugural Lecture" (Cambridge: Hilliard and Metcalf, 1810), I, 14.

[20] Adams, *Letters on Silesia,* p. 377.

[21] John Quincy Adams, *An Address Delivered July 4, 1821, Washington, D. C.* (Cambridge: Hilliard and Metcalf, 1821), p. 5; hereafter cited as Adams, *July 4th, 1821 Address.*

tributed according to the color of one's skin,[22] true reason would not accept such an idea. Also pure reason identified religion as the product of the necessities of human nature, as a veritable "appetite," rejecting "the Trinity, the Divinity of Christ, the whole doctrine of atonement, all miracles, the Immaculate Conception of Jesus, and a devil maintaining war against Omnipotence,. . . [and] the Real Presence of the Eucharist." [23] And reason produced the principle that proclaimed privateering to be robbery, a violation of the sanctity of private property.[24] There were certain sectors, however, in which reason did not necessarily operate to produce beneficial results. On one occasion Adams observed that reason did not govern the international affairs of mankind. Reason might protect the liberties of men within nations, but among nations force and the will to use it were freedom's protectors.[25] The force of reason produced in Adams an "overruling consciousness of rectitude" as to his principles.

Such a consciousness of a superior moral position accounted for the belief, which he egotistically asserted, that failure in the presidential election constituted a more serious vote of censure upon him than upon the other contestants.[26] Since his reason revealed to him true principle, to reject him was to censure the truth. His complete and unquestioning belief in his principles was naive. He assumed that his reputation and position should not require being "pampered and cosseted"; his country and posterity should sanction his principles on the basis of their *a priori* intrinsic correctness.[27]

Although he was disdainful of "dogmatical and bigoted" clerics,[28] his assertion of his own principles or of the principles, "inaccessible to human power," upon which he thought government in the United States to be founded was just as dogmatic in the realm of the secular as that of the cleric in the realm of religion.[29] With complete assurance of sound position, upon being reminded by the Spanish Minister

[22] *Memoirs*, March 2, 1820, V, 10–11.

[23] *Ibid.*, April 12, 1812, II, 356–357.

[24] I "Marcellus," *Writings*, I, 138.

[25] To William Vans Murray, Berlin, July 22, 1798, *ibid.*, II, 344. Other, less anarchical, ideas on international order will be adduced below.

[26] Quincy, *op. cit.*, p. 138.

[27] To Edward Everett, Washington, D. C., January 31, 1822, *Writings*, VII, 205.

[28] *Memoirs*, April 12, 1817, III, 498.

[29] Adams, *Cincinnati Oration*, p. 13.

that truth is eternal and reason governed by unchanging principle, he asserted that he needed no such reminder and implied that assertions of principle contrary to his own would not prevail through stubbornness of contention nor "repetition of error." [30]   His mind turned to authority for the derivation of principle; it found a definite pre-eminence of truth in the texts of publicists and authorities.   The support of his own reason was usually sufficient to establish him in a state of invulnerable conviction.   Rather early in life he arrived at the belief that his own deliberate judgments were more reliable than the heated prejudices of constitutents or critics and that he must put more trust in his own conclusions. [31]   He found nothing remarkable in the assertion that in both public and private affairs he pursued an unalterable determination to conform to the personal principles that had always guided him. [32]

He assessed the failures of political opponents in terms of their deviations from what he considered consistency of true principle. Moral considerations and high principle, he held, must come more thoroughly to guide statesmen and under that condition government would become wiser and more valid.   His own merit of literary production or political action he held to derive from his constant application of a correct standard of right and wrong that, with surprising naïveté, he concluded protected him from the pitfalls of sophistry, especially since, given the desire for truth, the human mind had a natural affinity for truth and justice. [33]   Such a quality of mind, or such an intellectual method, made it difficult for him to be a party man. [34]   When it was suggested that he might use money to suppress rumors circulated or charges made concerning his political past, he was so confident of invulnerable position that he refused to spend "one dollar" for any such suppression. [35]   His father chided him for becoming a champion of a religious orthodoxy without more study, and he answered that a shorter route to a trust in God and the

[30] State Department, *Notes to Foreign Legations*, II, 283.

[31] To Abigail Adams, St. Petersburg, October 2, 1811, *Writings*, IV, 227–228.

[32] To Skelton Jones, Boston, April 17, 1809, *ibid.*, III, 305.

[33] To Edward Everett, Washington, D. C., *ibid.*, VII, 202.

[34] To William Plumer, St. Petersburg, October 6, 1810, *ibid.*, III, 508: He described the reason for his alienation from the Federalist Party as due to "their degeneracy form the just and honorable principles" which were the foundation of his attachment to the party.

[35] *Memoirs*, August 8, 1831, VIII, 393.

Sermon on the Mount was open to him than the sixty years his father had expended in achieving the same goal.[36] Such a conviction of rightness in the support of principles of his own choosing produced that testy political personality that was John Quincy Adams.

This dogmatic intellectual approach had political implications. He reminded a British professional man that Americans chose to support the principles of international law as they existed, not as they could be warped to suit American interests.[37] He contemplated not replying to a British note on the fisheries question since its substance was "erroneous principle." [38] The representative of the Spanish King was reminded that Spain's failure to ratify the Florida treaty violated "every principle of natural right." [39] He favored those among his fellow politicians who, he judged, lived by "excellent principles," invariably in accord with his own,[40] and he suspected others because they had "weak . . . unsettled . . . [or] erroneous principles." [41] He referred to Socrates with approval because of his adherence to principle in refusing to escape from prison.[42] In a similar fashion, he followed his unremitting course, undeterred by the "intrigue, hatred, and slander" that surrounded him.[43] While he was a member of the Monroe Administration, although he accepted a duty to support the policy of the government, he determined to withdraw if sacrifice of principle should be the price of cooperation.[44]

Adams's life was one of inquiry and inspection of the causes of

[36] To John Adams, Ealing, January 3, 1817, *Writings,* VI, 134.

[37] To John Adams, London, December 29, 1795, *ibid.,* I, 474.

[38] *Memoirs,* January 16, 1816, III, 279.

[39] To Don Francisco Dionisio Vivés, State Department, Washington, D. C., *Writings,* VII, 18.

[40] *Memoirs,* September 16, 1841, XI, 19.

[41] To George William Erving, St. Petersburg, June 6, 1811, *Writings,* IV, 111. *Memoirs,* March 5, 1845, XII, 179: "I had voted against the thanks to Jones. The testimony to his unpartiality was too broad a lie for me to swallow. But I shook hands with him now—as I did with McKay, and told him it was to part from him forever for his baseness in defeating the appropriation of forty thousand dollars for a sea-wall in Boston Harbor." *Memoirs,* November 29, 1833, IX, 40: He wrote that he must terminate all "confidential correspondence" with Richard Rush, his Secretary of the Treasury, for working against Anti-Masonry in Pennsylvania, thereby showing he could not endure a minority position and that his principles rested light upon him. *Memoirs,* March 2, 1831, VIII, 332: "Calhoun veers around in his politics, to be always before the wind, and makes his intellect the pander to his will."

[42] *Memoirs,* October 13, 1811, II, 316–317.

[43] Nevins, *op. cit.,* p. XV.

[44] *Memoirs,* April 17, 1817, III, 504.

things in the realm of science, wherein his method, in the manner of Locke, was empirical and rejected large generalizations and *a priori* affirmations.   But just as clearly as Locke, through failure to inspect first principles, he saw no contradiction between his empiricism, on the one hand, and his natural law, natural rights doctrine, on the other.   He admired the inquiring mind, but he was as vulnerable as Locke to Hume's criticism that the tentative judgments to which the inquiring mind may subscribe cannot be transformed into dogma. With respect to the realm of philosophical values, as apart from science, John Quincy Adams was perhaps less given to questioning the reasons for things than John Adams, with whom he discussed the issue.[45]   His theory was not one that took delight "in reasoning high upon 'Fix'd fate, free will, [or] foreknowledge absolute.'"   His scientific practice was, it is true, another matter; in this regard he was filled with a desire for new knowledge, but such activity was always carried on within the framework of a system which he did not question.   His search for theoretical authority placed a surprising reliance upon the capacity of the rational mind to arrive at truth through discussion, a truth discoverable through the logical inspection of principles.[46]   He had little more than contempt for what he called the "political empirics." [47]   Whatever the genius, success, or grandeur of purpose of Napoleon, he was an inadequate man, since he was not under the control of a superior morality.[48]   Adams came to admire Lafayette for his incomparable sacrifices to the "*moral* principles of political action." [49]   Adams asserted that the only sacrifice of opinion that he would make to the interest of party or faction was one that did not involve "a *dereliction of principle*." [50]

His inspection of principle and the world about him produced a conviction that in the "counsels of Omnipotence" there was an assurance of progress and an improvement in the condition of man, most especially in the moral sphere.   His view of the inexorable operation of the natural order assumed that physical or material improvements

[45] To John Adams, Little Boston House, Ealing, October 29, 1816, *Writings*, VI, 111–112.

[46] Adams, *Lectures on Rhetoric and Oratory*, "Inaugural Oration," p. 23.

[47] *Memoirs*, May 24, 1819, IV, 370.

[48] *Ibid.*, June 22, 1828, VIII, 40.

[49] Adams, *Eulogy on Lafayette*, pp. 7–8.

[50] To William Plumer, St. Petersburg, October 6, 1810, *Writings*, III, 511.

in the condition of man would be matched by "*moral* improvement"
in the condition of man.[51]   That slavery would inevitably disappear,
however terrible the catastrophe that would excise it, he had no
doubt.[52]   Moral improvement would come as an unfolding of a
larger universal purpose, not at the behest of legislative fiat.   Man
would achieve virtue under the pressure of conscience and inborn
will.[53]   On similar grounds he refused to submit to a religious test
as Boylston Professor at Harvard, holding it safe to confine the matter
of his faith to the category of those things important to him and his
maker alone.   He was quite willing to extend the same indulgence to
others.[54]   In the world about him, as we shall see, he was quite ready
to make use of the government and legislation of men to work improvement.   He had great optimism, at least in his younger years,
concerning progress in both the moral and material spheres.   In the
former, however, he had little confidence in the capacity of power
to accomplish any purpose.

On morality and moral questions on the level of everyday social
intercourse, Adams presented the pattern of belief in many respects
normal in the New England Puritan.   He warned young Americans
to avoid the atmosphere of Europe, because it was infectious to
morals; inciting to dissipation, intemperance, sensuality, and idleness;
and destructive of the will to self-control and self-denial.[55]   He himself complained of an inability to withstand the tendency to dissipation in the atmosphere of Paris that made hard work and application
difficult.[56]   With almost precious moral purity he noted during his
residence in Prussia a monument to a bastard son of the King of
Prussia, costly and elegant, a record in marble of "egregious virtues." [57]
Adams attacked David Hume for writing as historian in terms of
cold detachment of the misery and horror of the conquest of Ireland
by Henry II aided by the renegade, Dermott MacMorrogh, king of
Leinster, and then summing up his evaluation of Henry in terms of

[51] Adams, *Newburyport Oration, 1837,* p. 59.

[52] *Memoirs,* December 13, 1838, X, 63.

[53] John Quincy Adams, *Address to the Norfolk County Temperance Society
at Their Meeting at Quincy, 29 September, 1842* (Boston: Russell and Cutler,
1842), p. 23.

[54] To Samuel Dexter, Quincy, October 6, 1805, *Writings,* III, 125.

[55] To Francis Calley Gray, Washington, D. C., August 3, 1818, *ibid.,* VI, 414.

[56] *Memoirs,* February 12, 1815, III, 154.

[57] *Ibid.,* June 7, 1801, I, 243–244.

eulogy. Hume should have taught the "virtues of conjugal fidelity, of genuine piety," and of patriotism rather than condone MacMorrogh's giving up his country to a foreign invader through the agency of "violated marriage vows, unprincipled ambition, and religious imposture." [58]

Adams's moral system was based upon a religious view with much larger implications than as a source of the rules of everyday conduct. Very near the end of his life he reaffirmed his belief in the existence of a creating deity, the grantor of the spark of immortal life in each individual, although he confessed "involuntary and agonizing doubts." [59]   As Brooks Adams asserted, his faith in an assisting deity had diminished following his failure to put into application his principles as a result of his failure of re-election to the Presidency, but to the very end he never abandoned a high degree of reliance upon "the laws of Nature and of Nature's God."   Jefferson's liberal non-religious thinking was one of the factors in Adams's distrust of him.[60] As a young man John Quincy's major comment on Gibbon was that the historian had been antipathetic to Christianity.[61]   And it is safe to say that Adams never was able to abandon the premises of Christianity that were foundation-pieces of his entire intellectual system.

According to Adams, the religion of Jesus Christ was the source of two basic principles of morality and therefore of a complete philosophical system. One was the principle of "life and immortality" and the other the principle of "brotherly love," out of which derived precepts of equality, peace, and humanitarianism.[62]   Adams believed that natural religion, which in this view included in broad outline the concepts of a personal god, immortality, and retribution, was not the product of a spontaneous understanding in the heart but was a learned body of principles in the keeping of society and brought to each generation by the forces of civic education.   Closely associated with his understanding of the tenets of Christianity was his concept of liberty, for he held that Jesus had come to teach men and not to

[58] John Quincy Adams, *Dermott MacMorrogh* (Boston: Carter, Hendee and Co., 1832), "Dedication and Preface," pp. XIII–XIV.

[59] *Memoirs,* March 19, 1843, XI, 341.

[60] *Ibid.,* January 11, 1831, VIII, 270.

[61] Adams, *Life in a New England Town,* March 24, 1788, p. 112.

[62] John Quincy Adams, *A Discourse on Education,* delivered at Braintree, Thursday, October 24, 1839 (Boston: Perkins & Marvin, 1840), p. 13.

compel them.[63] Although Adams conceded that men, or a man, might be the instrument of the visitation of God's anger upon earth,[64] he held that the spirit of peace, which is the essence of Christianity, could become dominant only as it was established by missionary work in the hearts of peoples and rulers.[65] A related view, emphasizing the heart and conscience, made him reject the idea of a religious test as a condition of his occupancy of the professorship at Harvard.

Christian principles were the best and only real source of the constitutional principles for a commonwealth desiring to establish a "perfect rule." [66] These Christian principles naturally imparted to such a system a concept of the "natural equality of mankind" and of inherent and "inalienable rights." Such had been the doctrine of the early Puritan colonists. The colonists had resorted to such a concept of inalienable rights when the Mother Country had violated the precepts of "Nature's God" as well as of Nature and therefore had violated the covenant between God and man.[67]

Adams's religion at times manifested a purist formality and asceticism, as when he registered disdainful surprise that a statue to the bastard son of a king of Prussia should be found in a Christian church. Religion and temperance were natural allies, the former being the major force controlling the appetites of man, the only creature not having appetites apportioned to his wants.[68] On the other hand, although John Quincy opposed "transcendental and rationalistic impiety," he rejected likewise the low estimate of human nature that he found in the orthodox clergy.[69] The clergy's view of sin and the

[63] Adams, *A Discourse on Education,* pp. 9, 18.

[64] To Abigail Adams, St. Petersburg, November 30, 1812, *Writings,* IV, 413: He noted that the tide had turned against Napoleon, so long "an instrument of divine wrath to scourge mankind."

[65] To Alexander Hill Everett, London, December 6, 1815, *ibid.,* V, 437.

[66] John Quincy Adams, *The New England Confederacy of MDCXLIII,* A Discourse delivered before The Massachusetts Historical Society at Boston on the 29th of May, 1843 (Boston: C. C. Little and J. Brown, 1843), p. 24.

[67] Adams, *Newburyport Oration, 1837,* pp. 18–19.

[68] Adams, *Address to the Norfolk County Temperance Society,* pp. 7–8.

[69] Samuel Hanson Cox, *Interviews, Memorable and Useful,* from diary and memory reproduced, "Interview III, John Quincy Adams," (New York: Harper and Brothers, 1855), p. 222 *et passim:* Dr. Cox, in the interview here recorded, found much to admire in Adams, but reported the interview with the main purpose of demonstrating the validity of his own dogma and the fallacy of that of the layman. If Adams was correctly reported, his ideas show a much greater liberality than those of the Pastor of the First Presbyterian Church of Brooklyn.

sinning he ascribed to "a latent vanity of [their] minds." They should recognize in all humility the true fact of man's smallness on an "atom world" in an infinite solar system. God in all the vastness of space very likely could not be concerned with our smallness, nor have time to expend His wrath upon the sinful to the degree threatened by the clergy. Asserting his right to judge of and interpret God differently from the orthodox clergy, Adams concluded that the deity would be too good to consign men to eternal punishment. Roger Williams, the "polemical porcupine from Oxford," despite his principle of a free conscience, was not admired by Adams.[70] Yet the latter assigned as the major significance of religion its effect upon human conduct and found no importance in controversies over "Trinity or Unity, or [concerning] the single or double personal nature of Christ." [71]

Closely associated with his religion was his doctrine of human perfectibility. The deity, moving according to certain laws, could be understood and discovered by scientific investigation; the knowledge thus derived, if properly used, could be used for the achievement of human perfection.[72] More specifically related to his social doctrines was his assertion that the direction of the energies of the nation toward the achievement of internal physical improvements served to release the "bounties of Providence." A social duty rested upon man to use his rational faculties in the service of the Lord, to release the energy stored in nature, and to raise all men above the level of want.[73] The Declaration of Independence was an event in the unfolding of the dispensation of the Scriptures as men trod the path toward the goal of a higher good.[74] Before the force of the Saviour's concept of brotherly love, applied in its ultimate sense, past empires and forms of government and institutions of evil, viz. war and slavery, had fallen and would fall in the due course of time. Though it might in the dispensation of Providence take a *long* time, they would eventually

[70] *Memoirs,* May 19, 1843, XI, 376–377.

[71] To George Sullivan, Washington, D. C., January 20, 1821, *Writings,* VII, 90. See also, *Memoirs,* April 12, 1812, II, 356–357.

[72] Henry Adams, *op. cit.,* pp. 30–31: In his old age his doctrine of human perfectibility was severely shaken as he saw science put to the service of slavery, land exploitation, etc.

[73] To Rev. Charles W. Upham, Washington, D. C., February 2, 1837, quoted in Henry Adams, *op. cit.,* pp. 24–25, 26.

[74] To Rev. J. Edwards, Quincy, July 13, 1837, quoted in *ibid.,* pp. 29–30.

"fall prostrate [and] crumble into dust." [75] The community of
Christian nations represented a step beyond the condition of the
whole community of nations, for in their relations they added to the
laws of nature the "laws of humanity and mutual benevolence taught
in the gospel of Christ." [76] These nations represented in their religious faith an advance in the progress of men toward a higher order.
The Christian nations had at their disposal the "fundamental maxim
of nature" that men should "do unto others as [they] would that
[others] should do unto [them]" that would solve all political, as well
as individual, problems. [77]

In spite of his antipathy for too great an emphasis upon doctrinal
complexities, Adams nevertheless felt religious differences keenly and
expressed them with pungency and directness: "There is something
in the dress, in the gait, in the deportment, in the expression of counte-
nance, and, above all, in the eye, of these clergymen of the most excellent church [the Church of England], that imparts arrogance,
intolerance, and all that is the reverse of Christian humility." [78] In
addition to adding to his stature as an observer, his strictures upon
the growing Irish Catholic influence in the cities of the United States,
and the conflict of those of that confession with native American poor
whites, and their consequent pernicious influence upon urban elections indicated his readiness to see political problems in terms of
religious divergence. [79] He viewed the Reformation as a great advance in the development of man's comprehension of his rights and
duties, particularly of his right to use the power of reason. Unfortunately, however, the sword still protected the tiara and the crown
in Europe, and rebellion against their oppressive weight had but
partially succeeded in Britain. [80] He looked upon bigotry and despotism as companions; he particularly despised Roman Catholicism,
dominant in those countries where the "sceptered tyrant" could give
protection to the theology of the "canonized fanatic, of whom nothing now remains but the name, in the calendar of antiquated supersti-

[75] Joseph C. and Owen Lovejoy, *Memoirs of the Rev. Elijah P. Lovejoy*, with
an introduction by John Quincy Adams (New York: John S. Taylor, 1838), pp.
3–4.

[76] Adams, *Newburyport Oration, 1837*, p. 17.

[77] III "Columbus," *Writings*, I, 164.

[78] *Memoirs*, August 20, 1815, III, 260.

[79] *Ibid.*, May 9, 1844, XII, 24.

[80] Adams, *July 4th, 1821 Address*, pp. 5–6, 7.

tion." [81] He rejected the authority of the fisherman's ring and refused to attribute infallibility to any living man.[82]

Adams associated the evil Spanish colonial system with the corruption of power by which a Bishop of Rome granted half the world to a despotical power with the purpose of bringing the "most benevolent of all religions" to its native inhabitants.[83] Noting the difficulty of supporting the principle of religious liberty in Catholic countries, he was highly gratified to see that the new constitution of Columbia recognized the principle, for the authoritative control of the Pope, he wrote, would be as foreign as that of the Spanish King. Positing the idea of an American system, he affirmed religious liberty as a fundamental component of that system, as a prerequisite of civil liberty.[84] The arm of government required the initial reform, however, for when the tyranny of soldiers was removed, the rule of monks and Jesuits would have no foundation upon which to act.[85] There was disapproval of tyranny in his observation of an insurrection in Spain against "Ferdinand the Beloved" and his anticipation that the Inquisition would efficiently suppress it and restore the "social order." [86] He was distressed to witness the invasion of Spain by the French armies with the purpose of re-establishing "bigotry and despotic sway" upon "the bowed neck of [that country] to the end of destroying the . . . constitution." [87] There can, in short, be no questioning the fact that he felt strong sectarian, if not doctrinal, prejudices in matters religious, but it is likewise true that in a final sense he subscribed to the ideal of freedom of religious opinion, even that which he most vigorously rejected. This degree of religious toleration in Adams was opposed to that religious dogmatism which obstructed the inquiring mind devoted to science.[88]

[81] John Quincy Adams, *An Oration Pronounced July 4, 1793 at the Request of the Inhabitants of the Town of Boston* (Boston: Benjamin Edes and Son, 1793), pp. 5–6, hereafter cited as Adams, *July 4th Oration, 1793.*

[82] Adams, *The New England Confederacy of MDCXLIII*, p. 3.

[83] To Richard C. Anderson, State Department, Washington, D. C., May 27, 1823, *Writings*, VII, 442–443.

[84] To Richard C. Anderson, State Department, Washington, D. C., May 27, 1823, *ibid.,* VII, 465–467.

[85] To John Adams, Ealing, August 1, 1816, *ibid.,* V, 59.

[86] To William Plumer, Ealing near London, October 5, 1815, *ibid.,* p. 403.

[87] National Archives, Records of the Department of State, *Diplomatic Instructions, All Countries,* IX, 188.

[88] To Robert Walsh, Jr., Washington, D. C., July 10, 1821, *Writings*, VII, 117: "But I take it for granted that at this day, the usurpation of the ecclesiastical

Adams had a high regard for the study of science. His respect for the trained scientist was deep.[89] In the field of science were made the greatest discoveries by the "incomprehensible energies of the human intellect." [90] Not only pure science but technology had his interest and support.[91] Nor did he view science entirely separate from the study of man, his mind and morality. In his thought there existed a "common chain, which unites, as with links of adamant, the whole circle of the sciences, and the liberal arts. . . ." [92]

This scientific approach was, as we have indicated, the source of his differences with religious dogmatists, for his comprehension of an infinite universe precluded his acceptance of man as its center.[93] Even as a young man his observation of the world produced in him a high degree of skepticism, in significant contrast with his natural law concepts. In Newburyport, pondering upon the interesting theme of "nothing," he expounded finally as follows:

In the physical world, what are sensual gratifications, what is the earth, and all it contains, what is life itself?—nothing. In the moral world, what is honour, what is honesty, what is religion?—nothing. In the political world, what is liberty, what is power and grandeur?—nothing. The universe is an atom, and its creator is all in all. Of him, except that he exists, we know nothing, and consequently our knowledge is nothing. Perhaps the greatest truth of all is, that for this half hour I have been doing nothing.[94]

---

power during the middle ages may be descanted upon without departing from that liberality which should be observed toward all religious opinions"; it was substantially a belief in "freedom of thought against organized power." See Adams, *Discourse on Education*, p. 25.

[89] John Quincy Adams, *An Oration Spoken at the Request of the ΦBK Society at Cambridge*, September 5th, 1788 (typed copy of the address presented to the Massachusetts Historical Society by Worthington C. Ford), p. 6: ". . . yet the generous and humane will ever esteem the passage through the portico of Science, to be the most honourable avenue to the temple of Fame." This was, to be sure, a statement to an academic audience, but it is in keeping with Adams's sincere views.

[90] Adams, *July 4th, 1821 Address*, p. 5.

[91] *Memoirs*, October 15, 1812, II, 413: He expended a good deal of effort in attempts to interest Alexander I's government in the use of Mr. Fulton's steamboat in Russia.

[92] Adams, *Cincinnati Oration*, pp. 34, 38.

[93] Cox, *op. cit.*, pp. 225–226.

[94] Adams, *Life in a New England Town*, January 4, 1788, p. 79.

In this, of course, Adams heralds the coming dilemma of the Victorian era caught between its old faiths and the insights which science was making possible.

Adams clung to the old faiths, but he became the champion of public support of scientific endeavor and investigation. Despite his despairing that the people of the United States would ever support and promote science, he indulged "dreams" that in the future they would enjoy the improvements that would result from such support.[95] All that a single individual in public position could do he did. Not only was the *Report on Weights and Measures* an achievement in itself, but he took pains to describe his conclusions to Rush, our Minister in London, especially indicating those conclusions that had come from his own experiment and that he thought would be of benefit to the British.[96] He became an especially enthusiastic guardian of the national obligation to make fitting use of the bequest of James Smithson to the United States according to the terms of the Englishman's will. As chairman of a select committee on the message of the President relating to the bequest, he rendered a report which emphasized the great obligation the United States had to carry out the high and noble purpose of assisting "the increase and diffusion of knowledge among men."[97] He opposed including provisions for the investment of the fund in a bill which related to West Point and objected particularly to granting the Secretary of the Treasury discretion to invest the fund in state stocks.[98] He proposed using the fund for an astronomical observatory for the extension of the "sublimest of the physical sciences," an observatory that would surpass all others.[99] Man's reason was his immortal part, and its best use must be in the inquiry into relations between unseen causes and observable effects, with the heavens the proper object of initial in-

[95] *Memoirs,* November 24, 1843, XI, 441.

[96] National Archives, Records of the Department of State, *Diplomatic Instructions,* All Countries, IX, 104–105.

[97] *Report from Select Committee on the message of the President relating to the bequest of James Smithson,* 26th Cong., 1st sess., H. Rept. 277, pp. 6–9; out of this request grew the present-day Smithsonian Institution.

[98] 25th Cong., 3rd sess., H. Doc. 11, Executive, "Letter from John Quincy Adams to the Secretary of State, John Forsyth, Esq.," Quincy, October 8, 1838, pp. 2–3.

[99] *Ibid.,* "Letter from John Quincy Adams to the Secretary of State, John Forsyth, Esq.," Quincy, October 11, 1838, p. 5.

quiry.[100]   In further illustration of his interest, we find him request-
ing leave to make a favorable report on behalf of a select committee
appointed to consider a memorial of the American Philosophical
Society that requested aid from the government for the purpose of
carrying out geological observations.[101]   On other occasions, he was
active on behalf of appropriations to establish stations to make observations of terrestrial magnetism, or for meteorological and geological observations.[102]   His curiosity was immense but not an end
in itself, for he always viewed scientific knowledge as a major source
of the public good.

The public good was unquestionably the goal of all his public
actions.   The writer has no doubt that the pages that have preceded
and those that will follow will reveal this to be the case.   There remains the question of whether or not that goal of the public good
was an abstract end, or was embodied in a feeling for men in a warm,
personal sense.   On the score of his regard for humanity, of deep
importance to the spirit of his political philosophy, the record is
ambiguous and complex.   It will suffice here merely to introduce
the subject, which will be dealt with in other contexts at greater
length.   The record indicates that his humanity and charity deepened
as he grew older, even though the asperity of his temper may have
been sharpened.

As a young man in Newburyport observing the political scene in
Massachusetts and noting a shift of popular sentiments during the
preceding year, he wrote that he was not surprised, since it could
be a surprise only for one "unacquainted with the weakness, the
follies, and the vices of human nature." [103]   On another occasion,
perceiving a tone and temper that he disliked in a newspaper, the
Centinel, he remarked that he had known too long the quality of
human nature and the "particular hearts of individuals" to be aston-
ished.[104]   He warned himself to be sure to choose a course doubtful
and suspicious of human nature.[105]   While conjecturing on the ad-

100 Adams, *Cincinnati Oration,* pp. 16–17.
101 *Congressional Globe,* 26th Cong., 1st sess., July 1, 1840, p. 497.
102 *Ibid.,* July 2, 1840, p. 499.   *Ibid.,* July 18, 1840, p. 541.
103 Adams, *Life in a New England Town,* April 7, 1788, p. 119.
104 To William Plumer, St. Petersburg, October 6, 1810, *Writings,* III, 510.
105 Adams, *Life in a New England Town,* November 23, 1787, p. 65: "Human

vantages and disadvantages of a public career, he voiced his fear of being placed within the power of the people in a lifelong dependence upon them.[106]

He graded the people, particularly in his early life, in a hierarchy and disdainfully held forth that "the idle and extravagant, and consequently the poor" complain of oppressive government, while "the men of property and consideration" fear the granting of liberty "to the unprincipled citizens, to the prejudice of the honest and industrious."[107]   He feared the mob, not as "the subjects of praise or blame" but as the wielder of a tremendous force dangerous to social stability.[108]   This great force, which in his view might be unleashed with particular ease in the United States, could be moved by the "pimping to the popular passions" that he declared he despised.[109] The "popular passions" were an unstable element that made it difficult, particularly in time of crisis, to forecast what the public will would demand.[110]

Advance in years, on the other hand, produced a mellower view. Observing the inclination of President Monroe to fear the fickleness of the people, Adams held himself in contrast to be willing to brave "popular prejudices" on the basis of a greater confidence "in the calm and deliberate judgment of the people. . . ."[111]   But more than that he developed, if he did not always possess, a genuine dislike of harsh government.   A strong emotion was produced by his discovery that Napoleon was attempting to preserve public peace in the face of famine by shooting people, women as well as men.[112] Ironically he suggested that the British government would be sup-

nature, how inexplicable art thou!   Oh, may I learn before I advance upon the political stage (if I ever do) not to put my trust in thee!"

[106] To John Adams, Boston, April 12, 1794, *Writings*, I, 185–186.

[107] To Abigail Adams, Cambridge, December 30, 1786, *ibid.*, I, 29: these views were normal to a man of his class in his day.

[108] V "Publicola," *ibid.*, p. 82; such conclusions will be considered at greater length in the following pages.   Here they are indicated as a measure of Adams's intellectual temper.

[109] To Thomas Boylston Adams, July 11, 1800, *ibid.*, II, 464.

[110] To the Secretary of State (Edmund Randolph), The Hague, November 7, 1794, *ibid.*, I, 221.To John Adams, Quincy, January 5, 1794, *ibid.*, p. 177: "The public is a lady having so many admirers, that a favor is not to be obtained from her by one of them with impunity."

[111] *Memoirs*, August 9, 1823, IV, 170.

[112] To Abigail Adams, St. Petersburg, April 30, 1812, *Writings*, IV, 320.

ported in its policy of shooting rioting men, women, and children stung to violence by hunger.[113]　Even before, during the Silesian journey, he was oppressed by the sight of the wretched lives of the people, oppressed by rich fortune-seeking merchants, whilst the former could barely procure enough bread.　He deplored the people's being swindled by the artful traders out of the true returns of their industry.[114]　In rich and powerful Britain, he reported that he often saw cases of starving beggars, and he was moved to compassion by the sight.[115]　The years brought a warmer feeling for the more humble in society.　John Quincy Adams took pride in the government of the United States because he thought that American statesmen had origins primarily among trading people and shopkeepers, as well as professional groups.[116]　The proper conclusion is, no doubt, that human sympathy, as well as principle, moved Adams to seek change.　In investigating these questions, however, it is necessary to be concerned with both the substance of and the transitions in his thought.　That study will be one of the purposes of the following chapter.

[113] To Thomas Boylston Adams, St. Petersburg, May 22, 1812, *Writings,* p. 333.
[114] Adams, *Letters on Silesia,* p. 157.
[115] *Memoirs,* November 8, 1816, III, 447–448.
[116] John Quincy Adams, *The Lives of James Madison and James Monroe* (Boston: Phillips, Sampson and Co., 1850), p. 206.

PART THREE

Men, Society, and Change

5

Social Origins and Social Solidarity

There are several subjects upon which the public mind in this country is taking a turn which alarms me greatly for the continuance of this Union—the bank; the currency; the internal improvement question; the extension or repression of slavery. . . .
—MEMOIRS, *January 2, 1820*

The general background, environmental and personal, has been drawn. Against that background the more specific doctrines of John Quincy Adams will stand out in clearer relief. At this point his precepts with respect to society in general may be introduced. This discussion will make it possible to comprehend Adams's emphases with respect to fundamental social forces and what he believed to have been the motivations in man's nature combining to make him a social being.[1] On that foundation may be established the structure of his values concerning men and things within society. In turn, this analysis will reveal his classifications of men in the social order and the interests that he thought men, related socially, represented and created. His views of the problem of the relations of races will be relevant to this analysis, for therein lay much of importance to his theory of social organization. And finally, his views

[1] John Quincy Adams, *The Social Compact, Exemplified in the Constitution of the Commonwealth of Massachusetts; with Remarks on the Theories of Divine Right of Hobbes and of Filmer, and the Counter Theories of Sidney, Locke, Montesquieu, and Rousseau, concerning the Origin and Nature of Government,* a lecture delivered before the Franklin Lyceum at Providence, R. I., November 25, 1842 (Providence: Knowles and Vose, 1842), p. 12, hereafter cited as Adams, *The Social Compact:* "Man is therefore by the law of nature's God, a social being . . . ;" in Adams's thought, man, from his earliest use of his intelligence, was thrown into association with his fellows, a beginning society. This view greatly reduced the importance of the state of nature in Adams's theory.

of the tempo, means, and quality of social change are closely related to an understanding of what he held important in the life that he lived. The purpose of this chapter will be, therefore, not only to indicate what he valued in his own era but also to state the conditions whence he thought man had come and the conditions toward which he thought man was evolving. In the analysis of Adams's thought in this connection especial attention has been given to what appears consistent; yet the aberrations have been noted and identified. In those areas wherein Adams's thought grew and developed, particular care has been taken to note such development, but we must constantly recall that Adams is more notable for the consistency of his thought than for his susceptibility to change. As a man from youth given to speculation concerning his values, he was early aware of his premises. They were changed only under the severest impact. A major thesis of this study is that Adams, in contrast with the typical political practitioner, made few concessions in theory and practice to necessity and opportunity. Where, therefore, a particular source has been adduced to indicate a particular facet of his thought, one may have confidence that the point made is valid as a part of Adams's general philosophy and not merely as an *ad hoc* reaction to a particular situation.

Adams's ideal social order was in no manner one of idyllic simplicity. He was far too impressed with man's capacity to create a better world out of the abundance stored in nature by the deity. The first stanza of his poem "The Wants of Man" genuinely reflects the store he put in material accomplishment:

> Man wants but little here below
> 　Nor wants that little long.
> 'Tis not with ME exactly so,
> 　But 'tis so in the song.
> My wants are many, and if told
> 　Would muster many a score;
> And were each wish a mint of gold,
> 　I still should long for more.[2]

This human society or social order was not an artificial creation, nor was it created on the foundation of a rational decision made by men

[2] Adams, *Poems of Religion and Society*, p. 15.

at a particular point in history or prehistory. Viewing life as inherently social, he found in man's very simplest associations the germs of a social order, and he thereby placed himself apart from typical eighteenth century theorists of a state of nature that men transformed into a state of society by a social compact. Since the capacity of men for individual self-government was inadequate to order their lives in association with each other, bonds of a higher order than those founded upon the individual alone were inherently necessary.[3] The important fact is that Adams, herein departing in emphasis from Locke—otherwise a powerful influence in his thinking—held against the idea of society as the product of an act of special creation. Adams's theory contained a concept of a natural progression of relationships between the sexes and among men from the simple to the complex, very early in which appeared the germ of government. The natural relationship of the sexes founded the order of natural society. Their establishment of a permanent abode and cohabitation founded domestic society; the relations of parent and offspring constituted simple government with authority to require obedience. As the off-spring grew older, the authority of the parent, originally almost absolute, became softened into a respectful association, until finally the child founded a family of his own and civil society appeared involving the association of two or more families. Government was more formally instituted as this process continues "multiplying [the] relations between man and man, how superadded to those between man and things."[4] Society and government were not only natural but necessary safeguards of culture, relationships, and standards.[5] Each generation must, through the devices that are inherent in human association, provide for the "birth, nurture, and support"

[3] Adams, *The Social Compact*, p. 12.
[4] Adams, *Report on Weights and Measures*, p. 9.
[5] *Ibid.*, pp. 10, 11. Probably Henry Clay and John Quincy Adams strongly influenced each other with respect to internal improvements and the powers and purposes of government. cf. Two speeches of Henry Clay on internal improvements in the House of Representatives, dated February 4, 1817, and March 13, 1818, *in* David Mallory, ed., *The Life and Speeches of the Honorable Henry Clay* (New York: A. S. Barnes and Company, 1857), I, 250–352, 356–376. In these speeches Clay expressed opinions identical on the matters in question with those of Adams, indicated similar views concerning the powers of the general government under the Constitution, and struck with equal vehemence against the States' rights view. During the Adams Administration Clay, as Secretary of State, unquestionably frequently exchanged views with Adams on these subjects.

of a succeeding generation. The accomplishment of these purposes constitutes the "end of existence" for the great majority of mankind.[6]

As the social order progressed toward greater complexity, special problems of social and individual obligation arose out of that complexity.[7] Adams was preoccupied with the appearance of stresses and strains in the unity of society. For that reason he was doubtful of the advantage of a given society's growing to include a large territory, a swarming population, and diverse races with the accompanying diversity of principles, and prejudices, for he recalled the weakening of the Roman Empire under the impact of hordes of barbarians.[8] He feared the development of revolutionary madness of the masses in convulsions of the social system engendered by "conflicting interests and absorbing passions."[9] The social order must be based upon a solid, organic community of interests and reciprocal advantages; force and power alone could not maintain it.[10] Although the beggar must receive the same justice as the prince, "substantial justice," in this view, required that the maxim should apply just as thoroughly the other way.[11] There was a superior unity that must be based upon the entire interests of society itself, a unity that could be upheld only by the recognition of all interests in a measure commensurate with their importance. In these emphases Adams manifested a kinship with Burkean views of community continuity and traditional order. Further, Adams's stress upon the importance of the community brings to mind Rousseau's similar stress with its recognition of the individual as a social product.

This is not the appropriate point to describe the Adams view of democracy, but it is material to reveal the conditions which he imposed upon popular government in the interest of social solidarity. That solidarity demanded, indeed his view of truth demanded, that the "constitution of government" should emanate from an entire people.[12] He referred to the preparation and adoption of the Massa-

---

[6] "Letters to my children," *Writings,* II, 10–11.

[7] *Ibid.,* p. 11.

[8] Adams, *The New England Confederacy of MDCXLIII,* p. 6.

[9] Adams, *Eulogy on Lafayette,* p. 19.

[10] To John Thornton Kirkland, Ealing near London, November 30, 1815, *Writings,* V, 430–431; to John Adams, B. H. Ealing, December 16, 1815, *ibid.,* p. 447.

[11] Adams, *Letters on Silesia,* p. 111.

[12] Adams, *Newburyport Oration, 1837,* p. 31: It will be clear in the discussion

chusetts constitution as being by the whole people. Adams did not necessarily mean by this action of the "whole people" popular participation in constitution-making and voting in the modern sense, but in so far as the participation of that "whole people" in these processes could be accomplished by a gradual enlargement of the franchise without disruption of "the harmony of the community" or society he favored such an enlargement.[13] He claimed that the enunciation of the principles of the Declaration of Independence had been part of a process of forging the American people into a nation.[14] But he feared that, since the popular voice was *varium et mutabile* "even in America," popular government would create social instability.[15] There was a tendency for free governments to be governments of "opinion" and therefore of parties or factions representing only portions of the community.[16] Recognizing that the vehicle of democracy must be parties, he feared that "the spirit of party" would polarize the community.[17] That conflict within society or the community based on the division between the poor, on the one hand, and the men of "wealth and abilities and of integrity," on the other, was particularly abhorrent to him.[18] This reaction embraced an apprehension that since "*Democracy*" as a shibboleth was particularly appealing to the multitude as a promise to them of absolute power, it would set the masses apart from other groups in society.[19] The view denied that democracy, to the degree that it might be accepted, should imply the rule of numbers only, but held that it should rest upon a solid foundation of association among various groups, particularly families, within society.[20]

---

of his view of the social compact below that he did not require unanimity as did Rousseau, but he preferred a high degree of popular agreement. And yet, of course, Adams always expected, and was chagrined when he did not receive, the unanimous support of the people for his own principles and projects.

[13] Adams, *The Social Compact,* p. 5.

[14] Adams, *July 4th, 1821, Address,* p. 23.

[15] To John Adams, The Hague, July 21, 1796, *Writings,* II, 4.

[16] To Abigail Adams, July 30, 1795, *ibid.,* I, 385, n. 1: The use of the word "opinion" in this reference is significant, since, in Adams's conception, that which governed the functioning of an entire community must be law and principle, not mere "opinion."

[17] *Memoirs,* December 31, 1803, I, 283.

[18] To Thomas Boylston Adams, Boston, February 1, 1792, *Writings,* I, 113.

[19] Adams, *The Social Compact,* p. 31.

[20] Ibid., p. 19: In this connection, a conversation which he had with Bentham is most interesting. He suggested that Bentham's pampering of democratic

Clearly, Adams's social philosophy placed great emphasis upon order and stability. The social order had an organic relationship with qualities inherent in man's nature and factors and conditions inherent in the association of men together. With this idea in mind, we may appropriately analyze his conception of the social compact and its relation to antecedent and subsequent conditions. The succession of years and different practical situations produced modifications in his views of the social compact and of the conditions that brought it into being. A dual compact should not be expected, one part creating a social order and another creating government. The social compact was to Adams historical, and, if a social compact creating a particular social order of government could not be pointed out in history, he could assume one from existing conditions.

At any rate he placed great reliance upon government being "an affair of compact."[21] And, although he contended on one occasion that the British people unfortunately traced their rights back to particular donations of kings;[22] on another, on the basis of the principle "*ex nihilo, nihil fit,*" he asserted that the existence of British rights and a conception of rights proved "the formation of a social compact" antecedent to the existence of those rights, even though no such compact was recorded in history.[23] In fact, he was convinced that a deliberate and conscious decision and determination of the British people had established the terms upon which the supreme powers of government were to be exercised over them.[24]

As Secretary of State, speaking of the South American revolutions, he held that they as well as our own revolution illustrated the fact and "the doctrine that voluntary agreement is the only legitimate source of authority among men, and that all just Government is a compact."[25] He judged the new South American republics and

---

forces would lead to the, perhaps violent, overthrow of other interests in society, the monarchical and the aristocratic. He remarked that the disfranchisement of Old Sarum would violate the principle of "*uti posseditis.*" *Memoirs,* May 22, 1817, III, 538–539.

[21] *Memoirs,* March 1, 1817, III, 475: The reference describes a discussion with Lord Harrowby in which Adams attempts to extract an admission that government was so founded.

[22] Adams, *July 4th, 1821, Address,* p. 7.

[23] VI "Publicola," *Writings,* I, 87.

[24] Adams, *Quincy Oration, 1831,* p. 10.

[25] National Archives, Records of the Department of State, *Diplomatic Instructions,* All Countries, IX, 275.

their rulers according to the degree to which they appeared to recognize principles deriving from a compact. In our own history the charters granted by the King to the colonists had been original contracts recognizing fundamental rights inhering in British subjects.[26] He referred to the Plymouth Colony as remarkable for being "the first example in modern times of a social compact or system of government instituted by voluntary agreement. . . ." The Mayflower Compact had created a civil society out of an original state of nature in which no law had governed.[27] He did not clearly indicate, any more than did Locke, whether the social compact created government or the social order. The generalizations are ambiguous and inexact, but a weighing of the evidence indicates that Adams, emphasizing as he did that society is natural to man, could hardly conceive a politically unorganized society. The best interpretation is that the social compact was a device used for the creation of that political organization without which society would have no vitality. The social compact seems to become equated with constitutions, even though loose generalizations in the writings will confuse those seeking a clear interpretation of Adams's meaning. The state of nature that preceded the Mayflower Compact is almost the solitary reference thereto in Adams's writings; and, weighed against his analyses of the origins of society in man's earliest associations, the allusion is reduced to minor importance, although it indicates the tradition of his political thinking. Moreover, the state of nature in which the Pilgrims found themselves was easily distinguished from the hypothetical states of nature of Locke or Hobbes. He anticipated with joy, although he had some fears and doubts concerning the results, the eventual combination on this continent of the largest population ever associated under one social compact.[28]

In this theory, the social compact itself was, as we have seen, preceded by authority in the family based upon the nuptial bond and made necessary by man's inadequate capacity for self-government.

---

[26] Adams, *Quincy Oration, 1831*, p. 10. It is true that on another occasion, illustrating the care that must be taken to balance one statement off against another, he asserted that the power exercised by British kings to grant power and rights "for the exercise of colonial governments" was "assumed but never legalized." Adams, *The New England Confederacy of MDCXLIII*, p. 17.

[27] Adams, *The New England Confederacy of MDCXLIII*, pp. 17, 20.

[28] To Abigail Adams, St. Petersburg, June 30, 1811, *Writings*, IV, 128: Here the allusion is quite obviously, from the context, to the Constitution.

The degree of authority exercised within the family was not absolute and varied depending upon the particular family relationship involved.[29]　The conjugal relationship implied an authority in the husband and a lesser but reciprocal authority in the wife.　The parental authority of the father was very great and that of the mother limited only by the conditions inherent in the nuptial bond. Adams, easily discovering *a priori* explanations of the social relationships and conditions of his own day, explained the unavoidable inferior position of women in the nuptial bond as deriving from the first woman's "disobedience to the divine command."[30]　Thus there existed a figure in the family capable of standing sponsor for all others, wife, unmarried daughters, minor sons, and his posterity for the duration of the compact.　That figure was the authoritative, although nondespotic, father.　Hence the family compact underlying the social compact invested the father with authority to subscribe to the social compact for the individuals under his authority upon whom the social compact might also operate in creating a body politic as well as for himself.[31]　Adams considered this compact to be simply a constitution of government, and the act of adherence to it consisted in assisting in its formulation or in assenting to it in the electoral process.　The family and the family compact, basic components of the social order, antedate the social compact and the body politic.　The social compact could not, therefore, under such circumstances create the social order, which was antecedent to it; it created the government necessary to the maintenance of safety and stability in a social order that was growing more complicated.

Women, children, foreigners, and slaves could have no "direct agency" in the formation of this voluntary compact creating the "body politic."　Since the compact was voluntary it presupposed the exercise of the *"will"* as well as the "capacity" to contract.[32]　Since the individual wills of members of the family, other than that of the father, were subordinate, and therefore not entirely free, those

[29] Adams, *The Social Compact*, p. 13.

[30] *Loc. cit.*

[31] *Ibid.*, p. 8.

[32] Adams, *The Social Compact*, pp. 8–9: This further makes the case for the view that in Adams's theory the social compact created government, for the social order in his theory did not arise from an act of "will" but from the necessity of living together.

members of the family subordinate to the father could take no part in the formulation of and adherence to the basic social agreement. To hold otherwise, Adams asserted, might result in the unnatural annulment of the vote of the husband by the wife, in contradiction of the husband's superior position.[33]

Once the government was constituted by this process, this agency of the people was confined to action permitted by the people through the process of election.[34]   However, the people empowered to covenant—the heads of families—could never amount to more than one in five in the population, even with what Adams would consider an extreme of democracy.   Adams, in keeping with his times, subscribed to the theory of a limited male suffrage, except in so far as it might be extended gradually, for he avowed that the "protection and security of property is not less the purpose of the social compact than that of persons." [35]   Tax and property qualifications would assure the presence at the polls and in office of those most likely to fulfill this purpose of property protection.   But Adams emphasized strongly that the limited group thus enfranchised did not possess any discretion to bargain away the fundamental rights of any person in the community, for, since the Protestant Reformation a widespread understanding had developed of what he considered a basic principle —that unlimited obedience could not be required to the "commandments of men" and that theories of the divine right of king or patriarch were untenable in the presence of inalienable individual rights.[36]

Although Adams denied the doctrine of Rousseau that the social compact is formed by unanimous agreement of individuals, which a representative body or a limited electorate could not render,[37] he was adamant in his assertion that power over a territory and people could not be legitimately acquired without that people's consent.   His acceptance of a limited suffrage that involved a predominant power

[33] *Ibid.*, p. 19.
[34] *Ibid.*, pp. 13–14.
[35] *Ibid.*, p. 20.
[36] *Ibid.*, pp. 21, 22.
[37] III "Publicola," *Writings*, I, 76: Adams thus to some degree avoids Rousseau's semimystical and romantic conception of an association of individuals. There is thus more foundation in Adams's theory for a pluralistic conception of the locus of power, a conception not incompatible with democracy, even though Adams in his own day might subscribe to a limited suffrage.

in the head of the family over the members thereof and a paramountcy of some heads of families over others indicated that he did
not equate the rendering of consent with a democratic mandate.
He referred to the consent that was rendered in the fashion of his
own day on the basis of a limited franchise and a "virtual representation" in a Burkean sense.   He carried on a bitter campaign against
the annexation of Texas on the ground that the consent of the people,
so understood, had not been received, and went so far as further to
assert that our own Union would be dissolved in the event of annexation.   "We might form another; but the people of a nation, the immortal mind, could not form a political union with another people
without their consent." [38]   Although we shall not at this point inspect
completely Adams's attitude toward revolution, it is essential to stress
his doctrine, one of his central republican principles, that "the sovereign power originally resides in the people [in a collective sense],
and can be delegated only by their free consent." [39]   This idea of
delegation was essential to his view of the social compact.   In addition to influencing his attitude toward the annexation of Texas, this
belief was the basis for his opposition to the purchase and annexation
of Louisiana, which he had accepted only as a *fait accompli*.   Before
the power of this idea he anticipated the crumbling into atoms of
the "magic talisman of despotism" and "the spell of prescriptive
tyranny." [40]

Every human being was born with rights, even against the pa-
triarchal powers of the father.   This idea, in addition to his aversion
to the brutal spectacle of the institution, was central to Adam's rejection of slavery and, further, to his loathing of any despot, whether
it be a Napoleon or a Paris mob, or even a majority determined to
disregard rights.   Any government that imposed itself by force
and conquest could legitimately be resisted by the people, and so
Adams denied the central Hobbesian thesis.[41]   Although he admitted the plausibility of Filmer's theory of the derivation of the
power of a monarch as the father of his people from the original

[38] *Congressional Globe*, 28th Cong., 2nd sess., January 24, 1845, p. 189: What
the fate of the "immortal mind" of the people would be in event of a dissolution
of the Union is a question here unanswered.   In any event, the reference to an
"immortal mind" does suggest, *mutatis mutandis,* the tradition of Rousseau.

[39] To John Adams, St. Petersburg, August 31, 1811, *Writings,* IV, 204–205.

[40] Adams, *July 4th Oration, 1793*, p. 19.

[41] Adams, *The Social Compact*, p. 23.

power of the father in the family, he located the fallacy in Filmer's assumption that the father's power was superior to inalienable rights inhering in members of the family.[42]   In keeping with this doctrine, he justified the American Revolution as a result of the colonists' failure to get British adherence to the social compact and the principles of the Great Charter.[43]   Under the principles of the Declaration of Independence, it became not only the right but the duty of men to throw off the yoke of "incorrigibly oppressive" government, for no people could *consent* to be governed oppressively, and, as the law of the Hebrews affirmed, the consent of the ruled—based on rights—was the only legitimate foundation of authority.[44]

Since government was instituted for the general security of natural human rights, the social compact could not act as an immutably binding force upon the rights of posterity.   In an extremity, Adams was ready to sanction the violence of revolution; in the presence of general governmental incompetence to achieve its purpose he was ready to sanction alterations in the details of the social compact on the terms of which government was founded, for a posterity could be bound orly by its own consent.   Having agreed to the operation of this principle, Adams maintained that it should be called upon only in moments of urgency, especially if the demand was made for complete dissolution of the bonds of civil society.[45]   And a people judging of the competence of their rulers must be certain of judging on the basis of principle, not passion; on the basis of principle a people, although they may have the power, have not the right to do whatever they choose, since they must act in accordance with the limitation of principle.[46]   On the basis of the compact, moreover, the rights of citizens and the duties of rulers being reciprocal, where the government offers protection equally to all, as its duty demands, it may expect the people to maintain a dutiful allegiance, as a matter of a right inhering in the sovereign.[47]   Thus Adams revealed his further indebtedness to Locke who likewise stressed a kind of vested

[42] *Ibid.*, p. 24.
[43] Adams, *Newburyport Oration, 1837*, p. 18.
[44] *Ibid.*, pp. 19, 20.
[45] II "Publicola," *Writings*, I, 72–73.
[46] IV "Publicola," *ibid.*, pp. 78–79.
[47] To William Plumer, St. Petersburg, August 13, 1813, *ibid.*, IV, 505–506; this discussion is in anticipation of a more complete development of his view of revolution, in particular the revolutionary events of his own day, which will be discussed later in this chapter.

right of government in the loyalty of the people as long as it performed its duties.

Adams's view of the social compact, nonartificial because historical,
combined with a concept of an organic social order as implicit in the
very nature of men, their necessities, and their association, no doubt
derived from or was related to the ardor of his nationalism. We may
postpone describing the various manifestations of his nationalism at
this point, but the nationalistic spirit is relevant here because of its
importance to the social cohesion that was a primary goal of his
public career. He was conscious that there were larger ties of sympathy than those comprehended within the family and the nation,
that those ties implicit in the common humanity of all men were not
less sacred than closer ties, but, to him those relations with the more
immediate institutions of experience were more natural and more
enduring. The bonds of the immediate community were combined
"with that instructive and mysterious connexion between man and
physical nature, which binds the first perceptions of childhood in a
chain of sympathy with the last gasp of expiring age, to the spot of
our nativity, and the natural objects by which it is surrounded."
"These sympathies belonged and were indispensable to the relations
ordained by nature between the individual and his country." [48]

His nationalism was more than merely theoretical. Relating a
conversation with Dr. Adams, one of the British commissioners at
Ghent, in which the matter of coats of arms had been discussed, he
recorded that, although Dr. Adams's might be a red cross, he himself was satisfied with the "stripes and stars." [49] Despite his long
European residence and experience, he could agree with Voltaire,
"Plus je vis d'étrangers, plus j'aimai ma patrie." [50] He asserted that
the greatest danger to a republic was "the intrusion of a foreign influence." [51] In conversation in London with a British official, Mr.
Hammond, he was irritated by that official's references to "Virginians,
the Southern people, the Democrats." "What sort of a soul does this
man suppose I have? . . . I let him know that I consider them all in
no other light than as Americans." [52] The American union, he wrote

[48] Adams, *July 4th, 1821, Address,* pp. 13–14.
[49] To Abigail Adams, Ghent, August 18, 1814, *Writings,* V, 75, n. 2.
[50] *Memoirs,* April 26, 1837, IX, 353–354.
[51] II "Columbus," *Writings,* I, 157–158.
[52] *Memoirs,* December 1, 1795, I, 142.

many times, was his most precious object of loyalty.[53]   He would preserve it at all cost against the corrosions of mere faction and foreign influence.[54]   The threat of disunion was a prospect of "hideous shape." [55]

In politics he held himself to have been the servant of the whole union and recognized that this approach would make it difficult for him to become a sectional favorite.[56]   As an American nationalist he rejected with contempt the champions of states' rights,[57] and on the same grounds he rejected Jefferson's doctrine of nullification.[58]   "We the People" in the Constitution was to him a sublime thought; the Constitution had been established, he asserted, as a decision of one people, not as a decision of a number of peoples confederated together.[59]   He reserved the bitterest of his language for "dirty, cadaverous nullification" with its white standard of those who in the service of an economic interest would destroy the organic unity of the nation.[60]   His break with the Federalist Party was facilitated by his belief that members of that party had laid plans for a rebellion by state authority against the government of the nation.[61]   Learning that William Plumer projected a history of the United States, he advised him to teach the doctrine of the indissolubility of the union.[62] He endured the humiliation of military reverses with greater comfort in the hope that the unity of the national spirit might be improved under their impact.[63]   Adams's nationalism was of a variety that became ever more widespread in the 19th century.   In him it was qualified, however, by other principles that limited it as a threat to peace and international solidarity.[64]

---

[53] E.g., to Nahum Parker, Boston, December 5, 1808, *Writings*, III, 259.

[54] To George Washington, The Hague, February 11, 1797, *ibid.*, II, 119–120.

[55] To Louisa Catherine Adams, Ghent, November 29, 1814, *ibid.*, V, 219.

[56] To Robert Walsh, Washington, D. C., November 27, 1822, *ibid.*, VII, 332.

[57] *Memoirs*, December 25, 1818, IV, 198.

[58] Adams, *The Lives of James Madison and James Monroe*, pp. 64, 65.

[59] *Register of Debates*, 22nd Cong., 2nd sess., February 4, 1833, II, 1612.

[60] *Memoirs*, February 4, 1841, X, 516.

[61] To Ezekiel Bacon, Boston, November 17, 1808, *Writings*, III, 250–251. To Nahum Parker, Boston, December 5, 1808, *ibid.*, p. 257.   To John Adams, St. Petersburg, July 13, 1812, *ibid.*, IV, 369–370.

[62] To William Plumer, written at sea, August 16, 1809, *ibid.*, III, 340–341.

[63] To Louisa Catherine Adams, Ghent, October 4, 1814, *ibid.*, V, 148–151.

[64] *Register of Debates*, 22nd Cong., 1st sess., June 30, 1832, III, 3833: Adams's nationalism was not exclusive; he was no protagonist of a tribal god.   He objected to a reference to "Asiatic" cholera in a joint resolution of Congress, for, he

Adams the nationalist was likewise the Puritan who counseled that the morals and character of a nation would benefit as much from affliction as would those of an individual.[65] A nation—which he referred to on occasion as having an "immortal mind"—might just as thoroughly benefit from discipline as a single individual. Courage in the individual required determination to conform to principle "to the last extremity," courage in the nation demanded determination to resist encroachment to the same degree.[66] Although he took comfort in what he deemed to be the greater virtue and morality of the American people, he respected the people of Britain, despite his Anglophobia, for the single-minded "national spirit" with which they were suffused.[67] Each people was possessed of a national character prepared for a particular type of political institutions and ideas.[68]

Social unity and cohesion in the United States, for him a symbol of correct principle until antislavery sentiments overruled the idea, derived from the equality of citizenship of all members of the community united under a great social compact.[69] There existed a unity of interest in the community as a whole in its constant defense of the equality of each individual—with respect to an immortal soul—against the continuing threat of government that would return man to the condition of an animal.[70] He found among the Puritans a "moral principle of equal and inalienable rights" that united them as a community against the pretensions of a parent church.[71] The same principles made the Puritans determined opponents of a pretentious

---

maintained, such a pestilence could be considered peculiar to no particular country. He suggested that we would object to any reference to an "American scourge." Adams, *Argument in United States v. Cinque* [16 Peters 518], p. 59: he excused the ardent demands of the Chevalier d'Argaiz on behalf of his countrymen, holding sympathy and partiality on behalf of one's countrymen to be pardonable and natural. To John Adams, Ealing, August 1, 1816, *Writings,* VI, 61: "I disdain as unsound all patriotism incompatible with the principles of eternal justice.

[65] To Thomas Boylston Adams, St. Petersburg, July 31, 1811, *Writings,* IV, 160.

[66] To Abigail Adams, Ghent, October 25, 1814, *ibid.,* V, 166.

[67] To Abigail Adams, St. Petersburg, April 7, 1813, *ibid.,* IV, 466.

[68] To the Secretary of State (Edmund Randolph), No. 26, The Hague, February 19, 1795, *ibid.,* I, 295.

[69] John Quincy Adams, *An Address to the Members of the Massachusetts Charitable Fire Society at their Annual Meeting, May 28, 1802* (Boston: Russell and Cutler, 1802), p. 23.

[70] John Quincy Adams, *Letter Read at the Recent Celebration of West India Emancipation in Bangor* (*Me.*), Quincy, July 4, 1843, p. 2.

[71] Adams, *The New England Confederacy of MDCXLIII,* p. 12.

government. The affirmation of equality in the Declaration of Independence was a major force in the creation of an American community or "nation." [72] The primary justification of the American Revolution lay in the general appeal of the revolutionaries to the "self-evident truths" of human equality.[73] Popular consciousness of a common and equal possession of rights was a unifying factor, which should lead men to a determination to protect their heritage at all costs.[74]

The ideal of social cohesion to which he subscribed was one served by the principle of political equality, but Adams saw likewise that some equalization of economic return was necessary to social stability. He saw in the accumulation of large masses of individuals in urban centers, thus multiplying the types of occupation, an increase in the precariousness of human subsistence.[75] At the same time that this possibility of urban poverty was increasing, there resulted from the division of labor the creation of a superfluous prosperity in other sectors of the community supported "by contributons levied upon the rest." With the increase of poverty among some individuals their obligations to society diminished, thereby weakening social solidarity, until the basic law of self-preservation alone governed their actions, and the community, in order to safeguard itself, was forced to assume responsibility for their care. Adams never lost sight of the importance of a prosperous and happy laboring class to a stable society. A major purpose of the program of internal improvement projected during his Presidency, which will be discussed below, was the creation of such happy conditions.[76] These conditions were necessary to insulate the laboring masses against destructive theorists who would question basic social principles and thus influence the masses to hatred and violent action against proprietors, e.g. members of the sophistical "transcendental school." [77] He

[72] Adams, *July 4th 1821, Address,* p. 23.

[73] Adams, *Cincinnati Oration,* pp. 12–13.

[74] *Ibid.,* pp. 13–15. On the other hand, Adams on one occasion, with respect to the French Revolution, had occasion to record horror at the excesses of which a people could be guilty in the name of equality. To John Adams, London, September 21, 1797, *Writings,* II, 214.

[75] "Letters to my children," *Memoirs,* II, 11.

[76] Tatum, "Ten Unpublished Letters of John Quincy Adams, 1796–1837," pp. 382–383.

[77] *Memoirs,* August 23, 1840, X, 349–350: this does not qualify his essential

animadverted upon the demogogue who stirred up the poor against the rich,[78] but he early became aware of the importance of maintaining a system in which laboring people felt psychologically, on the basis of security and contentment, an organic relationship and identification with the community interest.[79] He feared a working class entirely dependent upon the class of owners and contended, rather, for the ideal of an independent working class proud of its role in society. Only on such a basis could an economically and politically healthy community, united in economic and political endeavor, support the strong union that was his ideal.[80]

Adams's life is a revelation of his suspicion of the political technique that cultivated popular support and set the people against what he considered legitimate interests. He wrote disparagingly of Jefferson's susceptibility to popular opinion and willingness to work for the people's favor in seeking personal advancement.[81] Viewing tides of popular opinion as often reflective of divisions in the community, he took pride in asserting that his entire life had been spent in stemming such tides, often with considerable success,[82] although one such tide swept him out of office after one term in the Presidency. In his oppositions and struggles, he viewed himself as fighting against "political sectarians," those unaware of the national interest. His severest strictures, against not only the Jeffersonian school but also the Jacksonians, were based on the conviction that they had sacrificed the interests of the "General Government" and the Union in favor of the states' and other special interests.[83] Holding to a view

---

conservatism, but it surely places him in the ranks of those conservatives who recognize that reform cannot be avoided.

[78] *Memoirs*, October 13, 1837, IX, 406.

[79] Adams, *Letters on Silesia*, p. 17: Observing the absence of a *"division of labour"* in Silesia, he took occasion to remark that, whatever the truth of Adam Smith's principles concerning the resulting increase in quantity of goods produced resulting from the division, he doubted that it would benefit so many people as the older relationships he observed during his Silesian journeys.

[80] *Register of Debates*, 22nd Cong., 1st sess., III, Appendix, p. 83 *et seq.*: In his "Report on Manufactures," here cited, he made a strong plea for recognition of all the economic interests of the community and offered compromises when, for example, the support of the tariff interest became the injury of others.

[81] Adams, *The Lives of James Madison and James Monroe*, p. 65.

[82] *Memoirs*, November 21, 1831, VIII, 427–428: Adams opposed the popular agitation against imprisonment for debt until another "substitute [could be found] for the security which it gives to credit."

[83] *Ibid.*, January 13, 1831, p. 273: Adams himself was not always consistent

that the Southern and Western agrarian interests and the manufacturing interests of the community had to be compromised for the sake of unity, he supported a reduction of the tariff that would leave the "principle of protection unimpaired," [84] but he opposed the tariff doctrine of Jackson as ruinous to business, an interest that he was determined to protect. [85] The whole program of internal improvements of which he was the most ardent supporter had as one of its ends the consolidation of the national point of view; he identified any opposition to it with selfish sectional desires. [86] He found dire threats to the union and failure properly to use the bounties of Providence in the conspiracies among sectional groups in which concessions were traded and false alliances were created on foundations of selfishness, to the detriment of internal improvements. [87]

---

as to the best means of securing national solidarity.   For example, in the present reference he maintained that the "entire discharge of the national debt will dissolve one of the strongest ties which hold the Union together; . . ."   Later in the same year he concluded that President Jackson should be supported in his purpose of paying off the entire national debt.   It would be a "glorious day" when such a goal was accomplished.   In arriving at this conclusion, he parted company with Clay on the same issue. *Ibid.*, December 28, 1831, p. 447.

[84] *Register of Debates*, 22nd Cong., 1st sess., III, June 5, 1832, p. 3268.

[85] *Memoirs*, December 31, 1832, VIII, 515.

[86] *Ibid.*, December 13, 1832, p. 504.

[87] *Ibid.*, December 5, 1832, p. 503.   *Ibid.*, July 30, 1834, IX, 162.

6

The Political and Economic Hierarchy

"But no popularity lives long in a democracy."
—MEMOIRS, *May 12, 1820*

It is impossible to discover in Adams's writings a clear-cut statement or development of his view of the social order or hierarchy. The whole temper of the man, which sought unity and coordination in society and a united approach to the solution of social problems, was one that, at least in explicit doctrine, would deny rather than affirm the existence of class differences.[1] It is true that as the slavery crisis deepened he often saw the slaveholding planter class as a separate class threatening to dominate the nation in the interest of selfish ambition and avarice based upon cruel exploitation. However, classes were dealt with only in the most indirect fashion in his writings. His view of the social structure, even in broad outline, may only be inferred from those indirect references. And much of this endeavor must be devoted to the inspection of Adams's references to the broad mass of the people in general in order to determine the relative degrees of aristocratic and democratic emphases his thinking contained, and consequently his consciousness of classes.

There was a degree of aristocratic disdain in his refusal to recognize political reality and campaign for public office, in his assump-

[1] To John Adams, Boston, October 19, 1790, *Writings*, I, 63: "The farmer, the tradesman, the mechanic and the merchant, are all mutually so dependent upon another for their prosperity, that I really know not whether most to pity the ignorance or to lament the absurdity of the partial politicians [who saw matters in terms of party or faction rather than principle], who are constantly erecting an imaginary wall of separation between them."

tion that the high moral quality of his principles and record should speak for themselves. This attitude was manifested in his refusal to engage in electioneering practices designed to win the plaudits of the people; this anti-electioneering view was an important basis of his hatred of the Jacksonian forces, and he even criticized Clay for "peddling for popularity" in a tour of the North.[2] No doubt Adams, disturbed by the wide popular appeal of Jacksonianism, was influenced because of its success against the Adams forces to condemn more severely the political means that the new popular movement employed. It is clear, on the other hand, that democratic and more equalitarian ideas struggled, not always unsuccessfully, for manifestation in his thinking. He took pride in the realization that shopkeepers and tradesmen were transformed into statesmen in the United States.[3] Such reactions, of course, usually were manifested by Adams when he had occasion to contrast the social order of the United States with that of Europe. On the Silesian tour he noted with great approval that in one prosperous town he found no capitalist ownership of large establishments employing a miserable class of workers at subsistence wages.[4] He was quick to observe any class, even the most humble, that might by force of circumstance be suffering hardships. He viewed sympathetically the condition of the small farmer in Britain following the Napoleonic wars, borne down with undue severity by the load of taxation.[5] The picture of his thinking is varied and complex; he mirrors the contending forces of his age.

In the discussion of the social compact above it was revealed that Adams accepted the idea of a compact adhered to by a limited number of heads of families in the community. Since he thought it essential to give representation to property as well as persons, he advocated limiting the suffrage to those with sufficient property to warrant its being represented. Only in this way could his general goal be accomplished. Men of property would really represent more thoroughly than the propertyless the whole complex of interests in the community. He was, quite in keeping with the temper of his

[2] *Memoirs*, October 22, 1833, IX, 25.

[3] Adams, *The Lives of James Madison and James Monroe*, p. 206.

[4] Adams, *Letters on Silesia*, p. 17.

[5] To the Secretary of State (James Monroe), London, April 9, 1816, *Writings*, VI, 5.

day, always opposed to the union of popular or mass interests, as opposed to the total interests of the community, which might work to the disadvantage of the whole community and find expression in the establishment of single powerful assemblies and "invisible executives." [6] He feared, just as did the framers of the Constitution, a system that would give expression to the will of a tyrannical popular majority. The idea of balance in the Constitution was the logical response to this fear of democratic excesses, in which the aristocratic or oligarchical was balanced against the popular or democratic. He feared usurpation of governmental power by popular clubs and societies,[7] and he wrote disturbed letters home to his government from Holland remarking the spread in that country of these organizations "so notorious in France." [8] In this view the potential anarchy in the general populace was a fearsome thing, and he was revolted by "that summary justice" that was meted out by the unleashed masses regardless of the prescriptive and natural order in society.[9] He was suspicious of the consequences that would follow a violent attack upon an established order by a population in the name of high-sounding rights and liberties.[10] He took little satisfaction in the ephemeral nature of popularity in a democracy, in the fact that "the affections of the multitude [soon] cloy upon satiety and [are] ever bent upon change." [11]

On other occasions, for the most part after the fears engendered by the French Revolution had subsided, Adams showed a singular willingness to rely on the considered judgment of the people. He wrote that, the constitutional power of choosing a President having been placed in the people, he could await without fear their "calm and deliberate judgment. . . ." [12] In his polemic against Genêt he echoed the affirmation of Junius that "the people are seldom mistaken in their opinions, in their sentiments they are never wrong." [13] Per-

[6] To Alexander Hill Everett, Washington, D. C., October 15, 1817, *ibid.*, VI, 224–225.

[7] To Charles Adams, Helvoetsluys, November 4, 1795, *ibid.*, I, 426.

[8] To the Secretary of State [Edmund Randolph], The Hague, June 24, 1795, *ibid.*, p. 363.

[9] Adams, *Eulogy on Lafayette*, pp. 16, 17. V "Publicola," *Writings*, I, 82.

[10] To John Adams, London, September 21, 1797, *Writings*, II, 214.

[11] *Memoirs*, May 12, 1820, V, 112.

[12] To Joel Lewis, Washington, D. C., February 20, 1822, *Writings*, VII, 208.

[13] II "Columbus," *ibid.*, I, 150.

ceiving that the foundation strength of the Constitution lay in the intelligence and support of the people, he asserted that, though those forces might appear weak, they had never been known to fail.[14]

To continue this inspection by considering some of his allusions to so-called aristocratic elements, it would be well to allow Adams to speak entirely for himself. The following quotation certainly does not reflect his whole point of view, which was eclectic, but it is significant in showing his realism in viewing those who pretended to gentility:

> The town is not so much crowded this day, as it was yesterday. That class of people which is called by some persons the *rabble*, (by which word is meant people who have neither a fortune nor an education at our university, *alias* a liberal education) went off chiefly last night; and there now remains nothing but the genteel company, or otherwise people who have no business to call them from scenes of dissipation.[15]

This was Adams writing as a young man, but his capacity for suspicion of some qualities of the upper classes increased as he grew older. A minor sign, but not without importance, was his decision to discontinue the use of arms on his seal because they were emblematic historically of hereditary titles of honor of which he disapproved.[16] But, not only was his reaction to the mass of the people ambiguous, his views of the upper classes varied in like degree. As the author of "Publicola," he had been charged with favoring monarchy and aristocracy, a charge that had been made frequently against his father.[17] The charge, as subsequent discussions in this text will show, cannot be substantiated with regard to John Quincy Adams, but he did deny to a people the right "to lay violent hands upon . . . [a] Constitution . . ." that protected their liberties, despite the

[14] To William Vans Murray, January 27, 1801, *ibid.*, II, 495: He did not deny that on occasion the people might wrongly desert their government.

[15] Adams, *Life in a New England Town,* October 25, 1787, p. 53.

[16] *Memoirs,* January 26, 1819, IV, 233. Having seen what he described as a wretched play, *Othello, ou le More de Venise,* by Ducis, he related that it had the merit, nevertheless, of offering strictures upon aristocracy. *Ibid.*, August 13, 1796, I, 180.

[17] *Writings,* I, 65–66, n. 1. Later a controversy broke out over the question of whether or not letters written by John Adams to Samuel Adams had supported the idea of a monarchy and hereditary nobility in the United States. John Quincy Adams derides the controversy as an attempt at slander. To Thomas Boylston Adams, Boston, August 27, 1802, *ibid.*, III, 6.

fact that that same constitution might keep a king in office, or an aristocracy in a special status.[18]   He was considerably disturbed to learn in a conversation with Bentham of the Englishman's unconcern for what might happen to the monarchy and aristocracy in the event of a "democratic ascendancy."   In particular Bentham's willingness that the solution be worked out in the violence of "civil war" upset him.[19]   Holding a prescriptive theory similar to Burke's, he would not altogether subscribe to the idea that "the titles of Kings and nobles, and the wealth of Bishops, were all usurpations and robberies committed upon . . ." the people, for natural and prescriptive rights would then interpose but a weak barrier to popular passions.[20]   Even more significant, in the early days of the French Revolution he wrote, "A nobility and a clergy, church and state levelled to the ground in one year's time; rights not inconsistent with those of man, established by a prescription incontrovertible, if any prescription can be so; rights like these blown to the winds by the single breath of a triumphant democracy, are inauspicious omens for the erection of an equitable government of laws." [21]   These are surely not the words of a democrat in the tradition of Paine.   Many years passed before he came to admit the power of democratic arguments, but even then not to the degree argued for by Brooks and Henry Adams.[22]   Five years later, worse to confound confusion, in a conversation with the Prussian *chargé d'affaires* concluding that aristocratic and feudal institutions could not be accommodated within a system founded upon rights, he then went on to express doubt that man was capable of living in a society "clearly deducible from a theory of rights. . . ." [23]

Toward the end of his life the conflict between his aristocratic inclinations and his recognition of equalitarian trends became obvious.   Referring to Hamilton's plan of a constitution, he asserted that, although it was theoretically better than the Constitution adopted, one could no longer propound its principles even behind closed doors as a serious matter of speculation in view of the in-

---

[18] IV "Publicola," *Writings*, I, 78–79.

[19] *Memoirs*, May 22, 1817, III, 538–539.

[20] V "Publicola," *Writings*, I, 83: This was written during the French Revolution when his fears were particularly great.

[21] To John Adams, Boston, October 19, 1790, *ibid.*, I, 64.

[22] Henry Adams, *The Degradation of the Democratic Dogma, passim:* See Chapter IV.

[23] *Memoirs*, March 12, 1795, I, 88–89.

creasing democratic sentiment in the nation.[24]   In the same year he proposed that the study of literature was of and by its nature aristocratic, "that democracy of numbers and literature were self-contradictory." [25]   A political opponent was described as encrusted with "rabblement filth." [26]   He recognized the existence of classes in growingly democratic America and expressed dismay that the "gentry of New England," "the highest class of capitalists" should be involved, as they were in one case, in an unsavory conspiracy to bribe the officers of the customs.[27]   On another occasion he took time to note that there were no members of the "aristocracy" of Boston in attendance at a meeting of Antimasons.[28]   Not only political difference but aristocratic disdain lay behind his resentment that Harvard, his beloved *alma mater*, should grant an honorary degree to President Jackson.[29]

However, his political impulses and his political insights had a marked effect upon his aristocratic inclinations.   In keeping with his attitudes toward Southern economy and the "peculiar institution," he declined to agree that "wealthy land-holders" were the fundamental prop of society and the best friends of liberty.[30]   He recognized that one of the causes of the weakness of the Federalists was the aristocratic component of their body of principles.[31]   Political principle—which he firmly adhered to when it was fully formed in his mind—caused him, when he had patronage to dispense, to resent the importunings of certain families for public jobs, and he thus informed Judge Thruston who claimed a government position for his son.[32]   What should be the final assessment is difficult to say.   The

[24] *Memoirs,* April 3, 1837, IX, 345.   On the occasion of the death of George III, he expatiated upon the King's role as the protagonist of "the absurd and artificial distinctions of hereditary rank . . . [contrary to] the tendencies of the age to the common level of democracy." *Ibid.,* March 14, 1820, V, 23.

[25] *Ibid.,* October 21, 1837, IX, 416.

[26] *Ibid.,* December 17, 1838, X, 66.

[27] *Congressional Globe,* 27th Cong., 2nd sess., April 30, 1842, p. 461.

[28] *Memoirs,* July 11, 1831, VIII, 379.

[29] *Ibid.,* June 18, 1833, p. 546: "I could therefore not accept an invitation to attend upon this occasion.   And, independent of that [his own political differences with Jackson], as myself an affectionate child of our Alma Mater, I would not be present to witness her disgrace in conferring her highest literary honors upon a barbarian who could not write a sentence of grammar and hardly could spell his own name."

[30] Quincy, *op. cit.,* p. 211.

[31] Adams, *Parties in the United States,* p. 9.

[32] *Memoirs,* October 26, 1827, VII, 346.

picture should be considered confused and contradictory. His conditioned impulses inclined to be aristocratic and, in a passion, they would be revealed, despite the discipline of his intelligence that was aware of the trends of his age and the incongruities of hereditary position. Perhaps the best indication of his most considered inclination was his instruction to our Minister, going to Bogota, to inform the Columbian minister of foreign affairs that any European pressure on behalf of aristocratic institutions in Columbia should be resisted as incompatible with the American way.[33]

The economic order and values to which Adams subscribed cannot, of course, be separated from his system of political values, except for purposes of analysis. The system was coherent, even though not systematically expressed, and normal for the era in which he lived. As a student of Locke and the thinkers of the just-previous generation of American statesmen, Adams greatly emphasized in his scheme of human rights the right of private property. The earth was given to man by the "Creator" and all lower creatures were given likewise for the improvement of the prosperity of the possessor. In fact, the power that was given to man over things was greater than that which he could rightly possess over his fellows. The possession of things must naturally be an exclusive possession, illustrated by the exclusive occupation of the earth necessary for tillage during a season. By the law of nature the exclusive right of the first occupant and owner became vested on the basis of continuous tillage or use from season to season, and thus a proprietary right emerged giving to the occupant the power of enclosure and exclusion of others. This basis of prescriptive right to use the soil for tillage was superior to the right of hunters; free-running animals were contrary to the interests of agriculture, and hunting could be done only where the land was unoccupied. Thus the Indians had to give way before the pressure of the European settler.[34] A similar process would establish the right of man in the exclusive use of any type of property.

There was a peculiar equivocality in his view of property, for, although respect for the right of private property was essential to the system of freedom that he espoused, he maintained on occasion that certain institutions not usually associated with such freedoms were the best protectors of property. For example, remarking the parallels between the humble origins of Burke and Cicero and the defense they offered for existing aristocracies, he asserted those aristocracies were the institutions "upon which alone the *protection of property* subsisted." [35] Elsewhere he noted that various rights, including rights of property, were the main defenses against the assaults of the people upon the prescriptive rights of kings, nobles, and bishops.[36] Or he placed all the champions of property at a certain juncture in the struggle between France and Britain in the same ranks with the champions of ancient institutions on the British side, and he declared those who were thirsting for revolution anticipated feasting upon the "plunder" of dispossessed proprietors.[37] In correspondence with Monroe discussing the revolutions of 1830 in Europe, he expressed the view that the general European result would be heightened democracy with similar repercussions in America and a proportionate diminution of the "securities of property." [38] In a discussion of the party forces contending for superiority at the time of the establishment of the first state governments on the basis of the old colonies, he found that the main collision of interests was between "the relative rights of persons and of property—between aristocracy and democracy." [39] Thus he suggested a conflict between democracy and the "securities of property."

Yet he cannot be depicted as a champion of a great fund of inherited private property in society, for he took exception to an article in the *Edinburgh Review* that held that general standards would improve in America when wealth became more "inherited" than "acquired." [40] Many woes, he wrote, would then be transferred to the United States. Moreover, he early asserted, in analyzing the British constitution, that the British people were in possession of rights to life, liberty, and property and that they would be justified in appeal-

---

[35] To John Adams, London, September 11, 1797, *Writings*, II, 206–207: freedom in his theory, it is true, was freedom of prescriptive interests as well as individuals.

[36] V "Publicola," *ibid.*, I, 83.

[37] To John Adams, The Hague, February 3, 1797, *ibid.*, II, 102.

[38] *Memoirs*, January 10, 1831, VIII, 269–270.

[39] Adams, *Parties in the United States*, p. 4.

[40] To Alexander Hill Everett, St. Petersburg, April 10, 1812, *Writings*, IV, 310–311.

ing to their own strength against the tyranny of rulers who might support inequitable distribution of those benefits.[41]   The issue of the revolting colonists in controversy with the British King was the principle that property could not be taken from the people except by a body that represented them.[42]   The revolutionaries, in a popular movement, based their action on the "natural right of property," as well as the principles of the Great Charter.[43]   On the same basis, Adams suggested approval of the work of the National Assembly in France in basing representation upon property, as well as upon persons and places.[44]

The ambiguity of his position with regard to property may be further analyzed.   He berated the politicians who, in giving way before popular opinions, forgot the effect of their policies upon the safety of property.   His championship of the right of property went even to the length of questioning a bill to amend an act for the relief of sufferers in a New York fire.   He argued that it would take "away from a portion of the citizens of the United States, vested rights— rights of property," even though Congress was merely trying to remedy a situation in which it had granted more than it had intended.[45]   The controlling fact in Adams's mind was that it was contrary to the spirit of the Constitution to take away rights in property that had been vested by a previous act.   Yet, as absolute as this attitude might seem to make such rights, he averred that the greater one's property the greater was one's obligation to family, community, government, and nation.   He berated the idleness of the rich and prosperous, "mere burdens of human society, mere cumberers of the ground." [46]   A sufficient competency was for him, on the contrary, the basis of opportunity to follow either the honorable course of

[41] III "Publicola," *Writings,* I, 75.
[42] Adams, *Quincy Oration, 1831,* p. 10.
[43] Adams, *Newburyport Oration, 1837,* p. 10.
[44] VIII "Publicola," *Writings,* I, 97.
[45] *Congressional Globe,* 24th Cong., 1st sess., April 5, 1836, pp. 322–323.
[46] "Letters to my children," *Memoirs,* II, 12–13.   In one attack upon slavery, Adams pointed out that the constitutional safeguards that had been offered to the wealthy slaveholders had been entirely gratuitous, that they performed no services for society in return for privileges as had the holders of horses—"granted by God to man as men could never be—" in feudal society.   This was an assertion, in a special context, of an obligation upon wealth.   John Quincy Adams, "Speech delivered at Northbridgewater, on Wednesday, November 6th," *Boston Courier,* November 11, 1844.

politics or the study of the arts and sciences.[47]   He was quick to note
when a man of means did good with his fortune, although he might
suspect his motives.[48]   Nor did he hesitate to assert his willingness
to take issue with vast "associated wealth" where that wealth represented values that he could not accept.[49]   Right in property, then,
was fundamental to Adams.   He feared the impact of democracy
upon property; yet he deemed property essential to a fully developed
body of freedoms, likewise essential to democracy.   As an institution its best defenses might be classes often found inimical to freedom, and he would defend those very classes in their prescriptive
rights in things, although not in men, against the attack of a revolting
people.   His right in property was nearly absolute, yet it imposed
social obligations, and he was contemptuous of those who did not
assume them.   The doctrine is not clear, or perhaps it would be best
to record that his speculations concerning property do not offer any
final conclusions.

As for his view of the great toiling masses, we have already recorded his reactions to the picture of depressed working people in
Silesia.   He was far from immune to sympathy for working people.
A goal underlying his lifelong support of internal improvements was
the purpose of providing "high wages and constant employment to
hundreds of thousands of labourers . . ." throughout the land.[50]   In
his scheme labor was a most honorable activity, an assumption of a
great purpose in life necessary to all men.   After a man had provided
for his own wants, Adams asserted, with the spirit of Calvin, that it
was wrong for him to live in idleness.   On the other hand, his organic
view of society obstructed his becoming the defender of a mere sector
of that society to the neglect of other sectors.   He was extremely
aware of the division of the nation into debtor and creditor portions,
and, anticipating the controversies of the present generation, he
rejected the views of those political economists who held that a large
debt was not a burden to the nation on the ground that the nation—
as an entity—was both debtor and creditor, for he said it was more

[47] "Letters to my children," *Memoirs*, II, 13–14.

[48] Adams, *Life in a New England Town*, August 21, 1787, p. 18.

[49] *Ibid.*, October 12, 1787, p. 46.   *Memoirs*, November 12, 1842, XI, 267–268.

[50] Letter to Charles W. Upham, Washington, February 2, 1837, Tatum, *op. cit.*, pp. 382–383.

correct to see one half the nation as the creditor of the other with the government as the agent of collection.[51]   In the struggles between these two halves of the nation, particularly during depression, he feared the bitterness of political controversy, but he feared even more the remedies prepared by the "political empirics" to meet situations of depression—projects for paper money and the like.[52]   He blamed the banks for exacerbating the relations between debtor and creditor by using sneaking and evading bankruptcies.   This action led to political pressures from below that worked to violate the principles of political economy, since the debtors by their numbers were bound to dominate the press of the country.[53]

Under this sort of popular pressure, the country, Adams thought, had suffered from its greatest "scourge . . .—speculation in paper currency," often taking the form of banks in "great multiplication" and being manifested in the unnatural increase and sudden reduction of "fictitious capital."   This fluctuation in the value of money often resulted in an unnatural reduction in the prices of goods suitable for export or increased the possibility of competition from foreign goods supported by a depressed working class.   American workingmen often being "loaded with high wages," there was a consequent reduction of American trade and commerce due to higher costs and an increase in debt that strained credit.[54]   This sort of pressure made the working people susceptible to the influence of agitators stirring them up against proprietors.[55]   One of the subordinate causes of Adams's resentment against the slavocracy was his opposition to their "preachments of insurrections to the laborers of the North."[56]

[51] To the Secretary of State (James Monroe), No. 39, London, April 9, 1816, *Writings*, VI, 8.

[52] *Memoirs*, May 24, 1819, IV, 370.

[53] *Ibid.*, June 10, 1819, p. 391: this was a period of depression during the Monroe Administration.

[54] *Ibid.*, May 22, 1820, V, 128.

[55] *Ibid.*, August 23, 1840, X, 349–350.   Noting an attack by Van Buren upon "associated wealth," he asserted that a republic, in the very derivation of the word, is associated wealth, and suggested, here showing a considerable insight into the foundations of reaction among the masses so observable today, that "associated wealth" was perhaps less anti-republican than "associated poverty." John Quincy Adams, "Letter to the Citizens of the United States, whose Petitions, Memorials and Remonstrances, have been entrusted to me, to be presented to the House of Representatives of the United States, at the third session of the 25th Congress."   Quincy, May 21, 1838, Letter II, *Boston Courier*, June 6, 1839.

[56] *Ibid.*, October 12, 1837, IX, 403.

He noted one colleague in the House (Moore) as a "servile tool of the executive. . . . [who had twice] attempted a great effort to bring out his whole system of insurrection against the rich. . . ." [57]

Adams concluded with some satisfaction that the agricultural population seldom failed to procure its necessary subsistence, even though the tiller of the soil seldom managed to gather more than that, and he saw an unfortunate contrast between this position and the more precarious position of the worker in the city. [58] However, he rejected Jefferson's view that urban dwellers added little or nothing to society. [59] And he noted the fact that an agricultural economic system had produced slavery and an "infamous traffic of human flesh." [60] The community must be viewed whole and no sector of it should be preferred to another. In contrast with the skeptic Jefferson, Adams was bound to view the growth of the community as in keeping with a divinely ordained course. Whenever any portion of the community was in distress, the supreme political counsels must work to bring relief. [61] It was in aiding this function that we may find Adams acting as the means of submitting numerous petitions from laborers, particularly in Washington, asking the House of Representatives for relief. The mere submission of a petition by Adams does not mean that he endorsed the purpose of the petition, but in these cases he took a very sympathetic interest in the laborers' cause. He pointed out on one occasion that it should be remembered that these men possessed only their labor and he suggested that payment be made to them in compensation for time lost due to failure of the house to act on appropriations. [62] On another he opposed a cut in an

[57] *Ibid.*, October 13, 1837, IX, 406.
[58] "Letters to my children," *ibid.*, XII, 11.
[59] V "Publius Valerius," *Writings*, III, 77.
[60] *Ibid.*
[61] To the Secretary of State (James Monroe), No. 39, London, April 9, 1816, *ibid.*, VI, 6–7: He was quick to note the distress of landholders. In this reference, Adams noted the bad effect that the tax policy of the British government was having upon landholders and agriculture in general in contrast with the fundholders, who were prospering greatly.
[62] *Congressional Globe*, 25th Cong., 3rd sess., December 20, 1838, p. 52. *Ibid.*, 26th Cong., 2nd sess., January 12, 1841, p. 96. *Ibid.*, 27th Cong., 1st sess., August 7, 1841, p. 306. *Ibid.*, 27th Cong., 2nd sess., May 3, 1842, p. 469: Most of these petitions were from stonecutters or general laborers on the public buildings in Washington. It is true that Adams had become the great champion of the right of petition, but he often identified himself with the cause of the petitions he presented.

appropriation bill as a miserable attempt to defraud poor working-men out of their daily wages.[63]   His sympathies were not limited; they were eclectic.

He possessed a singular grasp of the operation of economic forces, as his dispatches to his government, particularly while he was United States representative in Britain, amply reveal.[64]   He did not always accept the economic development of his day as necessarily providing the best for man, for he was pleased, as we have seen, to observe in one town on his Silesian journeys that no large, capitalistically owned projects sharply divided ownership from workmanship. Expressing ideas having singular relevance to our own day, he refused to accept the argument, in this case with respect to Britain, that the economic distresses of the country were owing to "excessive plenty" at a time when a considerable part of the population was "nearly perishing with famine." [65]

He took great joy and a great interest in the growth of manufacturing in the United States.   Very early he remarked in a letter to his father with ample detail and illustration the growth of manufacturing in Massachusetts.[66]   One of the chief objects of the Silesian tour was to gather information concerning the manufactures of that province for the use of American manufacturers.   Being forced to interdict, when he was President, the acceptance by Mrs. Adams of presents of articles from their manufacturers, he said he found it difficult to do so, especially when these gifts indicated the extent or ingenuity of production in the United States.[67]   One of the great purposes of his program of internal improvements was the stimulation of domestic industry to the fullest extent.[68]   He always noted with

[63] *Memoirs,* May 3, 1840, X, 281.

[64] See, for example, letter to the Secretary of State (James Monroe), No. 39, London, April 9, 1816, *Writings,* VI, 5–8, in which he described in fine detail Britain's economic condition.   He found an overabundance combined with a great tax burden bearing upon the small farmers.   They were forced by factors to reduce the value of their stock by one half.   There was a consequent falling off in rent and tithe payments, a reduction in wages for village laborers, greater numbers of rural peoples supported by the poor rates, a reduction in landlord income, etc.—a developing vicious circle.   Adams proceeded to describe the degenerative process with keen analytical powers, in the course of which discussion his economic premises are implied.

[65] To Abigail Adams, Ealing, August 30, 1816, *Writings,* VI, 78.

[66] To John Adams, Boston, October 19, 1790, *ibid.,* I, 62–63.

[67] *Memoirs,* March 6, 1821, V, 319.

[68] *Ibid.,* January 13, 1831, VIII, 273.

distress the periodic depressions of industry, as well as commerce and agriculture.[69] But, for all the distress he saw resulting from failures in the wisdom and virtue of men, he doubted that the "growth and prosperity" of the United States could be offset.[70] He had an earnest desire to stimulate the growth of manufacturing because he saw it as a fundamental bulwark of our commerce and our foreign policy, a fundamental aid in our competition with the mistress of manufacturing and commerce, Great Britain.[71] And one of his greatest sorrows was that the manufacturing interests of the North should suffer through the combined efforts of the "slave breeders and the Northern democracy." [72]

Although Adams was perhaps never forgiven by the New England commercial interests for his support of Jefferson's Embargo,[73] he remained throughout his life a foremost champion of the commercial interests. While he was American Minister to Prussia, viewing as usual the whole prospect of affairs, he described to the Secretary of State the growing importance to the United States of Mediterranean commerce in which the new nation had up to that time scarcely participated at all.[74] In a letter to his father, observing that Austria was in control of Venetia and had thus become of increased importance commercially in the Mediterranean and consequently to the United States, he held that it was the purpose of Britain and France to reduce American commerce with other European states.[75] Nor did he find the obstacles to the prosperity of American commerce entirely in foreign influences; he was determined to fight any undue burden of taxation or government upon the commercial states.[76] He was quick to resent any implication of an attack upon commerce during consideration of tariff measures in the House.[77] Speculations engaged in with his father concerning the advantages of an increased navy

[69] *Ibid.,* May 24, 1819, IV, 370.

[70] To John Adams, December 24, 1804, *Writings,* III, 100–101.

[71] *Memoirs,* June 20, 1822, VI, 25.

[72] *Ibid.,* December 7, 1841, XI, 34.

[73] Henry Adams, *The Education of Henry Adams* (New York: The Modern Library, 1931), p. 21.

[74] To the Secretary of State (Timothy Pickering), Berlin, November 10, 1797, *Writings,* II, 223.

[75] To John Adams, Berlin, January 31, 1798, *ibid.,* p. 250.

[76] Speech prepared in connection with a Proposed Amendment to the Constitution on Representation, Ely's Motion, *ibid.,* III, 96.

[77] *Register of Debates,* 22nd Cong., 1st sess., III, June 27, 1832, p. 3801.

to the United States turned on the implications of such an increase for our commerce.[78]   One of the articles of difference between John Quincy Adams and Jefferson was the aversion of the latter to a navy, the most important use of which was, in Adams's view, the protection of commercial interests.   He took exception to the priority to be inferred from Jefferson's inaugural wherein he referred to the "encouragement of agriculture, and of commerce as its handmaid." [79] With ironical implication, he reminded his readers that this had been a primary axiom of the Tories in Britain, a strange consideration in view of the fact that Mr. Jefferson, in the great cleavage that had divided America as well as Europe, had been the leader of the American "Whigs," just as Napoleon was the leader of the European "Whigs." [80]

In his significant emphasis upon the importance of the commercial interests to the United States, he held that the United States, "conceived in the spirit of the Declaration of Independence," had established a precedent of "just and magnanimous" commercial dealings with other states in a commercial treaty with an absolute monarchy, France.[81]   In his statements, he was quick to point out the commercial advantages that would accrue to the United States from abstention from war while other nations were so engaged.   "As the natural consequence of war, the necessities of all the belligerent powers must increase in proportion as their means of supply will diminish, and the profits, which must infallibly flow to us from their wants, can have no other limitation than the extent of our capacity to provide for them." [82]   He constantly called attention to the pos-

[78] To John Adams, St. Petersburg, October 14, 1811, *Writings*, IV, 242–243: A strange contention in this letter reads as follows: "But from all that I have seen and all that I have heard and read of commerce, in this or in former ages, in my own or in any other quarter of the globe, commerce is the very last constituent interest in the nation, upon which I would bestow power."   In the light of his lifetime support for commercial interests, this statement must be denoted an aberration.

[79] Adams, *Parties in the United States,* pp. 22, 39.

[80] *Ibid.*, p. 105.

[81] To George Washington Campbell, State Department, Washington, D. C., June 28, 1818, *Writings*, VI, 368.   In the preamble of the French treaty of February 6, 1778, there had been contained the principle of the "equality of the most favoured nation . . . ," which he held should be the manual of every American negotiator.   National Archives, Records of the Department of State, *Diplomatic Instructions*, All Countries, IX, 262.

[82] II "Marcellus," *Writings*, I, 140–141.

sible advantage to our commerce from this neutrality in the presence of war.[83] Believing that the British, particularly the "Percival-Wellesley" groups, feared the Yankees more as commercial rivals than they did the French,[84] and that they would persist in their monopolistic commercial practices even during peacetime,[85] he counseled a policy toward Britain that would lead her to follow a more liberal course of commercial relations—similar to that of the United States—particularly with respect to her colonies.[86] His consistent policy or principle was an ideal of general commercial liberty in the interest of American commerce,[87] "a liberal principle of commercial intercourse with foreign nations . . . [as an ingredient] of our national independence."[88] He thought this course had been the consistently one pursued by the United States.[89] Of course, his principles of liberal commercial intercourse did not include a willingness to dispense with tariffs, and he counseled that the United States should wait to observe the British application of the principles of free trade before acceding to a British proposal that she adopt such principles.[90] A similar regard for the safety and prosperity of American commerce made Adams the author of a proposed convention—offered to the British—for the abolition of "private war upon the Sea," that is, privateering and depradations upon neutral shipping.[91]

Another economic interest with which Adams was closely asso-

[83] *Ibid.*, p. 142. To Thomas Boylston Adams, St. Petersburg, May 1/13, 1811, *ibid.*, IV, 68–69. He opposed a bill calling for the severance of commercial relations with St. Domingo because of the danger it would entail with France. "Believing it as I do, and that no needless interference of the Government with the regular course of commercial transactions ought ever to be countenanced, I hope the gentleman from Pennsylvania (Mr. Logan) will not have leave to bring in this bill." *Annals of Congress*, 9th Cong., 1st sess., pp. 29–30.

[84] To George William Erving, St. Petersburg, August 13, 1811, *Writings*, IV, 175.

[85] To William Plumer, Ealing near London, October 5, 1815, *ibid.*, V, 401.

[86] National Archives, Records of the Department of State, *Diplomatic Instructions, All Countries*, VIII, 196. *Ibid.*, p. 212.

[87] To Richard C. Anderson, State Department, Washington, D. C., May 27, 1823, *Writings*, VII, 466–467.

[88] *Memoirs*, November 28, 1821, V, 427.

[89] John Quincy Adams, "Inaugural Address," *in* James D. Richardson (ed.), *A Compilation of the Messages and Papers of the Presidents, 1789–1897* (Published by Authority of Congress, 1900), II, 300.

[90] *Congressional Globe*, 27th Cong., 1st sess., June 23, 1841, p. 98.

[91] National Archives, Records of the Department of State, *Diplomatic Instructions, All Countries*, X, 80.

ciated, the United States Bank, had a more partisan significance, and Adams, as a champion of that institution, revealed himself as an antagonist of the democratic forces surrounding Jackson.   Adams's behavior in the controversies surrounding the bank issue reveals his orientation on social questions.   Here it is sufficient to observe that he had quite early after his return from Europe begun to worry over the turn of the public mind upon the issue of the Bank.   He soon found his own political opposition among those who differed with him on the major issue of the Bank, and also what he considered the closely related issues of the national currency, internal improvement, slavery, and sectional cleavages.   He later had occasion to deny the accusation made in the House that he was an unrelenting champion of the Bank,[92] but he did line himself up with those interests that opposed what he called the "base persecution of N. Biddle and the bank directors"; that is, Adams was on the side of the financial interests.[93]   His party affiliations, such as they were, made this orientation normal, just as did his social antecedents, his place of birth, and his relations with other political figures of the day, particularly Jackson, who became the symbol of all that Adams rejected.   With this summary we may turn to another issue of his day—slavery—his stand upon which was consistent with his other principles, including support of the Bank, especially in view of the Jacksonian association with the alliance between the Southern slavocracy and frontier agrarianism.

[92] *Congressional Globe,* 26th Cong., 1st sess., May 1, 1840, p. 371.
[93] *Memoirs,* December 26, 1833, IX, 61.   *Ibid.,* January 9, 1834, p. 73.

7

Race: Slavery, the Vice of the American System

If slavery be the destined sword in the hand of the destroying angel which is to sever the ties of this Union, the same sword will cut in sunder the bonds of slavery itself.
—MEMOIRS, *November 29, 1820*

The cohesion and organization of a society are markedly influenced by the racial complexion of the group. In the absence of racial homogeneity significant social stresses and strains are apt to be present. In the presence of such homogeneity the problem of social cohesion is less difficult to solve. In addition to the *fact* of the racial structure of a group, the *attitudes* of the people themselves toward racial differences are of importance, on the old ground that it is not so much the nature of the fact as what people think is the fact that is important. Therefore, John Quincy Adams's views of race and of any particular status in society based upon race are an important guide in the process of assessing his general social views. We may with profit discuss this sector of his thinking, whereof his attitudes upon slavery and its effects will form an important part.

On his general views on race not so much may be written, for there was in his writings no explicitly stated doctrine. As Chief Executive, he expressed himself as always willing to see any person of color, whether Indian or Negro, and said that he would much prefer to see them than time-consuming placeseekers.[1] He consigned the Indians to a permanently inferior position, since he thought them

[1] *Memoirs*, March 7, 1828, VII, 465.

121

permanently unreconciled to any condition except that of wandering hunters.[2]   Furthermore, he once agreed with Clay that they were an inferior race, declining in virility, and perhaps not worth preserving.[3]

With respect to Jews, his references are ambiguous.   On one occasion he remarked that a town in Silesia had the peculiar characteristics that mark all those towns where many Jews live, "and to express which, I suppose, resort must be had to the Hebrew language: the English, at least, is inadequate to it; for the word *filth* conveys an idea of spotless purity in comparison with Jewish nastiness."[4]   And yet on another occasion he noted with disfavor that a Silesian town was still unashamed to prohibit the entrance of any Jew within its confines.[5]   Although not in explicit terms, he wrote in derogatory fashion of M. M. Noah, the editor of the *New York Advocate,* who had formulated a project for settling Jews in this country.[6]   He had many occasions to refer to Levy, the delegate from Florida, who, Adams wrote, was described by his enemies as, not only a Jew, but part Negro.   Adams noted acidly that in the minds of these enemies the latter condition was a "more formidable disqualification."[7]   His references to Levy, because the latter represented interests to which Adams was unfriendly, were often critical and in such terms as "the Jew delegate from Florida,"[8] the "alien Jew delegate,"[9] "the squeaking of the Jew delegate from Florida,"[10] or "Levy, the Jew, blustered up again with his motion of Saturday. . . ."[11]   Some indication of suspicion of Jews should probably be attributed to his references to "Jew-brokering tricks upon the Royal Exchange,"[12] or to the notice that he took of the fact that the Lord Mayor of London was going to dine with 500 Jews.[13]   Nothing

[2] *Memoirs,* September 1, 1814, II, 27–28.

[3] *Ibid.,* December 22, 1825, III, 90: In this discussion Clay asserted the superiority of the Anglo-Saxon race.

[4] Adams, *Letters on Silesia,* pp. 5–6.

[5] *Ibid.,* p. 183.

[6] *Memoirs,* September 7, 1820, V, 173.

[7] *Ibid.,* June 21, 1841, X, 483: He slyly suggested that this was *sub rosa* the case with more than a single member of the House.

[8] *Ibid.,* May 16, 1842, XI, 155.

[9] *Ibid.,* May 26, 1842, p. 162.

[10] *Ibid.,* January 14, 1843, p. 294.

[11] *Ibid.,* February 5, 1844, p. 502.

[12] To George Joy, Ghent, September 13, 1814, *Writings,* V, 138.

[13] *Memoirs,* March 21, 1816, III, 317.

conclusive may be drawn from these references, but the singling out of Jews as a special category often associated with tricks or a special manner was presumptive of prejudice.

Noting with disdain, furthermore, a speech of Dr. Duncan of Cincinnati asserting the inferiority of Negroes, he merely held the contention irrelevant to the question of slavery.[14]   For all that, the question of slavery apart, he often went out of his way to protest against injustices done to free Negroes, as when he opposed a Virginia law that permitted the imprisonment of a free Negro on the presumption that he was a slave,[15] or when he objected to a law of the state of South Carolina prohibiting under penalties the entry into that state of free Negroes.[16]

The above gives cause for believing that he graded races in a rather vague scheme of priority or relative merit.[17]   He was prepared to ascribe an excellence to the Anglo-Saxon character, but he stopped far short of being willing to discriminate positively against groups on the basis of racial difference.   He would have preferred racial homogeneity,[18] but in its absence he opposed those discriminations that increased the cleavages that may exist in the presence of various racial groups.   For example, he looked upon slavery as a violation of fundamental principles that were necessary to a cohesive social order in America.

Adams was never officially an abolitionist.   Even though he might

[14] *Memoirs,* January 6, 1844, III, 477–478.
[15] *Congressional Globe,* 28th Cong., 1st sess., December 29, 1843, pp. 88–89. *Ibid.,* 27th Cong., 2nd sess., June 2, 1842, pp. 569–570.   With respect to a charter amendment for the town of Alexandria, he moved to strike out the qualification "white" for the franchise, on the ground that it was much more sensible to allow the best colored citizens to vote than the dregs of the white population.   Quincy, *op. cit.,* pp. 112–113: he proposed that, as long as colored citizens from Massachusetts were denied the right to vote in Missouri, white citizens of Missouri should be denied the rights of citizenship in Massachusetts.
[16] *Memoirs,* June 7, 1824, VI, 376.
[17] *Ibid.,* October 17, 1820, V, 187: He spoke of Mr. Manuel Torres of Columbia as having all "that patelinage that belongs to the Spanish character."
[18] Adams, *The New England Confederacy of MDCXLIII,* p. 6: "With the expansion of the surface of soil, to be cultivated and replenished by the swarming myriads of our future population, men of other races, the children of other blood, bred to other opinions, accustomed to other institutions, trained to other prejudices, and disciplined to other principles, have been invested with the community of our rights, and mingled with the tide of our common concerns. It was by the accession of foreign conquered nations to the rights and privileges of Roman citizens, that the republic degenerated into an empire, and the empire itself was overrun and extinguished by hordes of foreign barbarians."

support the right of petition in a long struggle against Southern attempts to obstruct the right, he professed to be opposed to the pleas of such petitions that slavery be abolished, even in the District of Columbia.[19]   Although he held that immediate abolition was impracticable, he at a later date expressed the hope that before his "lamp [was] burnt out . . ." his opinions concerning the approaching abolition of slavery throughout the world should be declared and made clearly known.[20]   As his end grew nearer, he grew more definite in stating that his greatest sorrow was his country's deviation, under the influence of "slavery and the slave-representation," [21] from its basic creed of freedom.   Even though he knew himself to be disavowed by the sectarian abolitionists, yet he asserted that the whole venom of the South was poured upon him because of his position "as the head of the anti-slavery movement in this country. . . ." [22] His suspicion of the slave interests was so great that he even found it difficult to accept without protest their support of principles to which he subscribed.[23]

In Adams's view slavery was a violation of basic moral, political, and religious principles, principles of the Declaration of Independence that ascribed to man a common humanity and brotherhood on a plane of equality in the possession of an immortal soul.[24]   The religion of Jesus as he understood it left no room for slavery.[25]   The

[19] *Memoirs*, December 12, 1831, VIII, 434.

[20] *Ibid.*, August 10, 1843, XI, 406.

[21] *Ibid.*, May 29, 1844, XII, 37.   Earlier he had noted that the greatest danger to the country was its size plus slavery. *Ibid.*, April 13, 1820, V, 68.   As indicated above, Adams was never directly associated with the Abolitionists.   He would have striven as long as possible to oppose civil war, but from 1820 he feared it was inevitable, and he developed a doctrine, from which derived Lincoln's Emancipation Proclamation, whereby the final catastrophe could be made use of to emancipate the slaves.   Clark, *op. cit.*, p. 9.

[22] *Memoirs*, January 1, 1845, XII, 135–136.

[23] *Ibid.*, April 24, 1842, XI, 140: "This sudden Virginian overflow of zeal for the patronage of the navy comes reeking hot from the furnace of slavery. 'Tis a wholesome stream from a polluted fountain."

[24] Adams, *Letter Read at the Recent Celebration of West India Emancipation in Bangor* (*Me.*), pp. 1–2.   Declaring that the slaveholders were sophisticating even to the point of holding the tenets of the Declaration of Independence unsound, he declared that it was the same thing as holding the right to revolution which we asserted against Britain to be unsound.   Adams, "Letter to the Citizens of the United States, Whose Petitions, Memorials and Remonstrances, have been entrusted to me, to be presented to the House of Representatives of the United States, at the third session of the 25th Congress," Quincy, May 21, 1839, Letter II.

[25] Adams, *Discourse on Education*, p. 13.

Declaration of Independence had been, for the United States, an event in the inevitable progress of unifying principles directly antithetical to slavery.[26] Before the universal law of mankind, commanding brotherly love, slavery must eventually disappear.[27] This law established that all men were as of one blood, a principle denoted a "self-evident" truth in one of our first instruments.[28] The institution of slavery stood as a direct violation of this principle. The rising tide of democracy was shaking slavery to its foundation,[29] and the slaveholders were guilty of a shocking inconsistency in holding the principles of the Declaration of Independence in one hand and the slavery scourge in the other.[30] The immutable precepts of justice were as applicable to Africans as to any other people.[31] It was as Christian to abandon slavery as war, and they both must go in the course of the moral improvement of man.[32] The power men exercised over slaves was tyrannical; in the words of Junius, "The arguments of tyranny are as despicable as its power is dreadful." [33] Slavery tainted "the very sources of moral principle, . . . [and perverted] human reason" in heartlessly making human rights depend upon the color of one's skin.[34]

Passionately he thought that the actual effect of slavery upon the United States was disastrous. Adams saw the "Constitution [as] a menstruous rag, and the Union . . . sinking into a military monarchy. . . ." [35] Among the other divisive effects of slavery was the

[26] Henry Adams, *The Degradation of the Democratic Dogma*, pp. 29–30.

[27] *Memoir of the Rev. Elijah P. Lovejoy*, Adams's "Introduction," pp. 3–4. National Archives, Records of the Department of State, *Diplomatic Instructions, All Countries*, X, 69–70.

[28] *Memoir of the Rev. Elijah P. Lovejoy*, Adams's "Introduction," p. 7–8.

[29] *Memoirs*, August 11, 1835, IX, 251, 255.

[30] *Ibid.*, December 27, 1819, IV, 492. He noted the strange preference of "negro keepers" for "French democracy," and he predicted that they too would be cured of the malady "only by having the druggist's shop pass through them." A forecast of revolution or civil war to root out slavery is implicit here, coming singularly early in Adams's career. To William Vans Murray, August 4, 1798, *Writings*, II, 350, n. 2.

[31] *Memoirs*, February 24, 1841, X, 431. Adams, *Argument in United States v. Cinque* [15 Peters 518], pp. 6, 88.

[32] Adams, *Newburyport Oration, 1837*, pp. 59–61.

[33] *Memoirs*, May 24, 1839, X, 123.

[34] *Ibid.*, March 2, 1820, V, 11–12.

[35] *Ibid.*, February 19, 1845, XII, 171. In his later years he saw slavery as the force driving us on to the acquisition of additional territories—Mexico and West Indian islands—and forcing us to become a "maritime, colonizing, slave-tainted monarchy" with freedom extinguished. *Ibid.*, June 10, 1844, p. 49.

cleavage of the population into a superior class of slaveholders and an inferior class of nonslaveholders, with the former having a vote for each of themselves and for "3 of every 5 of [their] slaves," while the nonslaveholders contributed ten times as much to the support of government.[36] The fiery sensitiveness of Southerners concerning slavery obstructed the proper consideration of national problems by men of the North.[37] Thus the slave interests stood in the way of a policy of internal improvement.[38] Moreover, in defense of the institution of slavery these groups would defeat the general right freely to petition government for redress of grievances, out of fear that some petitions might concern their economic interests.[39] Slavery thus became a force inimical to the rights of all citizens of the United States. South Carolina would have the union governed as that state governed its slaves.[40] South Carolina and the slave interests were likewise the source of the divisive influence of "the mongrel brood of doctrinal nullification." [41]

In the face of the cleavages and movements produced by the institution of slavery, Adams at first proposed to adhere as long as possible to the terms of the constitutional compact that implicitly prohibited all attempts to aid the abolition of slavery or the insurrection of slaves.[42] On this ground, he had reluctantly favored the Missouri Compromise, but at the time he asked himself whether, if the union must founder, it could do so on a better issue than that of slavery.[43] In the same year, 1820, he had asserted even more strongly that there was no remedy that would obviate the "dishonorable compromise with slavery. . . ." except a complete reorganization of the

[36] V "Publius Valerius," *Writings,* III, 70–71.

[37] *Memoirs,* June 18, 1842, XI, 180.

[38] Henry Adams, *The Degradation of the Democratic Dogma,* p. 26.

[39] *Congressional Globe,* 24th Cong., 2nd sess., appendix, pp. 260–263.

[40] *Memoirs,* June 1, 1830, VIII, 230.

[41] *Ibid.,* June 20, 1840, VIII, 315–316.

[42] Letter to S. Sampson, Collector of the Custom—Plymouth, Mass.—Washington, D. C., May 21, 1836, Worthington C. Ford, *John Quincy Adams, His Connection with the Monroe Doctrine* (1823) and with Charles Francis Adams, *Emancipation under Martial Law* (1819–1842), [Reprinted from the Proceedings of the Massachusetts Historical Society, for January, 1902],(Cambridge: J. Wilson and Son, 1902), p. 83.

[43] *Memoirs,* March 3, 1820, V, 12. He held that the dissolution of the Union on the slavery issue would result in a servile rebellion and a war between the halves of the union with the resultant destruction of slavery. A harsh course, but to be desired. *Ibid.,* November 29, 1820, pp. 209–210.

union on the basis of concerted action by the nonslave states, and he speculated on the paradox that the unifying effect of slavery in the slave states was more powerful than the unifying effect of freedom in the whole union.[44] He was slowly losing his fear of slavery as a source of division; he was coming to think of a temporary division as a means of eradicating slavery and a prelude to greater unity. Refusing the compromises that would bring Texas or Florida into the union as slave states,[45] he rejected and resented the alignments between Northern interests struggling to achieve political power and votes and Southern forces agonizing "under sophistical argumentation" to safeguard their interests.[46] Adams saw in the annexation of Texas the threat of an "immediate crisis of a great struggle between slavery and freedom throughout the world." [47]

Not only did Adams come to accept disruption of the Union as preferable to the maintenance of slavery, he gradually came to realize that civil war was inevitable. The cause of human liberty was inevitably coming into conflict with slavery.[48] The holocaust would be terrible; the progress of man might be reversed for a time before he moved forward again. These ideas drove Adams on and made of him the most effective single antislavery force of his day. From an early period he thought that the union could not endure on the basis of slavery. At first he opposed attempts to move against slavery in the face of its constitutional safeguards, but, as he grew older, he came to believe that a civil war should be sought as a means of rooting out the evil.

[44] *Memoirs,* March 2, 1820, V, 4.
[45] *Ibid.,* March 31, 1820, p. 54. Adams bemoaned as a desecration the spectacle of President Tyler "and his Cabinet of slave drivers" attending the celebration of the completion of a monument on Bunker Hill. *Ibid.,* June 17, 1843, XI, 383.
[46] *Ibid.,* April 19, 1837, IX, 349–350. *Ibid.,* March 26, 1842, XI, 117.
[47] *Ibid.,* May 4, 1844, XII, 22.
[48] *Ibid.,* April 17, 1843, XI, 363.

8

Social Change: Evolution and Revolution

I said it seemed to me that the French were unable to combine all the simple ideas that were essential to constitute the complex idea of liberty.

—MEMOIRS, *March 6, 1817*

We have seen that Adams, devoted to the idea of human perfectibility and rejecting much that he saw in the world of his day, was not an enemy of social change *per se*. In this particular regard, however, investigation will reveal perhaps a greater transformation of point of view than in any other. He reversed the usual fact, and, instead of growing more conservative with respect to social change as he grew older, he became less devoted to the *status quo*. This fact was revealed in the vicissitudes of his party relationships, his view of evolving democracy, and particularly the transformation of his ideas on slavery in the context of the economic struggle between North and South. Discussion of these points has already been developed or will be developed elsewhere, but it will be worth while at this point to discuss more in detail his attitudes toward change, reform, evolution, and revolution, actual and theoretical. Again the report will or may be ambiguous or contradictory, but a general picture will be possible, a general category will be delineated into which Adams will fall without undue discomfort.

He recognized the changes that were wrought "by the slow but ceaseless hand of time." [1] The whole Adams doctrine of internal

[1] Adams, *July 4th Oration, 1793,* p. 9.

128

improvement showed that he was far from being merely a conservative opponent of change. The affairs and conditions of men were ephemeral, a fact that he admitted in more objective philosophical moments.[2] The propensity that the multitudes had for change might be regrettable, but he embodied one of his basic lessons in life that he called his "first canto of mutability," in a letter to his mother, in which he reflected on the revolutions in fortunes that had raised high many of the figures he had known in Europe and then cast them down.[3] This reversal of condition should teach that Fortune does not lavish her favors and must be recognized the one time she looks upon you.[4]

The world of the early nineteenth century was one in which the common man was becoming the possessor of political knowledge, and to diffuse such knowledge widely was one of the greatest obligations of a republic. The fact of popular emancipation contained a lesson for all rulers, one that had not been learned by the Bourbons returning to power, for they had not made people forget the yoke of monarchy through improvements and a liberalization of policy.[5] Some situations call for basic changes and cannot be met by mere palliatives, which Adams thought were all the Whigs offered in Britain in the years following the final defeat of Napoleon.[6] There was no threat, he asserted to the Earl of Westmorland, in reforms, particularly measures that might extend the suffrage to those paying direct taxes so as to make it practically universal, and he shrewdly suggested that widening the suffrage would not endanger the established order.[7] As he grew older, he reserved stringent criticisms for those who attempted to preserve anachronistic institutions in the face of growing democracy.[8] Yet he preferred the change that comes in response to the pressure of time working slowly on the minds of men, and he never had occasion to withdraw his criticism of Paine who had thought it as easy for a nation to change governments as a man his

[2] *Memoirs,* July 7, 1794, I, 33–34.
[3] To Abigail Adams, St. Petersburg, March 19, 1811, *Writings,* IV, 26.
[4] To the Secretary of State (Monroe), St. Petersburg, February 2, 1812, *ibid.,* p. 432.
[5] Adams, *Eulogy on Lafayette,* p. 25.
[6] To Abigail Adams, Ealing, August 24, 1816, *Writings,* VI, 71.
[7] *Memoirs,* March 6, 1817, III, 482.
[8] *Ibid.,* March 14, 1820, V, 23.

coat.[9]   Time could be counted on to demonstrate the fallacy or truth of principle; the faith of one generation becomes the heresy of the next.

In the Burkean sense, Adams asked that men look behind the façade of constitutions to ascertain the spirit of institutions as a basis of judging those constitutions.   Constitutions were easily made, but an effective constitution must be a response to the ethos of a people.[10] Political difficulties arose not so much from the defects of constitutions as from the state of society.[11]   Adams had little confidence in projects for constitution-making based on the assumption that good constitutions might easily remedy political evil, and for this reason he criticized Bentham's *"mentis gratissimus error"* in his project to circularize the governors in the United States with proposals for codification and public instruction.[12]   Such a view made it possible for him to conclude that, whatever the theory of French constitution-making, it was more remote from democracy than the "practice of the English House of Commons." [13]   Adams was not opposed to change, but change should come gradually more as a response to than as a disturbance of "the harmony of the community." [14]   He condemned the lack of principle of the "political empirics," an epithet he frequently applied to those who, without sufficient regard for principle, were willing to engage in a high degree of social experimentation under popular pressure.   Often change was obstructed by the very attempt to force it; the "situation" and the "course of nature" were more nearly the source of change.[15]   Old constitutions should not be so much destroyed as modified under the impact of a "single luminous principle" concerning the rights of man.[16]   Inexorable political evolution rather than catastrophic revolution was the process of change to which he most thoroughly subscribed.[17]   He

[9] IV "Publicola," *Writings,* I, 81.
[10] To John Adams, The Hague, September 12, 1795, *ibid.,* I, 414.
[11] IV "Publicola," *ibid.,* p. 81.
[12] To James Madison, Washington, December 15, 1817, *ibid.,* VI, 272.
[13] VIII "Publicola," *ibid.,* I, 95.
[14] Adams, *The Social Compact,* p. 5.
[15] To John Adams, December 24, 1804, *Writings,* III, 100–101.
[16] To John Adams, The Hague, April 1, 1795, *ibid.,* I, 312.
[17] To Albert Gallatin and Richard Rush, State Department, Washington, July 28, 1818, *ibid.,* VI, 396: "Every system established upon a condition of things essentially transient and temporary must be accommodated to the changes produced by time."

had great faith in the capacity of time working upon organized society to produce more worthwhile change than could the passions of revolution.

As to revolution, an alternative to evolutionary change, no simple, unqualified generalizations can entirely represent Adams's point of view.   We can observe a marked change in attitude, a transition from the antirevolutionary bias of the young man to the more acute awareness of the transitional nature of his era in the older man.   In the context of the American and European revolutionary era itself he was a champion of order.   As his own participation in political battles became deeper, his rejection of certain institutions and principles became vigorous and general enough to cause him even to entertain the idea of violence as a means of eradicating them.   Even this transition is qualified, however, for at no time was he an extremist, either as a champion of order or as an adversary thereof.

In opposition to an attempt of a majority faction in Boston to prohibit theatrical entertainments Adams, in the minority, held that the prohibition was unconstitutional, that every individual in the community had the same right as the legislature to interpret the constitution, that if the individual's construction was contrary to that of the legislature he could violate the laws based upon their construction. For example, Adams counseled going to the theater in defiance of a law he held unconstitutional.[18]   He took time to observe that the violence of revolution generally derived from the desire for revenge in individuals who had long suffered oppression,[19] and he was aware of the importance of prosperity to the public peace as a means of removing such consciousness of oppression.[20]   The causes of revolution would be found, in other words, in social conditions, not merely in the perverse desire for change of the people and their leaders. Government could not "draw the reins of power [too] tight" and expect to avoid explosions.[21]   He early expressed agreement with the "prophecy of Rousseau" that the ancient institutions of Europe were inevitably to be transformed, even though he might insist that the political ideas seeking to replace them were "wild [and] discord-

[18] "Menander," *Writings,* I, 127–128.
[19] To John Adams, April 1, 1795, *ibid.,* p. 314.
[20] To John Adams, October 19, 1790, *ibid.,* p. 63.
[21] *Memoirs,* October 25, 1794, I, 54.

ant." [22]   Sympathy for and understanding of the common people,
however, were not the dominant features of his early views of revolution or disturbance of the public peace.   The insurrection in western
Pennsylvania worried him because of its effect upon "the credit and
reputation of America, . . . [and because it violated] the perfect
image of united liberty and submission." [23]   The partisans of monarchy took delight in our discomfiture.   The same people who took
pleasure in the revolt delighted in attacks upon President Washington.   A later rebellion reported in Northumberland County, Pennsylvania, elicited from Adams the suggestion that force should be
used to put down the spirit of insurrection in that region, since insurrections injured the reputation of the United States. [24]   Particular
alarm stirred him as he received reports that the French were planning to revolutionize "the whole world," [25] although he said that it
was perhaps best for the loyalty of the people to the American government for it to be brought to the test, in order that its reliability
might be proved. [26]   He rejected Paine's *Rights of Man* as working
for the revolutionizing of all mankind, including the United States. [27]
The revolutionizing of Europe by France was being accompanied
by the plundering of Europe, a result which Adams, as an ardent
champion of the right to property, could not but abhor.   The French
were playing the same game in the United States that Mr. Burke had
foretold they would play in all countries. [28]   To illustrate the fact that
the revolutionary spirit was working its way insidiously into high
places, Adams reported that a highborn Prussian lady had announced

---

[22] To John Adams, The Hague, July 27, 1795, *Writings*, I, 388–389.   Implicit
in his social compact theory was, of course, the right of revolution.   He acknowledged in the people a "dissolving" as well as a "constituent power . . . [to] be
exercised by them only under the tie of conscience, binding them to the retribu-
tive justice of Heaven."   John Quincy Adams, *The Jubilee of the Constitution,
a Discourse Delivered at the Request of The New York Historical Society, in the
City of New York on Tuesday, the 30th of April 1839; being the Fifteenth Anniversary of the Inauguration of George Washington as President of the United
States, on Thursday, the 30th of April, 1789* (New York: Samuel Colman, 1839),
p. 69.   Hereafter cited as Adams, *The Jubilee of the Constitution.*
   [23] To the Secretary of State (Edmund Randolph), No. 5, The Hague, November 7, 1794, *Writings*, I, 223–224.
   [24] To Abigail Adams, May 7, 1799, *ibid.*, II, 417.
   [25] To John Adams, The Hague, August 13, 1796, *ibid.*, p. 25.
   [26] To Joseph Pitcairn, The Hague, March 3, 1797, *ibid.*, p. 133.
   [27] II "Publicola," *ibid.*, I, 72.
   [28] To John Adams, London, September 19, 1797, *ibid.*, II, 209.

that she had come to see the ceremony for the taking of oaths of allegiance to the new Prussian King because it was likely to be one of the last examples of such a ceremony.[29]   He took particular note of the knowing smile that had passed around the circle in response to the lady's remark.   Even in the United States the President (Jefferson) had an itch for popularity, a new component of the revolutionary spirit that Adams noted spreading into Massachusetts.[30]

Looking away from France to Britain, he questioned, with some inconsistency, the right of Englishmen "fundamentally to demolish their present form of government," for their competence so to do could be exercised only if and when their government showed "clearly" its inability to accomplish its fundamental purposes.[31]   He distrusted the "Jacobins" of France and every other country, or the mob that, although it cannot be blamed for its excesses, cannot create but can only destroy.[32]   With great approval he observed that the "sober, cautious, thrifty" Dutch were keeping their "political enthusiasm . . . subordinate to the steady manners and national spirit of good husbandry." [33]   It was wrong that the people should be taught that they can do anything they desire, rather should they be taught that constitutional defects flow generally from the defects of spirit and morality of the people "which a revolution in government could not reform." [34]   He saw an alliance between the anarchy of revolution and despotism,[35] and he professed to see all peaceful and humane forces ranged against revolution.[36]   But even though he found the peaceful and humane ranged against revolution and despotism, he saw nothing incongruous in his accepting Alexander I, the Russian autocrat, as promising in his character "much for the relief of our species . . ." from the threat of future revolution.[37]

A change was worked, however, by age and experience.   As

[29] To William Vans Murray [Berlin], July 7, 1798, *ibid.*, II, 335.
[30] To John Adams, November, 1804, *ibid.*, III, 81.
[31] III "Publicola," *ibid.*, I, 73, 75: This point of view showed his reliance upon Locke who, likewise, after stressing the ultimate right of a people to alter their form of government, held that they should do so only when government had clearly not fulfilled its obligations.
[32] V "Publicola," *ibid.*, p. 82.
[33] To Louisa Catherine Adams, Ghent, June 28, 1814, *ibid.*, V, 53–54.
[34] VIII "Publicola," *ibid.*, I, 95.
[35] To John Adams, The Hague, May 4, 1795, *ibid.*, p. 344.
[36] To John Adams, The Hague, February 3, 1797, *ibid.*, II, 102.
[37] To Abigail Adams, St. Petersburg, April 7, 1813, *ibid.*, IV, 467.

Secretary of State in a letter of instructions to Henry Middleton going
to Russia as American Minister, he expressed doubt that the European powers understood the revolutionary temper of the weapons
with which they were assailed, for, he wrote, the age was characterized by war, not so much among nations, but war between peoples
and their rulers.[38]   The transition in his thinking came slowly and
imperceptibly, for as early as 1814 he asserted that the catastrophe
brought by France upon Europe was a product of the spirit of
the times or the inexorable drift of history, rather than of the
rational wills of men.[39]   Previously he had thought that men guided
by false principles perversely chose the course of revolution; here
we see that he understood that a whole historical trend may sweep
men along.   And when revolution comes to seem unavoidable, it
is, of course, less to be condemned.   Transporting the application
of these views to the Western Hemisphere he described the world
struggle as one between a general American concept of "inalienable
right" and a European concept of "inalienable allegiance." [40]   He,
in fact, came to see the United States in the vanguard of the forces
struggling on behalf of freedom against despotism.

On the basis of the "inalienable right" to the "exercise of his own
reason" man has a responsibility to inspect the foundations of civil
society in search of his rights and, in so doing, he would find
that they did not come as donations from governments and rulers
above.[41]   This idea was the revolutionary principle of the day.
The struggle for its realization had begun with the Reformation,
and Adams came to expect this revolutionary struggle to continue
in his own day.   The republican spirit of the United States, he
wrote, must be in sympathy with peoples in South America struggling in a cause so nearly like our own, and this spirit could only

[38] National Archives, Records of the Department of State, *Diplomatic Instructions,* IX, 19: This is an interesting point in Adams, an essential principle
of Marxism, and shows that he could go beyond nationalist idealism, so fundamental a part of his point of view.   He came to see the revolutionary struggles
as international civil wars.

[39] John Quincy Adams, "Letter to Abigail Adams, Reval, May 12, 1814," *Proceedings of the American Antiquarian Society,* New Series, XXIII (April 9,
1913–October 15, 1913), p. 169.

[40] National Archives, Records of the Department of State, *Diplomatic Instructions,* IX, 283.

[41] Adams, *July 4, 1821 Oration,* pp. 6–7.

oppose the reversion of Europe to the "opposite principle of monkery and despotism." [42] Although "abstract truth" must be modified in the face of surrounding dangers and necessities, there was the highest truth in Lafayette's principle that "Rebellion to tyrants is obedience to God." [43]

Although Adams sought always a compromise between change and stability, and found some safeguard of this compromise in the principle that the "primitive right of insurrection" should be used only sparingly, held very much in reserve,[44] he came more and more, particularly in speculating about the origins of government in the United States, to affirm the right to revolt against tyranny.[45] There was a "moral supremacy of the people." [46] Truths that were self-evident conveyed principles and rights bestowed by God; these rights were inalienable, and no government could ravish men of them.[47]

Following the subsidence of the impact of the French Revolution on our institutions, Adams's fears of revolution diminished, and he himself became in a degree a theorist of revolution. The United States, of course, under the Constitution represented the highest development of political principles. When the French threat to those principles was reduced, he became less fearful of revolution as such, and became an advocate of an American type of revolution, which would serve to spread his country's high principles. We need not investigate here in detail his theory of the American Revolution, but it is important to note that he came to think of

[42] To John Adams, Washington, D. C., December 21, 1817, *Writings,* VI, 276.

[43] Adams, *Eulogy on Lafayette,* p. 26. He noted on another occasion that he had attempted to convince Lafayette that he should have nothing to do with further revolutionary projects in France. *Memoirs,* August 27, 1825, VII, 49.

[44] Letter to Messrs. H. G. Otis, Israil Thorndike, T. H. Perkins, William Prescott, Daniel Sargent, John Lowell, William Sullivan, Charles Jackson, Warren Dutton, Benjamin Peckman, Henry Cabot, C. C. Parsons and Franklin Dexter, Washington, D. C., December 30, 1828, *Correspondence between John Quincy Adams, Esquire, President of the United States, and Several Citizens of Massachusetts concerning the Charge of a Design to Dissolve the Union, alleged to have existed in that State* (Boston: Press of the *Boston Daily Advertiser,* 1829), p. 22.

[45] Adams, *The Social Compact,* p. 24.

[46] Adams, *Newburyport Oration, 1837,* p. 26.

[47] Adams, *Cincinnati Oration,* pp. 12–13. This idea, common for the time, is suggestive of modern sociological views that find in the community an authority superior to any authority that may exist in government. See R. M. MacIver, *The Web of Government* (New York: Macmillan, 1947), *passim.*

the wave of revolution as reversed, reacting again upon Europe. The Spanish-American revolution was after the North American model, which, moreover, continued as a model, and stimulated revolutions in Europe "against all the ancient governments." [48] Adams, therefore, was influenced in his views with regard to revolution by the quality and the conjunction of particular events. As the ideological and economic struggle between the North and the South became more critical, Adams, realizing that the Constitution was being made to protect a dispensation violating his fundamental principles, came to accept the idea of violence as a means of exorcising the evil. But, whatever the influence of the times, it is important to note that he did not grow less amenable to change as he grew older.

It is now possible to turn in more detail to the political doctrines of Adams. Despite a high order of consistency in his system, it is obvious, from the above, that the transitions in his thought must be marked, and we shall proceed with that caution in mind. Part III has dealt generally with his broad social point of view. The chapters following will deal with those doctrines with greater refinement in the political context. In view of the fact that Adams's emphases were usually political in nature, there will be a close relationship with much that has been already discussed.

[48] To Charles Jared Ingersoll, Washington, D. C., June 19, 1823, *Writings*, VII, 488.

PART FOUR

The Political Cosmos

9

Government: An Instrument
of God

*We soon concluded that aristocracy, feudality, nobility, could
not be reconciled with a Government founded upon rights.*
—MEMOIRS, *March 12, 1795*

THE PURPOSE OF GOVERNMENT

The study of John Quincy Adams offers the opportunity to draw
certain interesting parallels between his ideas and relative place in
the American politics of his country and similar factors with respect
to American statesmen of the twentieth century. In a true sense
representing an older, more conservative dispensation than that of
Jackson, who came to power riding the crest of a popular wave,
Adams may more than superficially be compared with Herbert
Hoover as to relative positions in their respective countries, just as
Jackson has been compared with Franklin Roosevelt. The analogies
should not be relied upon too heavily, however, for an inspection of
the substance of the ideas of the men will require the statement of
major contrasts as well as similarities. Adams as a personality, forbidding, austere, even harsh, surely suggests the distant, rather cold
personality of Hoover more than the ebullience of Roosevelt, but in
some respects the political views of Adams were more akin to Roosevelt's ideas than were Jackson's.

Adams was with reason called the champion of "a great, magnificent Government," a fact that he and his political friends recognized
to be a political liability in some parts of the country. No significant
references will be found in his writings or statements to the "state."

139

The reference was uniformly to "government." When he used the term "government," however, it must be assumed that he very often comprehended not merely a complex of governmental organs, but rather the community as politically organized. Government, which he described as "the exercise of power directing or controlling the will of human beings," [1] was not in Adams's opinion an unfriendly, inimical force to be kept at a minimum. There was much that was dramatic and good, and even magnificent, that government should do, in fact must do, if it was to fulfill its purpose. In this emphasis Adams differed from the general spirit of his day, which was manifested either in a conservative desire for a government only strong enough to keep the enemies of the social order in harness, or a more radical opposition to strong government, except in so far as it must be used to keep the economic oligarchy from tyranny, an opposition to strong government that was the essence of Jacksonianism. In Adams's theory, on the other hand, the Creator had made man a "sociable being," had blended his happiness with that of his fellow man, and government was a necessary instrumentality for the effectuating of this liaison. [2] In the main, this chapter will demonstrate that Adams held a theory that government should combine strength with limitation, effectiveness with respect for the individual personality, capacity to realize principle with concern for God-given rights.

According to Adams, civil government emerged early in the evolution of man's civil society for the purpose of placing a reliable confirmation upon the standards of weights and measures that society required as a basis of order and symmetry. [3] Moreover, not only was all properly organized government founded upon basic principles, such as those stated in the Declaration of Independence, but government was the means of realizing those principles and effecting national cohesion based upon respect for them. [4] Government must exist as the means of expressing the "unalienable sovereignty of the people," [5] and just as the will of the people, expressed in an Adamsian sense, was the source of all just government, so must the happiness

---

[1] Adams, *The Social Compact*, p. 11.
[2] Adams, *The Lives of James Madison and James Monroe*, p. 35.
[3] Adams, *Report on Weights and Measures*, p. 10.
[4] Adams, *July 4th, 1821, Address*, pp. 22, 23.
[5] To John Adams, London, September 19, 1797, *Writings*, II, 208.

of the people be the end of all government.[6] At the very least, it was necessary for governments to learn "that the exercise of power among men can be justified only by the blessings it confers. . . ." [7]

But Adams was suspicious of any government that brought benefits and order to society at the expense of numerous imposed burdens. Although he was the protagonist of strong government, it must at the same time be benevolent and benign government.[8] Only in this way might men achieve the relative happiness and comfort that was the most they could hope for. Thus in this respect Adams was a relativist. Although he justified the American Revolution on the basis of principle, he was, particularly in calmer moments, willing in some circumstances to compromise principles. He wrote: "Had the Sovereigns of England pursued the policy prescribed by their interest, had they not provoked the hostilities of their Colonists against the feeble fortress of their authority they might perhaps have retained to this day an Empire which would have been but the more durable, for resting only upon the foundation of immemorial custom, and national affection." [9]

Generally Adams would have left moral standards free of governmental restriction.[10] As much as he might admire Plato, he found the philosopher's projects pregnant with proposals and laws to regulate too much in the community, particularly the trivial.[11]

In achieving the happiness of its people, in conferring blessings upon them, in seeking popular allegiance, a government or a sovereign must, by the terms of the social compact, offer protection to all

[6] Adams, "Inaugural Address," *in* Richardson, ed., *A Compilation of the Messages and Papers of the Presidents, 1789–1897,* II, 296.

[7] Adams, "First Annual Message," *ibid.,* p. 300.

[8] To the President [Monroe], Washington, D. C., August 23, 1818, *Writings,* VI, 439. He supported the opinion that the practice of having all warrants of execution signed by the President should be adhered to and that executions should not be held immediately following a verdict, for in the interest of humanity "the last and most precious right [should be] reserved to the culprit. . . ."; on one occasion, however, he defended Jackson and his vigorous actions in Florida as supporting "with an excess of energy the cause of justice and humanity." *Memoirs,* December 3, 1821, V, 441.

[9] Adams, *July 4th Oration, 1793,* pp. 7–8: This is an interesting forecast of the spirit of the later British Commonwealth.

[10] *Memoirs,* June 27, 1839, X, 126: "This license law [15 gallon license law] is an ill-advised measure, intended to promote the virtue of temperance, but infringing the personal freedom and habits of the people."

[11] *Ibid.,* November 10, 1811, II, 323–324.

its citizens. This purpose, in Adams's view, amounted to more than protection against external danger or domestic violence. Government must be more than a simple policeman. A free government, which had not usurped its authority, must preserve by positive and forthright action "popular representation and periodical election, [effectuate] the subordination of the military to the civil authority, the suppression of ecclesiastical supremacy, the freedom of the press, and the security of personal liberty." [12] A government that usurped its authority in violation of popular rights and basic principle would not provide these safeguards. A free government must do so, for only by so doing could it demonstrate that it was not a usurpation. The accomplishment of these ends constituted a necessary protection of the people. By the preservation of such conditions, the government was, in effect, preserving in the people's possession the means of preventing the abuse of power in the community. With these means, the people could forever prevent the permanent and unqualified delegation of the "whole power" of the community to their rulers.[13] More specifically, only by preserving such means could government achieve the purposes stated in the Preamble of the Constitution, "the great and transcendental objects of all legitimate governments." [14]

Not only must government preserve the people in the equal enjoyment of the conditions of freedom, it must preserve the various interests in the community in their right to a fair participation.[15]

[12] To Caesar Augustus Rodney, State Department, Washington, D. C., May 17, 1823, *Writings,* VII, 432–433. National Archives, Records of the Department of State, *Diplomatic Instructions,* All Countries, IX, 258: Further discussion will more thoroughly accent this point.

[13] VII "Publicola," *Writings,* I, 90–91: One of his fundamental criticisms of the French following the Revolution was based upon the contention that they had placed the whole power of the nation in the hands of the government. To John Adams, London, October 23, 1794, *ibid.,* pp. 208–209. Government must rather protect the people in their use of the means to resist government. Similar reasoning prevented his supporting the imposition of American rule on the people of the Louisiana territory acquired from France. Since those people had been given no opportunity to render their consent to the bargain or its results, they had been denied their basic soverign right to establish the terms under which they would be ruled and to see to it that the means of preserving their sovereignty would be maintained. See "Notes on Speech on Motion," *ibid.,* III, 28, and to John Adams, St. Petersburg, August 31, 1811, *ibid.,* X, 204–205.

[14] Adams, *The Jubilee of the Constitution,* p. 48. *Cincinnati Oration,* p. 13.

[15] *Memoirs,* August 6, 1827, VII, 318: He wrote in high praise of Burke.

For example, he contended to Bentham that the latter should seek only to restore the democratic forces, which might be expressed through a reformed parliament, to an "equal share of power" in the British community, not seek to raise them to a position of ascendancy over aristocracy and executive.[16]   Moreover, democracy, which will be discussed more at length elsewhere, was not to Adams merely the rule of numbers of individuals, for democratic government was based likewise upon family or group interest.[17] No doubt a free government should "render real service to the public," but that should not consist of "flattering their prejudices, . . . ministering to their passions, . . . [or] humoring their transient and changeable opinions."[18]   The interests of all groups, from minor ones to the broad group, that must be represented if democracy was to be realized, must be reflected in the policy of government, but it was essential to prevent government from becoming the mere creature of "popular societies," which are efficacious in destroying a system of interests but incapable of creating.[19] Therefore, although Adams stated in so many words that government must be based upon the "unalienable sovereignty of the people," that sovereignty was not unlimited and should not be exercised, even though it might have the power, to extinguish inalienable rights.[20]   The Constitution was established to achieve the realization of justice, a purpose comprehending all the other subordinate purposes and defined as a "constant and perpetual will of securing to every one his right. . . ."[21]

Government, the vehicle of popular sovereignty, must do only what is in keeping with principle.   Although government, of right, must restrain and regulate human action, there were limits upon its legitimate power to restrain.   For example, Adams held that the government had no right to issue paper money, on the ground that

[16] *Ibid.,* May 22, 1817, III, 538–539.
[17] Adams, *The Social Compact,* p. 19.
[18] V "Publius Valerius," *Writings,* III, 69.
[19] To Abigail Adams, The Hague, April 25, 1795, *Writings,* I, 331–333.   For this reason he feared the impact of democracy upon the "securities of property. . . ."   *Memoirs,* January 10, 1831, VIII, 269–270.
[20] II "Publicola," *Writings,* I, 70–71.   See Vernon Louis Parrington, *Main Currents in American Thought* (New York: Harcourt, Brace, 1930), I, 325–326.
[21] Adams, *The Jubilee of the Constitution,* p. 70.

"governments have no right to take anything without giving [the people] a *quid pro quo*. . . ." [22] A free government in a republic, an association of wealth, should not identify itself with any partial association reflecting only partial interests.[23] Among the reasons that he gave for opposing any American interference in Europe's convulsions, which he conceived as mainly struggles between "*Power* and *Right*," was his fear that our involvement would transform our system from one of "liberty" into one of unrestrained "power." [24]

Despite the circumscriptions that Adams placed around government in defense of principles or interests to which he was loyal, he remained a protagonist of strong, effective government. As a nationalist, proud of the heritage and potential of the American continent, he looked upon government as a weapon in the struggle for great national goals. Partially on these grounds, he opposed the Southern "nullifiers." [25] He did not hesitate to support "a systematic combination of measures" as the real substance of government.[26] He was opposed to extravagant government, but he opposed retrenchment where important tasks had to be accomplished. He opposed the "inexorable economy" of government that would not permit maintaining its dignity in the eyes of the world. Niggardly government could not earn his respect.[27]

One great responsibility that he thought should be undertaken by government was the subsidization of education. Only if government assumed such a responsibility would the people come to understand the basic principles in conformity with which they might achieve legitimate goals. For the most part filled with religious conviction, although experiencing moments of grave doubt, he believed religious culture and understandings were the products of education rather than revelation. Education, therefore, was the vehicle that would bring to the people a sound religious belief.

[22] To Peter Paul Francis De Grand, Washington, D. C., November 16, 1818, *Writings*, VI, 473.

[23] Adams, "Letter to the Citizens of the United States, whose Petitions, Memorials, and Remonstrances, have been entrusted to me, to be presented to the House of Representatives of the United States, at the third session of the 25th Congress," Letter II.

[24] To Edward Everett, Washington, January 31, 1822, *Writings*, VII, 201.

[25] *Memoirs*, December 5, 1832, VIII, 503. *Ibid.*, June 20, 1840, X, 315–316.

[26] To William Plumer, St. Petersburg, October 6, 1810, *Writings*, III, 511.

[27] To Richard Rush, Washington, D. C., May 28, 1818, *ibid.*, VI, 339.

And he referred approvingly to the partnership of religion and education in New England.[28]

In addition, Adams believed that to "diffuse political knowledge through the mass of society . . . [was] among the greatest services that can be rendered to a Republican People." [29] Thus the educational process was fused with the political and governmental. He observed with considerable displeasure that Congress would subsidize a school such as West Point, for the making of soldiers, but would not support other, nonmilitary schools.[30] As a young man he had been impressed by the lack of Russian educational facilities, which added to the vast cleavage between the Princes and the "slaves" in that country.[31] Education was, therefore, a means of bringing to a people an understanding of a common cultural heritage that would reduce social cleavages. A republican government was charged with reducing these cleavages through support for the educational process. Even the military monarchy of Frederick the Great had established a glorious record in the field of education.[32] In a lecture on the Smithsonian fund he called upon the government to exercise judicious care in using the bequest and asserted that "To furnish the means of acquiring knowledge is, therefore, the greatest benefit that can be conferred upon mankind." [33] His charge was that the American people did not sufficiently realize the importance of patronizing and promoting "the progress of the mind." [34] One of the considerable debts he owed to the example and inspiration of George Washington was this belief in government support of education, for Washington, likewise, advocated a national university to produce a collective national mind. In such a fashion a government, using its power to diffuse knowledge, would be taking

[28] Adams, *Discourse on Education,* p. 9.

[29] Letter to Richard Rush, Washington, D. C., February 9, 1821, Tatum, ed., "Ten Unpublished Letters of John Quincy Adams, 1769–1837," pp. 379–381.

[30] *Memoirs,* August 26, 1826, VII, 146.

[31] To John Adams, St. Petersburg, October 12/23, 1781, *Writings,* I, 6 n.

[32] Adams, *Letters on Silesia,* p. 372. Quincy, *Memoirs of the Life of John Quincy Adams,* pp. 21–22.

[33] John Quincy Adams, *Two Lectures on the Bequest of James Smithson to the United States of America, for the Increase and Diffusion of Knowledge among Men,* Lecture I delivered at the Masonic Temple, Boston, before the Mechanic Apprentices Library Association, November 14, 1839 (Boston, 1839), newspaper cutting located in Harvard University Library.

[34] *Memoirs,* November 24, 1843, XI, 559.

a sure way to the goal of general social improvement, which it was the duty of every government to pursue.

Adams's doctrine of internal improvement also had a central relationship to his conception of the role and purpose of government. The doctrine anticipated the views of future generations on the function of government; in developing it Adams was at variance with the general attitude of his generation toward the purpose of government. He asserted that it was man's duty to act through government for the improvement of his condition. Only thus might the rights of all be realized through the efforts of all. All citizens must devote their energies to the improvement of their country and mankind.[35] "The first duty of a nation . . . [is] that of bettering its own condition by internal improvement." [36] "By the law of nature, independent of all revelation, and by the concurrent testimony of holy writ in the narrative of creation, the earth was given by the Creator to the family of man, for the purpose of improving the condition of its possessor. . . ." [37] In keeping with this conception he introduced a resolution into the Senate on February 23, 1807, embodying the doctrine and asserting the power of the general government to engage in such activities of internal improvement.[38] Of course Adams was many years ahead of his time in this respect. He supported vigorously the conventional projects of internal improvement, such as roads and canals in the service of commerce, but a reading of his writings shows that he would have gone far beyond such projects to include government planning of city construction and of measures to improve and aid business by a wide variety of means, or to include taking any measures that would make proper use of the bounties of providence.

[35] Adams, *Cincinnati Oration*, pp. 14–16: "It is God, the grants of whose favor, are instruments of beneficent power, and who in imparting them to his rational offspring, exacts the twofold return of thanks, and use."

[36] To James Lloyd, Washington, D. C., October 1, 1822, *Writings*, VII, 313.

[37] Adams, *The New England Confederacy of MDCXLIII*, p. 12.

[38] Henry Adams, *The Degradation of the Democratic Dogma*, p. 21: "Resolved, That the Secretary of the Treasury be directed to prepare and report to the Senate, at their next session, a plan for the application of such means as are constitutionally within the power of Congress, to the purposes of opening roads, for removing obstructions in rivers, and making canals; together with a statement of the undertakings of that nature now existing within the United States which, as objects of public improvement, may require and deserve the aid of government."

Many of the political antipathies that he felt in his career had their origin in this question. He opposed the Jeffersonian and Madisonian doctrine that the Congress had no power to do what was not "expressly delegated" and pointed out the incongruity between their scolding about "implied powers" and their assertions of power with respect to Louisiana and the United States Bank.[39] He took issue with General Scott who held that Congress might appropriate money for purposes of internal improvement but not actually engage in such activities on the ground that he "was saying that they [Congress] had the right to use the means, but not to enjoy the end." [40] His own conception, which he attempted to realize in the policy of his Administration, called for the use of the "national domain [as the] inexhaustible fund for progressive and unceasing internal improvement. . . ." [41] Any governmental system that deprived "itself of the faculty of multiplying its own blessings, would be as wise as a Creator who should undertake to constitute a human being without a heart." [42] The Constitution of the United States did contain such a power, and he deemed it a fundamental error to give it up through nonuse. Not only had he occasion to disagree with the earlier Presidents of the Virginia dynasty, he noted with disfavor that Monroe, in whose Administration he served, was willing to contend before Congress that there was no constitutional power to make internal improvements.[43]

The doctrine had its aesthetic component: "The transitions of an extensive region of the globe, from a land of hunters to a land of planters, is the metamorphosis of a wilderness into a garden." [44] There was a high degree of optimism in the very assertion of the point of view and a full-bodied respect for the capacities of man that belied the dour front with which he faced the world. It was a venturing spirit that called for the devotion of the "national energies" to

[39] *Memoirs,* October 20, 1821, V, 365.

[40] *Ibid.,* June 16, 1822, VI, 22.

[41] *Ibid.,* July 30, 1834, IX, 162.

[42] Quincy, *Memoir of the Life of John Quincy Adams,* p. 137, quoting from a letter in *Niles' Register,* XXVI, 251–328.

[43] *Memoirs,* May 4, 1822, V, 281. Monroe did not, of course, oppose internal improvements as such but held that the power did not exist. He considered recommending an amendment to Congress that would grant the power. *Ibid.,* December 4, 1819, IV, 462–463.

[44] Adams, *The New England Confederacy of MDCXLIII,* p. 15.

the end of releasing "the bounties of Providence." Adams recognized the great potential of America's "material heritage and saw in it boundless resources for the promotion of the general interest. . . ." [45] Disdainful of the sectarian clannishness that he thought would reduce the influence of New England in the councils of the nation, he rejoiced in "the excellent race of people" who were moving westward from that area to open up and improve the vast areas of the continent, unaffected by such a "narrow and contracted" spirit. [46] A similar sectarian spirit among the Jeffersonian anti-Federalists, he wrote, "in [a state of] ghastly horror at the phantom of consolidation," rejected or impeded the progress of internal improvements. [47]

From the time of the Monroe Administration onward Adams fought a battle on behalf of internal improvements, this issue becoming unfortunately entangled with others. Even though some of his colleagues in the Monroe cabinet, including Calhoun, seemed to agree with him that the policy of internal improvements constituted "the only path to increasing comforts and well-being, to honor, to glory, and finally to the general improvement of the condition of mankind," many of them, including the South Carolina statesman, subsequently turned their backs upon it. And, although Jackson in the scramble for Western votes had at first favored the policy, he too came into opposition, for the reason, Adams caustically concluded, that success would have added to his (Adams's) reputation. [48] From the very time that he supported action by Congress to permit the President "to obtain and cause to be remitted to the United States the funds bequeathed to them by James Smithson for the establishment at Washington of an institution for the increase and diffusion of knowledge among men," [49] he ascribed the opposition to the acceptance or the proper use of the fund to the same limited spirit that opposed internal improvements. [50] He struggled with equal energy on behalf of proj-

[45] George S. Counts, *Prospects of American Democracy* (New York: John Day, 1938), p. 68.
[46] To Benjamin Waterhouse, St. Petersburg, October 24, 1813, *Writings*, IV, 526–527.
[47] Adams, *Parties in the United States*, p. 105.
[48] *Memoirs*, June 25, 1830, VIII, 233.
[49] *Ibid.*, January 12, 1836, IX, 270.
[50] *Ibid.*, March 25, 1839, X, 109: He noted that Cambreling had "swindled" into a bill a provision to take $10,000.00 from the fund to pay for "expenses and charges of procuring the [Smithson] money." He was "deeply mortified not to have detected this dirty trick."

ects to aid the progress of the mind and to improve the land internally. In connection with his rather ostentatious journey to Cincinnati, designed to dramatize these values and goals so important in his life, he emphasized the point again that those who opposed the spread of human knowledge likewise opposed internal improvements.

Adams made his two most emphatic statements of the doctrine of internal improvements during his Presidential term. He held that it was from the policy of internal improvement that "the unborn millions of our posterity who are in future ages to people this continent will derive their most fervent gratitude to the founders of the Union; that in which the beneficent action of its Government will be most deeply felt and acknowledged." The public works of Rome were her most glorious achievement. It was true that honest doubt might exist concerning the powers of Congress, but Adams was sure that patient deliberation would remove the last remaining constitutional doubts from "enlightened minds." [51] He charged the lawmakers in no event to transcend the powers granted by the Constitution: [52]

But [he went on] if the power to exercise exclusive legislation in all cases whatsoever over the District of Columbia; if the power to lay and collect taxes, duties, imposts, and excises, to pay the debts and provide for the common defense and general welfare of the United States; if the power to regulate commerce with foreign nations and among the several States and with the Indian tribes, to fix the standard of weights and measures, to establish post-offices and post-roads, to declare war, to raise and support armies, to provide and maintain a navy, to dispose of and make all needful rules and regulations respecting the territory or other property belonging to the United States, and to make all laws which shall be necessary and proper for carrying these powers into execution—if these powers and others enumerated in the Constitution may be effectually brought into action by laws promoting the improvement of agriculture, commerce, and manufactures, the cultivation and encouragement of the mechanic and of the elegant arts, the advancement of literature, and the progress of the sciences, ornamental and profound, to refrain from exercising them for the benefit of the people themselves would be to hide in the earth the talent committed to our charge—would be treachery to the most sacred of trusts. [53]

[51] Adams, "Inaugural Address," *in* Richardson, *op. cit.*, II, 298–299.
[52] Adams, "First Annual Message," *ibid.*, pp. 315–316.
[53] *Ibid.*, pp. 315–316. In 1824 he rejected Governor Eustis's contention that Congress did not have power to make internal improvements and that such

Here is contained a broad view of constitutional power, but it is also a grand view of the duty of government to act vigorously in seeking social improvement.   John Quincy Adams, understood as devoted to this kind of doctrine, no longer is merely the leader of a displaced oligarchy routed by the democrat, Jackson; for in this regard he anticipated the experimenting twentieth century much more than did Jackson.

The times and the political climate were not favorable to this view. He early noted that members of his Administration were unfavorably disposed to internal improvements.   Secretary of the Navy Barbour was opposed to all internal improvement, he recorded, and Clay to some, including a national university.[54]   Following his Administration he experienced one of the major disappointments of his life in the coming to power of Jackson, who was by then totally out of sympathy with his doctrine.   He continued, however, to promote conceptions of governmental power that he said must be used to lift man above the "brute creation" and, in particular, fulfill the purposes of the Constitution.[55]   He asked Webster whether or not the National Republicans would support the "reservation of five millions a year for the purposes of internal improvement." [56]   But, for the most part, he looked upon his retirement from the Presidency as the defeat of a lifetime's goal of "the improvement, physical, moral, and intellectual, of . . . [his] country." [57]   Jackson's policy, he feared, would cause both internal improvements and domestic industry to lag.   The national Administration was becoming "vitiated"; he was apprehensive that the Union itself could not last.

I fear I have done and can do little good in the world—and my life will end in disappointment of the good which I would have done had I been

---

a program would endanger the Union.   His advice to the lawmakers to inspect well constitutional powers before acting was a purely tactical admonition, since his own mind was fully convinced that the constitutional power existed.   *Memoirs,* October 22, 1824, VI, 418.

[54] *Memoirs,* November 25, 1825, and November 26, 1825, VII, 61–62.

[55] *Register of Debates,* 22nd Cong., 1st sess., III, appendix, "Report on Manufactures," May 23, 1832, pp. 85–86: The report, of course, had generally to do with the tariff question, but it contained the same arguments concerning governmental power that he used to support internal improvements.

[56] *Memoirs,* December 18, 1831, VIII, 438–439; two days later he notified the Treasury that he would propose the reservation of $5,000,000 for internal improvement and asked that it be urged upon the President as a means of strengthening the country's defenses.   *Ibid.,* December 20, 1831, p. 439.

[57] *Ibid.,* February 28, 1829, p. 100.

permitted. The great effort of my administration was to mature into a permanent and regular system the application of all the superfluous revenue of the Union to internal improvements.[58]

There even was a danger that the Jacksonian project for extinguishing the national debt would be a signal for the complete abandonment of all plans for national internal improvement. In connection with proposals that the general government assume the debts of the states, Adams pointed out that the debts of the states had become so great because they had been called upon to assume the burden of internal improvements refused by the general government.[59] Although he at first opposed the assumption of the states' debts, he later maintained that the project was a call upon the general government to aid the states for "laudable purposes, and for objects of general utility," and he could not understand the Whigs for opposing it.[60]

He found it impossible to avoid the conclusion that his plans for internal improvements would be ruined. Tyler, an acting President cast up by chance, was "a political sectarian of the slave-driving, Virginian, Jeffersonian school; principled against all improvement. . . ."[61] The main political force that Adams saw following his Administration, working against the manufacturing interests as well as general internal improvements, was a combination between the "slaveholders of the South" and the West bribed by the offer of the Western public lands.[62] Long before the end of his Administration he had seen a threat coming from Senator T. H. Benton who was stirring up the people to "madness for the public lands," the great national fund which Adams thought should support general improvement.[63] Later these forces were joined by the Governor of Illinois, Ninion Edwards.[64] Adams wrote that the "thirst of a tiger for blood is the fittest emblem of the rapacity with which the members of all the new States fly at the public lands."[65] At the same time he rejected the thesis that the right of the community in the public lands could be purchased at

[58] Letter to Charles W. Upham, Washington, D. C., February 2, 1837, Tatum, "Ten Unpublished Letters of John Quincy Adams, 1796–1837," pp. 382–383.

[59] *Congressional Globe,* 26th Cong., 2nd sess., appendix, p. 324.

[60] *Ibid.,* 27th Cong., 3rd sess., February 10, 1843, p. 269.

[61] Quincy, *op. cit.,* p. 329. Tyler was against "improvement in the condition of man." *Memoirs,* April 6, 1841, X, 459.

[62] *Memoirs,* August 6, 1835, IX, 247–248.

[63] *Ibid.,* December 1, 1826, VII, 194.

[64] *Ibid.,* December 31, 1828, VIII, 88.

[65] *Ibid.,* June 14, 1838, X, 19.

the lowest price merely upon the basis of "occupancy and labor" and denied the argument that the squatter's right was the same as that of the fisherman upon the water.[66]

Adams believed that his doctrine of internal improvement had more than an American application. It was more than a political, administrative, or engineering program. It was basic to his whole political philosophy. He was filled with admiration for Peter the Great as the genius who had built St. Petersburg according to a magnificent plan. Peter applied his magnificent energies through government to build a new city, a capital suited to the genius that was reorienting Russia in a new direction. The Secretary of State admonished the Columbians to think little of Columbia as a center of empire but to give due regard to the bounties of nature. "God to thee has done his part—do thine." [67] No negative suspicion of government limited his conception of what men could accomplish through its agency. It was the collective means through which God's gifts could and should be exploited and developed. He enjoined all men of all lands to apply their skills through government to the task of internal improvement. His vision was prophetic and in the grand style as he assured a Colonel Beneski that he would use all his patronage and constitutional powers in support of a canal from the sea of the Antilles to the Pacific Ocean by way of the lake of Nicaragua, a project that he said was of interest to the whole Union.[68] The vision was of an inevitable unfolding of a divine plan for the improvement of the lot of man with government as the agency. The disappointments that he suffered in this regard in his old age were a threat both to his confidence in America's future and to his religious beliefs.

Adams's concept of government's duty to seek internal improvement was more than a concept of government building roads and canals. Government had an important function in the "promotion of domestic industry. . . ." [69] Government should engage in extensive projects to increase wages, maintain constant employment, and supplement the "limping gait of State legislation and private adventure. . . ." [70]

[66] *Memoirs,* June 12, 1838, p. 16.

[67] National Archives, Records of the Department of State, *Diplomatic Instructions,* All Countries, IX, 297–298.

[68] *Memoirs,* August 17, 1826, VII, 145.

[69] *Ibid.,* January 13, 1831, VIII, 273.

[70] Letter to Charles W. Upham, Washington, D. C., February 2, 1837, Tatum, "Ten Unpublished Letters of John Quincy Adams, 1796–1837," pp. 382–383.

Although he might assert on occasion that government should never be countenanced in a needless interference with "commercial transactions," [71] he was a strong supporter of Jefferson's Embargo, a tremendous intereference with commerce, which he later held had greatly stimulated manufacturing. [72] Commerce was an important object to government, and effective governmental action, including the building and use of a strong navy as a part of a program of improvement, should be undertaken to protect it. [73] His support of the Embargo was based in great measure upon political considerations. His later defense of it as an aid to manufacturing was a rationalization and, no doubt, also a reflection of his nationalism. Adams's support of the Embargo cannot be interpreted as an evidence of his opposition to commercial interests.

The very substance of a republic to Adams was "associated wealth." [74] The achieving of internal improvements would add to such wealth. The government of a republic might well be expected, in this view, to safeguard its very foundation. The United States Bank was a constitutional and intelligent instrument of general improvement and increasing the "associated wealth" of the Republic, and he objected, in defense of the Bank—shades of a more recent time—to inquisitorial legislative committee investigations into the operations of the institution. [75]

[71] *Annals of Congress*, 9th Cong., 1st sess., December 20, 1805, pp. 29–30.

[72] *Register of Debates*, 22nd Cong., 1st sess., appendix, p. 83. He also supported the Nonimportation Act, even after he thought the need of it had passed, out of deference to the judgment of the Executive. To Joseph Hall, Washington, D. C., December 11, 1807, *Writings*, III, 165.

[73] Adams, *Parties in the United States*, p. 47. Of course, not only his advocacy of a strong navy, but also his support of a liberal policy of commercial intercourse, should be mentioned here, even though the latter was a less positive aspect of the doctrine of governmental action to assist commerce. *Memoirs*, November 28, 1821, V, 427. This policy involved abstention from prohibitions upon commerce with particular countries, export taxes, etc. Adams, "First Annual Message," in Richardson, *op. cit.*, II, 300. Of course, it is a mistake to generalize too strongly on Adams's support of government assistance to commerce. He expressed doubt on at least one occasion concerning the wisdom of building a strong navy that might embroil the United States with Britain. To John Adams, St. Petersburg, October 14, 1811, *Writings*, IV, 240–241; he wondered if commerce was worth the cost of a large navy. *Ibid.*, pp. 242–243. Yet this train of thought was unusual.

[74] Adams, "Letter to the Citizens of the United States, whose Petition, Memorials and Remonstrances, have been entrusted to me, to be presented to the House of Representatives of the United States, at the third session of the 25th Congress," Quincy, May 21, 1839, Letter II.

[75] *Register of Debates*, 22nd Cong., 1st sess., appendix, pp. 54–55.

Nor was the problem of internal improvement merely one of aiding industry and commerce and building roads and canals. In the ultimate sense, government was obliged to improve the moral condition of man, to root out evil where it could be found. The moral problem of "the extinction of Slavery" was also a political problem that, in Adams's day, rocked the foundations of "human society." The government of the United States in particular, because of its origin in the American Revolution, was not a government that could pretend to require unlimited obedience, but must rather assist every human being within its power to realize social equality expressive of the equality of their immortal souls.[76] In the expression of such an obligation, the government of the United States had assisted in the suppression of the slave trade. For similar reasons, while not at this point actually asserting the power of Congress to interfere with slavery, Adams opposed the Atherton resolution, which declared that Congress had no such power.[77] Increasing democracy was inevitably shaking slavery, and government expressing the "theory of the rights of man" would inevitably move against it.[78] Government must strive to do justice to all, to bring to every man his due.

THE POWER OF GOVERNMENT

The foregoing section has dealt primarily with Adams's view of the areas with which government ought to be concerned. The following section will treat of his concept of the power and vigor that rightfully should be at the disposal of government in the areas wherein it is called upon to act. A succeeding section will deal in turn with the principles that should be applied as corrective restraints upon government. No hard and fast line separates one discussion from the others, but there are important distinctions in emphasis that can only be made by so ordering and systematizing Adams's thought upon these matters. The discussion which follows will be in large measure a continuation of the introductory portions of this chapter wherein his general conceptions concerning the role of government are indicated.

[76] Adams, *Letter Read at the Recent Celebration of West India Emancipation in Bangor* (Me.), p. 2.
[77] *Congressional Globe*, 25th Cong., 3rd sess., December 11, 1838, pp. 21–22.
[78] *Memoirs*, August 11, 1835, IX, 251.

At this point it is proposed to analyze in greater detail the legitimate power of government as Adams saw it.

In this theory, government was never absolute if it reflected true principle. Government could be absolute only where it had degraded "the natural dignity of mankind." [79] Its real function, on the basis of which it earned popular allegiance, was to afford protection. Upon the failure of governments to afford protection, as we have seen, Adams believed that the people have the right to "provide new guards for their future security." [80] And no government based upon the voluntary agreement of the people, which is the only source of legitimate authority, could be absolute.[81]

Yet, although Adams based a theory of limited government upon the foundation of popular sovereignty, he did not believe that the nation or the community, representing the whole body of the people, possessed unlimited authority: "This principle, that a whole nation has a right to do whatever it pleases, cannot in any sense whatever be admitted as true." [82] Both the community and government were restricted by the "eternal and immutable laws of justice and morality. . . ." [83] Although it was certainly within the *power* of government to violate these laws, it could never be within the *right* of government to do so.[84] "The perpetual, unalienable sovereignty of the *people*" might exist as a principle, but that principle could not imply that the people, or any majority speaking for them, could do anything guided "only by their pleasure." [85] Were this implication true, all the rights of man would fall before arbitrary power.[86] Sovereignty, even that of the whole people, could only do what was right.[87] The sovereign people could not escape the moral obligations imposed by the laws of nature. There were gradations of sovereignty, to be sure, beginning with the supreme sovereignty of God. Although governments were "subordinate to the *moral* supremacy of the Peo-

---

[79] Adams, *July 4th, Oration, 1793,* p. 5.
[80] Adams, *Newburyport Oration, 1837,* p. 19.
[81] National Archives, Records of the Department of State, *Diplomatic Instructions,* All Countries, IX, 275.
[82] II "Publicola," *Writings,* I, 70–71.
[83] *Loc. cit.*
[84] *Loc. cit.*
[85] To John Adams, London, September 19, 1797, *Writings,* II, 208.
[86] V "Publicola," *ibid.,* I, 83.
[87] Adams, *Newburyport Oration, 1837,* p. 31.

ple," the People were in turn subordinate to a moral law.[88]   In short, Adams rejected Blackstone's contention that there is "in all forms of government, however they began, or by what right soever they subsist, a supreme, irresistible, absolute, uncontrolled authority, in which the *jura summi imperii* or the rights of sovereignty, reside." [89]   Sovereignty did not partake of such infinite qualities, for "unlimited power belongs not to the nature of man" and is "incompatible with the first principle of natural right." [90]   Governments exercising such unlimited power exercised physical power given to man but not power of right inhering in him.   It was on such a basis, in deference to his own republican principles, that he had denied the right of the government of the United States to impose itself on Louisiana, unless an amendment to the Constitution and affirmative action on the part of the people of Louisiana rendered consent on the part of the two peoples to such an exercise of power.[91]   The action taken in acquiring Louisiana was an attempt by the government of the United States to exercise absolute and unlimited powers.

In his younger days Adams, influenced by his fears of the French Revolution and by Federalist ideas, came dangerously close to subscribing to unlimited government.   As a more extended subsequent discussion will indicate, however, this was a temporary or passing conception qualified by subsequent changes in this thinking.   During the Revolutionary Era he was interested in discovering a power in the community capable of restraining the revolutionary temper of the people.   In the "Letters of Publicola," in contest with Paine, he asserted that "whenever a number of individuals associate together, and form themselves into a body politic called a nation, the possession and the use of the whole power [at this point not meaning arbitrary or complete power] is the very object of their association." [92]   The whole power must reside somewhere and must be exercised for the benefit of the people.   The power of altering the constitution, there-

---

[88] Adams, *Newburyport Oration, 1837*, p. 26.

[89] Adams, *Quincy Oration, 1831*, pp. 12–14.

[90] Adams, *Newburyport Oration, 1837*, p. 9: It was against such governments based upon force and conquest that people had a right to revolt.   Adams, *The Social Compact*, p. 23.

[91] To John Adams, St. Petersburg, August 31, 1811, *Writings*, IV, 204–205: It is true that in this same letter he indicated that the consent of people can be "subsequent by their acquiescence as well as antecedent by express grant."

[92] VIII "Publicola," *ibid.*, I, 90–91.

fore, should be granted to the "common legislative authority, for, should this not be done, the nation would in effect abdicate its powers, since only government may be the nation's agent, or make them useless out of fear that they might be abused.[93]   There was a definite danger that such power might be abused; melancholy experience has always shown, that when the whole power has been thus delegated to one man, or to one body of men, it has invariably been grossly abused, and the sword of the people has been turned into a dagger against them." In consequence, the people have often severely limited their governments "without considering that the impotence of their supreme authority would certainly be very prejudicial to them, and perhaps as fatal as the abuse of power."   Experience would show the unwisdom of thus "annihilating the power of the nation. . . ."[94]   Adams, at this point, found a "whole power" in the community, which was the total power that could be rightly exercised in keeping with moral law. This "whole power" was the power to make or alter constitutions as well as to legislate in a subordinate fashion.   It was "sovereign" power in the limited sense in which Adams used the term "sovereign," and it should rightly be exercised by government without limitation from the people unless the government proved incompetent to act or abused its power.   Its limitation should come from the moral law and not from the people below.   He, therefore, located a supreme constituent power in government, and not more than a concurrent power in the people, yet he attempted to avoid tyranny by counseling "the distribution of those [supreme] powers in such a manner as shall, in its own operation, guard against the abuses which alone are dangerous to the people."[95]   Constituent power must be delegated, for the

[93] VIII "Publicola," *ibid.*, I, 90–91: "It is as if a man should bind himself never to wear a sword, lest he should turn it against his own breast."

[94] *Ibid.*, pp. 90–91.   "We know that bad laws exist in every country under Heaven, but it is strange reasoning, to infer from thence, that there ought not to exist in the nation a power to make good ones."   IX "Publicola," *ibid.*, p. 99. Adams, moreover, could justify much in the way of the exercise of power on the basis of "the great law of self-preservation."   X "Publicola," *ibid.*, pp. 105–106.

[95] VII "Publicola," *ibid.*, I, 90–91.   "Distribute the whole of your power in such a manner, as will necessarily prevent any one man, or body of men, or any possible combination of individual interests, from being arbitrary. . . ." *Ibid.*, pp. 92–93.   Yet "if the whole compass of human power could be concentrated in one arm, it would be impotent to take away, however it might ravish or prostrate those rights personified in the meanest individual of the breed of man, crawling upon the face of the earth."   Adams, *Cincinnati Oration,* pp. 12–13.

people may on occasion be precluded from acting in their original
capacity with sufficient expedition.   But here Adams offered another
safeguard to avoid abuse or failure of power.   The people should re-
tain a "concurrent power of altering the Constitution in . . . [their]
own persons. . . ," for on other occasions the legislature may be incompetent to act.[96]   Despite the granting of the constituent power to
government, therefore, abuse might be guarded against by a retention of an ultimate or "concurrent" power of altering the constitution
in the hands of the people.   Adams has difficulty maintaining a logical consistency in discussing sovereign power.   But it must be recalled that his sovereignty is limited.   It is, in final analysis, a competent power in government to alter its own constitution or to make
necessary laws.   It should be exercised in keeping with fundamental
moral principles.   Should such principles be violated, their violation
might better be endured to some degree rather than have the people
endure the disadvantage of an inadequate government.   If the government became incompetent to act or abused its powers too much, a
practical and concurrent power in the people might remedy the situation.   Adams, in other words, attempted to join the theoretical to the
practical, and occasionally his logic falters.

In addition to opposing such limitations of government as to render
it inadequate, Adams, in his concept of sovereignty limited by moral
law, opposed the frittering away of power among "municipalities or
local governments."   He was happy to note that a new French Constitution had avoided such dispersal of power.[97]   Such a weakening
of power had not been designed, he asserted, in the Constitution of
the United States, for it had left, he thought, "no such thing in the
. . . [state] constitutions as an absolute, irresistible, despotic power,
lurking *somewhere* under the cabalistic denomination of sovereignty."[98]   Thus, in Adam's sight, limited sovereignty was a sufficient

[96] VII "Publicola," *Writings*, I, 93–94. He believed that the United States
Constitution provided these necessary safeguards.   There is a possibility, of
course, of contradiction here between the idea of a delegated constituent power
and a retained concurrent constituent power in the people.   *Ibid.*, p. 91.   This
is borne out, by implication at least, in his criticism of the British Constitution,
wherein the whole power of the nation was exercised by Parliament by delegation,
because therein it prevented the British people from altering their constitution.
Ibid., p. 89.
[97] To John Adams, London, September 19, 1797, *ibid.*, II, 209.
[98] Adams, *Quincy Oration, 1831*, pp. 25–26.

basis for strong government, and in his theory a limited national sovereignty was superior to state sovereignty, and any pretensions of unlimited state sovereignty could only be an unwarranted means of interfering with powers granted by the whole people to the general government.

Against a background of this theory the theorist-statesman attempted to judge the events of his day. Adams recognized early that Napoleon, the aspiring military dictator, although still preserving in some degree the spirit of Jacobinism, was not a wholehearted opponent of kings and that, filled with the itch of a royal ambition, he was actually a pretender to absolute power.[99] Recognizing that a civilization-wide trend of catastrophe could not be the work of one man, Adams knew that the revolutionary spirit of the French nation created the dictator. He was the product of a social catastrophe that had upheaved the whole social fabric in disregard of moral law.[100] Adams foresaw clearly that, without a moral restraint on the "portentous anarchy" of the French masses, the result of the Revolution would be a "military government, by turns anarchical and despotic," itself unconfined by moral restraint, even though clothed with "democratic forms." [101]

[99] To Abigail Adams, Berlin, March 10, 1801, *Writings*, II, 514–515. What Adams most feared in the French Revolution was the authoritarian threat that could be based on the enfranchisement of the masses. He clearly saw the threat that exaggerated equality had for liberty, and that people often support a dictator. He saw as some modern writers do not, that exaggerated equality is a great danger to the liberty that is essential to democracy. He would never have obscured this conflict by using such a term as "totalitarian democracy." See Edward H. Carr, *The Soviet Impact on the Western World* (New York: Macmillan, 1947), p. 7.

[100] To Abigail Adams, Reval, May 12, 1814, *Writings*, V, 43. Adams could on occasion justify the man of action who transgressed the moral law, although too much should not be made of infrequent allusions: "There are exceptions to every rule of morality, and men may be in situations necessary to act upon such exceptions. But it is not given to every one to judge of these exceptions. Brutus did right in killing Caesar. Yet the act was against the most forcible moral obligations. I approve the conduct of Brutus, but I believe that I should not imitate him." To William Vans Murray, Berlin, July 17, 1798, *Ibid.*, II, 340.

[101] To John Adams, London, September 21, 1797, *ibid.*, II, 215–216. "The circumstances of the present period betoken an approach toward a simple, unqualified military government [in France], which seems to be the only possible issue to this portentous Revolution. . . ." To John Adams, London, September 11, 1797, *ibid.*, pp. 199–200. He noted a similar alternation between republican revolution and military despotism in Columbia as in the natural order of things and produced by the fact that revolutionary war requires military chieftains. *Memoirs*, March 30, 1830, VIII, 211.

His political theory did not, quite understandably, avoid moral conflicts. Although slavery in the District of Columbia was a violation of basic moral law, in his view it would have been arbitrary and despotic for Congress to abolish slavery there as long as a majority of the people were opposed to such an act.[102]

Going beyond his assertion already referred to that a government and a majority are limited by moral law, Adams held that in a civil society that is made up of adult human beings and in which the great authority of the father in the family is modified or replaced by a system of mutual human relations,[103] a minority can never be forced to sacrifice its rights, may even, where it finds government to be transgressing such rights, refuse to obey.[104]   On this basis he held that "in the abstract theory of our government the obedience of the citizen is not due to an unconstitutional law. He may lawfully resist its execution." [105]   Such disobedience would be justified, despite the fact that a clear majority might endorse the law.   In the application of this principle, he came to the defense even of groups of which he was definitely critical, for example, the Jesuits who had "been expelled [from Russia], turned adrift upon the world, and deprived of their property without a trial, by the mere will of the Emperor, upon secret investigations and accusation of enemies and rivals, to all appearance without having been allowed even a hearing to defend themselves. . . ." [106]   Moreover, the allegiance of men to any sovereign was not "intrinsic" nor "primitive."   Such allegiance would entail a doctrine of passive obedience, whereas, by the law of nature, any man could foreswear allegiance to any sovereign or prince.[107]

By these theoretical limitations upon governmental power.

[102] Adams, "Letter to the Citizens of the United States, whose Petitions, Memorials and Remonstrances, have been entrusted to me, to be presented to the House of Representatives of the United States, at the third session of the 25th Congress," Quincy, May 21, 1838, Letter II.

[103] Adams, *Report on Weights and Measures*, p. 9.

[104] "Menander," *Writings*, I, 127.

[105] Adams, "Letter to Messers. H. G. Otis, Israil Thorndike, T. H. Perkins, William Prescott, Daniel Sargent, John Lowell, William Sullivan, Charles Jackson, Warren Dutton, Benjamin Peckman, Henry Cabot, C. C. Parsons and Franklin Dexter, Washington, December 30, 1828," *Correspondence between John Quincy Adams, esquire, President of the United States and several Citizens of Massachusetts concerning the charge of a design to dissolve the union alleged to have existed in that state*, p. 18.

[106] To John Adams, Ealing, February 29, 1816, *Writings*, V, 520–521.

[107] Adams, *Life in a New England Town*, October 1, 1787, p. 43.

Adams exhibited healthy awareness that the stability of a constitutional system rested upon the fulfillment of principles, not upon adherence to mere "articles." [108]   The spirit of the people would be the best safeguard against the abuse of constitutional principles.[109] Wherever the attachment of people could not be earned by a government, it was perhaps better for that government to fall, even though its constitutional principles might be theoretically the best.[110]   Without the support of the *"good sense"* and "attachment" of the people, the support of the army alone remained.[111]   An army alone was a weak reliance, and to depend solely upon it might produce a resistant "nation in arms." [112]   Adams recognized that the loyalties of a people are complex, that people have attachments to many institutions in society which, although ultimately in the category of the political, were not to be explained entirely in terms of politics.   Adams recognized a hierarchy of human values with a single political apex but a pluralistic foundation.   Constitutions and the bare trappings of power are not enough to form a community.   A community is based upon a common acceptance, an unconscious acceptance, of the total pattern of life that the community comprehends.

On occasion, Adams, the theorist of internal improvements, manifested a warm admiration for efficiency, even that which might be gained at the sacrifice of rights.   When his letters were intercepted by French agents, he held that this illustrated their efficiency and remarked that it was France's advantage that she was governed by ministers who were not the creatures of mere "pleasure and indolence" nor mere subalterns.[113]   On one occasion, speculating on the threat of France to the United States, he suggested that a sound alternative to French domination would be "to engraft a *military spirit* upon our national character and become a *warlike people*,"

[108] III "Publicola," *Writings*, I, 75.

[109] VII "Publicola," *ibid.*, p. 93.

[110] To Joseph Pitcairn, The Hague, March 3, 1797, *ibid.*, II, 133.

[111] To William Vans Murray, January 27, 1801, *ibid.*, p. 495.

[112] To Benjamin Waterhouse, Boston House, Ealing, August 27, 1815, *ibid.*, V, 357: in this reference he notes the imposition of a government upon France by the "armed rabble of Europe."   This "armed rabble" was the armies of the Kings and Emperors who brought Napoleon to defeat.   Adams had little confidence that a solution that they might impose could long endure.   To the Secretary of State (James Monroe), London, April 9, 1816, *ibid.*, VI, 9.

[113] To Thomas Boylston Adams, St. Petersburg, July 14, 1812, *ibid.*, IV, 374.

the more efficiently to resist aggression.[114]   Taking pleasure in the fact that soldiers, ubiquitous in Prussia, did not everywhere accost one in Silesia, and showing considerable distaste for Prussia as a nation of soldiery,[115] he could nevertheless feel distress over the spectacle of the "last Agonies of a Great Man [Napoleon, the efficient military dictator], hunted to Death by Millions of little ones." [116] This conqueror might be preferable to the horde of "legitimates" who were being returned to their thrones.[117]

[114] To William Vans Murray, March 20, 1798, *Writings*, II, 272–273.   To William Harris Crawford, Ghent, September 14, 1814, *ibid.*, V, 140–141.

[115] Adams, *Letters on Silesia*, p. 202.

[116] Adams, "Letters to Abigail Adams, St. Petersburg, April 25, 1814," *Proceedings of the American Antiquarian Society*, New Series, XXIII (April 9, 1913–October 15, 1913), p. 168.

[117] To Abigail Adams, Ealing, March 4, 1816, *Writings*, V, 525.

10

✽✾✿✾✽

Government and the Moral Law

*The theory of the rights of man has taken deep root in the soil
of civil society.*

—MEMOIRS, *August 11, 1835*

AREAS OF FREEDOM

In the preceding pages Adams's concept of freedom and basic
rights has been referred to as a general matter related to his view of
revolution and the role of government.   At this point it is pertinent
to analyze substantively, in the light of Adams's political experience,
what was in his mind when he spoke or wrote of liberty or rights inhering in the individual or groups of individuals face to face with the
power of government.

There were occasions when he discussed "abundance of common-
place about liberty, equality and the rights of man" in terms of disdain.   He used such terms in discussing the condition of Holland
under the influence of French ideas during the revolutionary period.[1]
A similar attitude prompted his supercilious dismissal of French constitutional experiments as acceptable to the French people, if only
they "were ushered in with a proper seasoning of the words liberty,
equality, [and] representative system. . . ."[2]   But fundamentally
he was an ardent champion of liberty in the context of social arrangements he approved: "New England," he wrote, "is the child of that
puritan race, whom David Hume, with extorted reluctance, acknowl-
edges to have been the founders of *all* the liberties of the English
nation."[3]   There was a "holy temple of American Liberty, over the

---

[1] To John Adams, The Hague, June 27, 1795, *Writings,* I, 376.
[2] To William Vans Murray, January 6, 1800, *ibid.,* II, 447.
[3] Adams, *The New England Confederacy of MDCXLIII,* p. 9.   "In Braintree
I first beheld the light of Heaven—first breathed the atmosphere of your granite

tomb of departed tyranny." [4]   And he looked forward to the time
when such liberty should be universal among all peoples.   He might
depreciate the significance of the Alien and Sedition Laws as of "exceedingly limited operation" and merely "susceptible of being exhibited in odious colours to the people." [5]   It would be a normal
inclination in the younger Adams to assert that these important
legislative enactments of his father's Presidency had been overesti-
mated and misused by his father's enemies.   It is more important to
note that he expressed regret that the Bill of Rights had not been
written into the original Constitution and asserted that the defect had
not been fully remedied by the first ten articles of amendment.[6]
When he traveled in Europe he resented the signs he observed of the
police state.   Looking disdainfully upon the condition of man in
Europe of which he had seen so much, he declared that the rights set
forth in the Declaration of Independence were the natural rights
of mankind.[7]

The constitutional system of the United States was thus for Adams a
model.   Of course there existed on the foundations of that system a
government which by its nature must define and circumscribe areas
of freedom.   But in the Adams system there were assumptions that
are exceedingly germane to the creation of an "informing principle"
of civil liberties for today.   He assumed that the spirit and laws of
American institutions required that the repressive power of government should be applied only against "actual transgression," that even
odious projects should not be curtailed until they threaten immediately the social order.[8]   In this there was a clear relation with the

---

rocks—first sucked with my mother's milk the love of Liberty, and the reverence
for the Gospel of truth."   Adams, *Discourse on Education,* p. 5.

[4] Adams, *July 4th Oration, 1793,* p. 12.

[5] Adams, *Parties in the United States,* pp. 24–25.

[6] Adams, *The Jubilee of the Constitution,* p. 45.

[7] Adams, *The Jubilee of the Constitution,* p. 9.   "The Declaration of Independence justified itself as the only possible remedy for insufferable wrongs. . . .
As, between the two parties, the single question at issue was Independence—but
in the confederate existence of the North American Union, LIBERTY—not only
their own liberty but the vital principle to the whole race of civilized man, was
involved."   Adams, *Eulogy on Lafayette,* p. 6.

[8] To Hyde de Neuville, Washington, D. C., September 24, 1817, *Writings,* II,
190: "From the nature of the institutions and the laws of this [the United States]
country you will be aware that the repressive powers of the government, in their
application to the freedom of individuals, are limited to cases of actual transgression, and do not extend to projects which, however exceptionable in their

tradition of Justice Holmes's dissent in the *Abrams* case wherein Holmes made a neat application of his concept of "clear and present danger" to disagree with the Court in a case involving the relatively innocuous distribution of leftist pamphlets, which the government contended interfered with its prosecution of the war effort of the United States in World War I.[9] Adams maintained that personal liberty is "individual," based upon a right inhering in every individual as his own—*Jus Suum*, and not created by government.[10] The defense of such personal liberty—the personal liberty of sailors attacked by the "press gang"—was the cause of the War of 1812. The "sparing delegation and cautious distribution of power" in the American system "and the securities and hedges with which personal civil, political and religious liberty [were] surrounded" served as nowhere else in the world, he thought, to protect the individual's possession of such liberty.[11]

Adams held that the system of slavery constituted in the United States the great institutionalized violation of our own principles. Feelings of humanity, "Christian benevolence," and our basic doctrine of rights and liberty must inevitably shake that system. Slavery was falling "into convulsions at the approach of freedom," the freedom that must inevitably increase in the progress of the great moral improvement in the condition of man.[12]

This doctrine, quite conventionally, contained a "right to life, liberty, and the pursuit of happines." The exercise of such a right must not infringe "upon the same right of all other men."[13] Adams

---

character, have not been matured at least into an attempt or a commencement of execution."

[9] Abrams *v.* the United States, 250 U. S. 616.

[10] Adams, *Argument in United States v. Cinque* [15 Peters 518], p. 82. Adams, using this idea of the individual nature of freedom, came to the support of a liberal system by asserting that that nation would inevitably be the most powerful which was compounded by the most individuals enjoying "the most freedom." This line of reasoning was typically rationalist and places Adams in the tradition of the 18th century. Starting with a premise based on a preference, he expanded it into a principle, oversimple and not altogether regardful of practical facts. To James Lloyd, Washington, D. C., October 1, 1822, *Writings,* VII, 311–312.

[11] To James Lloyd, Washington, D. C., October 1, 1822, *Writings,* VII, 311–312.

[12] *Memoirs,* December 13, 1838, X, 63.

[13] Adams, *Letter Read at the Recent Celebration of West India Emancipation in Bangor* (*Me.*), p. 2.

envisaged a "perfect image of united liberty and submission." [14] He saw in America the opportunity for liberty and law to march hand in hand toward a higher order. [15] And, although liberty and freedom were in high degree individual, there was in social organization a resulting "treasure of public liberty" that was common property, every individual in society being required or obliged to contribute to its security. [16] Adams, therefore, in a manner consistent with his emphasis upon internal improvements, saw, in almost a modern sense, that positive freedom can be achieved only through a collective effort to improve the general warfare.

Adams saw and championed an American system that expressed a single principle of the "unalienable rights of human nature" of which doctrines of "civil, political, commercial and religious liberty . . . [were] but various modifications." [17] On this basis he opposed proposed Congressional legislation to govern, in particular to tax, the newly acquired population of Louisiana. There was a "natural right of property," to which government was obliged to give protection. [18] Further, although there might be inconvenience to the state in the warmth of our public discussions based upon a fundamental liberty, it was an inconvenience necessarily associated with the enjoyment of that liberty, and it was good that the "jealousy of one patriot [enjoying freedom of speech, should stand] as a guard over the ambition of another." [19] Freedom of speech was the "safety valve" that alone could preserve the American "political boiler from a fearful and fatal explosion." [20] Adams excoriated the attempts of Southern men in Congress to repress doctrines with respect to slavery contrary to their own, condemned their attempts to act as inquisitors of the thinking of the national legislators. [21]

[14] To the Secretary of State (Edmund Randolph), No. 5, The Hague, November 7, 1794, *Writings*, I, 224.

[15] Adams, "Inaugural Address," *in* Richardson, *op. cit.*, II, 295.

[16] I "Columbus," *Writings*, I, 149.

[17] To Richard C. Anderson, State Department, Washington, D. C., May 27, 1823, *ibid.*, VII, 466–467. This American system applied to a much wider area than the United States, for he assessed the quality of the leaders of the newly independent Latin American countries in terms of their recognition of the general "American" principles of civil liberty. National Archives, Records of the Department of State, *Diplomatic Instructions, All Countries*, IX, 258.

[18] Adams, *Newburyport Oration, 1837*, p. 10.

[19] II "Columbus," *Writings*, I, 159.

[20] Adams, *Newburyport Oration, 1837*, p. 56.

[21] *Congressional Globe*, 26th Cong., 1st sess., June 24, 1840, pp. 483–484: Adams offered a motion presenting a book on political economy to the House

With respect to the press, even in political contingencies in which deals with newspapers might have given him personal advantage, Adams endorsed fastidious standards and principles of freedom from control more honored in the breach than in conformity in his own day. Late in his presidential term, he told Walsh, the editor, that it was for him (Walsh) alone to decide whom to support in the coming election.[22] Several years earlier Adams had suggested that it was the duty of the same editor in an earlier political struggle to be independent, non-partisan, and disinterested, implying that a "public journalist" in enjoying a free press must present the issues, not personal biases.[23] He rejected a policy of seeking the services of the press to himself or his policies. For the most part Adams refused the assistance of a subsidized press serving special propaganda interests, although it was notable, in one of those obvious qualifications that the warmth of political struggle so often required, that Adams defended the right of the Bank of the United States to subsidize a friendly press as a means of safeguarding the interests of a minority.[24] Independent newspapers were exceedingly important, he thought, for they might raise the general level of the press, improve and influence the public mind to the support of "sound and useful principle," stimulate their readers to be just and generous, fair and good.[25] During his foreign journeys he observed with interest the degree of press freedom that existed,[26] and he was particularly irritated by any presumed servility of the press, of whatever nation, to foreign influence.[27] The tradition that he represented with respect to the press was that earlier tradition of the "penny press" that was partisan perhaps, but yet reflected principle and offered an opportunity even for the lowly, and above all a minority, to present their views. This tradition did not accept the type of partisanship, which is based upon size and eco-

---

of Representatives and requiring it to be deposited in the library of the House. Crabb of Alabama objected to the doctrine of the book, and Adams defended the principle of free access to ideas.

[22] *Memoirs*, March 31, 1828, VII, 492.

[23] To Louisa Catherine Adams, Washington, D. C., September 29, 1822, *Writings*, VII, 309.

[24] *Register of Debates*, 22nd Cong., 1st sess., appendix, p. 57.

[25] To Robert Walsh, Washington, D. C., November 27, 1822, *Writings*, VII, 330–331.

[26] To Thomas Boylston Adams, July 9, 1799, *ibid.*, II, 433: He concluded that there was as much press freedom in America as in Britain.

[27] To Abigail Adams, Berlin, January 9, 1798, *ibid.*, pp. 234–235.

nomic power and selfish support of special interests, characteristic of much of the modern press.

At least on one occasion Adams held that "among the securities in the political institutions of the Union deemed the most important and precious to individual liberty are the rules established to shield from oppression the rights of persons accused of crimes." The rights of the accused, of course, included the right of not having to answer any "other accusation than that of a grand jury," the right of being safeguarded against any sentence except one based upon "a verdict of a jury of trial," in a process presided over by judges answerable to the justice of "their country by the process of impeachment."[28] He asserted such rights in an exchange with the British Minister in the course of rejecting a British proposal for international tribunals. Although his major concern in such an exchange was to resist British pressure and not to guard against defective judicial processes, there is no doubt that the occasion offered an opportunity to emphasize principles for which he had a fundamental respect. He had occasion to call upon the rights of the accused in his own defense against a move in the House to censure him for presenting a petition from Benjamin Waterhouse and forty-five others from Haverhill, Massachusetts, that called for the peaceful dissolution of the union.[29] He said the House of Representatives could not receive resolutions calling for such a punishment without trial, since the preamble of the resolution of censure charged subornation of perjury and high treason.[30] He fought against violation of fundamental right to judicial safeguards in the *Amistad case*, which involved a demand by the Spanish Minister that certain Negroes claimed as escaped slaves be delivered up to Spanish authority.[31] The right of habeas corpus, which he thought in jeopardy in the case, he asserted to be the all-

[28] To Stratford Canning, State Department, Washington, D. C., August 15, 1821, *Writings*, VII, 174. He found this principle one of the bases for rejecting a British proposal for the establishment of international tribunals to try those accused of engaging in the slave trade.

[29] *Congressional Globe*, 27th Cong., 2nd sess., January 24, 1842, p. 168.

[30] *Ibid.*, p. 168.

[31] Adams, *Argument in United States v. Cinque* [15 Peters 518], p. 43: "Is it possible to speak of this demand in language of decency and moderation? Is there a law of Habeas Corpus in the land? Has the expunging process of black lives passed upon these two Declarations of Independence in their gilded frames? Has the 4th of July '76 become a day of ignominy and reproach?"

encompassing feature of British and American liberty, without which the power of arbitrary imprisonment could make all other rights a mockery.

This concept of civil liberty was imbedded in a religious premise: "But he [Jesus] came to teach, and not to compel. His law was a LAW of LIBERTY." True religion stood for "freedom of thought against organized power." [32] He thus rejected an application to himself of a religious test by the statutes governing the Boylston professorship at Harvard, not objecting to the doctrines prescribed, but to the very idea of a test. [33] In fact, Adams indicated a general belief in academic freedom. While in Holland, he manifested dismay that the existing regime was moving against faculty members of the University of Leyden, dismissing men even of distinguished learning. [34] "Freedom and communication of thought is paramount to all legislative authority. . . ." [35] He admired the Silesians, whose "manners and conversation" contained "a frankness, a cordiality, and good nature truly republican, or which at least [he wished] to consider as such. They speak with openness and freedom of their own government, which they praise and blame according as they think it deserves." [36] He opposed limitation on the right of people freely to assemble together. [37] Yet he feared the mob that "in tearing the lace from the garb of government, will tear the coat itself into a thousand rags." [38] Thus, rights must be defended against both government and the people unleashed, improperly influenced and moved themselves to destroy individual liberties. [39] Above all, the worth of the individual must be upheld and not lost sight of in

[32] Adams, *Discourse on Education*, pp. 18, 25.
[33] To Samuel Dexter, Quincy, August 6, 1805, *Writings*, III, 125.
[34] To the Secretary of State (Edmund Randolph), No. 27, The Hague, February 25, 1795, *ibid.*, I, 299: "Three of the Professors at the University of Leyden have been dismissed. One of them, Mr. Pestal, has been distinguished by several works relating to the Constitution of this Republic. Even the temple of the Muses is no sanctuary now, and the Patriots upon this occasion imitate an example of similar exclusion heretofore given by their adversaries."
[35] Adams, *The Lives of James Madison and James Monroe*, p. 27.
[36] Adams, *Letters on Silesia*, p. 22.
[37] Adams, "Letter to the Citizens of the United States, whose Petitions, Memorials and Remonstrances, have been entrusted to me, to be presented to the House of Representatives of the United States, at the third session of the 25th Congress," Quincy, May 21, 1839, Letter II.
[38] To John Adams, Boston, October 19, 1790, *Writings*, I, 64.
[39] V "Publicola," *ibid.*, p. 83.

the context of government and society, for, he wrote, "the principles of liberty are daily rendering the life of man more and more precious." [40]

His concept of liberty likewise assumed that fine balance between authority and recognized principles of freedom which underlay all his social and political thinking. He feared the stupidity of a government that was unnaturally oppressive and violated principles implicit in the facts of human individuality. At the same time, he feared the prospect of an imposition of the mass will through excesses and violence. He would always resist the enforcement of equality at the sacrifice of liberty. A neat balance between the two must be the major goal of a sound statecraft.

POPULAR CONTROL OF GOVERNMENT

As stated before, Adams did not reject the dominant influence of oligarchy in government. In his younger years, to be sure, he expressed the fear that the new federal constitution favored the "aristocratic party," [41] but later he found much to admire in the mixed system that this constitution had established, including democratic, aristocratic, monarchical, republican, and federalist elements. [42] He admired this system that had blended together "Federalism and aristocracy" and represented "a great majority of the men of wealth and education throughout the Union." [43] He easily understood why the French had chosen to refine carefully the representation in a new national assembly "to avoid the violence, the tumults, the riots which render almost all the populous towns in England a scene of war and blood at the period of Parliamentary elections. . . ." [44] He decried the tendency of all Administrations and parties in power in the United States, subject to popular pressure, to fall and to be pulled down. [45] There was aristocratic superiority in the delight he took in noting Jackson's lapses in syntax and orthography. [46]

On the other hand, with respect to his views of the function of

[40] *Memoirs,* April 26, 1840, X, 276.
[41] Adams, *Life in a New England Town,* October 12, 1787, p. 46.
[42] Adams, *The Social Compact,* p. 30.
[43] Adams, *Parties in the United States,* p. 9.
[44] VIII "Publicola," *Writings,* I, 98.
[45] *Memoirs,* July 28, 1818, IV, 120.
[46] *Ibid.,* March 22, 1828, VII, 483: He referred to such misspellings as "goverment," "solem," "secratary," "gurantee."

an aristocracy or an oligarchy as limitations upon popular control in government, no final, unambiguous generalization of Adams's views may be rendered. He stated that the long-delayed death of George III had prolonged the struggle between marching democracy and the absurd pretensions of hereditary aristocracy.[47] In defense of American borrowing of British political principles, he challenged the charge that he had any preference for monarchy or aristocracy.[48] For the people must judge of the incompetency of their rulers.[49] As Minister Resident in Holland he criticized secret manipulations and control in the new Assembly of Holland, dominated by a revolutionary committee, even though the new conditions in this legislature represented the application of the theory of popular sovereignty.[50]

Clearly the ambiguity of his position must qualify any claims he made of rejecting oligarchical control. Moreover, it must be borne in mind that the popular control or influence that he posited as against the influence of oligarchies might be of two types. He doubtless abhorred democracy in the form of undisciplined mass movements, whereas he would accept democracy as a manifestation of respect for the individual or if it were institutionalized in orderly elections or legislative processes. Also it must be consistently recalled that the limitation he put upon sovereignty expressed through government was inherently a limitation upon the right of the popular democratic will to do whatever it might desire.

With this introduction to the problem of popular control, considering the matter from the standpoint of the status of oligarchies, we may now turn to John Quincy Adams and his reactions to democracy. This approach is particularly important in order to evaluate the conclusion of Brooks Adams that his grandfather was especially notable as a champion of democracy.

This form of belief [democracy] was strong in my family a century ago, and found expression through my grandfather, John Quincy Adams, who made the realization thereof the work and ambition of his life and who,

[47] *Ibid.*, June 1, 1825, VII, 23.
[48] XI "Publicola," *Writings*, I, 108.
[49] IV "Publicola," *ibid.*, pp. 78–79.
[50] To the Secretary of State (Edmund Randolph), No. 25, The Hague, February 15, 1795, *ibid.*, p. 286.

when he grew old, practically gave his life for the cause. As an apostle of this doctrine, I take it, he must always be one of the most commanding figures in our history, when he comes to be fully understood.[51]

The record makes the unqualified assertion at least doubtful, unless by democracy is meant a rather special Adams variety of Whiggery, much in contrast with the popular forces finding expression in the Jacksonian revolution. A major part of this section will be devoted to an assessment of this thesis.

Adams's opposition to the taking of Louisiana, as it was accomplished, was, to be sure, based upon an acceptance of the authoritativeness of popular consent. But it is well to remember that he once chided the French for attaching the word "democratic" to a projected constitution, stating that "they still give it that epithet without any scruples. . . ."[52] At this time, when the French were so often busy constitution-making, Adams considered the word "democratic" to be a word of opprobrium. Shortly before, attacking what he called the "dreams" of Paine, he wrote, "To attempt to govern a nation like this [France], under the form of a democracy, to pretend to establish over such beings a government which according to Rousseau is calculated only for a republic of Gods . . . requires the continual exercise of virtues beyond the reach of human infirmity, even in its best estate. . . ."[53] Looking at the question of the respect due from governors to public opinion, an important component of the democratic spirit, he strongly asserted, "There is however one fundamental political error, from which France has not yet recovered; it is the unqualified submission, and the unwise veneration for the *opinion publique,* which is in its nature inconsistent with any regular permanent system of government or of policy."[54]

Adams's doubts about democracy were based on a conservative

[51] Brooks Adams, "Introductory Note," *in* Henry Adams, *The Degradation of the Democratic Dogma,* p. vi.

[52] To John Adams, The Hague, August 31, 1795, *Writings,* I, 400–401. He later said that the Constitution of the United States "was republican, and even democratic [when first established]." Adams, *The Jubilee of the Constitution,* p. 53.

[53] VIII "Publicola," *Writings,* I, 95.

[54] To Abigail Adams, The Hague, April 25, 1795, *Writings,* I, 333. To John Adams, The Hague, May 4, 1795, *ibid.,* p. 344.

respect for the past and the organic growth of society.[55]   He feared the enthusiasm with which the multitude saw its advantage in democracy.   He believed that the real power in government must always be that of a few.[56]   He even asserted the need for a strong and effective executive to curb the "impetuosities of the people." [57] The popular voice, forever "varium et mutabile," [58] was always bent upon change.[59]   Noting that his home town of Braintree had voted against him, he declared that "the people are a wayward master." [60] It was the "propensity of all free governments [to fall victim] to the convulsions of faction"; [61] "factious cabals [were] the besetting sin of all elective governments." [62]

Turning from the doctrinal references to the instances of direct, exclamatory reference, we find the assertions no less strong.   An important Dutch woman was declared to be acting "under a thin disguise of outrageous democracy." [63]   Much stronger was his reference to "that hideous monster of democracy, begotten by madness upon corruption, which produced such infinite mischief in Europe. . . ." [64]   In his own political life, he refused to hold his seat in the Senate "without exercising the most perfect freedom of agency, under the sole and exclusive control of . . . [his] own sense of right. . . ." [65]   Not only on general terms was he suspicious of the popular will, as a representative he insisted upon viewing his mandate as a charge to use his intelligence, his own sense of right and wrong, even though they might run counter to the popular will.   Wirt's submission to "popular humours" was described as a

[55] *Memoirs*, December 11, 1831, VIII, 433: "Democracy has no forefathers; it looks to no posterity; it is swallowed up in the present, and thinks of nothing but itself.   This is the vice of democracy; and it is incurable.   Democracy has no monuments; it strikes no medals; it bears the head of no man upon a coin; its very essence is iconoclastic."

[56] Adams, *The Social Compact*, pp. 10–11.

[57] Adams, *Eulogy on Lafayette*, p. 17.

[58] To John Adams, The Hague, July 21, 1796, *Writings*, I, 4.

[59] *Memoirs*, May 12, 1820, V, 112.

[60] *Ibid.*, November 15, 1842, XI, 269.

[61] Adams, *The Lives of James Madison and James Monroe*, p. 41.

[62] *Memoirs*, October 2, 1844, XII, 80.

[63] *Ibid.*, March 3, 1795, I, 84.

[64] To Abigail Adams, Berlin, May 25, 1800, *Writings*, II, 457: Of course, the allusion here is to the French type of democracy manifested in revolutionary upheaval.

[65] James Truslow Adams, *The Adams Family*, p. 138.

fault.[66] Calhoun's enthusiasm for the Greek cause was sentiment and constituted an undue regard for the "prevailing popular feeling."[67] Adams would not sacrifice one day's pay for the Greek cause, nor would he ask the President to do so.[68]

Adams came dangerously close to significant doubt concerning the validity of the democratic process when he wrote, "A stranger would think that the people of the United States have no other occupation than electioneering."[69] Electioneering was, of course, part of the process of stimulating the people to decision one way or another on important issues or political figures, an important part of the democratic process. His contempt for the electioneering process was surely not precisely democratic. And he expressed more than inhibition and shyness when, encountering a demonstration for him in Philadelphia shortly before election time, he responded thus abruptly: "Fellow-citizens, I thank you for this kind and friendly reception, and wish you all good night."[70] We have noted that he prided himself on having generally attempted to stem "currents of popular opinions,"[71] which so often through "waywardness and corruption" constituted an assault upon public prosperity.[72] He condemned Jefferson[73] for swimming with such currents and asserted that a similar subscription to "fraudulent democracy" likewise characterized Jackson and his disciples.[74] Isaac Hill and Martin Van Buren were demagogues, symbolizing the besetting sin of popular government, the latter figure having "a tincture of aristocracy," making of him "an amalgamated metal of lead and

[66] *Memoirs*, April 28, 1818, IV, 83.

[67] *Ibid.*, August 15, 1828, VI, 173. He even criticized Gallatin, whom he admired, for patronizing the Greek cause for the sake of popularity. There was in this attitude some contempt for popular feeling at home and the democratic cause of the Greeks. *Ibid.*, November 24, 1823, pp. 198–199.

[68] *Ibid.*, May 10, 1824, p. 324: His assertion that the contrary course would violate neutrality vis-a-vis the Turks was hardly compelling.

[69] *Ibid.*, August 5, 1828, VIII, 76.

[70] *Ibid.*, August 6, 1828, p. 76: Following this brief speech the crowd dispersed, unquestionably to the chagrin of his supporters in that city who were worried about his second term prospects. But Adams made no further concession to the necessities of democratic campaigning. *Ibid.*, p. 77.

[71] *Memoirs*, November 21, 1831, VIII, 427–428.

[72] *Ibid.*, October 9, 1834, IX, 187.

[73] Adams, *Lives of James Madison and James Monroe*, p. 65.

[74] *Memoirs*, April 13, 1836, IX, 276.

copper." [75] Adams looked with alarm and contempt upon the quality of the Congress, "the culled darlings of fifteen millions"; "the remarkable phenomenon that they . . . [presented was to him a reflection of] the level of [popular] intellect and of [popular] morals upon which they . . . [stood]." [76] Here was doubt concerning the quality of the statesmanship that democratic government could produce.

There was more than political ire and irritation in his references to his political opponents during and following Jackson's Administration: Robert Barnwell Rhett was "a South Carolina nullifier, of the absurdest stamp, a compound of wild democracy and iron-bound slavery. . . ." [77] Alexander Duncan of Cincinnati, "upwards of six feet high, made hideous by a wild, savage, and ferocious eye, . . . [was] the prime bully of the Kinderhook Democracy. . . . He has no perception of any moral distinction between truth and falsehood; but he has abundant sagacity to discern, and a brazen front to apply, that which will be sure to touch on the *ignorance,* the *envy,* and the *malignity* of the million. . . ." [78] Noting opposition to his project for a grant to the widow of General Jacob Brown, he wrote, "This bill was most vehemently contested by the spigot-sparing, bung-outpouring economists of both parties, and by the Kinderhook *ochlocracy.* . . ." [79] He found himself with his son among the ruins of the Whig Party having "to contend against the misrule of a triumphant, fraudulent, and reckless Democracy." [80]

The above materials serve to qualify the assertion of his grandson that John Quincy Adams was an unrelenting servant of the democratic ideal. True, he agreed that increasing democracy was attacking slavery, but he did so without registering approval of democracy itself. Further, he did reflect upon the impact that rising democracy

[75] *Ibid.,* October 9, 1834, p. 187.
[76] *Ibid.,* December 27, 1838, X, 78–79.
[77] *Ibid.,* June 20, 1840, X, 315–316.
[78] *Ibid.,* June 29, 1840, pp. 323–324; italics supplied.
[79] *Ibid.,* June 4, 1839, p. 87; italics supplied.
[80] *Ibid.,* November 16, 1842, XI, 270: It may be recognized that the "Democracy" referred to here has a capital "D," without agreeing that Adams in opposing it was friendly to democracy as such. It is true that Brooks and Henry Adams saw in Jacksonian democracy a "degradation," but it still may be questioned whether or not Adams was the forthright champion of the real democracy that they imagined.

was having upon Hamilton's political ideas in the late 1830's, but again without obvious approval.[81]   He regretted that he was not elected to the Presidency with more conclusive support, but it was the absence of unanimity he regretted more than the absence of a majority.   There was not much that was explicitly democratic in his support of the principle of national self-determination, although he did, as a good republican, regret that the Greeks had a monarchy stipulated for them.[82]   The same was true of his proposition that only the people, not the government, of Texas could accept annexation; and this issue was confused by the issue of slavery. It is true that he agreed with a Senate proposal to represent fractions in the House of Representatives on the ground that to do so would increase the number of representatives and thus more closely approach "pure democracy," [83] representation being that "expedient resorted to, for the purpose of attaining the substance" of the impracticable and realizing as closely as possible the consent of every man to his government and its decisions.[84]   But these assertions hardly obviate the significance of the many disapproving references he made to democracy.

We may turn now to another emphasis: a more detailed assessing of Adams's view of the practical responsibility of government to the people.   This discussion will in some degree, although not entirely, mitigate the asperities of his direct references to democracy.   Moreover, there will be involved a consideration of the processes without which democracy would be nonexistent.   He saw clearly that there existed a basic responsibility of the government to the people. In the absence of such an assumption, government would have no relationship to the pragmatic ends that a practical man must accept. It followed that an intelligent man must accept as fundamental certain processes, such as the legislative process, and the process of petitioning for redress of grievances, whereby such responsibilities might be realized.

Adams's doctrine of the right of petition was basically related to a theory of democracy.   He was, of course, the foremost champion

---

[81] *Memoirs,* April 3, 1837, IX, 345.
[82] *Ibid.,* January 19, 1830, VIII, 175.
[83] *Congressional Globe,* 27th Cong., 2nd sess., June 13, 1842, p. 620.
[84] *Loc. cit.*   VIII "Publicola," *Writings,* I, 98–99.

in our history of the right of persons to petition their government for redress of grievances or for the accomplishment of particular ends. He saw quite realistically that denial of the right on the ground that it might interfere with slavery was merely removed in degree, not in kind, from denial of the right on the ground of affiliation with a particular party.[85] The right of petition was not a mere political privilege, he asserted, but antedated the Constitution, which confirmed the right but did not create it: "My doctrine is, that this right belongs to humanity—that the right of petition is the right of prayer, not depending on the condition of the petitioner; and I say if you attempt to fix any limit to it, you lay the foundation for restriction to any extent that the madness of party spirit may carry it."[86] This statement was in effect the affirmation of the idea of a "hard core" of rights that should not be modified for reasons of political difference. He determined to present each petition that came to his hands, even though Congress might determine that such a petition contained a prayer for an unconstitutional result, since the right of petition was not related to the question of constitutionality.[87] There is no doubt that he held the right to be a popular right superior to the Constitution itself.[88] On such a ground, he proclaimed that he would present a petition even from a slave.[89] Determined to be consistent, he even presented a petition from Georgia asking that he, himself, be dismissed as chairman of the Committee on Foreign Relations of the House.[90] The decision of the legislature that might be based on the prayer of a petition

[85] *Congressional Globe*, 24th Cong., 2nd sess., Appendix, pp. 260–263. *Ibid.*, 25th Cong., 3rd sess., December 17, 1838, p. 39. *Ibid.*, 28th Cong., 1st sess., January 18, 1844, pp. 166–168.

[86] *Ibid.*, 28th Cong., 1st sess., January 18, 1844, pp. 166–168.

[87] *Ibid.*, 24th Cong., 1st sess., January 25, 1836, pp. 137–138. *Ibid.*, 27th Cong., 2nd sess., January 28, 1843, p. 192.

[88] *Congressional Globe*, 26th Cong., 1st sess., appendix, pp. 761–764: "The right of petition, therefore, is essential to the very existence of government; it is the right of the people over the Government; it is their right and they may not be deprived of it. . . . Will any man say that the right to petition would not exist unless written down in the Constitution?"

[89] *Ibid.*, 25th Cong., 2nd sess., June 23, 1838, p. 474. See *ibid.*, 24th Cong., 2nd sess., February 6, 1837, p. 164, *et seq.* for the record of a struggle precipitated by Adams when he asked whether or not a petition purporting to come from slaves came under the "gag" rule of the House.

[90] *Ibid.*, 27th Cong., 2nd sess., January 21, 1841, pp. 158–159. *Ibid.*, January 22, 1842, pp. 162–163.

was irrelevant; the basic popular right to petition must be safe-guarded at all costs. In defending the right of petition Adams stood out as a champion of a basic democratic right.

As noted previously, Adams's doctrine of "consent" was a view of "sovereign power"—even though limited—residing originally in the people, although "consent," in view of his acceptance of a limited suffrage and his concept of democracy, was a more intangible type than that which is rendered through modern democratic head-counting on the basis of universal suffrage. Love of order caused him to subscribe to a concept of "legitimacy," in a Lockean sense, but he asserted to Sir James Mackintosh that the rights of the people must be considered superior to any concept of "legitimacy." [91] The so-called legitimate government of the Bourbons brought back by the intercession of foreign arms was "an insult upon human speech, and an outrage upon the laws of God." [92] "Unalienable right" must ultimately overcome claims of legitimacy based upon doctrines of "unalienable allegiance." [93]

Yet Adams had a peculiarly formal view of "unalienable rights"; for, by the nature of his doctrine, the "unalienable rights" were the possession of individuals socially organized in a divinely ordained dispensation. Rights were enjoyed by virtue of being a member of a society known to and established by God and existing to fulfill his purposes. The isolated individual did not, by his nature alone, possess them, although, as we have seen, government did not create rights. Willful popular error could result in abuse, for the dispensation was an evolving one that would not displace error until the divine plan achieved perfect application. Therefore many manifestations of popular inclination, which were often considered expressive of democratic forces, might transgress upon "unalienable rights" as thoroughly as despotic government. The people might, by acting through a tyrannical majority, injure or destroy prescriptive rights in property, which also existed by virtue of the protection of a system evolving according to a divine plan.

Adams thus was often skeptical of mere public opinion. "In all

[91] *Memoirs,* June 2, 1816, III, 373.
[92] To John Adams, B. H. Ealing, December 16, 1815, *Writings,* V, 447.
[93] National Archives, Records of the Department of State, *Diplomatic Instructions,* All Countries, IX, 283.

ages of the world and in all countries," he wrote, "instability has been the most essential characteristic of popular opinions. It is so in America, and will infallibly become so more and more in proportion as the increase of population shall multiply the quantity of opinions." [94] Of course, as a student of the governmental process, he had to admit the essentiality of public opinion underlying stable government.[95] But he recognized that a public man "who gives himself voluntarily to the public has no right to ask for anything" [96] because he has accepted a master.

In his own election campaigns, despite his belief that high principle naturally should earn high place, Adams was singularly passive in the struggle for popular support. As we have noted, one of the great tragedies of his life existed in the fact that he had not been chosen for the Presidency by an overwhelming majority. "That confidence which the Constitution had reposed in the calm and deliberate judgement of the people, in a matter always of deep interest to them, I am assuredly not the man to deny them in the bearing which once or twice in the course of my life it may have upon myself." [97] On some occasions he expressed skepticism of the value of "popular elections," as when he prognosticated that the French would soon grow tired of them or affirmed that he was as sick as the French nation "of such reasoners as Dr. Priestley" who counseled frequent elections.[98] Although he might refer to the "Saturnalian electioneering holidays" in England,[99] he found American elections to be less corrupt.[100] And, at least following his Presidency, the loyalty of his constituency must have removed most doubts concerning the process of elections.

[94] To Charles Adams, The Hague, September 15, 1795, *Writings,* I, 418. To John Adams, May 4, 1795, *ibid.,* p. 344.

[95] *Memoirs,* March 6, 1817, III, 479–480. To John Adams, The Hague, September 12, 1795, *Writings,* I, 409.

[96] To Charles Jared Ingersoll, Washington, D. C., *Writings,* VII, 120.

[97] To Joel Lewis, Washington, D. C., February 20, 1822, *ibid.,* VII, 208. Later he expressed the view that the theory of frequent elections in the United States seemed to be based on the assumption "that power cannot be long trusted to the same hands, even of the wisest and the best." This opinion reflects an important aspect of Adams's aristocratic mind, but it should not be construed to mitigate his basic republicanism. *Memoirs,* April 28, 1841, X, 468.

[98] To John Adams, London, September 19, 1797, *Writings,* II, 210. To Abigail Adams, Berlin, May 25, 1800, *ibid.,* 459.

[99] To John Adams, The Hague, June 6, 1796, *ibid.,* I, 490.

[100] To Robert Walsh, Washington, D. C.. July 10, 1821, *ibid.,* VII, 116.

Adams placed a theoretical limitation on the power of democratic majorities by holding that a minority under a free government was never under an obligation to sacrifice its rights to the will of a majority. He was a loyal supporter of that republicanism of "virtue," the closest approach to pure democracy a large state could achieve, which would not produce tyrannical majorities.[101] As a very young man, having recently returned from a Europe that he had feared might modify his republican attachments, he was happy to proclaim himself the best republican he found.[102] Such a republican spirit, which formed the basis of the American system, excluded the absurdity of the monarchical principle. Such a spirit was conveyed by "manners and conversation" which contained "a frankness, a cordiality, and good nature truly republican." [103] The republican atmosphere in America was the creator of respect for certain basic constitutional principles; American diplomats abroad should return home periodically to avoid the decay of such respect. The Federalists, he wrote, showed an unfortunate opposition to republicanism.[104] Monroe feared that Adams's republicanism, evidenced in a note to Baron Tuyl, would offend the British and cause them to reject concerting with the United States against the Holy Alliance.[105] As Secretary of State Adams announced that our main purpose in Latin America was to insure republican institutions there against the influence of Europe.[106] Republican institutions combined a due regard for the security of individuals with an amplitude of authority.[107]

His theory of representation was, of course, a necessary part of

[101] Adams, *The Jubilee of the Constitution,* p. 54; he wrote that he rejected that kind of representative government based upon the idea, "Get out of your place and let me get in it." To William Vans Murray, Berlin, April 11, 1798, *Writings,* II, 275. To John Adams, London, September 21, 1797, *ibid.,* p. 214.

[102] To Abigail Adams, Cambridge, December 30, 1786, *Writings,* I, 29. In his commencement address at Harvard he showed a great attachment to republican principles. *Ibid.,* p. 34.

[103] Adams, *Letters on Silesia,* p. 22; republicanism conveyed to him an assumption of a prosperous citizenry. He remarked that our cities had "dwelling-houses suitable to the citizens of a republic." *Memoirs,* November 5, 1809, II, 53.

[104] "Review of the 'Works of Fisher Ames,' " *Writings,* III, 308.

[105] *Memoirs,* November 25, 1823, VI, 203.

[106] National Archives, Records of the Department of State, *Diplomatic Instructions,* All Countries, IX, 254. He called ours the "Republican Hemisphere." *Ibid.,* p. 301.

[107] *Memoirs,* October 13, 1821, V, 358.

his whole theory. Since all partial association, or associations in conflict with the spirit of the community as a whole, were anti-republican,[108] all partial representation of interests might be so considered. The system of representation, although never "fully [able to] answer the purpose of its institution, because every representative is actuated by several powerful motives, which could not operate upon his constituents," was an attempt to apply in a large state the principle that no freeman may be bound except with his own consent.[109] Adams recognized that the purposes or desires of constituents would be but partially accomplished through representative institutions, a condition that was less likely to be the case at least in a "natural democracy" wherein the intervention of representation was not present. Adams wrote, however, of representatives expressing the "sentiments," not the will, of their inhabitants, and called particular attention to the significance of the fact that a representative could not in a full degree represent those who have voted against him, and the further fact that suffrage qualification additionally restricted "natural democracy." In strict theory Adams might regret the practical limitation of the pure form, but in application he counseled such a distribution of powers among branches of the government and among legislative governing bodies as to prevent by balance the arbitrary tyranny of a single combination of interests.[110] At the same time he criticized the hampering of democracy in a French constitution through an indirect and complicated system of representation and the over representation of property.[111] Speaking later of the ethics of the representative, he considered more directly the relationship between representative and constituent and declared the former may follow the course of performing a "real service to the public," on the one hand, or the course of "proposing extraordinary solicitude for the people, on the other, by flattering their prejudices, by ministering to their passions, and by humoring their transient and changeable opinions."[112]   In

[108] Adams, "Letters to the Citizens of the United States, whose Petitions, Memorials and Remonstrances, have been entrusted to me, to be presented to the House of Representatives of the United States, at the third session of the 25th Congress," Quincy, May 21, 1839, Letter II.

[109] VIII "Publicola," *Writings*, I, 97–98.

[110] VII "Publicola," *ibid.*, pp. 92–93.

[111] VIII "Publicola," *ibid.*, pp. 96–97.

[112] V "Publius Valerius," *ibid.*, III, 69.

normal times unfortunately the latter type, the "patriot by profession," dominated. As for Adams, he felt strongly the obligation to public service; he believed in large representative bodies and small constituencies, in order more nearly to approach natural democracy,[113] but, as he showed when he resigned his Senate seat, he would not hold a representative position "without exercising the most perfect freedom of agency. . . ."[114] In fact, he would hazard "the reproach of madness or of worse" to rescue his contituents from what he might deem their perversity.[115] It is true that he chose to resign from the Senate rather than vote against his own principles, but this action revealed his belief that constituents could not dictate to a representative. A representative should be elected for his own "sound principles and sentiments," not merely on the basis of ability to act as an agent in a ministerial capacity.[116] He, himself, frankly affirmed a "denial of the duty of members of the House to be palsied by the will of their constituents. . . ."[117] Adams's theory of the discretion enjoyed by the legislative representative does in fact modify any concept of democracy to which he subscribed. Although he held that a representative should prefer the just interests of his own constituents to the interests of others,[118] he believed that the representative should determine what their just interests were.

Finally, his theory of political parties related closely to the question of popular control over government. Political opponents derided his claim "to be of *no party*" and to be possessed of a "discernment superior to both parties."[119] The Federalists of New England could never forgive Adams for opposing the party line in the Senate, particularly with regard to Jefferson's Embargo, for they

[113] Quincy, *op. cit.*, pp. 204–205.

[114] James Truslow Adams, *op. cit.*, p. 138.

[115] To Joseph Anderson, Boston, December 15, 1808, *Writings*, III, 269. This statement suggests John Winthrop's stewardship theory. See Parrington, *Main Currents in American Thought*, I, 46–47.

[116] To Joseph Hall, Washington, D. C., December 23, 1817, *Writings*, VI, 277.

[117] *Congressional Globe*, 26th Cong., 1st sess., April 27, 1840, p. 359.

[118] I "Publius Valerius," *Writings*, III, 47.

[119] John Quincy Adams, "Letter to the Federalists of the United States, Philadelphia, August 20, 1828," *The Conduct of John Quincy Adams considered in his relations, political and moral, towards the Federal Party*, originally printed in the *New York Evening Post*. In the Ridgway Library, Library Co. of Philadelphia, Pamphlet #4 in 50394, O..U. y 6. p. 2.

felt they had, in gratifying an Adams by sending him to the Senate, imposed upon him an obligation to support Federalist policy. It was deeply revealing of Adams's view of political parties that he felt no such obligation or felt it only slightly, which caused his erstwhile colleagues to charge him with conduct "worthy of Machiavel."[120] They should not have been surprised, for before electing him to the Massachusetts Senate they knew of "his restiveness in the trammels of party."[121] Adams did more than reject the discipline of parties, he attempted where possible to disregard party lines, for he had concluded that parties were not necessarily the organizations of legitimate popular aspirations. Indeed Adams evidenced not only disregard for, but perhaps even opposition to, the idea of parties. When he became President he agreed not to proscribe the Federalists, despite the fact that any favors extended to them would be interpreted by his supporters as concessions to political enemies and as a disregarding of the realities of politics.[122]

His real hope was that "the extremities of the times . . . [would] produce a coalition of parties and an administration combining all the respectable interests of the country. . . ."[123] In effect he would have preferred to remove the natural political divisions in terms of which parties may be understood and accepted. He accepted only incompletely and with regret the realization that a politician in the United States had to be "a man of party," whereas he, Adams, wished to be a "man of . . . [his] whole country."[124] He saw party conflict as a threat to the national union and a portent of the "unutterable horrors of civil war."[125] During the one-party period of the Monroe Administration, he expressed a feat that the situation

---

[120] Adams, "Letter to the Federalists of the United States, Philadelphia, August 20, 1828," pp. 3–4.

[121] Quincy, *op. cit.*, p. 26.

[122] *Memoirs,* February 7, 1825, VI, 500; he did recognize, however, that it would be difficult to favor them with appointments if they opposed him in the election. *Ibid.,* May 1, 1824, p. 313.

[123] To Louisa Catherine Adams, Ghent, November 29, 1814, *Writings,* V, 221; he noted with approval Monroe's purpose of bringing all parties together. *Memoirs,* August 31, 1824, VI, 415; he said that a "great object [of his Administration] would be to break up the remnant of the old party distinctions, and bring the whole people together in sentiment as much as possible." *Ibid.,* January 21, 1825, p. 474.

[124] *Memoirs,* January 28, 1802, I, 249.

[125] To John Adams, Ealing, April 8, 1816, *Writings,* VI, 2.

would be terminated by the emergence of a system of contending parties.[126]   As a young man in Holland he had observed with distaste the prevalence of the spirit of party, a spirit that was in great measure subservient to a foreign influence,[127] and he discerned a similar virulence of party struggle at home where an American party, the pro-French Republican party, mingled "with a foreign influence." [128]

Political parties were the refuge of those of "partial affection." [129] The true course should be to adhere to a true body of principles, loyalty to which would involve an intellectual stand above the partisanship of parties.   Opposing a move to resist Jefferson's Embargo, he asserted that the "whole truth" (a major practical and philosophical concern of his life) could not be discovered on the basis of personal view, "geographical position," "party bias," or "professional occupation." [130]   Inveteracy of political party difference offended him, particularly where justice could not temper the emotion associated with such difference,[131] and outlandish and contradictory epithets were directed at the opposition.[132]   Strangely enough, although Adams was possessed of a temperament given to vehement assertions of principle and the doctrinaire approach natural to the political partisan, he was at the same time philosophically so confident of the validity of his principles that he rejected the very party divisions with respect to these principles that would have been a fitting context for his partisanship.   The unhappy result was frustration in the statesman and depressing lack of ultimate success in the politician.

He would not grace some groups with the name of party, rather he concluded that there was a "propensity of all free governments

[126] *Memoirs,* July 28, 1818, IV, 119.

[127] To the Secretary of State (Edmund Randolph), No. 35, Amsterdam, May 1, 1795, *Writings,* I, 338.

[128] To Sylvanus Bourne, London, December 24, 1795, *ibid.,* I, 155.

[129] Adams, *The Jubilee of the Constitution,* pp. 55–56.

[130] To Harrison Gray Otis, Washington, March 31, 1808, *Writings,* III, 191–193.

[131] *Memoirs,* March 3, 1805, I, 370–371.

[132] To John Adams, The Hague, May 22, 1795, *Writings,* I, 358: "Everything done by them [the fallen executive committee in France] is an object of execration.   They are Jacobins, Terrorists, Royalists, drinkers of blood, robbers, scourges of the human race, everything that a victorious party can make of one that is defeated."

to the convulsions of faction. . . ."[133]   He looked with suspicion upon the appearance of popular party conventions as a political revolution, party movements that, and herein he revealed his failure fully to understand the necessity for parties, would become antagonistical and, if multiplied, lead to the deeper tragedy of civil war.[134]   Adams insisted that, although he would accept any office tendered him, the offer should be entirely the decision of the country uninfluenced by his own ambition manifested through party alignment.   No assistance should be sought by an individual in a political party, for he should not obtrude himself directly or indirectly, even with the assistance of friends (party), to gain political appointment or election.   It would not be true to say that Adams failed to recognize the tactical advantage of party affiliation; his principles simply forebade using the advantage.[135]   No "bargains," no "coalition," no "money" were his principles.[136]   On the occasion of his election to the Presidency, Adams was blissfully ignorant of the party manipulations, largely the project of Thurlow Weed, that figured so importantly in his election.[137]   He was congenitally incapable of heading a political party or remaining consistently within one.

In his political career, despite the fact that he occasionally expressed an awareness of the value of political parties to personal ambition, he showed an amazing consistency in disregarding the principles governing the operation and use of political parties, at least in his own day.   For example, it was beneath the rectitude of an Adams to reward one's supporters with political office, particularly if the support given was a major consideration.   Moreover, no

[133] Adams, *The Lives of James Madison and James Monroe,* p. 41.   "This tendency of all private associations to settle into factious cabals is the besetting sin of all elective governments."   *Memoirs,* October 2, 1844, XII, 80.

[134] *Memoirs,* August 29, 1840, X, 351–352.

[135] To John D. Heath, Washington, D. C., January 7, 1822, *Writings,* VII, 194–195: "For if the old prudential maxim that God helps those who help themselves is morally applicable to the pursuit of public honors and trust, I shall certainly be the most helpless candidate that ever was presented to the view of the American people."   Really, Adams believed himself to be rather unique as the above quotation reveals.   He recognized the inevitability of political parties in the election of a chief magistracy as well as of the next official in the direct line of succession.   Adams, *Parties in the United States,* p. 124.

[136] To Robert Walsh, Washington, D. C., June 21, 1822, *Writings,* VII, 272. Quincy, *op. cit.,* p. 168.   *Memoirs,* March 8, 1828, VII, 469–470.

[137] Clark, *John Quincy Adams,* p. 218.

consideration of disadvantage could deter him from appointing a qualified member of the opposition. He praised John Adams for refusing to bolster his popularity in his own party by associating himself with the war fever in that party.[138] We have remarked already the irritation he had caused in his party when he proposed allowing proportional representation in the Council about forty-eight hours after he had entered the Massachusetts Senate. In the face of the united opposition of his own party he voted for an eleven-million-dollar appropriation to carry out the treaty acquiring Louisiana.[139] In similar opposition to all the other Federalist senators, on November 24, 1807, he submitted and voted for a bill a section of which forbade British vessels from entering American harbors and waters except when they were in distress, in retreat from the dangers of the sea, or when in the public service.[140] How irritating it was to ardent Federalists to be told by him that, although there might be some question of the expediency of Jefferson's Non-importation Act, it should be supported as long as the responsible Executive branch deemed it necessary.[141] He determined to be guilty of the "inexpiable offense" of adhering to his own principles.[142] He preferred that to what he described as the complete absence of "candor, consistency, or even decency, in the spirit of party," that he thought had become characteristic of all parties in which personal ambition was supplanting principled opposition.[143] "But if our country has exhibited a new example of the instability of popular sentiments, the giddy habitations of the vulgar heart, it has still more forcibly proved to me the difficulty, as well as the

[138] To Thomas Boylston Adams, Berlin, December 20, 1800, *Writings*, II, 487.

[139] Quincy, *op. cit.*, pp. 30–31. Adams, "Letter to the Federalists of the United States, Philadelphia, August 20, 1828." *The Conduct of John Quincy Adams considered in his relations, political and moral, towards the Federal Party*, p. 21.

[140] Adams, "Letter to the Federalists of the United States, Philadelphia, August 20, 1828." *The Conduct of John Quincy Adams considered in his relations, political and moral, towards the Federal Party*, pp. 36–37. "Towards the close of his senatorial term he recorded, in reminiscence, that he had more often voted with the administration than with the opposition [his own party]." Morse, *op. cit.*, p. 35.

[141] To Joseph Hall, Washington, December 11, 1807, *Writings*, III, 165.

[142] *Memoirs*, December 31, 1804, I, 282–283.

[143] To Peter Paul Francis De Grand, Paris, April 28, 1815, *Writings*, V, 315. "As far as I know myself, the motives of my public conduct have always been pure and disinterested." To Skelton Jones, Boston, April 17, 1809, *ibid.*, III, 305.

duty, of maintaining oneself free from the shackles of dependence upon any party." [144]   He attempted to play the exciting game of politics in accordance with "rigid moral rules," a trial that would have vexed the temper of a man even more equable in disposition than Adams.[145]

From time to time outright necessity enjoined recognition of political expediency and party discipline.   When he was appointed Secretary of State, he admonished himself to recall constantly that he must consistently collaborate with his cabinet colleagues, that his position would remain "subordinate" to the requirements of the Administration.[146]   Secret and perpetual hostility of a member of an administration against its designs and projects in favor of a party opposition could not be endured.   This belief was a recognition of the impact of party needs upon his principle.   On the other hand, this emphasis on administration solidarity was also in some measure reflective of a skepticism of parties.   On occasion he expressed the idea that the Executive *represented* the best expressions of principle, and the legislature "the small motives [natural to parties] which turn the balance of deliberation upon great national concerns." [147]   An administration might represent sound principles, whereas the legislature dominated by parties might represent simply an amalgam of partial interests.   He once wrote that there was, unfortunately, a "perpetual tendency" of all administrations to fall and of all parties to struggle to pull them down.[148]   Even an Administration of Mr. Jefferson, who had been the chief opponent of his father, he wagered, would "inflexibly pursue the same general system of policy which . . . [had previously been] established." [149] Herein he expressed a belief that a Jeffersonian Administration could follow the dictates of principles rather than political and

---

[144] To William Plumer, St. Petersburg, October 6, 1810, *ibid.*, III, 511.

[145] Morse, *op. cit.*, p. 209.

[146] To Abigail Adams, London, April 23, 1817, *Writings*, VI, 182.

[147] *Memoirs*, September 29, 1837, IX, 384.   On one occasion Adams claimed that he had asked his own Secretary of the Navy to appoint friends as midshipmen and had been refused on all occasions but one as far as he could recall.   This acceptance of the decision of a subordinate Secretary indicates his acceptance of principle before party in guiding an administration.   *Congressional Globe*, 27th Cong., 2nd sess., July 22, 1842, p. 778.

[148] *Memoirs*, July 28, 1818, IV, 120.

[149] To Joseph Pitcairn, The Hague, November 13, 1796, *Writings*, II, 42.

partisan opportunity. Writing to his mother he expressed a hope that the American people would some day entrust their foreign negotiations entirely to the executive, which would be free to keep secret or divulge information as its view of national interest dictated, unburdened by a partisan legislative demand to know everything.[150] His loyalty to an ideal of cohesion within the Executive indicated a recognition of the need for party solidarity at least in that branch and a belief that the Executive might more naturally than a legislature represent an impartial, principled force above the arena of party squabbling.

The "spoils" system was quite naturally an abomination in this perspective.[151]

There are offices merely ministerial and of a subordinate character, easily filled, and requiring labor rather than talents to be filled in the best manner. These are usually sought after as a means of subsistence, and they ought to be reserved exclusively for meritorious indigence. They may be *wanted,* but can never be desired.[152]

These offices, which he suggests should be filled on the basis of merit, he filled during the early part of his own Administration by appointment from all parties. Much earlier he had written to President Madison to suggest the appointment of Benjamin Pickman, a Federalist "of the most decided cast" and perfect integrity who would support the Madison Administration wherever his judgment permitted.[153] This suggestion was in keeping with his doctrine that the proper attitude of a President was neutrality toward all parties. During his own Administration he put up with the disadvantage of numerous opponents in the Administration, particularly in the customs. Detesting the "self-eulogium" and "importunities of office seekers," [154] he remained largely unresponsive to complaints that

---

150 To Abigail Adams, June 22, 1798, *ibid.,* II, 318.

151 Nevins, *The Diary of John Quincy Adams, 1794–1845,* p. 344, n. 2.

152 "Letters to my children," *Memoirs,* II, 15.

153 To the President (James Madison), Boston, April 30, 1809, *Writings,* III, 311–312.

154 *Memoirs,* April 7, 1827, VII, 255. "A place or a subscription is the object of all the *new* acquaintance that I make, and if I could satisfy the seekers of the first of these classes as easily as I can those of the second, they would not have so much reason to complain of my *vinegar aspect* as they do." To Louisa Catherine Adams, Washington, D. C., August 5, 1822, *Writings,* VII, 288.

he was not rewarding friends of his own Administration.[155]   Even relatives, for all their chagrin at being refused, would not be appointed to public office under him.[156]   No persons would be excluded by reason of divergence of political belief or for personal opposition to him.[157]   And he held with great consistency to this article of faith, even though he finally agreed that the application should stop short of indulgence of "open and continual disparagement of the Administration and its head." [158]   Evidence, however, of positive acts of hostility must be produced,[159] as well as of substantiated official or moral misconduct.[160]   His Postmaster General, McLean, on these conditions for a long time served masters both inside and outside the Administration.   He asserted that executive officers should serve at the pleasure of the Executive commissioning them, but such power should not be used for patronage purposes.[161]   According to these principles the practices of Jackson were deeply immoral.   "Editors of the foulest presses," [162] "violent partisans" [163] were swept into office.   Yet Adams supported that Administration on the French question, showing the ease with which he could rise above partisan loyalty and thrust party considerations aside.[164]   He also supported the following Administration, almost equally execrable, in its request for money to fit an exploring expedition to the South Seas despite the fact that the issue had become a party matter.[165]

Adams, however much he disliked them, finally saw that parties in the United States were inevitable, the product of human propensities, a diverse population, divergent sectional interests, institutional factors, religious dissensions, and the issue of slavery.   But he rejected parties in principle, for they lay athwart the obligations of

[155] *Memoirs,* May 5, 1827, VII, 268.

[156] *Ibid.,* December 6, 1817, IV, 27.

[157] *Ibid.,* January 21, 1825, VI, 474.

[158] *Ibid.,* May 13, 1825, p. 546.

[159] *Ibid.,* October 27, 1826, VII, 103–104.

[160] *Ibid.,* December 28, 1827, p. 390.   He later admitted that such principles accounted for his not being more "successful in his political life."   *Congressional Globe,* 24th Cong., 1st sess., appendix, p. 395.

[161] *Memoirs,* February 7, 1828, VII, 424–425.

[162] *Ibid.,* April 16, 1829, VIII, 138.

[163] *Ibid.,* April 27, 1829, VIII, 145.

[164] *Ibid.,* March 7, 1835, IX, 217.

[165] *Congressional Globe,* 24th Cong., 2nd sess., February 2, 1837, p. 151.

stewardship.[166] The people need not organize to realize true principle in policy and government. His concept of democracy was limited to the degree that he failed practically to accept parties as necessary to democratic politics.

MORAL PRINCIPLES DELIMITING AND DIRECTING GOVERNMENT

A discussion has been given heretofore of Adams's concept of a natural order governed by natural law and natural reason and of proper government confined and circumscribed by such a system. Here we shall consider the obligations imposed upon government. Quite naturally it was easier for Adams, as it was for all other such theorists, to generalize such a theory than to indicate precisely the results of its application. Such a moral system implies a system of values in which emotion inevitably plays a large part. In company with other eighteenth-century rationalists, Adams did not see that his moral system was largely his preferences dressed up in a philosophical garb.

Free government, in contrast with usurpation, was under an obligation, according to Adams's moral system, to safeguard the areas of freedom of groups and individuals. "The principles of liberty must . . . [not] be the sport of arbitrary power. . . ."[167] Government so confined would inevitably seek the goal of "eternal justice," which is the repository of true values.[168] In the last extremity government might act under the license of the law of self defense, but generally it must operate under "the genuine maxims of moral subordination," the latter a principle to which Adams consistently adhered, at least rhetorically, throughout his life.[169] Such "moral subordination" constrained government to give protection to all those whose allegiance it claimed. Perhaps relative happiness was all that government could achieve for men, but it must abstain from violating moral principles, such as those embodied in the law of nations, to escape the charge of being an usurping despotism.[170]

---

[166] Adams, *Parties in the United States,* p. 2.

[167] II "Publicola," *Writings,* I, 70–71.

[168] To Hyde de Neuville, State Department, Washington, D. C., July 28, 1821, *ibid.,* VII, 158.

[169] Adams, *July 4th Oration, 1793,* p. 20.

[170] *Congressional Globe,* 23rd Cong., 2nd sess., II, February 20, 1835, pp.

Government was not only a negative moral restraint upon the individual or groups of individuals, it was under a positive moral obligation to maintain the degree of equality necessary to the enjoyment of liberty.[171] Only under such conditions of equality could justice secure to every one "his own right." [172] These moral concepts were interwoven with his religious views. The idea of the present imperfection of justice was in keeping with his acceptance of a future state of retribution.[173] If this were the only life, there was no room for a moral system operating upon governments or men, for then adherence to a moral system would produce no significant result. But since Adams believed almost unfalteringly in an afterlife, he subscribed to a universal moral system. Justice, deriving from this moral system, must guide governments in both domestic and foreign policy.[174] Even the most important component of war was the desire and search for justice.[175]

274–275: Adams denied the Federal government's right to set up an Indian territory, for, according to the law of nations by which relations with the Indians were governed, the Indians had self-government and to modify it was despotic.

[171] Adams, *Cincinnati Oration*, pp. 13–14.

[172] Adams, *Argument in United States v. Cinque* [15 Peters 518], p. 4.

[173] *Memoirs*, August 16, 1811, II, 297.

[174] To Joseph Hall, October 9, 1796, *Writings*, I, 33, n. In relations to a controversy with France on the matter of American commercial policy, he wrote, "No objection on the ground of natural justice or general policy has been, or it is believed can be alleged." Memorandum sent to Hyde de Neuville, State Department, Washington, D. C., April 26, 1821, *ibid.*, VII, 102–103.

[175] To Thomas Boylston Adams, St. Petersburg, July 31, 1811, *ibid.*, IV, 162.

11

The Institutionalizing of Political Power

I consulted also Leland's Demosthenes for the sentiment that abuses of government are usually discovered by impulses of private enmity; which is as true in these days as it was at Athens in her oratorical days.

MEMOIRS, *March 8, 1834*

Before presenting Adams's conceptions of the institutions and theories of American government—the subject of the next chapter—we will state in this chapter his general views of the institutions and forms and constitutions of government, as distinguished from the principles that should control government with which we have just dealt.

In the beginning of his career, when he was battling the protagonists of the French Revolution, John Quincy Adams showed great impatience with prolific paper constitution writers. This was a normal role for the young Federalist bitterly opposed to the tactics and ideals of the opposition to his father's Administration. He derided the fame of "the *Great* Sieyès," who had just produced a new constitution, describing the document as the work of a "prodigy of genius" who made complex arrangements more complex by adding a fourth legislative chamber.[1] New constitutions, on the contrary, must respond to the political understanding and ethos of a people in order to operate effectively. In the same temper he wrote that the ancient constitution of Holland, even though it might

[1] To John Adams, The Hague, August 31, 1795, *Writings*, I, 400–401.

protect anachronistic privileges and arrangements and contain a lack of internal logic, conceivably might produce more prosperity and liberty than could a new constitution.[2] In the "Letters of Publicola" in which he attacked Paine and defended the political order of Britain and the United States, he contradicted Paine's formalistic interpretation of Rousseau's principle requiring the unanimous consent of all members of the community to the constitution of government. Adams observed "that its [this principle's] operation would annihilate in an instant, all the power of the National Assembly [in France], and turn the whole body of the American Constitutions, the pride of man, the glory of the human understanding, into a mass of tyrannical and unfounded usurpations." [3] American constitutions, state and national, were based upon customary and conventional limitations of popular political rights and were "therefore" theoretically sound and preferable to the rationalistic constitutional devices of the French constitution-makers. Twenty-five years later, however, by which time he had become Secretary of State, the spokesman for an American system that he saw as the real enemy of outmoded European political usurpation, he wrote in great praise of a new "constitutional government" for Spain, meaning, by that phrase, government based upon a written constitution.[4] By this time he conceived of the American revolutionary spirit, rather than French revolutionary excess, as the real enemy of tyranny.[5] He bewailed Spain's loss of her new constitution under the attack of French armies that were re-establishing "bigotry and despotic sway." [6]

Of course, it is true that Adams was inescapably a champion of written constitutions when they represented true principle, but by the nature of his political philosophy he found the origins of government and civil society not only in historic social compacts (written constitutions) but in those relationships that are established whenever two men come into association. He did not subscribe to the

---

[2] To John Adams, The Hague, April 1, 1795, *ibid.*, I, 312–313.

[3] III "Publicola," *ibid.*, p. 76.

[4] To Don Francisco Dionisio Vivés, Washington, D. C., June 18, 1820, *Writings*, VII, 41.

[5] To Richard C. Anderson, State Department, Washington, D. C., May 27, 1823, *ibid.*, pp. 466–467.

[6] National Archives, Records of the Department of State, *Diplomatic Instructions, All Countries*, IX, 188.

artificial idea of a "state of nature." Adams took an amazingly
modern, sociological view of the origin of constitutional political
arrangements.[7]   "Paper constitutions" might mean something in the
United States, but for Europe "they are something like the Baltimore
schooners, which they say European sailors can not manage to
navigate." [8] He wrote that the British really had a constitution,
which they should not abolish merely because it could not be found
in written form.[9] The American Constitution was unique in being
written, but the ridiculous conclusion to be drawn from Paine's principles was that no nation had had a constitution before 1776,
whereas, in truth, there had been constitutions for centuries before
that time.[10] Speculating about constitutions during his Silesian
journey, he wrote,

By the word constitution, I do not here understand what commonly goes
by that name in our country.   The supreme power in this, as in other
Prussian provinces, is in the hands of a single person: it is a simple
monarchy; but it is governed by permanent laws, with regular forms;
and the various classes of inhabitants have privileges which every king,
upon receiving their homage, promises to protect and maintain.[11]

Regular forms, permanent laws, and existing privileges were of the
essence of a constitution.

No, Sir, the Constitution of a country is not the paper or parchment upon
which the compact is written, it is the system of fundamental law, by
which the people have consented to be governed, which is always sup-
posed to be impressed upon the mind of every individual, and of which
the written or printed copies are nothing more than the evidence.[12]

The fundamental principles of Britain's constitution were known
before Britons knew the "use of letters," and it was not necessary
to look for them "in a visible form." [13] A constitution, therefore,
in the broad sense could only be said not to exist where revolution,
as in France, had destroyed the basis of a community consensus.

[7] See Adams, *Report on Weights and Measures,* pp. 6–7.
[8] To William Eustis, Boston House, Ealing, August 31, 1815, *Writings,* V, 367.
[9] III "Publicola," *ibid.,* I, 75.   VI "Publicola," *ibid.,* p. 86.
[10] III "Publicola," *ibid.,* p. 74.
[11] Adams, *Letters on Silesia,* p. 338.
[12] III "Publicola," *Writings,* I, 75.
[13] VI "Publicola," *ibid.,* I, 86–88.

Nor could a fundamental and stable constitution be the product of a gratuitous donation of a king.[14] The community alone could create and maintain it. A constitution was, therefore, much broader than a written document; it was the political pattern according to which men lived in a community. In this respect Adams's position was a compromise between those of Locke and Rousseau. In the rationalist tradition, he emphasized those natural rights not created but confirmed by the social compact or constitution, but, at the same time he put great store in the continuing life of the community, which historically and organically created constitutional processes and rights.

With regard to the general form of constitutional dispensation which he preferred, there can be no doubt that John Quincy Adams was a devoted republican. In view of his devotion to his father, who influenced him strongly, the question of his relative attitudes toward republicanism and monarchy should be given consideration. The charge was often seriously made that John Adams had monarchical proclivities and there are, at least, textual reasons for so assuming.[15] Similar charges were made against the son, especially against the author of the "Letters of Publicola," [16] and in the first year of Adams's Presidency William Wirt, his Attorney General, warned him that his research on monarchies would be decried as a preference for that form of government.[17] But the following extract from a poem of John Quincy Adams genuinely states his attitude toward monarchy:

> Charles, seated upon all his thrones,
> With all his crowns upon his head,
> Built piles on piles of human bones,
> As if he meant to reign the sovereign of the dead.
> He kept the world in uproar forty years,
> And waded on bloody oceans through;
> Feasted on widows' and on orphans' tears,
> And cities sacked, and millions slew.

[14] Adams, *Eulogy on Lafayette*, p. 23.
[15] John Adams, *Works*, VI, 250–251. See also J. Mark Jacobson, *The Development of American Political Thought* (New York: The Century Co., 1932), p. 188.
[16] *Writings*, I, 66 n.
[17] *Memoirs*, November 28, 1825, VII, 65.

And all the pranks of conquering heroes play'd,
A master workman at the loyal trade,
The recipe approved time out of mind,
To win the hearts of all mankind.[18]

He denied that he or his father had monarchical preferences.[19] Filmer's theory of monarchical power was merely "plausible," not genuine.[20] In his earliest youth he expressed amazement that imbecilic, wicked kings could be supported merely because their fathers had been kings.[21]   International politics under monarchies too often became the product merely of a "sovereign's wanton ambition and lust of conquest." [22]   He pictured the trend to empire and hereditary titles under Napoleon as the turning of a terrible tragedy into a ridiculous "farce." [23]   Monarchy had a "natural propensity . . . toward arbitrary power." [24]   Adams did admire Alexander I of Russia, although he grew suspicious of that ruler's motives toward the end of his reign, but that admiration must be considered the reaction of a patriotic American who found in the Russian sovereign the only major friend of the United States in Europe during a critical juncture of our history.   But throughout his life he consistently remarked "the irremediable vices" of monarchy, which must give way eventually before growing democracy.[25]

Adams stated that the American Revolution was "essentially antimonarchical." [26]   This spirit, he thought, imbued the American system and must at all costs be maintained in both North and South

---

[18] Adams, "Charles the Fifth's Clocks," *Poems of Religion and Society,* pp. 32–33.

[19] IX "Publicola," *Writings,* I, 108.   To Thomas Boylston Adams, Boston, August 27, 1802, *ibid.,* III, 6.

[20] Adams, *The Social Compact,* p. 24.

[21] To Abigail Adams, The Hague, July 23, 1783, *Writings,* I, 9: this was his reaction to Christian VII of Denmark; he remarked what he thought was the stupid preference for the son in the direct line in France who might be a fool, in place of a brother who might be a "wise and good prince."   *Memoirs,* March 27, 1785, I, 15–16.   He wrote with contempt of the rude, illiterate George II and the licentious Louis XV, both kings by the operation of hereditary law. Adams, *Eulogy on Lafayette,* p. 3.

[22] Adams, *Eulogy on Lafayette,* pp. 4–5.

[23] To Louisa Catherine Adams, Quincy, July 19, 1804, *Writings,* III, 43.

[24] Adams, *July 4th Oration, 1793,* p. 9.

[25] Adams, *Newburyport Oration, 1837,* p. 9.

[26] Adams, *Parties in the United States,* pp. 119–120.

America. As the Revolution receded into the past, he finally concluded, although under the immediate impact of the French Revolution he would not have been liable to emphasize the point, that the colonial spirit had been basically republican.[27] Washington was to be admired because he had not sought a throne.[28] Adams, in his commencement address given at the time of his graduation from Harvard, had shown great preference for republicanism. He was a man of rather austere simplicity who took little delight in the company of nobility for its own sake, who found no reason for the "rational understanding to value" court ceremonial and "punctilio." [29] Adams's republican spirit underlay his "indignation against the relapses of Europe into the opposite principle of monkery and despotism." [30]

Irrespective of his opposition to despotism, Adams nevertheless accepted the necessity of an effective executive or leadership within the framework of the responsible, representative government in which he believed. In his younger years while he was closely associated with the Executive as an executive officer or supported the policy of the Executive, there was an emphasis in his thinking upon an independent, strong executive. Later, particularly after the end of his own Administration, when the Executive represented principles to which he was not able to subscribe, and after he began his long career in the House, Adams manifested much more suspicion of the executive power. Nevertheless these generalizations must be qualified, as they will be in the discussion below, wherein there will be an attempt to reflect the nature of Adams's view of executive power, and to render a valid judgment that can be based only on his references to such power throughout the course of his life.

Illustrating his early tendency to emphasize executive coordination and unity, shortly after his assignment to Holland he indicated pessimism about the success of a new French constitution partly because the executive therein was to consist of a Directory of five pre-

---

[27] Adams, *Quincy Oration, 1831*, p. 19.
[28] Adams, *The Jubilee of the Constitution*, p. 51.
[29] Quincy, *op. cit.*, pp. 47–48. *Memoirs*, May 17, 1811, II, 263; "Any court dress will answer the purpose just as well, and at any other place except at court either the uniform or the court dress would be as strange and as ludicrous as a Turkish caftan or a Roman toga." To Hugh Nelson, Washington, D. C., May 16, 1823, *Writings*, VII, 424.
[30] To John Adams, Washington, December 21, 1817, *Writings*, VI, 276.

sided over by each member alternately for three-month periods, to be without any veto power, and to be elected by the legislature.[31]   He was inclined always in fact to prefer energy in government, which the executive primarily could contribute.   As late as 1837 he found the emphasis on the strong executive to be an element of merit, theoretically if not politically practicable for the time, in the plan proposed to the constitutional convention by Alexander Hamilton.[32]   He wished to see the American Executive placed upon a level of dignity with European chiefs-of-state and he, therefore, praised Washington for insisting upon establishing the precedent that all foreign representatives should be referred initially to the Secretary of State.[33]   It was natural to emphasize this strong executive in the context of the French Revolution, since, although he sympathized with the French desire to rid themselves of arbitrary power in a single individual, an exaggerated sacrifice of such power might commit the land "to the custody of a lawless and desperate rabble." [34]   When he became more intimately associated with an administration, as Secretary of State, he wrote, "By our Constitution the Chief Magistrate is the first guardian of the public morals. . . ." [35]   This reference to "public morals," of course, is surely Adams of the early phase and assigns a positive role to the chief magistracy in accomplishing what, according to Adams's political metaphysics of the time, was the primary goal of government.

At the time of Shays's rebellion, he wrote that there had "appeared in the councils [of Massachusetts] a degree of timidity and irresolution, which does no honor to the executive power of a commonwealth." [36]   The rebellion occurred before the French Revolution but even before that Revolution he is to be found in the main in the ranks of the conservative defenders of the social order who became the

---

[31] To John Adams, The Hague, July 27, 1795, *Writings*, I, 383.   Reporting the rumor of a project to substitute a "directory" for the President of the United States, he objected on the ground of its weakening effect.   To John Adams, London, April 4, 1796, *ibid.*, I, 486.   "But if it be contended as a principle, that the President ought not to take any important step without consulting the other officers of government . . . I cannot admit it. . . . Such a system in effect would make our executive a Directory of five or six persons, and the President of the United States would be merely the President of a Council."   To Joseph Hall, Berlin, November 19, 1799, *ibid.*, VII, 441.

[32] *Memoirs*, April 3, 1837, IX, 345.

[33] Adams, *The Jubilee of the Constitution*, pp. 79–80.

[34] V "Publicola," *Writings*, I, 83.

[35] *Memoirs*, December 2, 1819, IV, 457–458.

[36] To Abigail Adams, December 30, 1786, *Writings*, I, 28.

architects of the Constitution. In his old age he wrote that there had been a regrettable anti-Federalist suspicion of Washington and executive power in the politics of the immediate post-1789 period. At the same time he contended that the executive power had been primarily responsible for the accomplishments in foreign affairs during Washington's Administration.[37] With respect to the executive power in foreign affairs—a field that he always tended to emphasize—when Jackson took Pensacola he stressed the point that the executive power could authorize "defensive acts of hostility." [38] The management of the affairs of foreign policy, requiring the "utmost secrecy and despatch," should naturally be "appropriated to the executive department" of government and often kept from the scrutiny of the legislature, particularly in the stages of negotiation.[39] In that connection he had pointed out an effort of a minority in the House of Representatives to "usurp upon the executive functions" in the realm of foreign policy in an attempt to direct our policy in support of revolutionary France.[40] This effort was part of a campaign that he later noted, using a peculiar term of particular importance here, to alienate the people of the United States "from their executive government." [41] Here he seems, in fact, to equate the idea of government with the executive. He condemned the opposition, particularly the anti-Federalists, from whom he was then far apart politically, for siding with the French in their attempts to alienate the American people from the "system of the Executive." [42] This same party was unwisely opposed to the increase of our naval establishment out of fear that it might "strengthen the Executive, an object of great terror to them." [43]

In diplomatic instructions to Albert Gallatin in 1820 Adams criticized the habit of Congressional committees to consult "the Executive

[37] Adams, *The Jubilee of the Constitution,* pp. 87–88.

[38] *Memoirs,* July 15, 1818, IV, 108: this was a euphemistic reference to Jackson's entry into Spanish territory.

[39] V "Publicola," *Writings,* I, 105–106. To Abigail Adams, June 22, 1798, *ibid.,* II, 318.

[40] To John Adams, The Hague, December 30, 1796, *ibid.,* II, 67.

[41] To the Secretary of State (Timothy Pickering), The Hague, February 1, 1797, *ibid.,* p. 99. A few weeks later he described with disfavor "the principal purposes for which they [the French] are now undertaking to negotiate *with* the House of Representatives *against* the *Executive* of the United States." To John Adams, The Hague, February 23, 1797, *ibid.,* p. 131.

[42] To John Adams, The Hague, January 14, 1797, *ibid.,* II, 82–83.

[43] To William Vans Murray, Berlin, April 11, 1798, *ibid.,* p. 273.

. . . [and then follow] their own ideas." [44]   The same year, while he
was an executive officer, he asserted that the Congress was constantly
encroaching upon the "powers and authorities of the President." [45]
He even went so far as to express regret that the Congress had been
given power to declare war, holding with Montesquieu that such a
declaration was naturally an executive act.[46]   The power of recognizing other governments was likewise a normal executive function that
should not be weakened by making Congress a party to it.   This attitude was a normal reaction for a Secretary of State.[47]   Adams ridiculed individuals who fancied themselves guardians "of the liberties
of the people against Executive encroachment." [48]

But there was a carry-over of this concern for executive power into
the period of his membership in the House.   The Senate was declared
mistaken in adding to an appropriation bill an amendment that was an
unconstitutional assertion that the President could not appoint diplomatic officers during a recess without its consent.[49]   On the occasion
of the Constitutional Jubilee he significantly pointed out that the executive powers were more general and extensive than the legislative
powers, which were enumerated.[50]   Even in his years of political opposition as a member of the House he supported this undefined executive power in its right to independent use of the secret fund,[51] and he
agreed that such an undefined executive power was probably necessary in politically turbulent France to "curb the impetuosities of the
people" of that country.[52]

Political irritations and opposition could impel him to attack the executive, mainly during the period following his Presidency when he
had become identified with the legislature and was in opposition in
principle and in practical politics to the contemporary Administrations.   He suggested unfavorably that the Whigs seemed to be losing

[44] National Archives, Records of the Department of State, *Diplomatic Instructions,* All Countries, IX, 44.

[45] *Memoirs,* January 8, 1820, IV, 497.

[46] *Ibid.,* December 30, 1817, p. 32.

[47] *Ibid.,* January 2, 1819, p. 206.

[48] *Ibid.,* February 16, 1821, V, 281.

[49] *Congressional Globe,* 23rd Cong., 2nd sess., II, March 3, 1835, pp. 326, 328:
it was the duty, he asserted, of the House to protect the executive branch against
encroachment.

[50] Adams, *The Jubilee of the Constitution,* pp. 70–71.

[51] *Congressional Globe,* 29th Cong., 1st sess., April 13, 1846, pp. 640–642.

[52] Adams, *Eulogy on Lafayette,* p. 17.

their opposition to executive power and might just as well exchange places with the Democrats.[53]   In 1842 he criticized the President for collecting taxes without authorization.[54]   Objecting to a reference to a letter in a House resolution, he said it would show a tendency to cower before the President.[55]   He opposed a measure reducing the tenure of territorial officials on the grounds that it would increase executive power and influence,[56] and he described the Jacksonian campaign against the Bank of the United States as executive tyranny.[57] Despite the fact that he was opposed generally to constitutional amendments, he held himself prepared to support such an amendment to reduce to a majority the number of votes necessary to override a presidential veto, and said he regretted that there existed a veto power.[58]   During these later years of his life, as well, he often vigorously asserted the right of the legislature to insist upon the transmission by the executive of papers needed or desired by the legislature. We can see that his criticisms of executive power were specific criticisms, not general in nature as were his assertions of executive power that he made earlier, and to a lesser extent later, in his career.   His criticisms were politically induced, and not so much the product of his system of political values, which in the main would strengthen and support executive leadership.   The one important example of his criticism of executive encroachment in his earlier career came in connection with his opposition to giving the President power to govern newly acquired Louisiana, but the real objection in that case was much broader and, in any event, manifested opposition to an Administration with which he was, as yet, far from sympathetic.

It is not necessary or warranted to discuss Adams's conception of legislative power in terms of its relationship to executive power, for that has been accomplished in the preceding pages.   At this point it is important to indicate substantively his conception of representative and legislative power.   In his early career he indicated "the *essential* principle upon which the representation of the people in the legisla-

[53] *Congressional Globe,* 27th Cong., 1st sess., June 1, 1841, p. 9.
[54] *Ibid.,* 27th Cong., 2nd sess., p. 788.
[55] *Register of Debates,* 22nd Cong., 1st sess., III, July 9, 1832, p. 3883.
[56] *Congressional Globe,* 25th Cong., 3rd sess., February 19, 1839, p. 177.
[57] *Register of Debates,* 23rd Cong., 1st sess., III, April 4, 1834, pp. 3477–3511.
[58] *Congressional Globe,* 27th Cong., 2nd sess., August 17, 1842, pp. 906–907: Adams's stand was not unexpected, since the veto had killed a provisional tariff measure that he had supported. *Ibid.,* p. 717.

ture is to be grounded." The principle was that no "Freeman" should be bound except with his own consent. In the absence of the physical possibility of every person's giving his own consent, voting by representation was invented, at best an "artificial democracy" in view of the varying and diverse motives that unescapably bear upon the representative.[59]

Adams's theory of representation held that the representative possessed a *"personal* trust" by which many authorized one to express their sentiments upon measures projected for the community. The very fact of representation, in addition to the necessity of determining representation by majority rather than unanimity and the existence of suffrage qualifications, constituted a qualification upon "natural democracy." [60] Adams stressed strongly that no one could be degraded by filling the role of the representative.

But, despite that assertion and the principle that legislatures represented the consent of the governed, he subscribed to a principle of divided legislative power to prevent legislative tyranny. Of a French constitutional experiment, he wrote, "The Legislative power, all concentrated in a single Assembly, was an incongruity still more glaring." [61] The early state constitutions contained as their worst error the tendency toward the establishment of unicameralism, based, he asserted, on a desire for simple arrangements and a prejudice against British bicameralism.[62] Experience, in fact, had shown the wisdom of bicameralism, as an almost immutable principle. Although as a young man contending with Paine, the champion of the French Revolution, he found nothing abhorrent in the fact that the British people had granted "their whole collective [constituent] power" to a legislature,[63] in his older years, when revolution became less odious to him and democracy more acceptable as a force resistant to tyranny whether executive or legislative, he rejected the idea of locating a *"jura summi imperii"* in a legislature.[64] His democracy, of course, was individualistic and required safeguards against the tyranny even of a legislature, which might represent merely the conjunction of a group of special interests. One means of preventing such a con-

[59] VIII "Publicola," *Writings,* I, 97–98.
[60] *Loc. cit.*
[61] Adams, *Eulogy on Lafayette,* p. 19.
[62] Adams, *Quincy Oration, 1831,* pp. 27–28.
[63] III "Publicola," *Writings,* I, 75.
[64] Adams, *Quincy Oration, 1831,* pp. 12–14.

junction of interests and forces was bicameralism. The importance of this safeguard had been illustrated in the trial of the impeachment against Samuel Chase, when the Senate checked "the impetuous violence of the House of Representatives." [65] The violation of fundamental political principles must be prevented at all costs, regardless of the source of violation.

The judicial power was for Adams a means, most important in the American system, of limiting the power of government, of protecting private and individual rights. He viewed with dismay the attempts, particularly of Giles, to impose a doctrine limiting the independence of the judiciary and asserting an unlimited right of the House of Representatives to impeach judges and of the Senate to try them.[66] At this juncture his Federalism was not yet completely impaired and he stood with his Federalist colleagues in opposition to Anti-Federalist assaults upon the judiciary as the shield of the Federalist system. In fact, changed political sentiments, alignments, or conditions did not alter his view of the function of the judicial power. At the time of Marshall's death, an encomium of the great Chief Justice set down in his diary avowed that Marshall had been a major defense against divisive Jeffersonian influences.[67]

Occasionally the exigencies of particular political events or situations pressed him to regard the judiciary as inadequate to meet a situation. In the expulsion case of Senator John Smith, he asserted "that the power of expelling a member [of Congress] must, in its nature, be discretionary, and in its exercise always more summary than the tardy process of judicial tribunals." [68] Later he decried the tendency of the judiciary "in the majority of cases to produce by inevitable necessity the sacrifice of substantial *justice* either to mere forms or to general rules." [69] A few years later, discussing with the Attorney-General the acquittal of a pirate in a trial at Baltimore, he said that he

[65] *Memoirs,* March 3, 1805, I, 370–371.

[66] *Ibid.,* December 21, 1804, I, 322, 324. *Ibid.,* March 3, 1805, pp. 370–371.

[67] *Ibid.,* July 10, 1835, IX, 243.

[68] "Report on Senator John Smith," *Writings,* III, 175. *Annals of Congress,* 10th Cong., 1st sess., I, December 31, 1807, p. 56 *passim.*

[69] To John Adams, St. Petersburg, July 21, 1811, *Writings,* IV, 145–146: Herein he wrote that he entertained heretical principles (not to the author's knowledge very fully expounded) with regard to the Common Law and its merits, to some degree revealed in his report on John Smith in the Senate, the popular reaction to which, he said, showed he could not win the people.

thought it was based upon "law logic—an artificial system of reasoning, exclusively used in Courts of justice, but good for nothing anywhere else." Although truth and justice were the end of human reasoning, in the courts the end was law. "Ita lex scripta est, and there is no reply." [70]

As to another manner of distributing and restraining power, there was more question in Adams's mind, for it did not always so much prevent tyrannical government as it often permitted sectional interests to obstruct. Very shortly after the establishment of the new general government, he became worried about the divisive effects of federalism. "It appears to me that the hostile character of our general and particular governments each against the other is increasing with accelerated rapidity." [71] Federalism, however, constituted a "nice and delicate interstructure," [72] but his theory, because he denied the necessity of the existence of the "*Jura summa imperii*," denied that federalism implied contradictory powers in establishing several governments over the same territory. [73] In Holland, when he was the bitter foe of the French Revolution, he indicated that he preferred even "a tyrannical, aristocratical, federal despotism" to a "rights-of-man government," indicating, however, that he looked upon federalism, despite his fears, as a defense against the tyranny of a government with all power in a single set of organs. [74] He hoped the Dutch would resist the French example of "totally dissolving every principle of federalism," for there was more safety under a "heterogeneous system." [75]

In supporting the separation of Maine from Massachusetts, Adams pointed out that the "objects of administration to which the state governments are generally confined may best be superintended by authorities encompassed within small local divisions." [76] In his day the vast number of social problems were neighborhood problems, and

---

[70] *Memoirs*, May 26, 1819, IV, 372–373: Daniels, the alleged pirate, had been indicted under an Act of Congress designed to preserve the neutrality of the United States in which Adams, at the time Secretary of State, was keenly interested.

[71] To John Adams, Newburyport, April 5, 1790, *Writings*, I, 50–51.

[72] II "Columbus," *ibid.*, p. 157.

[73] To the Secretary of State, July 17, 1796, *ibid.*, II, 13–14, n. 1.

[74] To William Branch, The Hague, November 29, 1796, *ibid.*, pp. 51–53.

[75] To John Adams, The Hague, November 25, 1796, *ibid.*, p. 47.

[76] To Joseph Hall, Ealing, near London, August 7, 1816, *ibid.*, VI, 65.

that fact combined with the adventitious existence of separate states in America and his theory of limited power made it reasonable to support the federal system.   Such a system accommodated the "adverse interests of soil, climate, and modes of domestic life." [77]   Still the system of the Articles of Confederation, which the Constitution supplanted, had suffered from "the mortifying inefficiency of the merely federative principle." [78]   It becomes clear that he supported a nice balance between unitary government, which he warned he did not think would succeed in the newly founded state of Columbia,[79] and the "merely federative" government of the Articles.   As President, even though he subscribed to the federal principle, he proposed to be President of the whole nation,[80] a nation empowered through its government to improve "its own condition by internal improvement." [81] With that premise in mind, it is logical to turn at this point to a discussion of Adams's views and ideas of American government.   The present chapter has indicated that Adams's system was essentially a system of balance between extremes of power and limitations, governmental scope and circumscription, political order and private right, executive leadership and legislative and judicial checks.   The American system that he supported in moments of optimism he conceived of as in high degree a model embodiment of these principles.

[77] Adams, "Inaugural Message," *in* Richardson, *op. cit.,* II, 297.
[78] Adams, *Lives of James Madison and James Monroe,* p. 19.
[79] National Archives, Records of the Department of State, *Diplomatic Instructions,* All Countries, IX, 284.
[80] *Memoirs,* May 1, 1824, VI, 313.
[81] To James Lloyd, Washington, D. C., October 1, 1822, *Writings,* VII, 311–313.

PART FIVE

The United States: Man's Greatest Political Accomplishment

12

The Constitution and the Union

"And all constitutional government is a compact."
—Memoirs, *February 16, 1833*

At this point we may logically begin a discussion of the Adams theory and concepts of American government. These ideas have been forecast in the preceding general theoretical analyses. There will of necessity exist some overlapping of generalization with previous discussions. It would be worth while to devote considerable space to direct exposition of and speculation concerning the origins and sources of his theories of American government, but, because we are mainly concerned with Adams's own writings and pronouncements, we are hampered by his failure to deal directly with the origins of his thought. We may reasonably assume that such questions are not customarily clear to the theorist himself, but may be more easily seen by those of a later day who can view a thinker in the whole perspective of his times. Wherever possible, therefore, these sources of his thought and this perspective will be indicated. Nevertheless the conditions of the subject matter require that a beginning be made with Adams's views of the American Revolution, the significance of the Declaration of Independence, the interim period of the Articles of Confederation, and the culmination of the struggle for political stability in the architectonic triumph, the Constitution. These views should be seen against the Colonial background, when it is relevant.

THE AMERICAN REVOLUTION

Adams, throughout his life, but particularly in his later years when the fires of the French Revolution had much subsided and his fears of social chaos with them, stressed the uniqueness and significance of the American Revolution.   This latter Revolution was first distinguished as the effort of freemen to defeat tyranny rather than the enslaved to throw off a yoke.[1]   Adams thus did not underrate the background of British liberties but claimed that the American Revolution was the means of transmitting to Europe, as a course of social action based on a theory of those liberties, a guiding body of principles to people who would be free.   The French learned from it, for example, that consent was the only true basis of government.   "The magic talisman of despotism was broken, the spell of prescriptive tyranny was dissolved, and the pompous pageant of their monarchy, instantaneously crumbled to atoms."[2]   Even during the very course of the French Revolution he wrote that, although he abhorred European disorder, "feudal absurdity has received an irrevocable wound. . . ."[3]   And later, although he persisted in charging that there was a distinction between the "inflammatory principles" of the French Revolution and the American, he agreed that he had modified his harsh opinions with regard to the former and thus found it easier to assert the stimulus to it of the American example.[4]   But the American revolutionary struggle remained the more pure and correct from the standpoint of principle,[5] and he even asserted that the events initiated in 1775 were different in nature from the revolts of the Spanish colonies, although the mutual struggle for independence was against similar forces of oppression.[6]

ORIGINS OF THE CONSTITUTION

As he grew older he came to dramatize the Revolution as the young Federalist would never have done: In his speech on the *Jubilee* he

[1] Adams, *July 4th Oration, 1793*, p. 17. In Adams's view, fifty years after the event, the American Revolution was stimulating revolutions against "all the ancient governments."   To Charles Jared Ingersoll, Washington, D. C., June 19, 1823, *Writings*, VII, 488.   Adams, *Letter Read at the Recent Celebration of West India Emancipation in Bangor* (*Me.*), p. 2.

[2] Adams, *July 4th Oration, 1793*, pp. 18–19.

[3] *Ibid.*, p. 19.

[4] Adams, To the Freeholders of Washington, Wythe, Grayson, Russell, Tazewell, Lee and Scott Counties, Virginia, *Writings*, VII, 337–338.

[5] To Friedrich Gentz, Berlin, June 16, 1800, *ibid.*, II, 463: there is no evidence that he ever abandoned the concept of the American Revolution as the paragon of revolutions, in many ways distinct from the French in principle, a point that he made in this letter.

[6] National Archives, Records of the Department of State, *Diplomatic Instructions, All Countries*, IX, 273–276.

wrote, "Resistance, instantaneous, unconcerted, sympathetic, inflexible resistance like an electric shock startled and roused the people of all the English colonies on this continent." [7] The Revolution had resulted in the "greatest enlargement of individual liberty with the most perfect preservation of public order. . . ." [8] Never before had the contest been more thoroughly drawn between the rights of people and authority. The Revolution, he asserted, had broad implications of principle from the beginning, in the minds of the leaders who undertook it. [9] The continuing tie of colonial subjection was incompatible with the existing capacity of the American colonies to protect themselves; the separation was in the moral order of things. [10] In this assertion he went beyond claiming that the Revolution had been precipitated by Britain's violation of stated principles. The Revolution would have happened in any event on the basis of moral necessity. This statement demonstrates that the theorist who is at the same time active in politics, only building a theoretical system as he reacts to events often widely separated in time, will justify the turn of these events at different times on the basis of different, even contradictory, fields of reference. Adams as a young man naturally justified breaking ties with Britain on the ground that Britain violated principles of the compact. Adams as the Secretary of State justified the Revolution in a more absolutist fashion as the inevitable course of destiny of the colonial peoples. Developed nationalism underlay the Secretary's assertion. [11] Of course the confusion was never resolved nor recognized by Adams. In 1831 and 1837 he proclaimed that the British Parliament's assertion of absolute power was the cause of the colonists' defection, thus implying that if the Parliament had restrained itself that defection would not have appeared. [12] In fact, on

[7] Adams, *The Jubilee of the Constitution,* p. 8.

[8] Adams, *Eulogy on Lafayette,* pp. 5–6.

[9] Adams, *Lives of James Madison and James Monroe,* pp. 12–13.

[10] Adams, *July 4th Oration, 1821,* p. 12. Adams, *Newburyport Oration, 1837,* p. 17.

[11] It is interesting to note in Soviet philosophy the growing assertion of absolutist concepts since the revolution has become established. Revolutionaries before they achieve power support the dispensation they propose to bring into being as an improvement upon the order they propose to disestablish. That is to say, their rationale is relative, and they may refer to the projected dispensation as transitional. Once the revolution is accomplished, there is an inevitable tendency to defend the goals accomplished absolutely in terms of their intrinsic validity.

[12] Adams, *Quincy Oration, 1831,* pp. 14–15. Adams, *Newburyport Oration, 1837,* p. 8.

the latter date, he pointed out that "the separation itself was a painful and distressing event; a measure resorted to by your forefathers with extreme reluctance, and justified by them, in their own eyes, only as a dictate of necessity.—They had gloried in the name of Britons. It was a passport of honour throughout the civilized world." [13] We had been driven to assert "unalienable right" against "unalienable allegiance."

The Declaration of Independence looms especially large in this theory.   Although it was a completely novel document, it was the fulfillment of the same motives that had led to the colonization. [14] On all appropriate occasions Adams asserted the principles of the Declaration in his contest with his political enemies.   At the time of presenting a memorial from Boston citizens calling for the removal of the national capital to the North, where the principles of the "Declaration of Independence . . . [were] not treated as a mere rhetorical flourish," he moved for reference to a select committee with instructions to consider and report on the powers of the national government to cede the District of Columbia to the states. [15] The Declaration had declared the truths of the Christian religion to be "self-evident," and its author, Thomas Jefferson, had stated doctrines that must spell the end of slavery and slaveholding. [16] If the slaveholders' doctrines were true, then the Declaration was a spurious instrument. [17] Adams said the slaveholders would hang an abolitionist with the temerity to utter in the South a part of the Declaration. [18] The principles of the instrument were a formidable political weapon in Adams's hands.

Adams held, in effect, that the Declaration was as much a part of the public law of the land as the Constitution, that it had established the proper relations among the states in the federal relationship, that the Constitution was the final fruition of the political evolution set in motion by the Declaration.   In defense of his clients, the Africans,

[13] Adams, *Newburyport Oration, 1837,* p. 10.

[14] Adams, *July 4th Oration, 1793,* p. 7.

[15] *Congressional Globe,* 25th Cong., 3rd sess., January 7, 1839, p. 99.

[16] *Memoirs,* December 27, 1819, IV, 492.

[17] Adams, "Letter to the Citizens of the United States, whose Petitions, Memorials and Remonstrances, have been entrusted to me, to be presented to the House of Representatives of the United States, at the third session of the 25th Congress," Quincy, May 21, 1839, Letter II.

[18] *Memoirs,* February 14, 1838, IX, 497.

in the case of the *Amistad,* before the Supreme Court, he relied on the Declaration of Independence, in the absence of statutes, constitutions, codes, treaties relating to the case; in reality the Declaration was the "Law of Nature and of Nature's God" and had been imported into the Constitution.[19]   The Declaration was a social compact "by which the whole people convenanted with each citizen of the United Colonies," to which union was as vital a principle as freedom or independence.[20]   From the hour of its issuance none of the states parties to it could withdraw from the "primitive compact," nor secede from association with the rest, for, while declared "united, free and independent," they were not declared sovereign as separate entities.[21] For a state to assert such sovereignty would violate the compact of a whole people.[22]   "Their union [in fact] preceded [and was not separable from] their independence. . . ."[23]   This interpretation could be derived from the language of the document;—it was especially noted that the colonies were not referred to by name or in terms of number.   They had in fact announced their constituents as a single people to the world.[24]   The people and not the states had covenanted to be the source of power;[25] no colony could have maintained itself in

[19] Adams, *Argument in the United States v. Cinque* [15 Peters 518], p. 9. Adams, *Newburyport Oration, 1837,* p. 19.

[20] Adams, *Quincy Oration, 1831,* p. 18.

[21] *Loc. cit.*   Different rhetoric on another occasion might seem to qualify these assertions: "The Declaration of Independence annulled the national character of the American people.   That character had been common to them all as subjects of one and the same sovereign, and that sovereign was a king."   Yet the real point is made clear as he continues, "The dissolution of that tie was pronounced by one act common to them all, and it left them as members of distinct communities in the relations towards each other, bound only by the obligations of the law of nature and of the Union, by which they had renounced their connexion with the mother country."   The essential bond of the "Union" remains here; but a degree of ambiguity is introduced by the reference to loss of "national character" and "distinct communities."   Adams, *The Lives of James Madison and James Monroe,* p. 15.   Similar ambiguity may be found elsewhere.   For example, he asserted that the Declaration had the effect of assuming for each of the colonies "the rights of a sovereign and independent community."   Adams, *Parties in the United States,* p. 3.   But in the same context he wrote that the document had changed the nature of the Union and made it permanent.   *Ibid.,* p. 2.   These statements are unquestionably rhetorical ambiguities.   The important fact is the assertion of the permanence of the Union.

[22] Adams, *Quincy Oration, 1831,* p. 18.

[23] *Ibid.,* pp. 6–7.

[24] *Loc. cit.*   Adams, *Newburyport Oration, 1837,* pp. 6, 16.

[25] Adams, *Newburyport Oration, 1837,* p. 15.

a claim to a right to secede.[26]   The Declaration had in fact been an announcement to the world of the foundations of government of the American people.[27]   The Constitution in turn embodied the principles of the Declaration of Independence.[28]   Adams showed no suspicion, as did later, more sophisticated students, that the Declaration and Constitution represented different forces in American society, revolutionary, in the first instance, and conservative, in the second. To him, both documents reflected basic characteristics of republican virtue.

The Articles of Confederation, on the other hand, represented an unnatural deviation from the principle that the Revolution had resulted in the establishment of a new and distinct, separate sovereignty encompassing all the colonies.[29]   In the course of the formulation of the Articles by the men who had enunciated the Declaration, the latter had been weakened, and thus the Articles constituted an attempt to modify the Union through the continuation of which alone the Declaration was understandable.[30]   The Articles gave liberty to sectionalism.[31]   They in fact symbolized the error of Blackstone's fatal fallacy of unlimited sovereignty, in this case presumed to reside in the separate states acting through their governments and enabled thereby to nullify the acts of the others states acting collectively.[32]   The failure of the Articles demonstrated the inadequacy of the principle of state sovereignty.   They represented an unauthorized intrusion by the state legislatures upon the power of the people, an attempt on the part of the states rather than the whole people to delegate to Congress.[33]   The result was merely a league of states, not in the main line of development, rather than a government as anticipated by the Declaration; [34] a diplomatic assembly, imbecile in nature, rather than

[26] Adams, *Newburyport Oration, 1837*, p. 11.

[27] Adams, *The Jubilee of the Constitution*, p. 12.

[28] *Ibid.*, p. 54.

[29] *Memoirs*, September 14, 1815, III, 257.   Adams, *The Jubilee of the Constitution*, p. 17.

[30] Adams, *Newburyport Oration, 1837*, pp. 34, 35, 43.

[31] *Ibid.*, p. 33.

[32] Adams, *Quincy Oration, 1831*, p. 23: this development of the doctrine with regard to the Articles appeared at the time of the controversy over nullification as propounded in the South, and as such constitutes an *a posteriori* assertion to meet a new political problem.

[33] Adams, *The Jubilee of the Constitution*, pp. 20, 23.

[34] Adams, *Parties in the United States*, pp. 120–121.   He stated a fear that

an effective Union.[35]   There was constituted during the operation of the Articles a conflict between the "party of the People" and "the party of the States." [36]   The result was humiliation and the appearance of great turmoil out of which finally came a "national Constitution" made by the people "in their original character," [37] a Constitution to consummate the work begun by the Declaration.[38]   Against the background of this theory, Adams's general and particular views of the United States Constitution may be outlined, a theory of nationalism and potent, albeit limited, government.

Although he was thought by some to be uncomfortably "Federal" in 1788,[39] until his father influenced him to become a protagonist of the new instrument of government, Adams records that he was thought by other associates of the time to be an "anti-federalist." [40] There is little doubt that the latter was the case, for Judge Cranch many years later showed him three of his youthful letters opposing the Constitution.[41]   He became, of course, a great champion of the instrument of government, interpreted strictly in the Adams sense. There were times of great doubt in his mind as to its survival value, times when the exigencies of the political contest evoked from him contradictory affirmations with respect to basic provisions.   In the course of a long political life complete consistency would have been a miracle.   The inconsistencies exist, but they do not conflict with the general climate of Adams's thought.

THE CONSTITUTION

His thinking on constitutional problems was sophisticated and rationalistic in the spirit of his times.   He believed that the Constitution could be understood only in terms of the theories of government under the auspices of which it had its birth.[42]   And, language being

---

Jackson was moving back to the imbecility of the ineffective dispensation of the Articles. *Memoirs,* January 30, 1831, VIII, 304.

[35] Adams, *Parties in the United States,* p. 5.

[36] Adams, *Newburyport Oration, 1837,* p. 37.

[37] IV "Publicola," *Writings,* I, 79–80.

[38] Adams, *The Jubilee of the Constitution,* p. 40.

[39] Adams, *Life in a New England Town,* April 25, 1788, p. 128.

[40] *Ibid.,* February 7, 1788, p. 93.

[41] *Memoirs,* July 9, 1827, VII, 307: He said it gave him "a lesson of humility and forbearance."

[42] Adams, *The Jubilee of the Constitution,* p. 61.

imperfect, the "extent of powers conferred . . . must in a very great degree depend upon the construction which it [the Constitution] received." [43]   Although, therefore, he recognized the importance of glosses on the instrument, the Constitution at the same time he considered a great culmination that rescued the nation from the "atrophy" into which it had fallen under the Articles, as well as a great beginning.[44]   There was an authoritative constitutional law that antedated the Constitutional document, as, for example, the law upholding the right of petition, which the Constitution confirmed but did not create.[45]   The document represented a great social compact embodying recognition of valid principles implicit in nature and known by nature's God, and nullification of its doctrines by sectional interests could only be in violation of those authoritative principles and productive of the same strife that was bringing trials to other lands.

The American Union thus inaugurated was "a moral person in the family of Nations," [46] which had as a great fundamental principle a balance of interests.[47]   The Constitution embodied the principles of the Declaration of Independence and thus balanced, one against the other, the fundamental rights of man, the sovereignty of the people, the rule of right and wrong, and responsibility of the supreme ruler of the Universe for the rightful use of power.[48]   With a typical eighteenth-century concept of right, justice, and natural law Adams came to see the Constitution as the source of any principle compatible with his system and as the instrument needed to withstand any impending threat.   A "charter of limited powers," [49] it set the government of the United States off from those other governments constitutionally enabled to act "gubernativamente." [50]   Moreover, on the basis of sound interpretations of Marshall, the Constitution rightfully restrained "the corporate action of States claiming to be Sovereign

[43] Adams, *Parties in the United States,* pp. 10–11.

[44] Adams, *The Jubilee of the Constitution,* p. 11.

[45] *Congressional Globe,* 27th Cong., 2nd sess., January 28, 1842, p. 192.

[46] Tatum, "Ten Unpublished Letters of John Quincy Adams, 1796–1837," pp. 382–383.

[47] To John Adams, St. Petersburg, June 25, 1811, *Writings,* IV, 120–121: the son ascribed the balance to the inspiration of the father.

[48] Adams, *The Jubilee of the Constitution,* p. 54.

[49] Adams, "First Annual Message," *in* Richardson, *ed., A Compilation of the Messages and Papers of the Presidents, 1789–1897,* II, 315–316.

[50] Adams, *Argument in United States v. Cinque* [15 Peters 518], p. 80.

and Independent." [51]   Particularly in opposition to the Southern States'-rights slavocracy, Adams insisted that the Constitution stood as a defense of the "constituent sovereignty of the people" as opposed to the "derivative sovereignty of the states." [52]   It represented a concentration of popular power at the center.   Since the powers under the Constitution were derived from the people, with a Lockean emphasis Adams insisted they could not be delegated by the government to the states.   Thus there existed a great moral bond between the people and the moral entity, the nation, which they had created, a moral bond that could be maintained only by the "heart" and not by "constraint." [53]

Of course, Adams did not worship the Constitution to the point of being unable to point out any defects in it.   Athough he might sanctimoniously state on occasion that "he had a general prejudice against any alteration of an instrument [the Constitution] that he regarded in so solemn and so sacred a light," [54] when the political controversy demanded it, he might bewail the "circumlocutions" in the document, or the "fig leaves under which these parts of the body politic [slaves and slavery] are decently concealed." [55]   Noting discriminations against colored citizens in Missouri, he counseled a denial—which would surely have been of questionable constitutionality—of rights in Massachusetts to white citizens of Missouri.[56] Despite his professed worship of the Constitution, he pointed out the limitations inherent in it that made, in his eyes, the Missouri Compromise the only available solution and he was willing to conclude that the Union and the Constitution could founder on no better issue than slavery.[57]   On another occasion as he went into embittered old age and the slavery issue exacerbated his view of all else, he charged that the Constitution was no safeguard against

[51] Adams, *Lives of James Madison and James Monroe*, p. 34.

[52] Adams, *The Jubilee of the Constitution*, p. 45.

[53] *Ibid.*, p. 69.

[54] *Congressional Globe*, 27th Cong., 2nd sess., August 17, 1842, p. 906.

[55] Adams, *Argument in United States v. Cinque* [15 Peters 518], p. 39.

[56] Quincy, *Memoirs of the Life of John Quincy Adams*, pp. 112–113.   *Memoirs*, November 29, 1820, V, 209–210.

[57] *Memoirs*, March 3, 1820, V, 12.   Adams, of course, could contemplate civil war and dissolution of the Union only as a prelude to its re-establishment on a sounder basis without the decaying influence of slavery.

our "sinking into a military monarchy." [58]   He had admitted that, under the Constitution, slaves escaping into states where slavery did not exist must be restored to their masters on demand, an admission that offended every principle of his general theory.[59]

THE UNION

The Union, an absolutely essential condition underlying our independence theoretically and practically, achieved its essential expression in the establishment of the Constitution.   An analysis of the Union and vicissitudes of its growth as observed by Adams from its constitutional establishment to the close of his political life is important.   His political orientations and goals and controversies are controlling in the analysis. The decline of his optimism concerning the future of the Union was especially noteworthy, a decline deriving from his fears concerning the disruptive effects of the slavery issue and party battles.   The following analysis, in order to show this transformation, will be chronological in approach, will not be so much a statement of a theory of national union as a developing reaction to the American political problem.

In the beginning, Adams noted, union came more easily because of the homogenous nature, racially and culturally, of the American community,[60] although he asserted that even in 1787 there were singular diversities of section, of economic interest, "of opinions, of manners, of habits and even of extraction" that made the framers somewhat discouraged about their capacity to create a single political entity.[61]   Yet from the earliest moment of the experiment, once he had concluded that union was a real culmination of the political evolutionary process, he stressed the importance of union and conciliation in the face of divisive commercial and agricultural opinion.   He resented foreigners' speaking in terms of "Virginians, the Southern people, the Democrats" rather than Americans.[62]   The nation would take "gigantic strides" toward greatness on the basis of national union.[63]   Foreign governments unfortunately, he sus-

[58] *Memoirs*, February 19, 1845, XII, 171.
[59] To Edward Perkins, London, April 6, 1816, *Writings*, VI, 1.
[60] Adams, *Parties in the United States*, p. 1.
[61] Adams, *Lives of James Madison and James Monroe*, p. 32.
[62] *Memoirs*, December 1, 1795, I, 142.
[63] To Charles Adams, The Hague, June 9, 1796, *Writings*, I, 494.

pected, founded their policy upon the project of dividing agricultural from commercial interests in the American community.[64] In the face of such threats he expressed the fervent hope that the value of union would appeal to the American people as an obstacle to the strength of factions. On the one hand he took hope in the fact that Thomas Jefferson, a political enemy then fighting against the elder Adams, expressed faith in the union.[65] On the other, John Quincy feared that the "unabated virulence" of factional controversy would blind his compatriots to the advantages of their political association and unity.[66] Although his father's defeat evoked the reaction of a temporarily reduced confidence in the future of the Constitution and the Union, he did not then really doubt the value of union in meeting external dangers and internecine strife.[67]

Adams condemned the demands of his fellow citizens of Massachusetts for resistance to the foreign policy of Jefferson, demands that the people and legislatures of the commercial states resist the Embargo. He reported with scorn that he had proof of the plans of such factions and sectional interests for insurrection against the national government.[68] In this period, the latter part of the first decade of the nineteenth century, he said independence and union were the foundation stones of his political creed. On the other hand, the Federalists had not only planned with "fanaticism" projects of disunion, they had "linked . . . their cause with Old England and her fortunes. . . ." [69] Elections and politics in Massachusetts and the fortunes of his former party were of great interest to him, for the success of that party presented the possibility of

[64] To John Adams, The Hague, August 13, 1796, *ibid.*, II, 24.

[65] To John Adams, The Hague, April 30, 1797, *ibid.*, p. 160.

[66] To Thomas Boylston Adams, Berlin, December 3, 1800, *ibid.*, II, 485.

[67] To Thomas Boylston Adams, February 14, 1801, *ibid.*, p. 501.

[68] To Ezekiel Bacon, Boston, November 17, 1808, *ibid.*, III, 250–251. To Abigail Adams, St. Petersburg, June 30, 1811, *ibid.*, IV, 127: The Federalists "seem so resolute for a little experiment upon the *energy* of the Union and its government. . . ." Adams, "Letters to Messers. H. G. Otis, Israil Thorndike, T. H. Perkins, William Prescott, Daniel Sargent, John Lowell, William Sullivan, Charles Jackson, Warren Dutton, Benjamin Peckman, Henry Cabot, C. C. Parsons and Franklin Dexter, Washington, D. C., December 30, 1828," *Correspondence between John Quincy Adams Esquire, President of the United States, and Several Citizens of Massachusetts concerning the Charge of a Design to Dissolve the Union, alleged to have existed in that State*, pp. 17, 20.

[69] To Joseph Hall, St. Petersburg, August 15/27, 1810, *Writings*, III, 473–474. To William Plumer, St. Petersburg, October 6, 1810, *ibid.*, p. 508.

numerous "petty clans and tribes at eternal war with one another," whereas its failure meant the possibility of a great populous nation dominating the continent.[70] The success of the "little and narrow" Federalist projects would be achieved, he wrote, only through a civil war, resulting in either many governmental forms and disunion or a "*military* and *arbitrary*" government under "a Jeroboam, Julius Caesar, a Cromwell, or some such ferocious animal."[71] Far better would it be for the American experiment to be defeated in united defense of "Union and glory, than to triumph in . . . [a condition] of dismemberment, disgrace and impotence."[72] The extent of his rejection of the Federalists was revealed when he wrote to Eustis that "you and I know full well that if Beelzebub had a plenipotentiary at Washington who should complain of ill treatment from the American government, the federalists of the Hartford Convention crew would cheer him and cry encore to his complai ts."[73]

The Federalists were a source of worry, but he never believed that they threatened disunion as an active, practical fact in the degree that later issues and political developments seemed to drive toward disunion, viz., "—the bank; the currency; the internal improvement question; the extension or repression of slavery; the conflicting ambition of the great States of New York and Virginia. . . ."[74] But more important, in moments of despair, Adams came to think of disunion as an alternative perhaps preferable to solutions on these matters contrary to his principles.[75] Indeed, on occasions when the course of events went contrary to his own beliefs, Adams expressed doubt concerning the value of the Union devoted to the protection of principles that he considered invalid. As he left the Presidency he felt that his failures came in large degree because of popular rejection of the principles upon which was based his own great loyalty to the Union. Jefferson birthday dinners witnessed toasts to anti-tariff forces and nullification. He

[70] To Abigail Adams, St. Petersburg, June 30, 1811, *Writings*, IV, 128.

[71] To John Adams, St. Petersburg, October 31, 1811, *ibid.*, p. 266. To John Adams, St. Petersburg, July 13, 1812, *ibid.*, pp. 369–370.

[72] To Alexander Hill Everett, Ghent, July 16, 1814, *ibid.*, V, 62–64.

[73] To William Eustis, Ealing, March 29, 1816, *ibid.*, V, 547.

[74] *Memoirs*, January 1, 1820, IV, 495.

[75] *Ibid.*, February 24, 1820, p. 531. *Ibid.*, March 2, 1820, V, 2, 3, 4. *Ibid.*, March 3, 1820, p. 12.

came to think of disunity as an inevitable vice of "confederacies." [76] He tried to stem this disruptive pressure by lecturing against nullification, and, following his Presidency, he emphatically expounded the nationalist interpretation of the Constitution.[77] He battled the Southern opponents of a protective tariff who held that such a tariff would lead to the dissolution of the Union,[78] and he himself implied that Northern forces would reject union at the price of sacrificing their economic interests.[79] In his mind prostration of the North under the attack of the "nullifiers of the South and the land-robbers of the West" assisted by unneutral national administrations threatened national unity.[80] He was growingly convinced that a Union half free and half slave was impossible.[81] The encompassing swirl of party politics, always distasteful to him, created a deep pessimism concerning the future of the united nation.

GOVERNMENT UNDER THE CONSTITUTION

Adams believed that the government created by the Constitution had "the great and transcendental objects of all legitimate government." [82] It is important to stress that he saw with the inauguration of this government the opening of a new era in the science of government and the history of mankind.[83] Although in bleaker moments he might have doubts, in the main he held that the Constitution provided a government designed to hold a tremendous and disparate union together.[84] The constitutional government of the United States was established after the people had recovered from their suspicions of strong government *per se* and had determined to fulfill the promise of the Declaration. Yet it

[76] *Ibid.,* March 12, 1831, VIII, 343.

[77] Adams, *Quincy Oration, 1831, passim.* Adams, *Newburyport Oration, 1837, passim.* Adams, *The Jubilee of the Constitution, passim.*

[78] *Register of Debates,* 22nd Cong., 1st sess., III, June 25, 1832, p. 3735.

[79] *Ibid.,* 22nd Cong., 2nd sess., II, February 4, 1833, pp. 1609–1610.

[80] *Memoirs,* December 5, 1832, VIII, 503.

[81] *Ibid.,* December 24, 1832, p. 510.

[82] Adams, *The Jubilee of the Constitution,* p. 48.

[83] Adams, *Lives of James Madison and James Monroe,* p. 15. He also emphasized that the American system was in its inception essentially extra-European. To Henry Middleton, State Department, Washington, D. C., July 5, 1820, *Writings,* VII, 49.

[84] *Memoirs,* October 10, 1815, III, 271.

was not a government that could rule by fiat; it was a government of laws.[85]   Being a government of laws, it had as its basic duty the definition of the rights and duties of citizens and the avoidance of departures from its principled course under the influence of popular fears and considerations of private interest.[86]   In such a light his expressed preference to be known as a constitutionalist rather than a democrat is understandable.   As a constitutionalist he looked upon the governmental system of the United States as compounded of many elements and forces, which the "phantom of universal suffrage" could not change.[87]   He declared that "this institution [the Constitution] was republican, and even democratic [when first established]," yet the order of the adjectives is significant and the emphasis upon democracy seems somewhat grudging.[88]

Adams did not stress democracy in this theoretical structure, but, rather, accented the constitutional complications of confederacy, heterogeneous population, and balance of powers.[89]   He realized that the real strength lay in the people's attachment to the system.[90]   Of course Adams, by the nature of his system, had great faith that the attachment of the people could only be founded upon the basis of popular respect for principle.   The realization of principle had resulted in a government for the United States as competent as any other "to all the purposes of restraint or of punishment, upon that enterprise which by transgressing . . . [the] laws [of the nation], would usurp upon the rights of others." [91]

It is necessary and relevant, therefore, to inspect Adams's views of the competence of the government of the United States, particularly the federal government, in terms of power to accomplish valid social and political ends.   On this subject, too, his point of view

[85] Adams, *Argument in the United States v. Cinque* [15 Peters 518], pp. 15, 38, 63, 80.

[86] Adams, "A Message to the House of Representatives, March 15, 1826," *in* Richardson, *op. cit.*, II, 339.

[87] Adams, *The Social Compact*, p. 31.

[88] Adams, *The Jubilee of the Constitution*, p. 53.

[89] *Ibid.*, p. 115.   Adams, "Speech delivered at Northbridgewater, on Wednesday, November 6, 1811," *Boston Courier*, November 11, 1844.

[90] To John Adams, London, September 19, 1797, *Writings*, II, 210.

[91] To Pierre De Poletica, State Department, Washington, D. C., April 24, 1822, *Writings*, VII, 246: Of course, Adams is here representing the United States' institutions to a foreign representative, but there is no doubt that this assertion represents his view of American government.

evolved, and that evolution must be outlined. Moreover, the impact of the political struggle must be considered wherever it is obvious. However, we must avoid assertions with regard to John Quincy Adams's thought that do not take into account the whole of that thought, the contradictions, the qualifications, and the reservations: for example, such generalizations as that of W. Hardy Wickwar, that "he [John Quincy Adams] did not believe that written constitutions should be superior to statute law." [92] Such a conclusion would appear to be warranted on the basis of the "Letters of Publicola" alone, a polemical attack upon Thomas Paine as the major protagonist of the French Revolution, but a review of the whole of Adams's writings will prove at the very least that the "Letters" must be read in the whole qualifying context of Adams's life and letters.

Adams clearly feared the emergence of a despotical government in the United States, an eventuality particularly to be feared if the Union grew too large under slaveholder influence.[93] He did not, however, view the Constitution as an obstacle to the accomplishment of important purposes. He derided the opponents of Jackson's actions in Florida who cried out for the defense of "the sacred Palladium of the Constitution." [94] Moreover, he held that the Constitution and the rights it conferred had not followed Jackson into Florida to protect American citizens from military power, for, he asserted that Jackson was the only effective power in Florida at the time, and that this power would have been weakened or destroyed by a blanket application of the Constitution.[95] But with these qualifying cautions in mind it is possible to maintain, Wickwar to the contrary notwithstanding, that Adams did conceive of the Constitution as a superior law not to be violated by statutory enactment. On certain occasions he made the definite point that his opposition to legislative measures derived from his view that they were un-

[92] W. Hardy Wickwar, "Foundations of American Conservatism," *The American Political Science Review*, XLI (December, 1947), p. 1109, n. 10.

[93] Adams, *The New England Confederacy of MDCXLIII*, p. 6. *Memoirs*, June 16, 1844, XII, 57.

[94] To John Adams, Washington, D. C., February 14, 1819, *Writings*, VI, 529.

[95] *Memoirs*, October 24, 1821, V, 369, 370, 372: Adams was an official defender of Jackson's career in Florida. He admitted that he had to work hard to create the latter's defense, but his argument on this occasion sheds significant light on his conception of constitutional power.

constitutional, as when he opposed a measure to set up an Indian territory.[96] In further support of his view of the superior law, Adams contended for a view of treaties as the supreme law of the land, so to be interpreted by the courts.[97] He went so far as to contend that the abstract theory of our system held that conformity with unconstitutional laws—that is, laws violating the superior law—was not required, that a citizen might resist their application.[98]

At to the extent of the power that had been granted under the Constitution as a superior law, on one occasion he held that the treaty-making power was unlimited,[99] thus seeming to admit that, should the medium of the treaty power be used, there was nothing that government might not do under it. If this had been his unqualified conclusion, he would then have been admitting the substance of unqualified power while denying it in theory. But such is not a proper conclusion. A few days later he adamantly contended that the government of the United States was not empowered even to make a treaty to extend our penal statutes beyond our borders to be applied in mixed courts of the United States and of foreign sovereigns for the suppression of the slave trade.[100] There were constitutional rights guaranteed to our citizens that could not be made subject to such tribunals and possibly violated thereby.[101] The Constitution of the United States had reserved decision con-

---

[96] *Congressional Globe*, 23rd Cong., 2nd sess., II, February 20, 1835, pp. 274–275: He asserted that relations with the Indians were regulated by the law of nations, by which they had self-government, to interfere with which would be despotic and antirepublican.

[97] To Don Luis De Onis, State Department, Washington, D. C., October 31, 1818, *Writings*, VI, 461. *Memoirs*, October 30, 1818, IV, 151. National Archives, Records of the Department of State, *Diplomatic Instructions, All Countries*, X, 216–218.

[98] Adams, "Letter to Messers. H. G. Otis, Israil Thorndike, T. H. Perkins, William Prescott, Daniel Sargent, John Lowell, William Sullivan, Charles Jackson, Warren Dutton, Benjamin Peckman, Henry Cabot, C. C. Parsons and Franklin Dexter, Washington, D. C., December 30, 1828," *Correspondence between John Quincy Adams Esquire, President of the United States, and Several Citizens of Massachusetts concerning the Charge of a Design to Dissolve the Union, alleged to have existed in that State*, p. 18.

[99] *Memoirs*, October 30, 1818, IV, 151.

[100] To Albert Gallatin and Richard Rush, State Department, Washington, D. C., November 2, 1818, *Writings*, VI, 470.

[101] To Stratford Canning, State Department, Washington, D. C., December 30, 1820, *ibid.*, VII, 85–86.

cerning the guilt or innocence of United States citizens to their own country-men.[102]

As to whether the power to be derived from the Constitution had been explicitly granted or rendered by implication or construction, Adams's position was unquestionably ambiguous, and decades of explaining did not obviate this ambiguity. The stand he took on the purchase of Louisiana was in practical conflict with his position on the constructive powers he would have exercised to accomplish internal improvements. When it suited the argument he affirmed that he was inclined "always against the assumption by Congress of any power not clearly granted." [103] He asserted a limited view of Congressional power in his opposition to the exercise of an inquisitorial power by the Congress over the accounts and the pecuniary transactions of the Bank of the United States. In this connection he held that no power granted to Congress might be used for any purpose than that for which it was granted.[104]

He challenged General Smyth to indicate otherwise than by "construction" the power in the Constitution that had been exercised in the acquisition of Louisiana.[105] Once this assertion of power had been made, Adams decried the precedent as making it in the future much more difficult "to set any bounds to the powers of Congress." [106] Although he admitted that the treaty power had been constitutionally exercised with respect to Louisiana, he at the time denied that Congress could implement the treaty by governing and taxing the people of Louisiana because, among other reasons, the Constitution had not delegated such authority.[107] There was a constitutional "constructive" power to take the territory consequent upon the power to make the treaty, but there could be no power to annex the

[102] State Department, *Notes to Foreign Legations*, III, 142–143.

[103] Adams, To the Freeholders of Washington, Wythe, Grayson, Russell, Tazewell, Lee and Scott Counties, Virginia, *Writings*, VII, 347.

[104] *Register of Debates*, 22nd Cong., 1st sess., appendix, p. 55.

[105] Adams, To the Freeholders of Washington, Wythe, Grayson, Russell, Tazewell, Lee and Scott Counties, Virginia, *Writings*, VII, 345: He did not deny the existence of constructive powers, but denied their existence in this case on the ground that powers of a "transcendental nature" could not be assumed by construction.

[106] Adams, *Parties in the United States*, pp. 37–38.

[107] Notes on Speech on Motion, *Writings*, III, 30: Actually Adams went much farther to hold that the Constitution could not grant such power since it would have constituted a violation of basic natural rights of the people of Louisiana.

inhabitants, for no such "constructive" power to modify individual rights without consent could be delegated. Yet, despite the fact that Adams, in terms of a doctrine of natural rights, opposed at the time the exercise of power in the annexation of Louisiana, he did not deem himself a strict constructionist of the Jeffersonian or Madisonian school, which he declared to be mistaken and whose inconsistency in the Louisiana controversy he derided. He wrote that the same party of strict constructionists and States' rightists that opposed internal improvements and the Bank had acquired Louisiana and ruled it with a "rod of Spanish colonial despotism." [108]

Adams wrote that he accepted the precedent of Louisiana as establishing the doctrine that the necessary and proper clause might "be understood as unlimited." [109] He had opposed this doctrine until he recognized that the whole authority of the Union and tacit popular consent had established the precedent. Then, in a remarkable statement seeming to make a concession without really doing so, he added, "Since which time, so far as this precedent goes, and no farther, I have considered the question as irrevocably settled." [110] In other words, he accepted the accomplished fact, but not its full implication as a precedent; we have the paradoxical picture of Adams, the broad constructionist, opposing strict constructionists in their assertion of great power in the general government, a kind of assertion that he as an ardent nationalist habitually favored. This limitation of the precedent made it possible for him to oppose the annexation of Texas as an usurpation of power reserved to the people, although he distinguished the situation on the ground that in the instance of Texas there was involved the entire people of a foreign government. [111]

Nevertheless in support of those goals to which he politically

[108] Adams, *The Jubilee of the Constitution*, p. 110. *Memoirs*, October 20, 1821, V, 363–365: He pointed out that Madison had signed the Bank bill, thus further demonstrating inconsistency.

[109] Adams, "Letter to Messers. H. G. Otis, Israil Thorndike, T. H. Perkins, William Prescott, Daniel Sargent, John Lowell, William Sullivan, Charles Jackson, Warren Dutton, Benjamin Peckman, Henry Cabot, C. C. Parsons and Franklin Dexter, Washington, D. C., December 30, 1828," *Correspondence between John Quincy Adams Esquire, President of the United States, and Several Citizens of Massachusetts concerning the Charge of a Design to Dissolve the Union, alleged to have existed in that State*, pp. 19–20.

[110] *Ibid.*, pp. 19–20.

[111] *Memoirs*, June 15, 1838, X, 20.

subscribed he was a broad constructionist. He urged upon the Congress that the enumerated powers plus the necessary and proper clause were sufficient to promote "the improvement of agriculture, commerce, and manufactures, the cultivation and encouragement of the mechanic and of the elegant arts, the advancement of literature, and the progress of the sciences, ornamental and profound. . . ." [112] He thought the power to make roads and canals had been given by the Constitution. [113] While he was in the Monroe cabinet he had occasion to note his disagreement with those who asserted that there was no express or implied power in the Constitution that could be used to prohibit slavery in a territory. [114] Adams found such a power in the provision for "needful rules" that should apply to the people of territories as well as to the land. [115]

The fullest Adams statement concerning Congressional powers and constitutional interpretation was set forth in a "Letter to Andrew Stevenson, Speaker of the House of Representatives, July 11, 1832." [116] Therein, in defense of his stand on the tariff issue, he expressed regret that he should be unjustly charged with "latitudinarian doctrines upon questions relating to the extent of the powers of Congress under the Constitution of the United States." Yet he proceeded to assert that the power to impose tariffs for the protection of domestic industry proceeded from the power to tax "to provide for the common defence and general welfare." He agreed that, as Madison and others contended, there was no substantive grant contained in the purpose stated of providing "for the common defence and general welfare." The grant of power was in the preceding words, "The Congress shall have power to lay and collect taxes, duties, imposts, and excises, to pay the debts. . . ." Yet he doubted that the words stating purposes for which the government must provide were mere harmless words, auxiliary only to the preceding enumerated powers. However, the power to "provide for the common defence and general welfare" was not unlimited power, nor even the power to charter the Bank

[112] Adams, "First Annual Message," *in* Richardson, *op. cit.*, II, 315–316.
[113] *Memoirs*, December 14, 1825, VII, 80.
[114] *Ibid.*, March 2, 1820, V, 5.
[115] *Ibid.*, p. 6.
[116] John Quincy Adams, "Letter to Andrew Stevenson, Speaker of the House of Representatives, July 11, 1832," *Daily National Intelligencer*, July 12, 1832.

of the United States. The taxing power and this "injunction and exposition of purposes" he had deemed enough to authorize the acquisition of Louisiana by purchase but not enough to warrant the governing of the people of that territory. But, particularly following popular acceptance of the purchase of Louisiana, it had become impossible to contend that the words indicating purpose had a narrow and contracted meaning.[117] They had not been expanded as the basis of an indefinite and substantive power, but they became words efficacious in themselves. They were not granting words, however; they were limiting words confining power to the purpose of accomplishing the "common defence and the general welfare." [118] And if these words of purpose could serve as a basis for the acquisition of new territory, they could with equal or higher justice warrant a protective tariff. Moreover, he agreed with Madison that a protective tariff might be founded on the commerce power. In either case there would be the exercise of an implied or constructive power. The power to charter a bank was not contained in these words of purpose but was sufficiently to be found in others. Adams appears thus as a broad constructionist but one sufficiently wary to preserve ground upon which to oppose the accomplishment of purposes to which he did not subscribe.[119]

In further analyzing the powers available under the Constitution, Adams asserted a much more unique principle. He stated that in the event of a servile insurrection and war the Congress would acquire complete and unlimited control over "the whole subject of slavery even to the emancipation of all the slaves in the State where such insurrection should break out." [120] As long as the slave states

---

[117] Adams was here making use of the precedent of the exercise of power with respect to Louisiana for his own purposes in support of a protective tariff.

[118] It is hard to believe that Adams is not here straining his sense of humor, for it is difficult to discover any substantial difference between words that convey power and those that have an efficacious meaning. Moreover, these words as limiting words did not acquire that function on the basis of the Louisiana precedent. It is impossible to avoid the conclusion that Adams in attempting to blend the requirements of principle with those of politics has become hopelessly enmeshed in a semantic quagmire.

[119] It is not charged that he was consciously manipulating constitutional doctrine to suit his purposes, but one so thoroughly addicted to natural law doctrines usually found it easy to manipulate principle to support a practical position.

[120] Worthington C. Ford, *John Quincy Adams, His Connection with the Monroe Doctrine* (1823) and with Charles Francis Adams, *Emancipation under Mar-*

were capable of maintaining their internal order the institution of slavery might be safe, but, should they require assistance in putting down the slaves in an insurrection or civil war, the war power of Congress would come into operation and would be plenary.[121] In time of war, international or civil, the Congress could do anything with regard to slavery, subject to the rules and laws of nations.[122] Even in peace time, he reminded his hearers, Congress had abolished the external slave trade. He presumed the South to be in a "panic terror" at the thought of eventual emancipation by martial law. Adams, therefore, had a liberal view of the war power, and, moreover, he may be credited with the earliest vigorous support of the principle upon which the Emancipation Proclamation was based.[123]

As to the amending power, Wickwar is correct in pointing out that in "Letters of Publicola" Adams contended for a complete delegation of the amending power to the legislature and assumed that it had been so delegated in the cases of the American national government and some of the states.[124] But it is far from certain that Adams was making a forthright assertion of the importance of parliamentary supremacy, after the British pattern, in order to bolster conservative resistance to popular control. Adams subscribed to the concept of the Constitution as a superior law in

---

tial Law (*1819–1842*), [Reprinted from the Proceedings of the Massachusetts Historical Society for January, 1902]. (Cambridge: J. Wilson and Son, 1902), pp. 73, 83.

[121] *Ibid.*, pp. 76–77. *Congressional Globe*, 27th Cong., 1st sess., June 9, 1841, p. 38. On February 21, 1839, Adams proposed in the Congress the abolition of hereditary slavery after July 4, 1842, that all children born on and after that date should be free; that there should never more, with the exception of Florida, be admitted a state tolerating slavery; and that after July 4, 1848, the slave trade or slavery should not be tolerated in the District of Columbia. Quincy, *op. cit.*, p. 294.

[122] *Congressional Globe*, 24th Cong., 1st sess., appendix, pp. 447–450.

[123] Surprisingly, Adams denied that the British during the War of 1812 could emancipate American slaves as an act of war. Yet it would seem that the power to emancipate slaves would exist more clearly, from a practical and legal standpoint, as between nations at war than in a civil war. In the former case there existed no such clear-cut limitation in law on the act of a state. In the case of a civil war, Adams had to make use of a liberal interpretation of the war power to conclude that the constitutional safeguards of slavery could be modified under that power.

[124] III "Publicola," *Writings*, I, 77. VII "Publicola," *ibid.*, pp. 90–91, 93. Wickwar, *op. cit.*, p. 1109.

the United States, and this would have precluded his ascribing un-limited power to the legislature, as contrasted with the people. He pointed out that a nation, that is, the "people" as he understood that term, might reserve to itself such power as it thought proper. Moreover, although he did so grudgingly at this point in his life because he was alarmed by the French Revolution, he admitted in the "Letters" that a nation might change its form of government if that government became "incompetent for the purposes for which all Governments were instituted." [125] At this juncture the matter was a practical one for Adams, not a question of immutable con-stitutional principle. He was contending in those chaotic times for a safeguarding arrangement placing within the control of the legislature the right to change constitutions and removing this right from the people to a considerable degree in the interest of vigorous action in time of crisis, despite danger of abuse.[126] The danger of abuse could be, and had been, reduced in the United States by a proper distribution of powers. He came dangerously near to con-tradiction, if he is not absolutely contradictory, with respect to the United States when he held that the amending power had been completely delegated but the people retained a fundamental reserve power to alter the Constitution.[127] It is the dilemma of one caught in the necessity of having to justify the American revolutionary tra-dition and yet fearing the implications of French revolutionary violence. As to Wickwar's generalization that Adams did not be-lieve in a superior law of the Constitution, which would be removed in large degree from legislative tampering, it is notable that Adams later asserted that from the beginning he had been completely op-posed to any amendment to the original document.[128] In fact, on the basis of his concept of constitutional law as superior law or "the law of the land," superior to *"an act of the legislature,"* Adams in 1792 counseled the good people of Boston who were friends of the theater to disregard an act of the legislature prohibiting theatrical entertainments, and thus to act upon their own construc-tion of the Constitution of the state in preference to that of the legislature.[129]

[125] III "Publicola," *Writings*, I, 77.
[126] VII "Publicola," *ibid.*, pp. 90–91, 93–94.
[127] *Ibid.*, p. 91.
[128] *Congressional Globe*, 27th Cong., 2nd sess., August 17, 1842, pp. 906–907.
[129] "Menander," *Writings*, I, 127.

Furthermore, Adams's view of the role of the judiciary as a safeguard of the Constitution is directly related to the question of whether he believed in the Constitution as a superior law, placed it at the mercy of a sovereign legislature, or at the mercy of a sovereign people. Wickwar contends that Adams did not believe in a "superior law" doctrine, that, at least in the general context of the "Letters of Publicola," he did not contend for "judicial trusteeship" or judicial supremacy.[130] The latter conclusion may be true for that context, but as early as 1793 Adams was contending for the power of judicial supervision as if it unquestionably existed, pointing out that the chief magistrate's arbitrary acts should not be feared, "for if the construction [of the Constitution], upon which his measures were grounded, should be erroneous, they [the people] had provided a judiciary power, competent to correct his mistakes."[131] Of course, later he accepted the accomplished fact of judicial review as the means of protecting the superior law from both popular and legislative tampering as well.[132]

Adams did not underestimate the difficulty of preserving the Constitution as a clear-cut superior law, even though the judiciary possessed the power of review. He saw the difficulty of maintaining the standards of constitutionality based upon powers not expressly granted as contrasted with the relative ease of doing so with respect to powers expressly granted.[133] He had occasion to assert that an unconstitutional act was null and void, inapplicable, and unbinding.[134] On one occasion, in controversy with those in the House who submitted a resolution declaring that the general government had no power over slavery, he submitted a counter resolution declaring that, since Congress's powers were conferred by the Constitution, no resolution of the Congress could add to them or deduct from them.[135] This was unquestionably an assertion of the superiority of the Constitution to the power of the legislature. In

---

[130] Wickwar, *op. cit.*, p. 1109, n. 10.

[131] II "Columbus," *Columbian Centinel,* December 4, 1793, *Writings,* I, 151.

[132] Adams, "Inaugural Address," in Richardson, *op. cit.*, II, 294: "A coordinate department of the judiciary has expounded the Constitution and the laws, settling in harmonious coincidence with the legislative will numerous weighty questions of construction which the imperfection of human language had rendered unavoidable."

[133] Adams, *Parties in the United States,* p. 99.

[134] *Congressional Globe,* 25th Cong., 2nd sess., February 6, 1838, p. 162.

[135] *Ibid.*, 3rd sess., December 13, 1838, p. 31.

answer one may claim that Adams preached doctrines that he did not find embodied in the Constitution, but the record shows that Adams looked upon the Constitution as a paragon of correct principle. Wickwar is correct in assuming that Adams was in great measure a conservative, but he sought relief from popular threat in the safety of a superior constitution rather than in legislative supremacy. The "Letters of Publicola" were at most a deviation, or a temporary point of view elicited by a particular situation, and not representative of his long range position on the relationship of constitutional and statutory law.

13

The Institutions of American Government

*A sovereign who countenances such vices is no longer a sovereign.
It is a virtual abdication of his authority. He is a sovereign for
that very purpose, to maintain justice and morality; and to give his
sanction to falsehood and injustice is, in substance, ceasing to
reign.*

MEMOIRS, *April 20, 1812*

BALANCE AND SEPARATION OF POWERS

In Adams's theory, as we have seen, the Constitution was a definition of adequate power. The safeguard against its abuse was the
proper institutional distribution of powers, in the interest of a safe
balance of social forces. Bicameralism and the traditional separation of powers were the means. For example, he found a significant
reason for criticism of Siéyès in the latter's opposition to bicameralism.[1] Adams continued to fear situations where single powerful
assemblies could dominate "invisible executives." [2] In particular he
was critical of the trend in the new state constitutions, produced by
"the overruling ascendancy of popular supremacy," toward "governments with legislatures in single assemblies." [3] In France's early
revolutionary constitutions, he had found the concentration of legislative power in a single chamber to be more incongruous and threatening than an "hereditary royal executive." [4] He considered sub-

[1] To John Adams, The Hague, August 31, 1795, *Writings*, I, 402.
[2] To Alexander Hill Everett, Washington, D. C., October 15, 1817, *ibid.*, VI, 224–225.
[3] Adams, *Parties in the United States*, p. 5.
[4] Adams, *Eulogy on Lafayette*, p. 19.

sequent French revolutionary constitutions, embodying the idea of balance in an abandonment of unicameralism, an improvement over the earlier experiments. Broadening the use of the principle of balance to include the organization of social forces as well as institutional arrangements, in argument with Jeremy Bentham, he declared the balance in Britain among "monarchical, aristocratical, and democratical branches" was the application of a sound principle in the British constitution. Here Adams enlarged the principle of balance to imply more than bicameralism.[5] He preferred the more definite and general balance achieved through the separation that existed in the governmental system of the United States, a preference that was made obvious in the asperity with which he noted the British Prince Regent's inability to comprehend a government in which the executive did not sit in the legislature.[6] The fact that he had accepted the judgment typical of his day that there existed a kind of institutional separation of powers in Britain was, of course, revealed in his discussion with Bentham. In his mind the more precise and complete arrangement in our system was a refinement on the British system. On occasion he might express doubt concerning the efficacy of the balance, but those moments were rare; for the most part he believed that the American system was the greatest improvement upon all the other forms of polity that had existed among men, especially in its "cautious *distribution*" of powers.[7] It provided the necessary obstacles to the domination of "one man, or body of men, or any possible combination of individual interests," yet it stopped short of shackling government.[8]

As to the separation of powers, in large measure the means of accomplishing the balance, Adams's views were realistic. Recognizing that the three powers, executive, legislative, and judicial, blend into each other so that no one can see the exact dividing line, he saw practically that there would be occasional encroachments by one upon another.[9] Even more, although he thought that

[5] *Memoirs*, May 22, 1817, III, 537.

[6] *Ibid.*, May 14, 1817, p. 530.

[7] To James Lloyd, Washington, D. C., October 1, 1822, *Writings*, VII, 311: italics supplied.

[8] VII "Publicola," *ibid.*, I, 92–93.

[9] Adams, *The Jubilee of the Constitution*, pp. 61–62.

there were inconveniences that would derive from the sitting of executive officers in the legislature, he speculated that the absence of a medium of communication between the executive and the legislative was a defect in our Constitution that might be remedied by the executive's having a representative in Congress.[10] He wrote, in fact, that there was nothing in the Constitution to prevent the President himself from appearing before either House.[11]

Observing Monroe's lack of control over Congress, Adams asserted the need for liaison and cooperation between executive and legislature as well as for strong executive leadership.[12] On the basis of long executive experience, particularly in foreign affairs, he condemned the Senate's striking out an appropriation to pay for the President's recess appointment of a minister to France.[13] He consistently championed the right of a President, even a bitter political enemy, to make appointments during a recess. The President was the paramount power in foreign affairs, and only in extreme cases should the legislature use its power over supply to influence the executive in this sphere.[14] That principle should even preclude the legislature from appropriating an outfit for a representative to a country before the Executive had seen fit to make such an appointment.[15]

In another sphere, Adams declaimed against a bill proposing to reduce the salary of a territorial governor and superintendent of Indian affairs as the product of a spurious economy of those who railed against executive patronage and were content with "nibbling at the salaries of subordinate officers." [16] The members of Congress were criticized by Adams for suggesting a special session before it was known what the newly elected President, General Harrison, would, on the basis of his prerogative, desire to do, and for turning

[10] *Memoirs,* November 29, 1819, IV, 457.

[11] *Ibid.,* May 15, 1820, V, 119.

[12] *Register of Debates,* 22nd Cong., 1st sess., II, April 28, 1832, p. 2645: He asserted that the branches of government could function only by cooperation and mutual control; he recognized this need, but the history of his own Administration demonstrates that he, perhaps more than any other President, was ignorant of the means of accomplishing it.

[13] *Ibid.,* April 27, 1832, pp. 2627–2628.

[14] *Congressional Globe,* 27th Cong., 1st sess., August 27, 1841, p. 394.

[15] National Archives, Records of the Department of State, *Diplomatic Instructions,* All Countries, VIII, 185.

[16] *Memoirs,* June 6, 1838, X, 11.

themselves into cabinet makers who would dictate the Executive's appointments.[17] Adams even suggested that it would be time enough to discuss the question of a National Bank when the President (General Harrison) recommended the establishment of one to Congress.[18] In other words, Adams, while an adherent of a separation of powers as an obstacle to tyranny, did not assert the doctrine as a means of obstructing an effective executive, even though he might fulminate on occasion against the power-pretensions of a Jackson or a Van Buren.

On the other hand, there was no unrelieved sympathy for the Executive in his view of the relationship between the two powers. Wherein the matter had to do with a clearcut legislative right or prerogative, he would have the legislature stand its ground. For example, he opposed the premise, which underlay the choice of Cambreling as chairman of the Committee on Foreign Affairs in the House in place of Edward Everett,[19] that a committee chairman should be favorable to the Administration. Indeed, a committee might even give orders to one of the presidential secretaries, although not the President himself, a doctrine that would come close to a violation of the separation of powers.[20] He bitterly noted Jackson's arrogant retorts to Clay's request for a communication with the Cabinet concerning the removal of deposits from the United States Bank.[21] Asserting that the House of Representatives had the power to call for any paper that came to the Executive or was in his possession, Adams said that this power included that of requisitioning papers concerning a secret negotiation, if they were to form the basis of an impeachment,[22] Washington's decision in 1796 notwithstanding. In such cases the Congress's powers were the same as those of a court of justice.[23]

However, when Adams was himself the President, he resented

[17] *Congregational Globe*, 26th Cong., 2nd sess., February 4, 1841, p. 146.
[18] *Ibid.*, appendix, p. 323.
[19] *Congressional Globe*, 23rd Cong., 2nd sess., II, January 21, 1835, p. 150.
[20] *Register of Debates*, 22nd Cong., 2nd sess., I, January 19, 1833, p. 1134: It would be an advantage to know precisely the definition of this power of direction, but it was not offered. It is important to note that he would contemplate the exertion of such legislative control over the Executive.
[21] *Memoirs*, December 12, 1833, IX, 51.
[22] *Congressional Globe*, 27th Cong., 2nd sess., June 4, 1842, pp. 580–581.
[23] *Ibid.*, July 2, 1842, p. 712.

a request from the Senate for papers that required him to designate those particular papers that had a bearing on current negotiations and should therefore be kept secret. He argued that such designation was a matter of his opinion and that senatorial disagreement with his decision might result in the publication of all the papers he submitted and a violation of the rules on executive business.[24] Normally he was sympathetic toward the Executive, particularly in the foreign field, but even here he could come close to a challenge. For example, while a member of the House, he called for more information concerning the need for certain foreign missions before he could vote for appropriations therefor, and asserted that it was a settled principle that the House of Representatives could exercise an independent judgment as to such a need.[25] But recognizing, as he did, the vagaries of the lines of separation between the three powers and the practical difficulties of its definition, Adams attempted to take a practical view of the matter in terms of historical and evolving prerogative and the necessities of government, even though, being human, he was naturally influenced in his attitudes at critical moments by political animosities. As Secretary of State he would have resented legislative importunities that he later supported as a legislator. He firmly believed in the tripartite arrangement in the American system, and we have seen that he early opposed an attack upon the judiciary because he considered the courts the major safeguard of the arrangement.

THE PRESIDENCY

In consideration of Adams's more direct views of the American Presidency, it should be remembered that the greater, if not the most significant, part of his official life was spent as an executive officer. There is a normal tendency for the student to consider his career a kind of inexorable preparation for the achievement of the highest executive office. He might refuse dinners in his honor to avoid giving the impression that he had engineered them in campaigning for the Presidency,[26] or insist that this office, more than all

[24] *Memoirs,* February 16, 1826, VII, 117.
[25] *Congressional Globe,* 23rd Cong., 1st sess., II, May 2, 1834, pp. 361–362: As we have seen, he later said this power of controlling supply should be used sparingly. *Ibid.,* 27th Cong., 1st sess., August 27, 1841, p. 394.
[26] *Memoirs,* September 9, 1824, VI, 416.

others, "ought to be most freely and spontaneously bestowed," [27] yet he took his own candidacy for granted, as befitted an Adams. Early in his career in the State Department he expressed regret that there was no one in the Congress to defend him against the onslaught of other candidates.[28] He held it unfortunate, if not tragic, for his own cause, that the situation seemed to require a department head to ingratiate himself with Congress, if he would become President.[29] He thought it especially tragic in his case, since his principles prevented him from attempting so to ingratiate himself. He viewed with waspishness the maneuvers of others in seeking the office, an irritation that it is hard to attribute merely to his resentment at the violation by those others of his self-created principle that the office should be spontaneously bestowed. His own ambitions were deeply involved. Crawford's ambition was the principal object of his ire. In the Secretary of the Treasury's importunings to the President to invite other department heads to the diplomatic dinners during Adams's tenure of the Department of State were found the "pantings of . . . [Crawford's] ambitions" for the succession.[30] Crawford's only talent was intrigue. His major motive in supporting certain legislative measures was to put officials within his power and thus increase his chances for the Presidency.[31] The means he employed were such that Adams said he could not stoop to meet them. Holding that Crawford was not above swearing to falsehoods in a court of justice, Adams said that the Treasury Secretary demonstrated the capacity of ambition to debauch memory.[32] In short, the Secretary of the Treasury, Adams's colleague, was a "worm preying upon the vitals of the Administration within its own body." [33] The Adams testimony to this baseness became so strong that it is impossible not to believe that his own personal aspirations were involved.

He himself professed determination to manifest no desire for the office. Not even in seeking the highest honor was it possible to

[27] *Memoirs*, March 18, 1818, IV, 64.
[28] *Ibid.*, January 5, 1819, p. 212.
[29] *Ibid.*, February 3, 1819, IV, 242.
[30] *Ibid.*, March 13, 1819, pp. 296–297.
[31] Brown, *The Missouri Compromises and Presidential Politics, 1820–1825*, letter to William Plumer, Sr., Washington, D. C., November 24, 1820, p. 57.
[32] *Memoirs*, November 4, 1821, V, 383.
[33] *Ibid.*, March 3, 1821, p. 315.

violate the principle that the country's suffrages should never be sought nor its call denied. No cabal, canvass for votes, money to editors, or scramble for patronage would underlie his rise to power. He declared he would not take advantage of the factors that had placed the Secretaryship of State in the main line of succession.[34] There would be no "bargains," nor "coalitions," [35] nor expenditures of money.[36] Yet there can be no gainsaying his interest in the office of the Presidency as the fruition of his life's work. He wrote that he, of all the candidates, had the greatest interest in the outcome of the 1824 election.[37] In fact, one must suspect that the vehemence with which he turned to attack Russell on the score of the "Duplicate Letters," even to the extent of working through the "warm dog-days" of a Washington summer, was due in some measure to concern over the effect of Russell's charges upon the public mind.[38] To the charges that his strictures upon Russell had been unduly severe he retorted that the nature of the offense had warranted the means employed. And as he further analyzed Russell's political depravity, he speculated as to whether he should not have even more thoroughly annihilated the by then discredited man.[39]

Jackson's charges of a "deal" between Clay and Adams are no longer credited by the historian. However, Adams did make note in the *Memoirs* of the *rapprochement* with the Kentucky gentleman. The two men had been in violent disagreement at Ghent over the disposition of official papers, and Adams wrote that Clay at one time marked him as the principal rival for the Presidency.[40] Particularly interesting, in the light of the charges of a "deal," is the approach to Adams by a third party, Wyer, to report that Clay was disposed to support Adams if he could at the same time benefit

---

[34] To John D. Heath, Washington, D. C., January 7, 1822, *Writings,* VII, 192–193.

[35] To Robert Walsh, Washington, D. C., June 21, 1822, *ibid.,* p. 272.

[36] *Memoirs,* March 8, 1828, VII, 469–478.

[37] Quincy, *op. cit.,* p. 138. *Memoirs,* May 8, 1824, VI, 323–324. In fact, Adams claimed the office on the basis of his performance, for he wrote that the greatest accomplishments of the Monroe Administration had been made through the Department of State. To Louisa Catherine Adams, Washington, D. C., October 7, 1822, *Writings,* VII, 316–317.

[38] To Louisa Catherine Adams, Washington, D. C., August 28, 1822, *Writings,* VII, 297.

[39] *Memoirs,* July 22, 1822, VI, 46.

[40] *Ibid.,* March 9, 1821, V, 325.

himself,[41] or a statement by Letcher that Clay's friends might be inclined to vote contrary to their instructions if Clay could be assured a prominent place in the Administration.[42] The entry for the meeting between the two at which the "deal" was presumed to have been set is vague and uncommunicative and serves to do only what the other entries and references with respect to this period do, to reveal the closeness and concern with which Adams was following the progress of the campaign and the turn of political maneuvers. Noting a rumor of his continuing Federalism, he asked John Reed if he thought it would cost him the election and was at pains to make it clear that he had abandoned Federalism years before.[43] Although he might "disdain the ignoble warfare" evident in the slanderous press attacks upon him, he could still pause to worry over their effect upon the election results.[44] He was in the quandary of being intellectually and philosophically incapable of campaigning normally for the office to which he thought he had a superior claim, but he could not avoid watching closely the campaign that was proceeding according to principles so antithetical to his own.

Adams continued to oppose electioneering for the highest office.[45] In particular he opposed both the "caucus conventions" and "party popular conventions" as means of designating candidates for the Presidency.[46] The Adams conception of the office, on the contrary, was of a superior tribuneship of the whole people, above the vulgarity and vicissitudes of party struggle, a symbol of high principle and rectitude. The occupant of the office should be elevated to it on the basis of a disinterested insight into principle possessed by the whole people. The Presidency, secured on this basis, was the ideal of achievement. This conception caused him to abhor the thought of Mr. Monroe's Administration bringing into existence a party *"adverse"* to it.[47] Adams saw the government of the United States becoming a cabal with many of the worst features of elective

[41] *Memoirs*, December 15, 1824, VI, 444.

[42] *Ibid.*, December 17, 1824, p. 447.

[43] *Ibid.*, May 1, 1824, p. 313.

[44] Quincy, *op. cit.*, p. 130.

[45] *Memoirs*, May 12, 1827, VII, 272, 273. *Ibid.*, February 6, 1830, VIII, 185.

[46] *Ibid.*, November 18, 1823, VI, 191. *Ibid.*, January 25, 1824, p. 237. *Ibid.*, August 29, 1840, X, 351–352. *Ibid.*, September 24, 1840, pp. 352–353.

[47] *Ibid.*, July 28, 1818, IV, 119.

monarchies.[48] His goal as President, at least on the high level of executive policy, was to bring all the people together in sentiment, a purpose that prevented him from proscribing "any party—political or geographical." [49] The Presidency, he contended, should be the "center of hopes and expectations," and his election with a majority against him was a major tragedy in his life.[50] Adams concluded that he, himself, could best produce this ideal of tribuneship. But he as a man supporting consistently the basic principles of the Republic was opposed by a "base and profligate combination. . . ." [51] Adams always took heart when he recognized signs that men generally seemed to be uniting behind a candidate for the Presidency or a President whose principles he could approve. Presidents whose principles and politics he rejected, on the other hand, could only affect to speak for the nation as tribune of the whole people.[52]

As his life drew to a close, Adams found in his own presidential career and the spectacle of marching events tragic evidence of the existence of new conditions of party strife and contention surrounding the Presidency that violated the principles that he thought should surround and support that office. "Military service" and "demagogue policy" had become the surest routes to success in a presidential election.[53] In fact, he concluded that the first Administration of Thomas Jefferson had ushered in the demagogue.[54] In his own political activity and in his political thinking Adams struggled to resolve the conflict between an ideal tribuneship and a practical political leadership that was forced to traffic in the passions of party strife.[55] He never abandoned his principles, even at the sacrifice of success; the bitterness of the conflict added an almost

[48] *Ibid.*, December 16, 1818 and December 17, 1818, p. 193.

[49] *Ibid.*, February 7, 1825, VI, 500.

[50] *Ibid.*, June 2, 1822, VI, 8.

[51] *Ibid.*, December 17, 1828, VII, 382–383.

[52] *Ibid.*, February 14, 1845, XII, 168: "He [Polk] has affected to speak, at Nashville and at Cincinnati, of being the President of the nation, and not of a party; but he is sold soul and body to that grim idol, half albino, half negro, the compound of Democracy and of slavery, which, by the slave-representation in Congress, rules and ruins·the Union."

[53] *Ibid.*, January 1, 1840, X, 182.   Quincy, *op. cit.*, p. 320.

[54] Quincy, *op. cit.*, p. 320.   To Thomas Boylston Adams, Berlin, December 20, 1800, *Writings*, II, 487.

[55] To Thomas Boylston Adams, Berlin, December 30, 1800, *Writings*, II, 487.

venomous component to the naturally caustic Adams temperament. It is only implied, but he would perhaps have preferred a non-elective executive magistracy.[56] At the least, he took exception to the two-term precedent, engrafted onto the Constitution by the Virginia Presidents and resulting in "furious electioneering."[57] The limitation was not in the Constitution and should not have been, nor should the retirement of Washington at the end of two terms been followed as a precedent. Even frequent elections, he concluded, which could never settle the succession to the chief magistracy "for the whole Union" to the satisfaction of the people, were based on the "theory that power cannot be trusted [for long] to the same hands, even of the wisest and the best."[58]

These conceptions of the Presidency accounted for Adam's refusal to take action against political opposition within his own Administration, even though he knew it might be fatal to his fortunes.[59] Adams did not, however, despite his own weakness as a President, conceive of the Presidency in weak terms, even though the record of his Administration places it in the category of the least effective of all Administrations. On the contrary, the obligation of seeing that the laws were faithfully executed required that "the discretionary power of removing all subordinate executive officers must necessarily be vested in . . . [the President]."[60] Moreover, he wrote that "the powers of the executive department, explicitly and emphatically concentrated in one person, are vastly more extensive and complicated than those of the legislature."[61] The legislative powers were limited by enumeration; the executive power was granted in general terms. During the Tyler Administration, which he decried bitterly, while opposing increasing expenditure for the navy, he stated that he had never criticized the Executive

[56] Adams, *Parties in the United States,* p. 124: "In all governments of which the chief magistrate is elective, the organization, the character and the movements of parties will depend in great degree upon the anticipation to the succession. . . ." This allusion in itself is not strong, but in the light of Adams's aversion to electioneering and parties, it indicates some doubts on his part concerning the value of elections to the chief magistracy.

[57] *Ibid.,* p. 123. *Memoirs,* November 27, 1819, IV, 451.

[58] *Memoirs,* April 28, 1841, X, 468.

[59] Quincy, *op. cit.,* pp. 147, 149.

[60] Adams, *The Jubilee of the Constitution,* p. 78.

[61] *Ibid.,* pp. 70–71.

for extravagance, for it was the duty of the Congress to pull the purse strings tight.[62]   The implication was that it was the responsibility of the Executive to lead positively, and that the Congress's control of the purse strings should not unduly hamper this leadership.   On another occasion, he expressed it as his view that Congress was constantly and unfortunately encroaching upon the Executive domain, the "powers and authorities of the President." [63]   With regret he observed that policy often was formed by Congressional humors rather than the judgment, will, or principles of the President.[64] The emphasis upon the importance of executive power was revealed in his reminder to his audience in the speech on *The Jubilee of the Constitution* that the executive power had been responsible for the benefits achieved in foreign affairs during Washington's Administration.[65]   The early orientation of his mind in this direction was embodied in a letter from Berlin, surveying the political scene in the United States, and expressing regret there was so much dread of executive power at home, for, until a great general change should take place in the reason of mankind, force (as represented by the executive) must underlie the government of the world.[66]

The giving of so much of the federative power, in the Lockean sense of the term, to the legislature in the United States was, he thought, unfortunate.[67]   An even greater mistake in the Constitution was the granting of the power to declare war to the Congress.[68]   During Jackson's activities in Florida, Adams, as a member of the Administration, had opposed an admission that the President had no power to order the taking of Pensacola, holding that such a disclaimer of power

[62] *Congressional Globe,* 28th Cong., 1st sess., December 27, 1843, pp. 78–79. He referred with disapproval to the habits that Congress showed of holding up general appropriation bills, taking care of itself and leaving other branches of the government to go begging.   *Ibid.,* 24th Cong., 1st sess., December 10, 1835, p. 20.

[63] *Memoirs,* January 8, 1820, IV, 497.

[64] Adams, *The Jubilee of the Constitution,* p. 115.

[65] *Ibid.,* p. 102.

[66] To William Vans Murray [Berlin], July 22, 1798, *Writings,* II, 344.

[67] *Loc. cit.*

[68] *Memoirs,* December 30, 1817, IV, 32.   It is true that later, while he was a member of the House of Representatives, he had offered resolutions to remind the Executive that the power to declare war rested with the Congress and to warn the President against flagrant violation of this principle.   *Congressional Globe,* 28th Cong., 1st sess., June 11, 1844, p. 710.

established a dangerous precedent.[69]   "Defensive acts of hostility" could be authorized by the Executive.[70]   Further, the power of recognition was an executive power and should not be weakened by making Congress a party to it.[71]   The President's request for an appropriation for a diplomatic mission to China was, he said, sufficient justification of its propriety, and it should not be subjected to restrictions.[72] While Secretary of State, he made it a point to see that the form of foreign diplomatic accreditation was correct and was directed to the President and not to Congress.

Adams viewed the President as a remote and exalted personage, a view quite in keeping with his own personality.   He approved of Washington's establishment of a precedent that, in Adams's opinion, precluded the President from going abroad into any private companies.[73]   He also believed it fortunate that Washington had established the precedent of referring all foreign representatives to the Secretary of State, thereby putting the office of the Presidency on a level with those of foreign chiefs-of-state.[74]   An antifederalist attitude toward Washington and executive power had caused suspicions of "trifles lighter than air on his personal deportment and domestic establishment" that promoted whispers of "monarchy." [75]   Adams, himself, felt no aversion for such trifles.   The President was not merely the president of a council, but the responsible Executive in his own person acting upon any advice he might wish to take or upon his own counsel or "his own conviction of expediency. . . ." [76]   Adams criticized Monroe for being slow, indecisive, and procrastinating in the domination of his cabinet council, the members of which must accept their subordinate position.[77]   He assumed that there was a col-

[69] *Memoirs,* July 21, 1818, IV, 114.

[70] *Ibid.,* July 15, 1818, p. 108.   Quincy, *op. cit.,* p. 108.

[71] *Memoirs,* January 2, 1819, IV, 206.

[72] *Congressional Globe,* 27th Cong., 3rd sess., February 21, 1843, p. 325.

[73] *Memoirs,* December 31, 1825, VII, 97.

[74] Adams, *The Jubilee of the Constitution,* pp. 79–80.

[75] *Ibid.,* pp. 87–88.

[76] To Joseph Hall, Berlin, November 19, 1799, *Writings,* II, 441.   *Memoirs,* November 26, 1819, IV, 449–450.

[77] To Abigail Adams, London, April 23, 1817, *Writings,* VI, 182.   As President Adams himself did not act according to his principles.   In spite of the responsibility that he felt as President, he allowed a projected message to Congress to be taken by members of his cabinet to allow them time to prepare objections to it.   *Memoirs,* November 29, 1826, VII, 190.   By reason of Clay's and Barbour's opposition to the report of the Board of Engineers on the Chesapeake and Ohio

lective responsibility of a cabinet to the President who appointed it, and he criticized Webster for remaining with Tyler after the death of Harrison in 1841.[78] And he recognized no claim that anyone might assert upon a President for appointment to office.[79] He opposed tenure bills limiting administrative tenure to four years, and he particularly resisted pleas for Senate confirmation of subordinate officials. Executive officers should be appointed by and hold office at the discretion of the Executive commissioning them.[80]

In this perspective, the President was not only the wielder of a censorial power over the "moral and official conduct" of members of the government appointed by him,[81] he was "the first guardian of the public morals." [82] However, he was not himself the embodiment of a moral standard, for the law of nature and the Constitution were his guides.[83] His discretion was closely circumscribed, he could not act outside the sphere of law.[84] He could not act except in accordance with the law, nor dispense with the laws except in the cases provided by the laws themselves. And, as we have stated before, in the heat of battle with an Executive (Jackson), Adams could recommend the limitation of the veto power by constitutional amendment to limit

---

Canal he struck out of his projected message the recommendations made in the report, although he favored them. *Ibid.*, November 30, 1826, pp. 190–191. He conceded his original position on the appointment of a minister to Columbia and the appointment of a Secretary of War, because he stood alone in the Administration, even though he considered the "public interest" was "made subordinate to individual accomodation." *Ibid.*, May 20, 1828, VIII, 4.

[78] *Memoirs*, March 17, 1843, XI, 339.

[79] *Ibid.*, May 21, 1818, IV, 99.

[80] *Ibid.*, February 7, 1828, VII, 424–425. A seemingly contradictory reference in the *Memoirs* stated that appointment and removal of postmasters were dependent upon the Postmaster General, probably to be accounted for as a means of brushing off an office-seeker. *Ibid.*, October 18, 1826, p. 154. He recognized, of course, that the subordinate *organization* of the executive establishment had been left to the "discretion of Congress." Adams, *The Jubilee of the Constitution*, p. 76. In the House he opposed a restriction upon the power of the President to staff a military unit with West Pointers as an interference with the power of the Executive. To say whom he should not appoint was to say whom he should appoint. *Congressional Globe*, 24th Cong., 1st sess., April 26, 1836, p. 402. Somewhat in qualification of his general view, he stated on one occasion that the Congress might designate a category of persons from whom the President must make a selection in filling a particular office. *Memoirs*, April 10, 1822, V, 488.

[81] *Memoirs*, June 23, 1820, V, 158.

[82] *Ibid.*, December 2, 1819, IV, 457–458.

[83] Adams, *Argument in the United States v. Cinque* [15 Peters 518], p. 82.

[84] *Ibid.*, pp. 38, 63.

further the President's censorial power and capacity to defend the Constitution.[85]

A strong, but limited and circumscribed, Executive was the ideal, particularly an Executive untainted with ambition for military power. Adams consistently evidenced opposition to a military government that would by its nature unduly emphasize the Executive. The Union was a means of reducing the military requirements upon the North American states, for without union each state would have to maintain a strong military power separately as a protection against each other.[86] Although Adams was aware of the great military potential of the United States, he saw a great threat to European stability coming from the spread of conscription and widespread arming of the people.[87] He might regret our humiliating failures in the War of 1812, attributable in great measure to "the miserable composition of our army, . . . an unreasonable reliance upon militia soldiers and militia officers," [88] yet he held that "an army is always a monarchy" and has "as its invariable tendency" that of making the government that supports it a monarchy.[89]

Adams, strong nationalist though he was, did not place the usual nationalist's emphasis upon military power. He wanted the Committee of the Whole to continue to consider the President's message in its entirety, in particular the portions having to do with military affairs; for, being suspicious of the military, he promised he would have ideas different from the Executive on the size of the army.[90] Shortly thereafter he opposed an increase in the army, adverting at the same time to the historic danger of a standing army, and of the military mind that had always wanted an increase in strength. He suggested the maintenance of a 6000-man army, believing the figure established

[85] *Congressional Globe*, 27th Cong., 2nd sess., August 16, 1842, pp. 894–896, August 17, 1842, pp. 906–907.

[86] To Abigail Adams, Berlin, July 3, 1799, *Writings*, II, 427–428. To Thomas Boylston Adams, February 14, 1801, *ibid.*, p. 501.

[87] To Thomas Boylston Adams, February 14, 1801, *Writings*, II, 500–501: Interestingly, Adams saw the necessity of conscription in Europe coming from the trend toward consolidation brought about by encroaching and aggressor states, against whom other states were required to defend themselves.

[88] To Joseph Hall, Boston House, Ealing, near London, September 9, 1815, *ibid.*, V, 375.

[89] Adams, *Parties in the United States*, pp. 119–120.

[90] *Congressional Globe*, 26th Cong., 2nd sess., December 31, 1840, p. 76.

for 1821 appropriate for the year 1842.[91]   The army had on one pretext or another, he announced, been growing out of all proportion, particularly in regiments of dragoons that cost twice the amount of infantry regiments.   "As to engineers, ordnance corps, and all the pride, pomp, and circumstance of war, he had been lately looking over the documents for the purpose of showing how this monster had been growing till it had reached a size enough to startle the country." [92]

The navy was not so much to be feared, and he had opposed its reduction.[93]   Early he had stressed the need for an enlarged naval force that would be sufficient to deter the hostilities of other powers, a burden to which he considered our resources were entirely adequate. He took a nationalist's delight in our naval success in the War of 1812,[94] with a navy inferior in size and made inadequate through the false naval economies of Mr. Jefferson.[95]   As President, Adams called for the establishment of a naval academy,[96] and stressed the point that our naval squadrons made our name favorably known wherever they were seen.[97]   The naval establishment should also be kept technologically proficient, and he supported a proposal to require the Secretary to procure at least two steamers for the new Home Squadron.[98] Of course, politics had their impact upon this pro-navy sentiment, and he could not forego the opportunity to decry the "new-born passion of the South for the increase of the navy," [99] as a "wholesome stream from a polluted fountain," [100] a Southern policy unwisely trying to build the United States navy to one half the size of Britain's navy.[101]   His politi-

---

[91] *Ibid.*, 27th Cong., 2nd sess., June 6, 1842, pp. 585–586.

[92] *Ibid.*, 27th Cong., 2nd sess., May 24, 1842, p. 528.

[93] *Loc. cit.*

[94] To Louisa Catherine Adams, United States Corvette John Adams, below Mingo, June 12, 1814, *ibid.*, V, 49.

[95] Adams, *Parties in the United States*, pp. 22, 33–34, 47.

[96] Adams, "First Annual Message," *in* Richardson, *op. cit.*, II, 310.

[97] Adams, "Second Annual Message," *in ibid.*, 367.

[98] *Congressional Globe*, 27th Cong., 1st sess., July 21, 1841, p. 238.

[99] *Memoirs*, February 18, 1842, XI, 95.

[100] *Ibid.*, April 24, 1842, p. 140.

[101] *Ibid.*, December 10, 1842, p. 277.   In 1844, opposing Southern naval zeal, part of which was directed against Britain, then suspected of designs on Texas, he objected to increasing expenditures for the navy.   He was ordinarily anti-British, but he counseled restraint in this case since British policy seemed to be in conflict with Southern policy and ambitions.   *Congressional Globe*, 28th Cong., 1st sess., March 21, 1844, p. 429.

cal conflict with the South was sufficiently deep to excuse him to resent Southern support of the navy.

THE CONGRESS

The most dramatic and admirable portion of Adams's career was spent in legislative halls, in spite of which fact fewer direct references are available in his writings, orations, and public pronouncements dealing with the power and position of the Congress than upon the power and position of other branches of the government in the United States. For he was basically a man of executive temperament who accepted the legislative forum as his arena only after he had been checked by defeat in 1828 in the accomplishment of the great designs for which he had worked in the Executive. In discussing the Constitution, we have analyzed in part his conception of the legislature, the separation of powers, and the Presidency. A brief discussion, however, of his infrequent allusions to the status of the legislature is necessary.

We have already pointed out, in refutation of Wickwar, that Adams held to the concept of a superior, constitutional law, impervious to the threat of statute law. In fact, he even went so far as to deny every pretense of omnipotent power in the British Parliament.[102] On the purely practical side, while he was Secretary of State, he made use of his opportunities to complain of the pretensions of Congress that it was entitled to know everything "doing by the Executive." [103] While he was a member of Congress, certain incidents afforded him "illustration of the utter recklessness with which deliberative assemblies in voting trample upon written Constitutions which every member of them is sworn to support." [104] Moreover, he found that universal mediocrity characterized the legislature upon which the liberties of the people depended. He felt hampered by the complex system of rules by which his activities in the House were circumscribed and suggested in exasperation that it would perhaps be better to have no rules.[105] One feels that he was easily exasperated with the obstacles and delays to be overcome in legislative life.

[102] Adams, *Quincy Oration, 1831*, pp. 12–15.
[103] *Memoirs*, February 19, 1819, IV, 270.
[104] *Ibid.*, December 10, 1838, X, 596.
[105] *Ibid.*, September 15, 1837, IX, 337: "I sometimes think there are already too many rules [of the House], and that it would be better to have none at all."

The evidence is sufficient to justify the generalization that he held a concept of strong executive leadership of the legislature, even though his own Administration fails to illustrate the principle. He complained that the committees of Congress, after consulting the Executive, perversely followed their own ideas.[106] He pressed the Russian government to clarify its position with regard to the northwest coast of the continent, before the matter became a matter of Congressional concern.[107] He admonished Congress to await executive leadership in financial matters.[108] It was unfortunate, to his mind, that "the exercise of actual control by the President over the opinions and wishes of a majority of the legislature . . . [would always be unpalatable] in what form soever it may be administered." [109] Ardent support of executive leadership in foreign affairs, opposition to captious legislative nibbling at executive control over administration, solicitude for the preservation of the line between the executive and legislative branches, resentment of the attention required to be given to Congressional whims in connection with presidential elections predominantly characterized his thinking.

Within these restrictive limits, natural to his intellectual prepossession, he was nevertheless vigorous in seeking a full realization of Congressional efficiency and power. Executive leadership was a goal worth seeking, but he would not force the Congress to organize itself in a manner favorable to the Executive.[110] The legislature should possess an amplitude of power, without the necessity of adhering to judicial procedure, to purge itself of members deemed morally inadequate,[111] and to limit the legislative rights of anyone whose credentials were not in order or whose election was contested.[112]

He experienced misgivings concerning Congressional caliber, especially after he entered the House, but he insisted that the body compared favorably as to the "free exercise of mind" with the British Par-

[106] National Archives, Records of the Department of State, Diplomatic Instructions, All Countries, IX, 44.

[107] *Ibid.*, X, 53.

[108] *Congressional Globe,* 26th Cong., 2nd sess., appendix, p. 323.

[109] To William Plumer, Washington, D. C., July 6, 1818, *Writings*, VI, 381.

[110] *Congressional Globe,* 23rd Cong., 2nd sess., II, January 21, 1835, p. 150.

[111] Report on Senator John Smith, *Writings*, III, 177. *Annals of Congress*, 10th Cong., 1st sess., I, December 31, 1807, p. 56.

[112] *Congressional Globe,* 25th Cong., 3rd sess., January 28, 1839, p. 143.

liament.[113]   We have seen that he felt no sense of degradation in the retirement from the Presidency and entry into his final legislative career.   The executive initiative in foreign affairs was championed, yet the Secretary of State took great pains to make no commitment infringing upon Congressional prerogative.   Although the Executive was responsible for successes in foreign affairs during Washington's Administration, he wrote that the Congress was mainly responsible for our domestic successes.[114]

In Adams's mind, republicanism was not an alternative to democracy, in the sense that it was to Hamilton; it was rather the closest practicable approach to the limited democracy he could endorse.   He disagreed with the Senate's proposal to decrease the number of representatives in the House and supported the Senate's proposal to represent fractions.   He was, as we have seen, no supporter of exaggerated or pure democracy; the American representative institutions were a compromise or "expedient resorted to, for the purpose of attaining the substance" of the impracticable.[115]   The Senate represented the States' rights and oligarchical corporations and interests, and it must not presume to dictate to the democratic branch, the numbers of which some day might for practical reasons be limited.[116]   For the moment the numbers in the House should be increased rather than decreased.[117]   Popular arguments did not affect the federative principle of equality of sovereignty underlying the Senate as they did the nature of representation in the House.   The former body's proper function as the aristocratic branch was to put "a check upon the impetuous violence of the House of Representatives."   This function was performed with "*coolness* and *firmness*" in the trial of Chase.[118]   During the French Revolution in particular, he saw the Executive and the Senate as representing the stable force of the American government and feared the effect of propaganda upon the loyalty of the peo-

[113] *Memoirs,* June 5, 1829, VIII, 154.

[114] Adams, *The Jubilee of the Constitution,* p. 102.

[115] *Congressional Globe,* 27th Cong., 2nd sess., June 13, 1842, pp. 620–621.

[116] *Loc. cit.* I "Publius Valerius," *Writings,* III, 47.

[117] *Congressional Globe,* 27th Cong., 2nd sess., June 13, 1842, pp. 620–621.

[118] *Memoirs,* March 3, 1805, I, 370–371: This is typical Federalist doctrine, although in Adams it was associated with a higher regard for the democratic branch than in many others.

ple to these institutions.[119] The House of Representatives at this time, sharing the indignation of the *"friends of liberty,"* was a danger to the stability of the government.[120] Bicameralism was essential to political stability, but occasionally it was almost inadequate to control popular emotions manifested in the House.

With respect to the potentiality of legislative tyranny, Adams's conception of the power of Congressional investigating committees has a peculiarly interesting relevance, as have many of Adams's views, to an important problem of the mid-twentieth century.   In a minority report on the Bank of the United States he strenuously excoriated a House committee of which he was a member for prying "into the accounts and pecuniary transactions of the Bank" and scrutinizing "the fortunes and characters of thousands of individual citizens of the Union, merely because they . . . [had] an account in the bank, which, in the examination of the books and the proceedings of the corporation, must incidentally be disclosed."   There had been no authority previously granted in the Bank charter to accomplish this purpose.[121] Moreover, no such power could be exercised without a violation of the fundamental liberties of citizens; therefore, the exercise of such inquisitorial powers was contrary to a higher law.   The transactions of private individuals—for example, editors—with the Bank were not any more within the purview of a Congressional committee "than the dwelling-house, the fireside, or the bed chamber of any one of them, . . . [places that had been since] the darkness of heathen antiquity . . . [the inviolable sites of] the altars of the household gods."   Accepting the depositions of private individuals that impugned the testimony of other private individuals with regard to their transactions with the Bank was contrary to principles of jus-

[119] To John Adams, London, September 19, 1797, *Writings,* II, 210. For the most part, the Executive and Senate stood together as a common defense against popular instability, but Adams had occasion to condemn the Senate's attempts to dictate appointments to the President, as, for example, the pressure of "a small junta of senators" dictating Robert Smith to Madison as Secretary of State. Adams, *Parties in the United States,* p. 108.

[120] To the Secretary of State (Timothy Pickering), Berlin, June 25, 1798, *Writings,* II, 322.

[121] *Register of Debates,* 22nd Cong., 1st sess., appendix, pp. 54–55: It is, of course, difficult to see how the powers established in the charter of the Bank of the United States could define the investigative powers of Congress with respect to that institution.

tice.[122]   Loans made to private individuals by the Bank were not a fit subject of investigation.[123]   Since there was no law prohibiting the Bank from subsidizing the press, it was inquisitorial to investigate the motives of the bank directors in granting a discount on a loan to the press.[124]   The directors quite rightly might use all legitimate means in working for a renewal of the Bank's charter, even collaboration with newspapers.[125]   Adams's principles, if applied consistently today, would seriously hamper Congressional committee investigations, in fact would very likely go beyond the desires of the most determined opponents of current committee methods.   Unfortunately there exists no other instance in Adams's legislative career of opposition to committee activity.   This absence is the more unfortunate because he was so emotionally involved with the Bank.   The given instance serves largely to indicate that he was on guard against legislative oppression of institutions and interests that he wished to safeguard.

THE JUDICIARY

The function and role of the judiciary in Adams's institutional scheme have been briefly referred to, especially the role of the judicial organs in preserving the balance and separation of powers.   Clearly, he was not a man whose temperament could be described as judicial, and it was for that reason, among others, that he refused the appointment to the Supreme Court offered to him by Madison.   Of course, it is not true that there is a judicial temperament completely separate from the political.   Adams did not fail to recognize the significance of political partisanship in the selection of judges, as well as in judicial decisions themselves, for he early commented to his father upon this

[122] *Register of Debates*, 22nd Cong., 1st sess., appendix, pp. 55–58: The particular liberties endangered here were not set forth, but it must be assumed that Adams had in mind the liberty to pursue financial transactions without their being scrutinized by the legislature or an agency of the legislature.   This point of view is not only related to the particular controversy but perhaps revealed a peculiar manifestation of a *laissez-faire* concept in Adams.

[123] *Loc. cit.*: In fact, Adams in the instant case placed such a circumscription around Congressional investigative power that it is difficult to defend it on practical grounds.   He does not attack the procedure alone, but the subject matter and substantive areas that might be investigated, and thus he severely limits an historical and necessary foundation of wise and efficient legislation.

[124] *Register of Debates*, 22nd Cong., 1st sess., appendix, pp. 48–59: This objection loses sight of the fact that adequate investigation is a necessary antecedent to adequate legislation.

[125] *Register of Debates*, 22nd Cong., 1st sess., appendix, p. 59.

factor.[126] Political motivations, however, would surely not have influenced Adams unduly as a judge. It is safer to say that he found
executive and legislative activities more compatible with his interest.
As President he made it clear, in conversation with Webster, that his
appointments to the bench took into account political factors.[127] Of
course, the anti-Republican attacks upon the Federalist judiciary and
its newly asserted power of judicial review he resisted and excoriated
at every opportunity.[128] He did not, however, exaggerate respect for
the courts and was quite capable of deprecating practical sacrifices of
"substantial justice" and the use of "law logic." [129]

John Quincy Adams possessed the very conservative and conventional view of the judiciary as that "coordinate branch" whose duty
was to interpret constitutions and laws and to settle, in conformity
with the legislative purpose, many questions that the inadequacies of
language left unsettled. Remarking the death of Marshall, he wrote
that the great Chief Justice had performed a great role in reducing the
divisive Jeffersonian influences.[130] The courts for the most part
served the interests and principles that Adams served; only rarely did
he have an opportunity to speculate negatively on judicial power by
reason of failure on the part of that power to serve those interests and
principles.[131]

THE STATES

Adams's nationalism and organically related contention against
overweening state claims have previously been analyzed. There is
available in the sources little discussion of the function of the states
as institutions, a fact that is not surprising in view of the emphasis

[126] To John Adams, Newburyport, April 5, 1790, *Writings*, I, 52.

[127] *Memoirs*, December 16, 1825, VII, 84: He described H. L. White, an
adamant foe of Jackson, as a man of determined integrity.

[128] *Ibid.*, December 27, 1804, I, 324. *Ibid.*, March 3, 1805, pp. 370–371. To
John Adams, Washington, D. C., March 8, 1805, *ibid.*, III, 108.

[129] To John Adams, St. Petersburg, July 21, 1811, *Writings*, IV, 146. *Memoirs*,
May 26, 1819, IV, 372.

[130] *Memoirs*, July 10, 1835, IX, 243.

[131] *Congressional Globe*, 27th Cong., 3rd sess., February 27, 1843, p. 359:
The slavery issue would have served to create conditions eventually that very
likely would have brought Adams into collision with the judicial role vis-a-vis
that issue. In the instant citation he asked leave to introduce a resolution
setting forth that all vacancies in the Supreme Court should be filled from the
nonslave states until four fifths of the positions should be so filled, a candid court-
packing proposal with a vengeance.

upon the national government in his theory. To Adams there was "no magnet of attraction in any league of Sovereign and Independent States which . . . [caused] the heart-strings of the individual man to vibrate in unison with those of his neighbor." [132] Even the Constitution, which had transformed a league into the organization of a nation, had not succeeded in establishing a perfect balance between the states and the general government. The enemies of a cohesive national spirit perversely associated republicanism with state sovereignty.[133] Adams's insistence was that the Constitution had created "not . . . a confederacy, but . . . a national government complicated with a federation." [134] This remark was as close to an assertion of centralization as the facts would permit him to make. In the political struggle of the early constitutional period, Adams associated opposition to Washington's Administration, theories of States' rights and restricted national powers, French democracy, sectional rivalry, and unfortunate individual ambitions in one anathematized category. *"The whole truth,"* or right principle, could, indeed, be given expression only through the national or general government.[135] Although on a rare occasion he could admit that the "objects of administration to which the state governments . . . [were] generally confined . . ." might best be administered by local authorities,[136] he could on the other hand describe a mere leaning toward States' rights as a fault in a public figure.[137] In public addresses as President he admitted the possible permanence of divisive factors based upon geography and the "inviolable duty" of the Union to respect and conserve the rights of the states,[138] but he confided to his diary his resentment against the "blustering, bullying style" of the state governments in their relations

[132] Adams, *Lives of James Madison and James Monroe*, p. 19.

[133] To Charles Adams, Helvoetsluys, November 4, 1795, *Writings*, I, 426–427.

[134] Adams, *Parties in the United States*, pp. 8, 12.

[135] To Harrison Gray Otis, Washington, D. C., March 31, 1808, *Writings*, III, 191–193.

[136] To Joseph Hall, Ealing, near London, August 7, 1816, *ibid.*, VI, 65. He could, of course, recognize practical necessity and admit the advantages of federalism. For example, he pointed out that the South American state, Columbia, could not succeed as a unitary state, because of its great size and population. National Archives, Records of the Department of State, *Diplomatic Instructions*, All Countries, IX, 284.

[137] *Memoirs*, April 28, 1818, IV, 83: Such a fault he ascribed to his close friend, Wirt.

[138] Adams, "Inaugural Address," *in* Richardson, *op. cit.*, II, 297.

with the "General Administration," against the insolence that was the means they chose for "demonstrating their sovereignty." [139]

He resented any suggestion that the states should have greater power to encourage literature and science than the general government.[140]   In fact, one gains the impression that he abhorred the concessions he was forced by the constitutional system to make to the states.   One of the most condemnatory charges he could make against Jackson was that he was in league with the state of Georgia as it defied the Chief Justice of the United States.[141]   He called upon his fellow members of Congress to contrast the sublimity of the reference to "We the People" in the Preamble of the Constitution with the decision of the South Carolina Convention.[142]   "State pride, State prejudice, State jealousy" were execrable forces that could be expressed only under the pretenses of "State sovereignty. . . ." [143]   His strongest condemnation of the latter was that "State sovereignty is but another name for knavery. . . ." [144]   The testimony is unrelieved.   If provided with a genuine opportunity, Adams, the nationalist, would have consigned the states to limbo. Adams's nationalism is an important factor to stress immediately prior to the analysis of his relative position in American politics that is to follow.

[139] *Memoirs,* February 8, 1828, VII, 427.
[140] *Ibid.,* January 16, 1830, VIII, 172.
[141] *Ibid.,* January 4, 1831, pp. 262–263.
[142] *Register of Debates,* 22nd Cong., 2nd sess., II, February 4, 1833, p. 1612.
[143] Adams, *Newburyport Oration, 1837,* p. 36.
[144] *Memoirs,* April 26, 1839, X, 110.

14

Adams's Politics

*One of these assemblies [political meetings] was held yesterday.
. . . I was invited also there, but did not attend. . . . Here is
a revolution in the habits and manners of the people. Where will
it end? . . . These meetings cannot be multiplied in numbers
and frequency without resulting in yet deeper tragedies. Their
manifest tendency is to civil war.*

MEMOIRS, *August 29, 1840*

Arthur M. Schlesinger, Jr., refers to John Quincy Adams and several
of his contemporaries as honest Jeffersonians.[1] The record testifies to
his honesty, but one must question the validity or propriety of cate-
gorizing Adams as a Jeffersonian. To be sure, the substance of his
doctrine, as revealed in his political life, must be inspected in any
effort to place Adams in the political context in the United States during its early history. Obvious bases in his career and theory exist for
the conclusion of Schlesinger, but other compelling factors in his
career argue to the contrary, not least of which was the superficial
Whiggery of his later political career. Moreover, inspection of the
written and spoken record even more thoroughly casts doubt upon the
wisdom of a facile generalization concerning Adams's political orientation. The material heretofore adduced may have provided adequate demonstration of this contention. However, in this chapter we
shall consider further data involved basically in the question of his
place in the whole picture of the period. We shall deal particularly
with explicit references by Adams to the political forces and figures of
his day. If these references are at all significant, they will indicate

[1] Arthur M. Schlesinger, Jr., *The Age of Jackson* (Boston: Little, Brown,
1945), p. 313.

that Adams became at best a hesitant Jeffersonian. The proper conclusion no doubt is that Adams defies classification, was peculiarly *sui generis*, not in the sense of espousing completely novel doctrines or principles but in the sense of working them into a synthesis unusual for his day.

He took advantage of an early opportunity to indicate sympathy for Federalist principles by manifesting tacit support for Hamilton's plan for the assumption of the debts of the states.[2] The Federalists, being nationalists, more closely represented his political position than their opponents; he belabored the first opposition to them as a "faction."[3] His nationalistic principles were permanent, of course, and his party affiliations in large measure turned upon the capacity of parties to reflect his interpretation of national interests, as opposed to sectional interests. Citizen Genêt, representing the principles of the French Revolution and attempting intervention in American domestic affairs, was a symbol of the forces assaulting the national interests of the United States.[4] The Federalist Party at the time was the most effective political opposition to such influence. Adams was thus in congenial company. Moreover, the first outright physical resistance to the new government, of which he early became an ardent supporter, was directed at the Federalist-dominated Administration of Washington. Adams noted that the infected areas and peoples were on the frontier, wherein the new party of opposition was arising.

The signs of defection from the Federalists on his own part, however, appeared early. In 1788 he heard with disfavor Theophilus Parson's tales of the intriguing maneuvers that outwitted the "anti-federalists" in the Massachusetts Convention.[5] In 1799 he indicated he would have no hesitation in leaving Federalist ranks should they split because one element in the party desired war at all costs.[6] Moreover, he wrote that there was in operation a Federal Jacobinism deriving from unfortunate English influence.[7] However, he was quick to credit the party with the great accomplishment of the Constitution, even at the risk of severe odium and obloquy in the popular mind

---

[2] To John Adams, Newburyport, March 19, 1790, *Writings*, I, 48.
[3] To John Adams, Boston, December 16, 1792, *ibid.*, p. 123.
[4] II "Coumbus," *Writings*, I, 155.
[5] Adams, *Life in a New England Town*, February 11, 1788, pp. 95–96.
[6] To William Vans Murray, December 10, 1799, *Writings*, II, 444.
[7] To William Vans Murray, December 15, 1799, *ibid.*, p. 445.

on charges of aristocratic tendencies.[8]   Furthermore, he emphasized that the party had seen more clearly than other American forces the alarming passions issuing from the French catastrophe.   The party likewise championed naval power.[9]   But these bases for loyalty were not enough to offset the record of the party under a leadership influenced unduly by the British: [10]

The effects of my letter [to Harrison Gray Otis] will, I hope, be what was intended—to promote Union at home, and urge to vigor against foreign hostile powers.   If federalism consists in looking to the British navy as the only palladium of our liberties, I must be a political heretic. If federalism will please to consist of a determination to defend our country, I still subscribe to its doctrines.[11]

But the party showed no promise of reform and abandonment of its antinationalism and Anglophilism.[12]   It continued with perversity and sectional emphasis to be duped by a pro-British faction.   Even more unfortunate, in Adams's eyes, the party seemed to have put itself in such a position as to make it impossible for its members to express "any other impulse than faction." [13]   As a faction they had become anti-Union, and that he could not forgive them.[14]   In Adams's system the Union was equated with a respect for a total system of principles, a "faction" could reflect only a loyalty to a partial system of principles.   The Federalists' projected launching of treasonable projects, which Adams charged were planned in association with the British, was heinous action that he, above all a nationalist, could not endure.[15]   These partisans of the British, particularly those of the "Hamiltonian school," were, moreover, the most seriously "stained with . . . [the] pollution" of "allying private stockjobbing with public office." [16]   Even in the 1830's his strictures upon the old Federalists were severe.   They were in league with hated Freemasonry,[17]

[8] Adams, *Parties in the United States*, pp. 5, 9.

[9] *Ibid.*, pp. 13–14, 47, 54.

[10] I "Publius Valerius," *Writings*, III, 48–49.

[11] To Abigail Adams, Washington, D. C., April 20, 1808, *ibid.*, p. 234.

[12] To Joseph Hall, St. Petersburg, August 15/27, 1810, *ibid.*, pp. 473–474.

[13] To William Eustis, St. Petersburg, August 24, 1811, *ibid.*, IV, 190–191.

[14] To William Plumer, St. Petersburg, October 6, 1810, *ibid.*, III, 508.

[15] To Abigail Adams, St. Petersburg, June 30, 1811, *ibid.*, IV, 127.   To William Eustis, Ealing, March 29, 1816, *ibid.*, V, 547.

[16] To Louisa Catherine Adams, Ghent, December 20, 1814, *ibid.*, V, 243.

[17] *Memoirs*, September 29, 1833, IX, 17.

still tainted with "Essex juntoism," and "Hartford Convention federalism." [18]   He noted the appointment of the Federalists, Baylies and Williams, as collectors at New Bedford, with almost ludicrous severity as being a political action "rank as the compost of a dunghill." [19]

To be sure, on the death of Chief Justice Marshall, Adams recorded the passing of a great Federalist who had used his high office to help preserve the Union, in contrast with many of his colleagues who had expressed the "crafty and quixotic Democracy of Jefferson." [20]   Long after leaving the party, Adams continued to recognize the party's service to the Union in making the Constitution, building a navy, and correctly analyzing revolutionary forces coming from abroad.   In the 1824 election he had had the support of New England and the remnants of the Federalist forces elsewhere.[21]   But there can be no doubt that he had abandoned his uneasy Federalist relationship in the first decade of the century.   And I think it is equally clear that, since he was never "a devotee of partisan politics," he did not become a Republican, notwithstanding his support of the Embargo, his appointment to Russia, and his subsequent career.[22]   When the Republican forces came to seem most closely identified with the national interest, he naturally gravitated toward them, but he continued to see both parties "in frequent and flagrant violation of their proposed principles." [23]   Although he continued to condemn the disunionist Federalists, he held the Jefferson Administration to be much to blame for their defection.[24]

Branded by his friends in 1787–88 as an Anti-Federalist, Adams patently was unable to associate himself with an organized party of that political temper at a time when their anti-Federalism took the form of overt opposition to the Constitution or sans-culottism.[25]   Although the group eventually accepted the accomplished fact of the Constitution, their pro-French bias continued for long to be expressed through an American Jacobinism combined with the art of "Dema-

[18] *Ibid.*, October 30, 1833, pp. 20, 27.
[19] *Ibid.*, December 9, 1837, pp. 446–447.
[20] *Ibid.*, July 10, 1835, IX, 243.
[21] Dwight Lowell Dumond, *A History of the United States* (New York: Henry Holt and Company, 1942), p. 252.
[22] *Ibid.*, p. 225.
[23] Adams, *Parties in the United States,* pp. 120–121.
[24] *Memoirs,* March 18, 1829, VIII, 115.
[25] To John Adams, Boston, May 26, 1794, *Writings,* I, 191.

gogie" learned from abroad.[26]   Mr. Thomas Paine, the international-ist-revolutionary execrated by the defenders of property interests on both sides of the water, wrote one of his most effective pamphlets ensconced in Mr. Monroe's residence in Paris.[27]   Adams reported that an attack upon Washington and the second part of the *Age of Reason* were written under the protection of Monroe.[28]   Deriding the Anti-Federalists for their support of France, he found it difficult to believe that any man at home or in France could dare to challenge Washington's system of administration "sanctioned, not only by his example, but by his retirement." [29]   But "the Blounts and the Randolphs, . . . too thickly sown in the fields of our legislation," produced "the pestilential principles of the terrible Republic." [30]   Perhaps even more objectionable, they opposed adequate protection for our trade.[31]

When the despised Anti-Federalist, or Republican, Party achieved power, Adams seemed undetermined as to the survival value of its political success.   In the same letter to Rufus King he remarked, on the one hand, the "sandy . . . foundation" of its lease of "democratic popularity," while, on the other, he asserted that the Party was in no "real danger," for its power rested on "a much stronger majority of the people throughout the Union than the former Administrations ever possessed since the first establishment of the Constitution." [32]   This period was doubtless one of dawning recognition on his part of the importance of popular support, made psychologically more easy for him by the apparent ebbing of the revolutionary tide in Europe, although he continued to execrate Jefferson's "itch for popularity." [33]   Adams's respect for the party could never increase merely because it represented numbers; principle prevented that.   Nor could he ever accept the Anti-Federalists' States' rights doctrines—their opposition to constructive powers, and the inferior position that they assigned to

[26] To Abigail Adams, The Hague, April 25, 1795, *ibid.,* pp. 331–333.   To John Adams, London, August 31, 1797, *ibid.,* II, 198.
[27] To John Adams, London, April 4, 1796, *ibid.,* I, 482.
[28] To John Adams, The Hague, May 11, 1797, *ibid.,* II, 166.
[29] To Joseph Pitcairn, The Hague, January 31, 1797, *ibid.,* II, 96.
[30] To William Vans Murray, Berlin, January 27, 1798, *ibid.,* pp. 244–245.
[31] To William Vans Murray, Berlin, April 11, 1798, *ibid.,* p. 273.
[32] To Rufus King, Boston, October 8, 1802, *ibid.,* III, 8, 9.
[33] To John Adams, November, 1804, *ibid.,* p. 81.   Adams, *Parties in the United States,* p. 105.

commercial interests.[34]   Adams was never an Anti-Federalist, and he never became a Republican.   That fact was understood when he was appointed to Russia by the Madison Administration.[35]   Although he admitted that Madison left the Union in a state of "prosperity and tranquillity," [36] the record shows that he blamed the Anti-Federalists for much of the Federalist defection from the Union.[37]   And in *The Jubilee of the Constitution* he referred to them as the party of "partial affection" for the Constitution, who affected to call themselves "Republicans." [38]

Since it is clear that Adams was neither a true Federalist nor a Republican at any time, it is necessary to pursue the inquiry further. Was there a broader sense in which he was a Jeffersonian, entirely removed from the matter of attachment to party movements?   Some indication has been given heretofore of his reaction to Jefferson personally, and this element cannot be separated from his reaction to Jefferson's principles.   Adams, doctrinaire figure that he was, was singularly capable of judging a man on the basis of his political principles.   The Federalists in 1808 wrote of him as "Mr. Jefferson's new disciple . . . [who] could not resist the temptation to ape his master," [39] but the almost entirely unqualified strictures by Adams upon Jefferson cannot be considered by any logical process the respectful utterances of a disciple with regard to his master.

Except for the instances referred to in Chapter II, Adams's references to Jefferson were highly critical.   Adams deplored Jefferson's letter to Mazzei in 1796 opposing an alleged pro-British orientation of the American Chief Executive.[40]   Jefferson was cavalier in the handling of facts and itched for the telling of "prodigies." [41]   When

---

[34] Adams, *Parties in the United States,* pp. 5, 9, 12, 47, 94.

[35] Dumond, *op. cit.,* p. 225.   While he was in Russia he showed his opposition to the Continental System, which he wrote was the cornerstone of the policy of the French favored by the Republicans, and derided the idea that he went to Russia to support it.   To John Adams, St. Petersburg, September 2, 1810, *Writings,* III, 482.

[36] To John Adams, L.B.H., Ealing, January 3, 1817, *Writings,* VI, 136.

[37] *Memoirs,* March 18, 1829, VIII, 115.

[38] Adams, *The Jubilee of the Constitution,* pp. 55–56.

[39] Anon., *Remarks and Criticisms on the Hon. John Quincy Adams's Letter to the Hon. Harrison Gray Otis* (Boston: Joshua Cushing, 1808), p. 7.

[40] To Abigail Adams, London, July 29, 1797, *Writings,* II, 194. Adams, *Parties in the United States,* p. 21.

[41] *Memoirs,* January 11, 1805, I, 330.

Adams's pen hit its most venomous stride, he could refer to Jefferson's "deep duplicity" and "perfidy worthy of Tiberius Caesar or Louis the Eleventh of France . . ." [42]   Although Jefferson's love of liberty was sincere and ardent,[43] he was not a legislator and had no constructive powers; he could destroy but not build.[44]   The success that he met in achieving high office was "a slur upon the moral government of the world." [45]   However regrettable were the want and penury of his declining years, which no just government should have permitted, this condition "was the natural consequences of the niggardly doctrines which his political system had imposed upon him, and which he had passed off upon the country for patriotism." [46]   This latter condemnation of Jefferson's principles was combined with a criticism of his ill treatment of Washington and John Adams, which to John Quincy's mind was equivalent to lack of patriotism.[47]   Testimony to such sentiments must far outweigh any assurances of respect that Adams tendered by letter to Jefferson.[48]   These sentiments were based upon an antipathy for man and principles that no praise from Jefferson, such as that for Adams's great letter of instruction to Erving in Madrid, could counteract.[49]

Was Adams unwittingly a Jeffersonian in the sense of subscribing to Jeffersonian doctrines with sufficient consistency and completeness to warrant his being placed in that category, even though he might protest the discomforts or even the agonies of such a position? No! A survey of the main components of the Jeffersonian system reveals that there was no major area of agreement between the two on peculiarly Jeffersonian doctrines.   With respect to government controls and planning, Jefferson "understood how the movement from simplicity to complexity—from freedom to regimentation—creates a psychology and an institutionalism that conducts straight to the leviathan state

[42] *Memoirs*, January 12, 1831, VIII, 272.

[43] *Ibid.*, January 27, 1831, VIII, 299.

[44] *Ibid.*, January 18, 1831, p. 284.

[45] *Ibid.*, July 29, 1836, IX, 306.

[46] *Ibid.*, August 30, 1836, pp. 306–307.

[47] *Loc. cit.*   Later he pointed out grudgingly and as damningly as he could in a public address that Jefferson had never wholly abandoned Washington. Adams, *The Jubilee of the Constitution*, p. 112.

[48] To Thomas Jefferson, Washington, D. C., October 11, 1817, *Writings*, VI, 219.

[49] *Memoirs*, January 23, 1819, IV, 227.

. . . serving the demands of exploitation. . . ." [50] He stood apart from his friend of the Physiocratic school, Du Pont, who "wanted things planned, ordered, consistent, directed from the top down. . . ." [51] In this respect, he differed likewise from Adams, who favored a program of internal improvements planned and carried forward by government. Adams saw as an early obstacle to such a program "the narrow jealousies and envious cringing of Jefferson's blighting breath. . . ." [52] Although Adams would make concessions to necessity, his great stress upon an immutable natural law and a set of principles, on which he based definite ideas about a positive governmental program, separated him to a significant degree from Jefferson's stand of "pragmatic empiricism"; which the latter derived in ample measure from Locke. [53] Adams owed his debt to Locke, but it was not to the empirical elements in Locke's thought. Adams was modern in his stress upon internal improvements. However, that stress was based upon an eighteenth-century concept of natural laws that became the disguise of his emotional preferences concerning the goals of government. Jefferson's empiricism led him, as he observed the tyrannies of his day and the miseries of urban populations, to reject more active government primarily serving commercial and manufacturing interests.

Jefferson, therefore, had become a major synthesizing agent in the creation of American agrarian democracy. [54] Democrat he was, for, although the ideological position was qualified by the emphasis he placed upon the agrarian as opposed to the urban community, he "from the outset cast his lot with poor, frontier farmers" rather than the planting aristocracy. [55] Adams was never the thoroughgoing doc-

[50] Parrington, *Main Currents in American Thought,* I, 345.

[51] A. Whitney Griswold, "The Agrarian Democracy of Thomas Jefferson," *The American Political Science Review,* XL (August, 1946), p. 669.

[52] Letter to Charles W. Upham, Washington, D. C., February 2, 1837, Tatum (ed.), "Ten Unpublished Letters of John Quincy Adams," 1796–1837, pp. 382–383; of course, both men agreed upon national support for education.

[53] Griswold, *op. cit.,* p. 669. The conflict over constructive or implied powers stood at the heart of the whole question of the proper role and purpose of government. In this regard, of course, despite some ambiguity in Adams's position forced upon him by political necessity, as discussed in Chapter XII, Adams and Jefferson stood poles apart. Adams, *Parties in the United States,* pp. 37–38.

[54] Parrington, *op. cit.,* I, 352.

[55] Griswold, *op. cit.,* p. 667. Adams likewise was suspicious of "wealthy

trinaire democrat, although he might recognize the marching forces of democracy, just as Jefferson came to see the inevitability of the expansion of commerce and manufacturing.[56] Adams described Jefferson as the protagonist of a "fraudulent democracy by the possession of which . . . [he] rose to power in this country, and of which he set the first successful example." [57] As a sounder theoretical and practical democrat, Jefferson also understood the nature and function of political parties and maneuvers, a fact that Adams saw but mislabeled "demagogue policy." [58] Adams, of course, never understood political parties, nor did he really ever understand or sympathize with the swelling democratic tides that made political parties of a new type necessary and normal. As to Jefferson's preference for the stability of an "agrarian economy," [59] Adams would have none of that and objected strenuously to Jefferson's thesis "that commerce was to be encouraged only as the handmaid of agriculture." [60]

Turning to another doctrine that may be described as typically Jeffersonian, we find one possible point of agreement between the two men. Jefferson could not avoid rejecting the principles underlying slavery. He knew that in the course of events the woeful institution was doomed. Yet even on this point Adams qualified his approval of Jefferson's stand. Adams also opposed slavery in principle and practice. He agreed that Jefferson "was above that execrable sophistry of the South Carolinian nullifiers, which would make of slavery the cornerstone to the temple of liberty." [61] Jefferson sincerely hated slavery, although he evidenced "the alloy of expediency" in founding the Colonization Society.[62] But this agreement on slavery was not enough to justify an assertion that Adams was in any significant respect a Jeffersonian.

Jeffersonian doctrine may be so denoted, of course, because Jeffer-

---

landholders" and a planting aristocracy, but his conscience Whiggery prompted that suspicion more than democratic instincts. Quincy, *A Memoir of the Life of John Quincy Adams,* p. 211.

[56] Griswold, *op. cit.,* p. 670.

[57] *Memoirs,* April 13, 1836, IX, 465.

[58] Quincy, *op. cit.,* p. 320. Parrington, *op. cit.,* I, 342.

[59] Parrington, *op. cit.,* I, 347. Griswold, *op. cit.,* p. 668.

[60] Adams, *Parties in the United States,* p. 47.

[61] *Memoirs,* January 27, 1831, VIII, 299–300.

[62] Adams, "Speech Delivered at North-Bridgewater, on Wednesday, November 6, 1844," *Boston Courier,* November 11, 1844.

son, its chief protagonist, towers intellectually and spiritually above his contemporaries of like persuasion. Jeffersonianism was not created *de nouveau;* it had its origin in the intellectual heritage from which Jefferson derived and which he shaped to fit an American environment.[63]

Why is there not a body of doctrine popularly called Adamsian with as strong an influence in American politics and life as the Jeffersonian? The fact that there is not cannot be ascribed to the absence of an Adamsian system or doctrine. It must be ascribed rather to the fact that Adams was both, on the one hand, behind his times in his views of democracy and political parties, and, on the other hand, ahead of his times regarding the role of government. Adams found no such response in his country as did Jefferson, because he was both ahead of and behind his times in his social theory. In fact there is reason to believe that a significant majority in the United States even today are closer to Jefferson's views of the responsibilities of government. It is remarkable that this should be true even in a century in which the Adams thesis of the government as a positive instrument to be used wherever needed for the accomplishment of the general social good seems more than ever an inevitable response to the necessities of man's living in society. Adams remains ahead of his time. He will perhaps come into his own in the understanding of Americans when they have accepted more fully and consciously the idea of a positive role for government as the chief instrument for serving the general welfare.

Adams was not, therefore, thoroughly associated with any major political movement when he was appointed Secretary of State. His career was always hindered by non-partisanship, in terms of party association, and an acidulous personality; but both factors were more than offset by consummate ability and technical mastery of the expertness required in the positions he was called upon to fill. But a catalytic agent was introduced into American politics, the personality of Andrew Jackson. He became the potent symbol of the developing frontier democracy that as a component of traditional American agrarian democracy was overshadowing the planter forces. The latter were not altogether in sympathy with the newer agrarian democracy, yet they were in a major degree maintaining alignment with

[63] Griswold, *op. cit.,* p. 658.

it under pressure of the slavery issue. The effect upon Adams was not to alter his attitude toward political parties but to keep him in secure but expedient association with the forces, many anachronistic, that opposed the Jacksonian revolution.

Adams's early championship of Jackson has been recorded. In the light of the subsequent bitter conflict between the two men, it is strange to recall that Adams in 1822 wrote that he could not contemplate the character of Jackson "without veneration." [64] Jackson's language, wrote Adams, might have been "impassioned and violent, his conduct . . . [was always] calm and deliberate." [65] Not only was he deliberate, but after listening to advice he made inflexible decisions; his policy always rested upon justice, the law of nations, and the public good. For those reasons Adams preferred him to all the other candidates for election in 1824.[66] Should Jackson not achieve the Presidency, Adams recorded he was willing to see him in the Vice-Presidency.[67] One of the great social events of 1824 was a ball given by the Adamses to celebrate General Jackson's victory at New Orleans.

The reaction was violent. Jackson's charges of collusion between Clay and Adams and the domination of the whole period of the Adams Administration by preparation for the coming election forced Adams to recognize the clear division of political forces. By 1827 in Adams's mind Jackson appeared incompetent by reason of ignorance and passion; he would be advised, if he became President, by incompetent men with nothing but a talent for intrigue. The opposition appeared to him as the "base and profligate combination against" him and Clay

[64] *Memoirs,* January 2, 1822, V, 473. Even his appraisal of Jackson's military career was somewhat modified by subsequent events. In 1828 he opposed the grant of one thousand dollars to Jackson by the Congress to pay a fine, plus the interest since 1815, imposed upon Jackson for imprisoning a judge under the power of martial law. Adams said the real reason behind the proposition was the glorification of the Battle of New Orleans. He, himself, had never justified such a use of the military power. *Congressional Globe,* 27th Cong., 3rd sess., January 6, 1843, pp. 128–129. And, in defense of General Brown's reputation, he wrote that Jackson had been aided by "fortune," and "egregious errors of the enemy." *Memoirs,* February 24, 1828, VII, 448.

[65] *Memoirs,* January 12, 1823, VI, 129.

[66] Brown, *The Missouri Compromises and Presidential Politics, 1820–1825,* Letter from William Plumer, Jr., to William Plumer, Sr., Washington, D. C., December 3, 1823, pp. 85, 87. This letter records the gist of a conversation between Plumer and Adams. Such a sentiment was not recorded in the *Memoirs.*

[67] *Memoirs,* April 2, 1824, VI, 274. *Ibid.,* May 27, 1824, p. 360.

that he early saw would succeed in bringing Jackson to the Presidency in the next election.[68]   Adams even came to regret that he had supported Jackson in the Seminole War; and for that defense he was later bitterly attacked.[69]   Despite attempts at *rapprochement,* the gulf between the two men became unbridgeable, not least of all because of Adams's intransigeant attitude, similar to that of contemporary liberals, formerly admirers of the Soviet Union, who, after determining that it has failed them, have become its most implacable foes.[70]

The breach was emotionally, as well as politically, based.   Jackson, in the assertion of Adams, was a semi-literate popular idol, inaugurated into the Presidency by the force of a popular, constitutional uprising; his entry into Washington was celebrated by the planning of a self-appointed committee.[71]   He was a barbarian to whom, regrettably, Harvard was stooping to grant honorary degrees, thus seeming to place its august approval upon the catastrophe.   In hurrying back to Washington from Boston on the claim of illness, the new popular idol, turning "disease to commodity," [72] was about to be "glorified into his grave." [73]   On the doctrinal level, Jackson symbolized a slanderous democracy working through the medium, for example, of Isaac Hill and his *New Hampshire Patriot,* provided with the weapons of attack by long-standing enemies, such as Jonathan Russell.   To the stemming of such forces, Adams asserted, he had devoted his life.

Jackson, more specifically, was the instrument of attack upon the interests protected by the Bank of the United States.   While decrying the Bank's electioneering against him, he was employing all the power of a government that had been captured by a reckless lot of plebeians to electioneer for himself by attacking the Bank.[74]   A reckless, popularly controlled "executive will," under Jackson's leadership an instrument to be feared, was substituted for Congressional or judicial action.[75]   The exalted office, in fact, had become the weapon of "a joint stock company."   He wrote as follows:

[68] *Memoirs,* December 17, 1827, VII, 382–383.
[69] *Ibid.,* April 29, 1830, VIII, 223.
[70] *Ibid.,* March 2, 1832, pp. 484–486.
[71] *Ibid.,* February 28, 1829, p. 101.
[72] *Ibid.,* June 27, 1833, IX, 5.
[73] *Ibid.,* June 25, 1833, p. 4.
[74] *Register of Debates,* 23rd Cong., 1st sess., III, April 4, 1834, pp. 3497–3500.
[75] *Ibid.,* p. 3505.

Jackson came in upon the trumpet tongue of military achievement. His presidency has been the reign of subaltern knaves, fattening upon land jobs and money jobs, who have made him believe that it was a heroic conception of his own to destroy the Bank of the United States. . . . Two political swindlers, Amos Kendall and Rueben M. Whitney, were the Empson and Dudley of our Solomon, and, by playing upon his vanity and his thirst of petty revenge, have got into their own hands the overflowing revenue of the country; with the temporary and illegal *use* of which they are replenishing their own coffers and making princely fortunes. Jackson has wearied out the sordid subserviency of his supporters, and Van Buren has had the address to persuade him that he is the only man who can preserve and perpetuate the principles of his Administration.[76]

Thus, Jackson's Administration had been based on democratic forces influenced by military popularity, and it had been corrupted by the support of Van Buren, the sycophant, and Kendall, "the ruling mind." [77] It meant abandonment of internal improvements and refusal to promote internal industry, lack of any pretense of control over the separate states,[78] an outright capitulation to sectional and special interests,[79] and neglect of all just standards with respect to official appointments.[80] Its moral tone was set by Van Buren's "pandering to palm a prostitute upon decent society. . . ." [81] "All other questions of public interest . . . [sank] into insignificance in comparison with that of arresting him [Jackson] in his career of ruin." [82]

The passion of such sentiments and beliefs drove Adams to closer association with political parties, association deriving in the main from the Clay-Adams partnership, although he maintained his extraordinary capacity to take the independent course when principles required it. Adams agreed that the course of the Jackson Administration required a new party alignment to represent the division of the country.[83] The National Republicans were the party that repre-

[76] *Memoirs,* October 11, 1836, IX, 311–312.
[77] *Ibid.,* December 4, 1840, X, 366.
[78] *Ibid.,* January 13, 1831, VIII, 273. *Ibid.,* December 31, 1832, p. 515. *Ibid.,* June 22, 1830, p. 232.
[79] *Ibid.,* June 22, 1830, p. 232.
[80] *Ibid.,* March 14, 1829, p. 113. *Ibid.,* January 19, 1830, p. 177.
[81] *Ibid.,* December 22, 1831, p. 440.
[82] *Ibid.,* January 9, 1834, IX, 73.
[83] *Ibid.,* January 24, 1830, VIII, 180.

sented the old Clay-Adams partnership and the major opposition to Jackson. Adams was therefore interested in the survival of this party and worried over the possible effects on it of a projected union with Antimasons and of his own Antimasonry, particularly on those National Republicans who were Masons.[84]

At one time Adams approved of the Freemasons. In a letter of instructions to Hugh Nelson, he claimed that the Masons in the United States had probably not supported the Cuban independence movement on the ground that American Masonic societies did not use political means.[85] Moved by the story of the murder of Morgan in New York, his reaction to the organization changed, and he claimed that it wielded an unfortunate political power in places high and low by means of political parties and public office.[86] The defect was not in the members but in the institution.[87] He was convinced that Washington if he had lived to view the subsequent history of Masonry would have changed his views.[88] Adams himself candidly admitted his Antimasonry. He accused the Masons of crimes and of unfairly and corruptly assisting members' political ambitions. They were, in fact, "if not the greatest, . . . [at least] one of the greatest moral and political evils, under which . . . [the] union . . . [was then] laboring." [89] There was even reason to believe that the order was unfriendly to civil authority.[90] In the face of that threat the Antimasonic Party, playing the same role with regard to Freemasonry that Protestantism played in relation to Catholicism, was formed to ward off the danger.[91] And Adams was associated with it.

[84] *Ibid.*, March 6, 1833, VIII, 535.

[85] National Archives, Records of the Department of State, *Diplomatic Instructions, All Countries*, IX, 193.

[86] John Quincy Adams, *Letters and Addresses on Freemasonry* (Dayton, Ohio: United Brethren Publishing House, 1875), Letter to Edward Ingersoll, Quincy, September 23, 1831, pp. 66–67.

[87] *Ibid.*, Letter to Edward Ingersoll, Quincy, September 22, 1831, p. 60.

[88] *Ibid.*, Letter to a Reviewer of Sheppard's Defense of the Masonic Institution, Quincy, August 22, 1831, p. 53.

[89] John Quincy Adams, *Letters to Edward Livingston, Grand High Priest of the General Grand Royal Arch Chapter of the United States, and Late Secretary of State of the Said States* (Boston: Connecticut Antimasonic Tract Association, 1833), Letter I, Washington, D. C., April 10, 1833, pp. 2–4.

[90] Adams, *Letters and Addresses on Freemasonry*, Letter to a Reviewer of Sheppard's Defense of the Masonic Institution, Quincy, August 22, 1831, p. 50.

[91] Adams, *Letters to Edward Livingston*, Letter II, Philadelphia, April 15, 1833, p. 9.

In addition to cooperation with the Antimasons, Adams was generally identified with the Whig Party, the outgrowth of the National Republican party and the forces that had supported the Adams Administration. The amazing fact, however, in view of the passion of his anti-Jackson bias, was Adams's maintenance of a high degree of independence from the political parties that opposed Jackson. As a so-called "conscience" Whig, he was no doubt widely divorced on the slavery issue from such Southern Whigs as W. P. Mangum and John M. Berrien,[92] but, furthermore, his Whiggery was generally too unstable to be termed close party loyalty. His conscience would assert itself with regard to more than slavery, and at such times no party tie could bind him. The nonpartisan quality of his political life was maintained in spite of the fact that he was always the dogmatist, as the discussion of his political and social system has revealed. Indeed, the political and social dogmatism remained, more immovable than would that based only upon undeviating party affiliation. Adams was to himself the singular example of all that was good. He was always the associate, never the obliging ally. The doings of all his contemporaries passed before him to be gratuitously judged. He expressed regret that the Antimasons did not manifest a "discretion" and a "plain dealing" and a "consistency . . . equal to the goodness of their cause." [93] Further, he placed them, as we have noted, in the main tradition with all the other groups in the country that were produced by a certain "restless and turbulent" spirit in those "who must always have something to quarrel about with their neighbors." [94]

The Whigs, on the other hand, were impregnated with "Clay Masonry." [95] There was, to begin with, a significant measure of incompatibility between Adams and the Whigs, who were "the champions of legislative deliberation as opposed to executive power." [96]

---

[92] Allan Nevins, *Ordeal of the Union* (New York: Charles Scribner's Sons, 1947), I, 8.

[93] Adams, *Letters and Addresses on Freemasonry,* Letter to Richard Rush, Quincy, October 25, 1831, p. 79.

[94] *Memoirs,* January 21, 1844, XI, 491.

[95] Adams, *Letters and Addresses on Freemasonry,* Letter to Edward Ingersoll, September 23, 1831, p. 70.

[96] Dumond, *op. cit.,* p. 252: Presumably, not even hatred of the Jacksonian revolution could destroy Adams's theoretical preference for executive power. Nevertheless, he did express regret over the weakened Whig opposition to executive power. The Democrats and Whigs might just as well change places under the circumstances. But here Adams was referring to the Jacksonian type of execu-

He showed his independence, as we have seen, in the controversy during Jackson's Administration over the $3,000,000 fortification measure, which the Whigs had opposed and Adams vigorously supported.[97]   Although he might regret the ruin of the Whig Party, leaving impotent the forces necessary "to contend against the misrule of a triumphant, fraudulent, and reckless Democracy," [98] he never hesitated to criticize that party for reasons he deemed sound.[99]   He would never have hesitated to take any party to ruin, if that was the only alternative to abandonment of his own principles. That willingness was a natural consequence, first, of his ignorance of the significance of parties, and, second, of his concept of a higher law with which Adams felt himself to be peculiarly *en rapport.*

Although John Quincy Adams may be considered a major contributor to the building of the American political and social Myth, it is surely not in the area of domestic affairs that he made his greatest contribution. He occupied a position apart; his was an eccentric or unique mind and philosophy. Perhaps his lonely position does not have the significance for his country that Brooks and Henry Adams asserted it had, but there will be few to deny his importance as a fashioner of American foreign policy. The principles that guided American statecraft for generations were in considerable measure those he had formulated while occupying high office. It is indeed remarkable that he was able to exert his influence so strongly upon United States foreign policy. He did not appraise the course of American domestic politics accurately, and yet he assisted in the setting of the national sights on targets of foreign policy that have proved until recently adequate to domestic needs. In this area his contribution to the building of the American political system was profoundly important. It is appropriate, therefore, to turn to Adams the practitioner in the realm of international relations.

---

tive leadership and power, which represented suspect and unprincipled forces. *Congressional Globe,* 27th Cong., 1st sess., June 1, 1841, p. 9.

[97] *Congressional Globe,* 24th Cong., 1st sess., appendix, p. 709.

[98] *Memoirs,* November 16, 1842, XI, 270.

[99] *Congressional Globe,* 27th Cong., 3rd sess., February 10, 1843, p. 269.

PART SIX

The United States, John Quincy Adams, and International Politics

15

The World of Nations

A man might profess to be perfectly independent, and to set at naught the opinions and wishes of others; but he could not get along without soon finding the inconvenience to himself of such a system. And so with nations.

—MEMOIRS, *March 21, 1820*

The area most congenial to Adams's talents, if not his temperament, was the diplomatic calling, statecraft on the international level. He brought to this field vast experience, the result of a conditioning in the art of diplomacy that began early and was most rare for a United States' citizen of his day, and an erudition that was extraordinary for the man of affairs even in the age of Jefferson and John Adams. It was the nation's good fortune that he possessed the capacity to observe widely and to develop a broad perspective from such observation. Of course, no analyst should overstress the uniqueness of any era's implications for the future. He must always remember that an eventful period results from forces and trends present in preceding periods that may have been outwardly calm. Nevertheless, Adams's diplomatic career coincided with a time of significant social upheaval in Europe to which America was forced to adjust. The assumptions underlying his policy, together with his view of policy, are of great importance, therefore, in relation to his whole social and political view.

Adams conceived of a nation as a "moral person" in a family of nations.[1] This moral person, in his view of the international law governing the subject, was possessed of external rights and obliga-

[1] Letter to Charles W. Upham, Washington, D. C., February 2, 1837, Tatum (ed.), "Ten Unpublished Letters of John Quincy Adams, 1796–1837," p. 383.

tions that remained unchanged by any "internal revolution of government."[2]   In this context, he described as a new maxim in the law of nations the principle, especially devised by the victors to apply to Napoleon but promising disadvantage to the victors in future contingencies, that a sovereign by the breach of a treaty should forfeit "all legal right to existence."[3]   Adams saw the obligations imposed upon the "moral person" of the nation usually in such a light as to favor the interests of the United States as he interpreted them.   This fact should not be the basis of a charge that Adams was any more guilty than other natural law theorists of confusing his preferences with so-called absolute values.   Such a confusion is inherent in a philosophical system that accepts natural laws.   In Adams's case, he identified his interpretation of the best interests of the United States with eternal verity.   For example, he conceived of the law of nature and nature's God as requiring the eventual achievement of most "liberal" principles of commercial relations and exchange, in particular resulting in the opening up of South American ports to the commerce of the world and in the relaxing of the whole system of imperial commercial restrictions.[4]   He especially importuned the British to liberalize their system, and propounded a policy of mutual exclusions upon British commerce in order to force concessions.[5] He praised the Russians for inaugurating and maintaining a regime

[2] National Archives, Records of the Department of State, *Diplomatic Instructions,* All Countries, IX, 8.   To Don Francisco Dionisio Vivés, State Department, Washington, D. C., May 8, 1820, *Writings,* VII, 18: He asserted that Spain could not be relieved of an obligation to ratify a treaty that had been signed by a plenipotentiary, even though he had acted on unqualified instructions of a sovereign whose authority was subsequently limited by a legislative body asserting a new constitutional power to pass on treaties.

[3] To Abigail Adams, Paris, April 22, 1815, *Writings,* V, 302.   Adams, without ever explicitly dealing with the point at length, distinguished between the sovereign "moral person," the nation, susceptible of no act incompatible with the necessities of the moral system of which it was a part, and the physical sovereign in a monarchy, who could be sovereign only in a fashion subordinate to the level of the nation.   *Annals of Congress,* 9th Cong., 1st sess., March 3, 1806, pp. 145–161.

[4] National Archives, Records of the Department of State, *Diplomatic Instructions,* All Countries, VIII, 196.

[5] *Ibid.,* VIII, 223; it is interesting to observe that in a speech before the *Massachusetts Historical Society* Adams, asserting that equality was the basis of relations among states, justified Britain's struggle to force acceptance of that principle by the Chinese.   Quincy, *Memoirs of the Life of John Quincy Adams,* pp. 336, 338.

of liberal commercial relations without especial favor,[6] but, in contrast, he saw in the mutual bartering of colonial commercial rights among the colonial powers a conspiracy against the United States, the only other extensive commercial and maritime power without colonies.[7] He described our own policy with regard to South America as based upon the two principles of "entire and unqualified reciprocity" and permanent most-favored-nation treatment, which were necessary to the achievement and maintenance of South American independence. Reminding the world that the states of the Union in their mutual relations "abstained altogether from prohibitions," he suggested that the same determination lay behind the Constitutional prohibition of export taxes and that they followed a policy of favoring "their own shipping by special preferences or exclusive privileges in their own ports" only to counteract similar practices by other nations.[8] In negotiating treaties of commerce, most important instruments in the preservation of peace, a nation should seek not only to satisfy its own interest but should also be willing "to concede liberally to that which is adapted to the interest of the other." [9] Adams asserted that an important reason for sending a delegation from the United States to a general American conference in Panama was the opportunity to familiarize the newly independent Latin Americans with the principles that should govern their independence, among which he listed the avoidance of special concessions to particular countries.[10] He conceived of the United States

[6] National Archives, Records of the Department of State, *Diplomatic Instructions, All Countries*, VIII, 205–206.

[7] National Archives, Records of the Department of State, *Diplomatic Instructions, All Countries*, VIII, 241. With an exquisite Adams touch, he asserted that American acceptance of "independence, Equality, and Reciprocity" as the basis of dealings with other nations meant that the United States rejected all "double dealing, overreaching, and corrupt caballing." *Ibid.*, IX, 288.

[8] Adams, "First Annual Message," *in* Richardson, ed., *A Compilation of the Messages and Papers of the Presidents, 1789–1897*, II, pp. 300, 302.

[9] Adams, "Third Annual Message," *in ibid.*, p. 380. Ordinarily this might be considered a mere platitudinous generalization, but coming from John Quincy Adams it undoubtedly has a deeper significance, for it was compatible with his whole view of commercial relations.

[10] Adams, "Message to the Senate, December 26, 1825," *in ibid.*, p. 318. For example, Adams denied that Buenos Aires could close its ports without cause, especially against one particular nation. Such an action would violate the provisions of international law. *Memoirs*, January 13, 1818, IV, 41.

as the leader in a general struggle for liberal, unrestricted, reciprocal relations among nations, especially commercial relations. Adams had his own peculiar concept of an American system of international relations that was anti-imperialist in the old-fashioned and liberal sense and should become the model for the stereotyped Old World. And by the nature of his intellectual system, the goals that he set for the United States in the realm of international affairs were generalized as valid goals implicit in the laws of nature themselves.

The most explicit manifestation of the order in nature governing the actions of nations was the body of international law. Adams defined it thus:

The laws of social intercourse between sovereign communities constitute the laws of nations, all derived from three sources:—the laws of nature, or in other words the dictates of justice; usages, sanctioned by custom; and treaties, or national covenants. Super-added to these, the *Christian* nations, between themselves, admit, with various latitudes of interpretation, and little consistency of practice, the laws of humanity and mutual benevolence taught in the gospel of Christ.[11]

It will be noted that Adams places the laws of nature with usages, and treaties as sources of the law of nations. This does not mean that there was no priority among them. Their order of listing is one indication, but an understanding of his philosophical system makes it clear that the basic source was the laws of nature, or the dictates of justice. That source would, of course, be to Adams the basic one. If one substituted commonsense as a criterion of what is the due of each nation for the dictates of justice, or the "laws of nature," and retained usages and treaties, the definition is adequate for today. By adding Christian principles as a support of the law of nations, Adams was designating as of primary importance the European system of which the Western Hemisphere was a part. The Christian component in this structure of law should not be depreciated. On the basis of the above definition Adams could conclude that the "rights of nations . . . [were] nothing more than an extension of the rights of individuals to the great societies, into which the different portions of mankind . . . [had] been combined. . . ."[12] These

---

[11] Adams, *Newburyport Oration, 1837*, p. 17.
[12] II "Marcellus," *Writings*, I, 139

rights were indirectly or directly drawn from the basic tenet that "the author of Christianity" had established to govern the power to enjoy liberty, the tenet that each individual should possess the right to do whatever does not interfere with the enjoyment of the rights of others. The rights, of course, remain to be defined, but we may assume them to be all those rights obviously compatible with Christianity that might be enjoyed without restricting others in the enjoyment of the same rights.

In the practical sphere, Adams used this tenet as the test when he attacked Ingersoll of Pennsylvania for an allegedly warmongering speech, asserting that he would rather have his country "in the right" than successful.[13] He ascribed a tremendous role to international law as he wrote, "The general history of mankind, for the last three thousand years, demonstrates beyond all contradiction the progressive improvement of the condition of man, by means of the establishment of principles of International Law, tending to social benevolence and humanity."[14] Only in comformity with such an evolution would a nation achieve greatness.

The difficulties of definition, of course, remain. But for Adams the necessity of defining either the conditions governing the application of the principles of the laws of nations or of nature—for example, the right of self-defense—or the principles themselves was never an insuperable obstacle. In defending General Jackson's actions in Florida in the great letter of instructions to Erving in Madrid, he found his vindication of the volatile General in "the first law of nature," entirely compatible with the law of nations, the right of self-defense.[15] The "first law of nature" was here naturally subject to any definition Adams chose to render. It is not that the natural law theorists consciously clothed their practical goals with the disguise of a formal natural law philosophy, but in accepting a natural law concept they were forced into a confusion of their value preferences with what they called the laws of nature. By way of further illustration, Adams denied that France could demand of "right" that the United States government deliver up deserters from French

[13] *Congressional Globe,* 27th Cong., 2nd sess., April 14, 1842, p. 424.

[14] National Archives, Records of the Department of State, *Diplomatic Instructions,* All Countries, X, 148.

[15] To George William Erving, State Department, Washington, D. C., November 28, 1818, *Writings,* VI, 486–487.

vessels, partly on the ground that France had set the precedent by refusing to deliver up American murderers and robbers, guilty of acts on the high seas.[16] The "right" here, based upon the law of nature, served to support Adams in his support of the United States against the French. He concluded that it was "settled by universal usage"[17] that a nation's jurisdiction in the execution of its revenue laws extended far beyond its territorial jurisdiction. As sources of the authority and the principles recognized in the intercourse of nations he recommended Smith, Montesquieu, Grotius, and Ward to the would-be diplomat. Vattel's *Droit des Gens,* written in a "popular and easy style," was recommended for matters of practical diplomacy. But, beyond those sources, the diplomat who would acquire expertness and an adequate background must study the "history, internal interests, and the external *relations*" of his own nation, as well as of other nations.[18]

[16] National Archives, Records of the Department of State, *Diplomatic Instructions,* All Countries, IX, 53.

[17] To the President (Monroe), Washington, D. C., July 17, 1821, *Writings,* VII, 119.

[18] To Christopher Hughes, Ealing, December 25, 1816, *Writings,* VI, 129.

16

Adams, a New-World Diplomat

There is, no doubt, great delicacy, and sometimes danger, in bestowing diplomatic confidences; but, crafty and fraudulent as the trade has the reputation of being, I give it as the result of my experience that confidence judiciously and cautiously bestowed is one of the most powerful and efficacious instruments of negotiation.

MEMOIRS, *May 28, 1819*

THE PRACTITIONER OF DIPLOMACY

His own experience, as we have seen, began as early as 1782 when he went to Russia with Judge Dana. In particular, his journey from St. Petersburg to The Hague afforded him an extraordinary opportunity, important in the training of the diplomat, to observe political and economic conditions. Surprisingly, he was able to develop a calm view of exotic habits and customs in foreign courts, as indicated, for example, by the matter-of-factness of his observation without criticism that the Emperor Alexander allowed no influence to the women by whom he had children.[1] The stern puritan moralist could with sufficient ease compartmentalize his view of the world. Adams was acutely conscious of the significance and implication of diplomatic maneuver, and his first contacts with the British government provided him with early experience in the art. Taking care to assess the diplomatic capacities and assets of those with whom he had to deal, he recorded his conclusions in the *Memoirs*: Bagot, for example, was the most successful British minister he had known. This fact surprised him because success was perhaps based

---

[1] *Memoirs*, January 9, 1810, II, 94.

on the minister's mediocre talents, and this possibility staggered Adams's "belief in the universality of the maxim that men of the greatest talents ought to be sought out for diplomatic missions." [2] Stratford Canning, with whom he had one of the most furious verbal exchanges of his career, he rated as a man of his word who possessed the most important quality for a diplomatist, sincerity, yet was seriously lacking in suppleness. [3] The diplomatic business was a serious one and should be, Adams stressed, so transacted, and by people in some manner prepared by temperament and training for it.

Diplomatic affairs were formerly managed by few persons. They were like a convent of monks, and accordingly there was some gravity in the manner of transacting business. But now [especially as he viewed the Congress of Vienna] there are so many *dilettanti* that I, for my part, cannot see through it. [4]

As American Secretary of State, Adams not only played to a great degree the role of *eminence grise* in the formulation of policy in the Monroe Administration, he took into serious account the motivations and necessities of his counterparts abroad. Discussing his belief that Mr. Canning (The British Secretary of State for Foreign Affairs) ought to desire to recognize the independence of Spanish America to the degree that its struggle for independence had achieved well-established success, he cautioned our minister not to press for it, since Britain might wish to appear to make such a move spontaneously. [5]

Adams clearly possessed great talent for diplomacy, accompanied by training and interest in this field of human endeavor. The wonder is that his acid and self-righteous temperament did not bring him to greater grief. Diplomacy is not merely one manifestation of the art of winning friends and influencing others, but a portion of that faculty in the chief architect of a nation's foreign policy would not be amiss. Adams's incapacity to win friends was unquestion-

---

[2] *Memoirs*, April 14, 1819, IV, 339.

[3] *Ibid.*, June 24, 1823, II, 157.

[4] *Ibid.*, August 19, 1813, II, 513. He did not counsel secret, surreptitious diplomacy, however, if we may draw broad implications from his rejection of a proposal to send secret agents to Greece and his assertion that American agents could never be secret. *Ibid.*, August 15, 1823, VI, 173.

[5] National Archives, Records of the Department of State, *Diplomatic Instructions*, All Countries, X, 125–126.

ably compensated for by great technical ability. The latter was his main reliance in influencing men and events. At Ghent his colleagues, one and all, came in for strictures: Russell, for trivial criticisms of Adams's drafts, "grammatical and verbal"; [6] Gallatin, for too great a fear of offending his colleagues; Clay, for a captious dislike for "figurative language." [7] The British plenipotentiaries, on the other side, held to trivial points. [8] There were sound bases for some of his criticisms, no doubt, but his general unwillingness to admit his own human failing was an irritating quality. To be sure, he might confess the vigor of his own temper, speculate as to whether he was not on occasion guilty of indiscretion in dealing with foreign representatives, or confess that an objection of Crawford to a harsh note in a dispatch might be sound, but such doubts were rarely stated.

Adams's jaundiced views of others did not obscure his conception of the practical and changing world about him. Diplomacy was, to him, largely a process of gathering empirical data for use in making the decisions of the observational science of government. In other words, when it came down to the actual practice in every-day terms of the art of diplomacy, Adams was not an impractical, doctrinaire theorist. Alert to political changes, imminent and accomplished, he watched world-wide developments intelligently. Early in his State Department tenure, he projected instructions (later deleted) to J. B. Prevost to go to the mouth of the Columbia River and there to assert United States sovereignty by any appropriate means short of force. [9] Several years later when the Russian threat had materialized in that part of the world, he was quick to instruct the American Minister to inform the Russian government that, although the United States Government had confidence in the utimate realization of justice, this government was surprised at Russian aggressions and did not propose to overlook them, because they affected the national rights and the citizens of the United States. [10] The Russian Imperial Ukaze establishing the 51st degree of north latitude

---

[6] *Memoirs*, August 13, 1814, III, 15.

[7] *Ibid.*, August 21, 1814, p. 21.

[8] *Ibid.*, December 23, 1814, p. 124.

[9] National Archives, Records of the Department of State, *Diplomatic Instructions*, All Countries, VIII, 149.

[10] *Ibid.*, X, 53.

as the line bounding their possessions and forbidding the vessels of other powers to approach within one hundred Italian miles of the territory was flatly rejected by Adams and the United States Minister was directed to press for a retraction.[11] He realistically assessed Britain's real desire in Spanish America as independence for the colonies in the interest of the commercial privileges to be gained for Britain.[12] His eyes were directed with particular concern toward Cuba with full understanding of the implications of internal political conditions in that island for the United States, the British Empire, and Spain.[13] He pressed the British government, having an early insight into its real interests in Spanish America, to keep him informed concerning the intention of the European Allies with respect to that part of the world.[14]

Observing the European scene as his early career gave him a firsthand opportunity to do, he demonstrated a keen insight into events and trends. He easily analyzed Napoleon's Continental System as working fundamentally in Britain's interest.[15] An Adams report to the State Department contains an astute early forecast that Napoleon would direct his attentions toward Russia, because of the new failures of the French in Spain and changed relations between the French and Austrians.[16] Later, following Napoleon's defeat, instructions from the Secretary of State contended truly that the triumphant European Alliance probably did not comprehend the revolutionary temper of the forces against which it was struggling. With perspicacity he also saw that Alexander of Russia, the only nation not affected by the new ferment and the one profiting most from the situation of European political disorder, possessed a temperament in complete accord with the conservative interests of his Empire.[17] Adams remarked that, on its face, it was peculiar that Castlereagh had announced in Parliament that the Prince Regent

[11] National Archives, Records of the Department of State, *Diplomatic Instructions*, All Countries, IX, 121–122.

[12] *Ibid.*, VIII, 193.

[13] *Ibid.*, IX, 186.

[14] *Memoirs,* June 25, 1818, IV, 103.

[15] *Ibid.*, December 26, 1809, II, 84. *Ibid.*, December 29, 1809, p. 91. *Ibid.*, August 8, 1810, p. 145.

[16] To the Secretary of State (James Monroe), St. Petersburg, June 22, 1811, *Writings*, IV, 115.

[17] National Archives, Records of the Department of State, *Diplomatic Instructions,* All Countries, IX, 19–20.

entirely approved the principles of the Holy Alliance, since the British constitution did not permit the sovereign of Great Britain to make personal compacts binding upon the country. He therefore concluded, stressing the fact that Britain's interests were diverging from those of Russia, that the Prince Regent's adherence had been rendered only to the degree permitted by the constitution and required by the international situation.[18] In 1818 he was unaware that Britain was not a secure member of the European or Quadruple Alliance, but when that fact became clear to him, he recognized the implications for British European and global policy. He then expressed hope that this insecurity would influence British statesmen to modify or review their previous policy on neutral and maritime rights, and he sought negotiations on that assumption.[19]

Adams firmly believed in sound training and expertness for a diplomat. Noting the changes of diplomatic assignment by the Jackson Administration, he wrote that no Administration could make bad appointments abroad "with impunity."[20] He rejected any conception, however, of American diplomatic careers that included living abroad for years at a time. He held that his own appointment to London should be short, for he believed that "every American who . . . [had] resided so long as five or six years in Europe ought to go home to be *new tempered.*"[21] He advised friends and subordinates of the propriety of this maxim. Diplomatic posts, "founded upon the nature of our institutions," could not be considered careers as in Europe.[22] The principles of our system would not permit missions abroad to be considered life establishments. Nevertheless, he wrote, it was regrettable that our government was so parsimonious in the support of the diplomatic and foreign service, and he found it tragic to report that no American Minister to Britain had found it possible "to limit his expenses within the public allowance of salary and outfit."[23] In consequence of

[18] To George Washington Campbell, State Department, Washington, D. C., June 28, 1818, *Writings*, VI, 375.

[19] National Archives, Records of the Department of State, *Diplomatic Instructions, All Countries*, X, 72.

[20] *Memoirs*, April 18, 1829, VIII, 139.

[21] To Alexander Hill Everett, London, July 27, 1815, *Writings*, V, 331.

[22] *Memoirs*, February 10, 1819, IV, 248–249.

[23] To the Secretary of State (James Monroe), London, July 12, 1816, *Writings*, VI, 52.

the general truth of that fact, among others, "an American mission abroad . . . [was] a perpetual lesson of humility, not to say of humiliation. It . . . [fixed] a man in the condition of a parasite, and then . . . [told] him to maintain his self-respect and the consideration of his country."[24] "Inexorable economy" and "parsimony" made for this result.[25] Adams would have preferred a competent and sufficient service, of which a growing republic could be proud, yet one that would maintain respect for republican principles and interests by avoiding career tenure abroad in contact with foreign influences.[26]

In the actual practice of the diplomatic art Adams stood out as an innovator as well as, in some sort, a model. As Secretary of State, he wisely planned an index for diplomatic correspondence and a register for consular correspondence.[27] With close attention to details, he admonished Jonathan Russell in Sweden and Middleton, who was bound for Russia, to number all diplomatic dispatches to permit their being more easily accounted for.[28] Complaining that he was constantly being obstructed in his work by lost papers, he despaired of instituting an improved system.[29] After a thorough study he recorded that he had partially "ascertained the causes of the deficiency in the appropriations" for the Department and promised to look for a remedy.[30]

The most arduous task of the Secretary was the drafting of instructions for American representatives abroad or on the point of departure for foreign posts. He established as an early goal the discovery of a "general principle" for drafting instructions to ministers, and the finding of "some particulars of instructions which

[24] To Abigail Adams, Ealing, June 6, 1816, *Writings,* VI, 44.

[25] To Richard Rush, Washington, D. C., May 29, 1818, *ibid.,* p. 339. To William Plumer, Washington, D. C., July 6, 1818, *ibid.,* p. 382.

[26] The low estate of the American service, he wrote, made it difficult to avoid following the European custom of giving gifts to departing diplomats, although republican principles required its rejection. *Memoirs,* May 21, 1811, II, 267; on the basis of the same scruples he, himself, would not accept a gift from a Mr. Raimbert, although Raimbert was a private citizen to receive a gift from whom would not establish a precedent. *Ibid.,* January 4, 1812, pp. 332–333.

[27] *Ibid.,* May 20, 1818, IV, 98.

[28] National Archives, Records of the Department of State, *Diplomatic Instructions,* All Countries, VIII, 181. *Ibid.,* IX, 16: Middleton was closely instructed as to the size of the margins of his dispatches.

[29] *Memoirs,* May 15, 1819, IV, 364.

[30] *Ibid.,* May 18, 1819, p. 366.

could be circular." [31]   Except when on leave or vacation Adams
drafted personally the great bulk of instructions, until shortly before
his entry into the White House, when other matters intervened.
This task forced him to add continuously to his vast knowledge of
affairs and to develop an astute "speculative foresight" concerning
what representatives should most thoroughly observe that would be
of interest to the United States.   The instructions contained vast
and perspicacious generalizations concerning the state of the world,
in particular Europe, by reference to which as perspective the representatives were to observe and judge what they saw. [32]   American
ministers were counseled to observe the relations of the countries
to which they were accredited with other countries, to observe the
relations among the nations generally, to keep up a correspondence
with other American representatives, and to keep on good terms with
other foreign ministers. [33]   Adams demanded reports in minute detail
based upon such observations. The instructions set forth not only the
Secretary's view of international affairs but lessons in the smaller
details of how to be a minister. [34]   Republican ministers were reminded of the importance of small courtesies to monarchs. [35]   Adams
should be remembered, therefore, not only for his great state papers
in the form of letters of instructions, but for his mentorship of the
United States foreign service in the little things of diplomacy.   He
set the sights in many ways.   For example, he was particularly aware
of the value of the knowledge of languages.   Finding that no one
in the United States could translate a dispatch written in Arabic, he

[31] *Memoirs*, October 1, 1817, IV, 12.

[32] E.g., To Henry Middleton, State Department, Washington, D. C., July 5,
1820, *Writings*, VII, 46–47.

[33] National Archives, Records of the Department of State, *Diplomatic Instructions*, All Countries, VIII, 162.

[34] *Ibid.*, IX, 142–148: Letter to General H. Dearborn.

[35] *Ibid.*, IX, 179.   Adams's burdens even included the writing of detailed
instructions to the members of the consular service for the purpose, among others,
of instructing them in the proper manner of following their duties.   He instructed American representatives abroad to follow the forms of official courtesy
existing in other places, not to stand too much on their dignity.   He did not
look with favor upon the pretended right of pre-eminence (right to be received
alone and a day in advance) asserted by British consuls and instructed that
United States' consuls should visit sovereigns on ceremonial occasions with the
British consul or not at all.   National Archives, Record Group No. 59, General
Records of the Department of State, Vol. II, Series, *Consular Instructions*, pp.
88–89.

sent Mr. Hodgson to Algiers to learn oriental languages.[36]   And he watched the diplomatic service closely after he left the Presidency, and took sardonic notice of failures, such as what he considered McLane's inability to prognosticate correctly the turn of events in Britain.[37]

AMERICAN GOVERNMENT AND FOREIGN AFFAIRS

In the realm of foreign affairs, according to Adams's theory, the Executive wielded a power that antedated the Constitution and was delimited by a law of its own.   Whereas, with respect to the law of nations, Congress might merely punish offenses and had no alterative power, the President had an unlimited power of "fulfilling all the duties and of exacting all the rights" of the nation in international intercourse.   Without being explicit, Adams indicated that the President had an alterative power with regard to international relations, a dictatorial power only partially limited by the Constitution, a power that was the remedy of the greatest deficiency of the Articles.[38]   In the exercise of this power there should be, he asserted, no hampering requirement of publication of the contingent or secret funds expenditures for foreign intercourse or limitation of presidential control thereof.[39]   The Congress, moreover, should hesitate to press too far for information with regard to delicate matters in international affairs,[40] avoid striking out appropriations for missions upon which the Executive had already decided,[41] and avoid applying restrictions upon the President's free use of funds appropriated for foreign missions.[42]   Adams wished the United States to stand powerful among the nations of the world, and strong Executive leadership in this sphere would help to accomplish this goal.

Only thus armed with strong Executive leadership might the United States with vigor require other nations to observe the amenities of international intercourse, such as the "alternative first naming"

[36] *Memoirs,* January 16, 1830, VIII, 170–171.

[37] *Ibid.,* March 13, 1831, p. 344.

[38] Adams, *The Jubilee of the Constitution,* pp. 71–72.

[39] *Congressional Globe,* 24th Cong., 1st sess., April 20, 1836, p. 380.   *Ibid.,* 29th Cong., 1st sess., April 13, 1846, pp. 640–642.

[40] *Ibid.,* 27th Cong., 1st sess., September 4, 1841, p. 428.

[41] *Memoirs,* September 10, 1841, XI, 12.

[42] *Ibid.,* February 21, 1843, XI, 325.

of the parties to treaties.[43] Only thus armed might we emphatically inform the British government that we proposed to be notified of European policy while matters were in progress, not after negotiations had been completed, as Adams did with respect to a projected European mediation between Spain and South America, which included a proposal for a naval patrol for the slave trade and a restricted right of search.[44] This powerful American Executive could object vigorously to a French note imputing "a grave error" to the United States in the seizure of a French vessel, the *Apollon*, held to be violating American customs laws.[45] He also could protest, with equal vigor, Spanish seizure of American vessels, the *Beaver* and *John Jacob Astor* of New York and the *Canton* of Salem, while seeking restitution, indemnities, and satisfaction for those injured.[46] This executive could afford to announce the American Government's great forebearance and self-restraint in awaiting satisfaction from a European power as an indication of strength rather than of weakness.[47]

Adams contributed hugely to the foundations upon which American statesmen have been able to convey to the world a conception and myth of a distinct American tradition and political process. The republican government of the United States, he asserted, had no less regard for the security of individuals than European governments. There was no want of authority in the government of the United States.[48] Britain was informed emphatically that she need not be surprised by the Senate's making alterations in a treaty signed with the United States.[49] He defended the constitutional provision that made such Senate action possible on the ground that

[43] *Ibid.*, February 19, 1819, IV, 271–272: It is difficult to believe that European states—least of all of the stature of Spain in the nineteenth century—would object in Adams's day as Secretary to such a practice and courtesy.

[44] National Archives, Records of the Department of State, *Diplomatic Instructions, All Countries*, VIII, 201.

[45] *Memoirs*, March 29, 1821, V, 337–338.

[46] National Archives, Records of the Department of State, *Diplomatic Instructions, All Countries*, VIII, 181.

[47] To Don Francisco Dionisio Vivés, State Department, Washington, D. C., May 8, 1820, *Writings*, VII, 23.

[48] *Memoirs*, October 13, 1821, V, 358: This assertion was made in connection with a request by Canning that we deliver up a Newfoundland captain who had run away with his ship and its cargo.

[49] National Archives, Records of the Department of State, *Diplomatic Instructions, All Countries*, X, 75.

treaties became in the United States the supreme law of the land and that the intervening ocean precluded giving plenary power to American negotiators, in contrast with the situation of Europe where agents could consult their governments with ease.[50] Similar grounds of constitutional rectitude he asserted to the British Minister in rejecting a British suggestion for multinational courts to try slave traders.[51] With considerable success Adams attempted to give the world confidence in the validity of an American political system.

THE SYSTEM OF THE WESTERN HEMISPHERE

This American system would be incompatible with any "preference for European connections . . . [or] predilections for European princes" on the part of an American statesman, whether of the United States or another Western Hemisphere nation.[52] And it is important to stress that he included the entire Western Hemisphere in the American system. Adams early displayed a conception of Europe as incorrigibly devoted to outmoded political practices. In contrast, new governments to be established on this side of the ocean should "be immutably founded upon the principles of freedom, and administered by the genuine maxims of moral subordination and political equality." [53] The status of independence in this hemisphere must be based on principles largely differing from those of the European system:[54]

Continental Spanish America must henceforth be considered in three different points of view. First, as composing, together with the United States, a distinct *American* portion of the human race:—connected with Europe by a mutual and *Independent* commercial intercourse by common principles of Religious faith and National morality; and by modes of social manners; habits and opinions, in many important essentials, the same, while as essentially differing from those of the two other quarters of the Globe:—but differing from Europe in the fundamental principles

[50] National Archives, Records of the Department of State, *Diplomatic Instructions,* All Countries, X, 216–218.

[51] To Stratford Canning, State Department, Washington, D. C., December 30, 1820, *Writings,* VII, 85–86.

[52] To Caesar Augustus Rodney, State Department, Washington, D. C., May 17, 1823, *ibid.,* pp. 432–433.

[53] Adams, *July 4th Oration, 1793,* p. 20.

[54] National Archives, Records of the Department of State, *Diplomatic Instructions,* All Countries, IX, 312.

upon which their respective Governments are founded. The basis upon which all the American Governments have arisen, and are arising, being the natural rights of mankind, and the sovereignty of the people; while the prevailing doctrines of Europe, consider the liberties of Nations as having their origin in the will of kings.[55]

This, the "Republican Hemisphere," must be founded upon principles of intercourse "benevolent and liberal in themselves, congenial to the spirit of our Institutions, and consistent with the duties of universal philanthropy." [56]

[55] *Ibid.*, X, 129–130.
[56] *Ibid.*, IX, 265, 301.

17

Adams and the Major Powers

The sceptres of all the European continental monarchs were turning to ashes in their hands. Their crowns were dropping from their heads; the very instruments of power upon which they were leaning pierced their hands and sides.
—MEMOIRS, *October 30, 1820*

ADAMS'S REACTIONS TO BRITAIN IN THE WORLD OF NATIONS

In addition to the above conceptions as influences on Adams's strategic views in international affairs, his reactions to the key nations as myth complexes and as symbols of social values are important. Some intimation of these reactions has already been conveyed in general terms; more detailed descriptions at this point will add to an understanding of the premises underlying the foreign policy and strategic goals of the United States as Adams viewed them.

For example, with minor variations that tended only slightly to modify his basic attitudes, he always retained an "ineradicable antipathy" for Britain. It can only appear fantastic to one knowing the record to learn that late in his career he was charged with being the head of a powerful English party in the United States.[1] He gave proper credit to the Motherland for her contributions of law, language, song, literature, customs, passion, prejudice, and philosophy.[2] One might reasonably suggest that Adams's attitude toward Britain was mainly an objective appraisal of Britain shortcomings. Such may have been his attitude, but the language he used suggests that

[1] *Congressional Globe*, 27th Cong., 2nd sess., January 27, 1841, p. 183.
[2] Adams, "Speech Delivered at North-Bridgewater, on Wednesday, November 6th, 1844," *Boston Courier*, November 11, 1844.

his feeling was stronger than that. On fitting occasions Adams could admit Britain's contributions; however, the overall picture of Britain that he depicted was somber and distrustful. The colonists, to be sure, had come "tempered by the tenderest and most attractive sympathies of English *patriotism*." [3] Although he did recognize the substantive value of the British contribution to the world, Adams throughout his life was an Anglophobe. The recitation of his strictures is overwhelming and conclusive: the British perversely refused to give up certain ports as stipulated in the treaty of peace. The United States would soon become their most dangerous commercial rival and in time their naval superior, and, in the light of that eventuality, it was absurd to expect from her moderation in victory or anything but insolence so long as she was secure in her "lordship of the waves." [4] Although Adams defended British institutions in the *Letters of Publicola* in answer to Paine, that defense must be considered apart from his antipathy for the British nation and apart from his conception of the British strategic position in the world.

Shortly after writing the *Letters* and arriving at The Hague as American Minister, Adams wrote with grave disapproval of the British control over the Dutch government. [5] The Dutch government's maritime and naval power, he wrote, would surely decline by degrees in a relationship of "subordinate intimacy with the self-entitled rulers of the waves." [6] His antipathy toward Britain extended beyond the government to include the British national character. [7] Such a prejudice, combined with his nationalism, allowed him to feel a double satisfaction at the spectacle of America growing stronger in peaceful pursuits and Britain being enervated by war. [8] Natural attraction and "motives of interest" combined to make the French more appealing, the British more repulsive. [9] Britain,

[3] Adams, *The New England Confederacy of MDCXLIII*, p. 10.

[4] *Memoirs,* July 11, 1794, I, 37–38.

[5] To John Adams, The Hague, December 21, 1794, *Writings*, I, 254.

[6] To the Secretary of State, The Hague, March 17, 1795, *ibid.*, p. 303.

[7] To John Adams, Helvoetsluys, October 31, 1795, *ibid.*, p. 424.

[8] To John Adams, February 1, 1796, *ibid.*, pp. 475–476. Amusingly, Adams accused the British of comparable sentiments, that is, the desire to see the tranquillity of the United States disturbed. To John Adams, London, February 10, 1796, *ibid.*, pp. 477–478. Gouverneur Morris described Adams as "absolutely mad" in h. wrath at the British government at this time. *Diary and Letters of Gouverneur Morris*, II, 157.

[9] To John Adams, The Hague, June 24, 1796, *Writings*, I, 506.

inspired by the shibboleth, "Rule Britannia! Britannia rule the waves!," [10] foisted upon the world a justice in maritime matters widely divergent from the requirements of "natural justice." [11] The combined purpose of all other commercial nations, Adams wrote, should be to counteract this overwhelming power of Britain.[12]

To multiply the evidence would be redundant and superfluous. An inspection of the materials running from the beginning of the nineteenth century until Adams's death shows an almost unrelieved anti-British attitude. The British did score slightly with him—for example, when French treatment of American commerce became even more severe than theirs.[13] He assessed their land on one occasion as that wherein genius and science had been most effectively combined to improve the arts and manufacturers.[14] On another, he referred to the melancholy spectacle of their superior political system being brought low by the imbecility of their rulers.[15] He could admit partial victory in Britain in the rebellion of the people against the sword that protected the crown and the tiara,[16] or affirm that the American colonists, feeling the name of Briton to be a "passport of honour throughout the civilized world," rebelled and sought independence with painful misgivings.[17] He might in a moment of effulgence agree that Britain had taken the lesson of the American Revolution to heart and was "under the red cross of St. George, overflowing from the white cliffs of Albion, and sweeping the slave trade and slavery from the face of the terraqueous globe." [18] He might with respect to the Northeastern boundary question assert that he "believed England more sinned against than sinning. . . ." [19] But this is small testimony in a political lifetime of over sixty years to weigh against the evidence of his firmly rooted antipathy. We must keep this antipathy as an underlying premise in his thinking

[10] To Rufus King, The Hague, October 3, 1796, *Writings*, II, 33.

[11] To Joseph Hall, October 9, 1796, *ibid.*, p. 33 n.

[12] To Joseph Pitcairn, The Hague, January 13, 1797, *ibid.*, p. 75.

[13] To Joseph Pitcairn, The Hague, May 2, 1797, *ibid.*, p. 163.

[14] Adams, *Letters on Silesia*, p. 161.

[15] To Thomas Boylston Adams, St. Petersburg, April 21, 1810, *Writings*, III, 421–422.

[16] Adams, *July 4th, 1812, Address*, p. 7.

[17] Adams, *Newburyport Oration, 1837*, p. 10.

[18] Adams, *The Jubilee of the Constitution*, pp. 3–5. *Memoirs*, February 15, 1843, XI, 319–320.

[19] *Memoirs*, December 9, 1841, XI, 36.

consistently in mind when considering his conceptions of international affairs.

France had a place in his mind that must be considered in relation to other, only partially associated, factors. France's position in his perspective depended largely upon the political and strategic situation. It was more relative, less intrinsic. We have noted that Adams felt some sympathy for the French national character, but in large degree France was seen as part of a general European problem, in relation to an overshadowing Britain, or in the context of an event with much wider than French implications, the French Revolution. Adams's antipathy for the British had the emotional quality of a family division. His view of the French was a rational assessment of a national phenomenon. The intensity of his feelings regarding the British was increased by his capacity to think in British terms. The French nation could be evaluated as an external problem.

Whereas France's immediate strategic impingement upon the United States was not a matter of much concern to him, except in so far as it modified the British position, Adams's main reaction to France was as a vehicle or harbinger of false or dangerous political principles and forces. The theories emanating from the Revolution, enjoying high reputation among many, were farther from true democracy, he contended, than the practice of the English lower house.[20] As we have seen, at this time he greatly feared the influence of "a nation [France] of fanatical atheists, all warriors." [21]

While retaining his distrust of the British, he charged the French with harboring a desire to change the United States Constitution, so as to enable them to wield an "effectual influence over our [the American] national executive." [22] Such a motive was combined with capacity for the "tactique," with rashness, insolence, and impetuosity in the public men of France that made it difficult to keep in mind the greater danger of British influence.[23] In the face

[20] VIII "Publicola," *Writings*, I, 95.
[21] To John Adams, Boston, April 12, 1794, *ibid.*, I, 184.
[22] To John Adams, The Hague, August 13, 1796, *ibid.*, II, 22. To Joseph Pitcairn, The Hague, January 31, 1797, *ibid.*, p. 96.
[23] To Joseph Pitcairn, The Hague, March 9, 1797, *ibid.*, pp. 140–141.

of the threat of French ideas and influence Americans must stand united, as the titanic struggle between Britain and France got under way. He even accused the French of fostering the project of a Southern pro-French republic, divided from the incorrigibly pro-British northeast.[24]

Adams feared not only the infiltration of French ideas; he recognized the danger of United States involvement in the general European war precipitated by the French Revolution. The United States has been concerned in the eighteenth as well as the twentieth century with the ideological, military, and strategic implication of Europe's wars. Adams recognized this to some degree, if not fully. Although a war with France might be a most unfortunate event, there was "a point beyond which every sacrifice to preserve Peace, only serves to defeat its own purpose." "Perfidy or dishonor . . . [were] too high a price to pay even for the first of national blessings."[25] Although, surveying the history of Napoleon, Adams could note that one of France's blessings was not to have been ruled by subalterns,[26] the Emperor's fall constituted the inevitable "catastrophe of the French Revolution."[27] As Napoleon's career drew toward its denouement, Adams observed that this development likewise meant the closing of a chapter in which France had been for years "the scourge of Europe . . . [manifesting an] ambitious, domineering, oppressive, and rapacious spirit."[28] The glory of the period should be judged on the basis of its origin in the Revolution and military power, all symbolized by one man whose guilt was indistinguishable from that of the nation. The opponents of France were no better, and the settlement they imposed was unwise and inexpedient.

It is of the greatest significance, however, that from this time forward, except for moments of irritation over alleged commercial discrimination and other minor vicissitudes of international relationship, in particular the prolonged negotiation over indemnities, Adams

[24] To John Adams, The Hague, April 3, 1797, *Writings,* pp. 155–157.
[25] Letter to Elbridge Gerry, Berlin, February 20, 1798, Tatum (ed.), *op. cit.,* p. 373. This was in reference to a breakdown in negotiations over the XYZ affair.
[26] To Thomas Boylston Adams, St. Petersburg, July 14, 1812, *Writings,* IV, 374.
[27] To John Adams, St. Petersburg, February 17, 1814, *ibid.,* V, 20.
[28] To Abigail Adams, Reval, May 12, 1814, *ibid.,* pp. 42–43.

did not manifest a continuing Galliphobia. After the French Revolution had spent itself in the burning out of the career of Napoleon, as long as Adams controlled American foreign policy, he was not influenced by any premise of antipathy for France. With the revolution dead or moribund, France no longer constituted the same degree or type of threat.

RUSSIA AS A GREAT POWER

Russia, the other major continental and land power, likewise did not appear to Adams as a continuing danger. There were times of irritation, but for the most part he preserved a friendly spirit toward this vast land. Prior to the emergence of the Holy Alliance, Russia's singular friendship for the United States served to temper any Adamsian strictures on the Russian political system. Moreover, although Adams did not depict the Emperor as a radical democrat, he considered Alexander a sovereign of genuine "moderation, . . . humanity, . . . [and] magnanimity." [29] The rigors of the autocracy he recognized, but the Russian government had become milder in the hands of this emperor.[30] Even after the creation of the Holy Alliance Adams maintained a policy of real solicitude for Russian sensibilities, taking care, for example, to have the Russian government informed that the return home of an American representative implied no lessening of friendly relations.[31] Even when many were interpreting the Holy Alliance and the European Concert as a preprandial manifestation of which the United States should be especially wary, Adams could write in sympathetic terms of Alexander's policy as derived from his genuine religious nature. He praised Alexander's preference for general systems of international order rather than partial systems as a basis of stability.[32] Russian power made partial and exclusive associations possible, but the Emperor refused, Adams wrote, to pursue a regional policy increasing the temptation to aggression against those excluded.[33] Adams was not

[29] To Louisa Catherine Adams, Ghent, July 2, 1814, *Writings*, V, 55.
[30] *Loc. cit.*
[31] To John Adams, Ealing, February 29, 1816, *ibid.*, pp. 520–521.
[32] National Archives, Records of the Department of State, *Diplomatic Instructions*, All Countries, VIII, 175–176.
[33] To Henry Middleton, State Department, Washington, D. C., July 5, 1820, *Writings*, VII, 48.

significantly frightened by a united Europe, even a Europe united under the aegis of a mighty land power. As to the threat to the Western Hemisphere, especially Spanish American, coming from the Holy Alliance, Adams's fears were mainly ideological, institutional, and commercial. Panic never seized him as it did many others in the Administration when they thought of the Holy Alliance and the European Concert.

18

Major Adamsian Concepts in International Politics

I occasionally answered his remarks, by observing to him [Alexander I] . . . that being at once a great commercial and a pacific nation, they [the United States] were greatly interested in the establishment of a system which should give security to the fair commerce of nations in time of war.

—MEMOIRS, *November 5, 1809*

THE MONROE DOCTRINE AND ADAMS'S STRATEGIC CONCEPTIONS

A study of the Monroe Doctrine, John Quincy Adams's authorship of which cannot be doubted, is most important for an understanding of his conception of the goals and conditions of United States foreign policy. The villain of the piece in the mind of the doctrine's architect was most probably Great Britain, a none too surprising judgment in view of his overriding anti-British prejudice. Almost thirty years earlier, in a letter from London, he had speculated upon the importance of a projected British expedition to Santo Domingo and remarked that its success should not be wished for by Americans. He had observed that the preparation of such an expedition showed that the real purpose of the British in the war they were then waging with France was the establishment of their commercial and maritime supremacy, that the realization of this goal vis-a-vis the United States required British domination of the West Indies and prevention of American penetration into that area.[1]

[1] To Timothy Pickering, London, December 22, 1795, *Writings*, I, 462–463.

299

From the beginning Adams opposed the taking of concerted measures with Britain "to promote the independence of South America," because, although there was no doubt that Britain favored that result, her purposes were different from those of the United States, which should not become identified with English purposes and thus endanger relations with other powers opposed to Britain.[2]   Moreover, the commercial supremacy and interests that Britain hoped to augment by her South American policy should not be strengthened by the identification of American diplomatic moves with hers.   The struggle for a peculiarly American hemisphere was more with Britain than any other power or group of powers.

Great Britain was warned by Adams that the United States did not expect any resistance on her part to American penetration to the "South Sea" (the Pacific) and reminded that she should be satisfied with her "undisturbed enjoyment of all her holds upon Europe, Asia, and Africa, [and] with all her actual possessions in this hemisphere." [3] He charged the British with evil designs and jealousy.   He was especially fearful that Cuba, of peculiar strategic importance to the United States,[4] would fall to Britain and preferred its retention by Spain.[5] Where Spain's rule had been patently terminated, the British threat could be met in a novel way, as through the Monroe Doctrine; otherwise Spain's retention of sovereignty was preferable to absorption by the world-girdling maritime empire whose power presented the most imminent threat.[6]

Adams did not rule out the possibility of intervention by continental European powers in the American continent.   He warned these nations that they could not settle South American affairs without the United States,[7] but that any mediation, which he interpreted as a type of intervention, proposing to accomplish any result short of complete commercial and political independence for that area must proceed

[2] *Memoirs,* May 13, 1818, IV, 92.

[3] National Archives, Records of the Department of State, *Diplomatic Instructions,* All Countries, VIII, 189–190.

[4] *Ibid.,* IX, 186.

[5] *Ibid.,* IX, 158–159.   *Memoirs,* May 20, 1819, IV, 367–368.

[6] To Hugh Nelson, State Department, Washington, D. C., *Writings,* VII, 377.

[7] *Memoirs,* May 1, 1818, IV, 86.   To Richard Rush, Department of State, Washington, D. C., May 20, 1818, *Writings,* VI, 325.

without American participation.[8]   Admittedly, he feared not only the mediation of these powers, but also their military threat.   He indicated that the United States opposed any Russian encroachments on this continent.   He devised a counterargument to the reasoning upon which the Russian actions were based,[9] agreeing that cannon might be more difficult to meet than arguments.[10]   But the fear of Britain was his most compelling concern.

To meet the threat of European encroachment in the earlier phases of the revolution in Spanish America, the Secretary of State had at hand the traditional American policy of neutrality, in this context put to the use of insuring European nonintervention.   If the European powers could be influenced to remain neutral in the struggle between Spain and the rebel governments in Spanish America, the possibility of a dangerous intervention was eliminated and independence for the rebels was brought nearer.   This was a purpose quite different from the conventional one of securing the safety of American commerce in the context of Europe's wars.   The American doctrine of neutrality was offered as an alternative policy for states conditioned by the recent events of the French revolution to intervention in the name of legitimacy.   In 1817, while still in London, he told General Dumouriez that United States policy with respect to South America was "absolute neutrality." [11]   By that term he did not mean to set forth a permanent or absolute policy; but before it could be abandoned, justice must be found on the side favored by the change.   An intervention involving an abandonment of neutrality could be justified only on the ground of a decision as to what side in the struggle in Spanish America served the cause of justice.   But Adams went even further in developing tactics to serve the cause of independence in that region.   He wrote that, as long as neutrality was maintained, the question of justice need not be decided, although, in the case at hand, he was convinced that it was not on the side of Spain.[12]   He called for the formulation of policy in the name of justice, but, as long as

[8] To Albert Gallatin, Department of State, Washington, D. C., May 19, 1818, *ibid.*, VI, 316–318.

[9] *Memoirs,* June 28, 1823, VI, 157.   National Archives, Records of the Department of State, *Diplomatic Instructions,* All Countries, X, 53–60.

[10] *Memoirs,* July 1, 1823, VI, 159.

[11] *Ibid.,* April 27, 1817, III, 511.

[12] National Archives, Records of the Department of State, *Diplomatic Instructions,* All Countries, VIII, 187.

neutrality served the rebel cause more than a decision concerning justice, he called for the maintenance of neutrality. This juncture found Adams at his best in relating theory to tactical needs.

The neutrality policy was a manifestation of the general policy of "reserve and caution" that Monroe and Adams pursued in handling this question.[13] The position was maintained against terrific pressure from Spanish Americans and their protagonists in the United States. Foreign representatives were told that abandonment of the policy could be accomplished only by the legislature.[14] Adams informed a Spanish American representative that abandonment of neutrality would not aid the revolting colonies,[15] but in a letter to Richard Rush he candidly admitted that United States neutrality worked to the disadvantage of Spain, in affording recognition of belligerent rights in the revolutionaries.[16] And Adams attempted to carry out a policy of neutrality. He remonstrated with revolutionary governments for issuing freebooters' commissions and authorizing the use of their flags contrary to the law of nations; [17] he revoked in biting terms the commission of Thomas L. Halsey as United States consul at Buenos Aires for being interested in privateers equipped and commissioned to sail against a nation (Spain) with whom his country was at peace.[18]

Although the United States government made a serious attempt to adhere to a neutral position, the Secretary described the relative positions of Europe and the United States as, on the one hand, neutrality with an inclination toward "authority and Spain," and, on the other, neutrality with an inclination toward "liberty and South America." [19] There was never an occasion to doubt the direction of the Secretary's sympathies. But this inclination could not soundly be enlarged through the forming of any engagements whatever with the revolting

[13] Nevins, *The Diary of John Quincy Adams, 1794–1845,* p. 199, n. 5.

[14] State Department, *Notes to Foreign Legations,* II, 382–383: Adams knew, indeed, that the power of recognition was in the President, yet, at least for tactical purposes, he chose to assert that neutrality with regard to the contenders in Spanish America could be abandoned only under legislative direction.

[15] *Loc. cit.*

[16] National Archives, Records of the Department of State, *Diplomatic Instructions,* All Countries, VIII, 297.

[17] National Archives, Record Group No. 59, General Records of the Department of State, Vol. 2, Series, *Consular Instructions,* pp. 72–75.

[18] *Ibid.,* p. 92.

[19] National Archives, Records of the Department of State, *Diplomatic Instructions,* All Countries, VIII, 338.

provinces until the groundwork had been laid for the next move. Adams's neutrality was essentially a policy based upon a firm realization of the material interests of the United States. Although he saw the Western Hemisphere evolving a political system to be distinguished from the system of "partial rights . . . and exclusive privileges" in Europe,[20] he looked upon the neutrality policy as basically vital to the liberties and union of the North American states. He had no illusions concerning the prospects of an early establishment of liberal institutions in Spanish America.[21] His confidence in the development of an American system did not cloud his vision of the actualities of the present with regard to political and social conditions among the United States southern neighbors.

Neutrality was designed to prevent European intervention. It constituted recognition of certain rights in the revolting provinces. While guiding the country in its role of a neutral Adams strove vigorously to achieve as soon as practicable a general recognition of the independence of the revolting Spanish colonies. The Russians were early informed that Americans sought the "total independence, political and commercial, of the colonies."[22] The United States should take the lead, he even wrote on one occasion, in recognizing South America, persuading Britain to act in concert but letting her know that this country would act independently.[23] The ability of the colonies to maintain their independence should be the intrinsic test of policy for all powers, including Spain itself.[24] He regarded American leadership in this effort to assist the rebels as participation in the building of a "remarkable era in the history of the world,"[25] the end achievement of which would be of greater implication than the downfall of the Roman Empire.[26]

Once the United States had determined to recognize the independ-

[20] *Ibid.,* IX, 301–303.

[21] *Memoirs,* March 9, 1821, V, 324–325.

[22] To George Washington Campbell, State Department, Washington, D. C., June 28, 1818, *Writings,* VI, 379.

[23] *Memoirs,* January 2, 1819, IV, 207.

[24] To Don Joaquin De Anduaga, State Department, Washington, D. C., April 6, 1824, *Writings,* VII, 218.

[25] To Caesar Augustus Rodney, State Department, Washington, D. C., May 17, 1823, *ibid.,* p. 424.

[26] National Archives, Records of the Department of State, *Diplomatic Instructions,* All Countries, IX, 301.

ence of South America, the course that the Secretary had always favored, he proposed to work vigorously for European recognition as well. This course of action was naturally necessary to protect the United States investment in the course she had decided candidly to pursue. The enunciation of the Monroe Doctrine, however, was considerably in advance of mere recognition of Spanish American independence and was an earnest of the deep United States commitment on behalf of that region against the threats, actual and potential, in the policies of European states. But it is a mistake to overrate Adams's fears of continental European power and policy and to underrate the effect of anti-British prejudice on his policy in connection with the Monroe Doctrine. He wrote in considerable disparagement of Monroe's and Calhoun's unnatural alarm that the Holy Alliance would re-establish Spanish power and criticized the President for indecision in the face of rumor to that effect.[27]

Admittedly, Adams took pains to minimize any substantive differences with the Alliance on other than American issues,[28] and the first hint of the doctrine did come in a statement to Baron Tuyl, the Russian Minister, on July 17, 1823, that the United States government would contest any Russian foothold on this continent, on the ground that the American continents were no longer subject to colonization.[29] A few days later he wrote a letter to the American Minister in London to the same effect, ordering transmission of this position to the British government; going farther, he asserted that European powers could, however, expect the extension of American territorial settlements in this hemisphere.[30] Moreover, this communication made clear that a great fear of the United States government was of the continuation of principles of colonial exclusion and maritime inequality, historically and potentially enforced more by Britain than any continental European power.[31] The Secretary thought a communication from Baron Tuyl afforded a "very suitable and convenient opportunity for us to take our stand against the Holy Alliance, and at the same time to decline the overture of Great Britain [for a joint declaration].

---

[27] *Memoirs,* November 13, 1823, VI, 185.

[28] *Ibid.,* November 26, 1823, pp. 204–205.

[29] Morse, *John Quincy Adams,* p. 132. *Memoirs,* July 17, 1823, VI, 103.

[30] National Archives, Records of the Department of State, *Diplomatic Instructions,* All Countries, X, 65.

[31] *Ibid.,* pp. 66–67.

It would be more candid, as well as more dignified, to avow our principles explicitly to Russia and France, than to come in as a cockboat in the wake of the British man-of-war." [32] This expression is more than a convenient figure; the British "man-of-war" was the symbol of an overriding British naval and commercial power, constantly fulfilling a policy that competed with American policy.

The Monroe Doctrine, by which the United States asserted the independence from European hegemony of the Western Hemisphere was designed as a defense against the most potent threat to that independence, the British Empire, especially threatening in the eyes of the Secretary of State. The United States did not propose to impose its principles upon Europe or any other continent, but expected Europe to entertain no ambitions to impose European principles in this hemisphere.[33] Adams opposed any indication of alarm in the President's Doctrine message; no gauntlet should be thrown down to Europe,[34] for the United States should fight only *in extremis,* after Europe had been put clearly in the wrong.[35] These admonitions were precautionary and did not indicate panic on Adams's part. On the other hand, a joint declaration with Great Britain would involve, very likely, the giving of a great deal in return for nothing.[36] The United States would be in danger of supporting a closed British system of commercial relations with Spanish America. Adams desired, on the contrary, a system without special privileges for any power, and he thought he could devise a policy which the British would support as the best alternative available.

The announcement of the Doctrine policy by the United States alone constituted a stronger warning to Britain and a stronger statement of American principles. Britain could choose to underwrite this policy as a lesser bargain preferable to colonial exclusion in the affected area. Britain's commercial opportunities in that region were great enough to warrant a modification of Britain's own practices of colonial exclusiveness elsewhere. Adams gave clear expression to the British in a communication to his view that commercial relations with Spanish America should be open, equal, and multilateral. He con-

[32] *Memoirs,* November 7, 1823, VI, 178–179.
[33] *Ibid.,* November 21, 1823, VI, 194.
[34] *Ibid.,* pp. 194–195.
[35] *Ibid.,* November 22, 1823, p. 197.
[36] *Ibid.,* November 7, 1823, pp. 177–178.

veyed therein, in addition to an emphasis upon the colonizing ban, the contention that, although the United States would not frown upon Spanish American commercial arrangements with other powers, she would insist upon commercial equality under the most-favored-nation principle.[37]　Adams, in fact, sought and achieved British maritime support of an American policy.　His desire was to transform a potentially exclusive British policy into an open and multilateral policy. Joint action with the British might have involved a weakening compromise.　The issues, significantly, about which Adams was most at pains to negotiate were those that could be resolved only in negotiation with Britain.

During this period the United States was willing to agree to the same principles of commercial equality with regard to Spanish America to which the Secretary sought European adherence; she disclaimed territorial ambitions.[38]　Moreover, Adams with consistency opposed the ambitions of Latin American nations to move against Spanish territories not in successful revolt, such as Florida.[39]　He made fun of the Portuguese representative's proposal of a project of an American system based upon the power of the "two great powers of the Western Hemisphere," Portugal and the United States.[40]　Having called for European recognition of a *status quo* in Spanish America, he was not prepared to support a contrary United States policy.　A Columbian project of a North and South American federation was rejected as more in the interest of Columbia's prestige than this country's,[41] although Adams indicated possible support of a Latin American federation more competent to guarantee republicanism in the face of European influence.[42]　A decision of the congress of San Salvador of December 5, 1822, calling for inclusion in the North American Union was noted by the Secretary, if without enthusiasm, as having major significance as a token of respect for the superior in-

[37] National Archives, Records of the Department of State, *Diplomatic Instructions*, All Countries, X, 120–123.

[38] *Loc. cit. Memoirs*, May 19, 1825, VII, 9–10.

[39] *Memoirs*, May 8, 1818, IV, 89.

[40] *Ibid.*, September 19, 1820, V, 176.

[41] National Archives, Records of the Department of State, *Diplomatic Instructions*, All Countries, IX, 253–254.

[42] *Ibid.*, p. 254.　A certain facet of isolationism was shown in a suggestion that Buenos Aires would be better off tending to internal affairs than working for a major federation of the old vice-royalty.

stitutions of the United States.[43]   The main goals of his policy in this area were commercial, for his most serious charge to American envoys was that they work for the most-favored-nation principle and guard against a successful search by Britain and France for special privileges.

ADAMS'S ISOLATIONISM

John Quincy Adams was in the main American isolationist tradition.   Although cosmopolitan in training and experience, he saw the issues of Europe's struggles as of small moment to the United States. Writing from The Hague, he asserted to his father that the war between France, the revolutionary force, and Britain, the protector of Europe's balance of power, was "nothing more in reality than a contest of national rivalship between France and Britain." [44]   Napoleon's attack upon Russia was interpreted as further warning that America should keep out of European affairs.[45]   Although he informed Madame de Staël that lack of means did not account for the failure of the United States to attack Napoleon, he added that he did not dread Napoleon's "universal monarchy" and that there was a fundamental principle of American policy prohibiting meddling in Europe.[46]   Britain and France presented two adequately formidable forces arrayed against each other—here Adams made a slight concession to the conception of a European balance—and, in any event, he "did not consider Britain at all the champion of the liberties of mankind, but as another tyrant pretending to exclusive dominion upon the ocean—a pretension full as detestable, and I trust in God full as chimerical, as the pretension of universal monarchy upon the land." [47]

Admitting American sympathies for people struggling for a great cause, such as republicanism, he at the same time criticized "ardent spirits for always rushing into the conflict, without looking to the consequences." [48]   The arguments, quite modern in tone, criticized the

---

[43] *Ibid.*, X, 194–198.

[44] To John Adams, The Hague, August 31, 1795, *Writings*, I, 405.

[45] To Thomas Boylston Adams, St. Petersburg, November 24, 1812, *ibid.*, IV, 407–408.

[46] To John Adams, St. Petersburg, March 22, 1813, *ibid.*, pp. 453–454.

[47] To John Adams, St. Petersburg, March 22, 1813, *ibid.*, IV, 453–454. He rejected the idea that America should actually participate in the "future political reformation of Europe."   To Robert Walsh, Jr., Washington, D. C., July 10, 1821, *ibid.*, VII, 117.

[48] To John Adams, Washington, D. C., December 21, 1817, *ibid.*, VI, 276.

Colonization Society (projected to resettle Negroes in Africa) for smuggling "in upon us a system of establishing Colonies beyond [the] sea, of the consequences of which the people of this country were little aware. . . ." [49] The political system of the United States, he averred, was essentially "extra-European." [50] The United States undoubtedly would have a difficult time avoiding European entanglements, particularly since the rights of a growing nation might be protected only according to "the energy with which they shall be asserted," [51] but Adams opposed any American ambitions to be admitted to the counsels of any European alliance. [52]

The major manifestation of this isolationism, understandable for the time although in contrast with other and contemporary views of American policy, was Adams's concept of neutrality with respect to Europe's affairs. This neutrality was designed to avoid danger for the United States, in conformity with, yet having different ends from, the neutrality he enjoined upon all citizens of the United States with respect to South America until the propitious moment for recognition and other stronger action had arrived. His general concept of neutrality with respect to European affairs was a continuation of the Washingtonian concept.

On the basis of such a policy Adams believed that the United States could await the inevitable triumph of the American system. [53] Forebodings of future events and American rationalizations thereof were contained in his advice to America to abstain from assistance to or war against either side in the long war between Britain and France, since both sides would probably go down to defeat. [54] Unwise veneration of one side and abhorrence for the other should be abjured. [55] "Justice" and "rights" should be sought from Britain on an equitable basis. "But no alliance with the British lion; no common cause

[49] *Memoirs,* April 29, 1819, IV, 354.

[50] To Henry Middleton, State Department, Washington, D. C., *Writings,* VII, 49.

[51] To the Secretary of State (James Monroe), London, January 31, 1816, *ibid.,* V, 496.

[52] National Archives, Records of the Department of State, *Diplomatic Instructions,* All Countries, X, 151.

[53] To the Secretary of State (Timothy Pickering), London, December 22, 1795, *Writings,* I, 465.

[54] To the Secretary of State (John Marshall), Berlin, February 21, 1801, *ibid.,* II, 504–505.

[55] "Review of the 'Works of Fisher Ames,'" *ibid.,* III, 307.

against the Corsican!" [56]   He concluded that neutrality was worth defending at considerable risk, for on one occasion he counseled the
sending of two frigates into the Baltic to restrain Denmark and to prevent predatory French and British methods from spreading too far.[57]
In fact, where American interests were clearly involved, he was at
pains not to rule out war to defend them.   His was no ostrich-cautious
neutrality, but was based upon the belief that the United States had
no obligation to determine the justice of Europe's causes and struggles.

The United States, he wrote, could not be entirely disconnected
from Europe's affairs because of this country's maritime interests,[58]
and because of the prominence of the principles of "civil liberty and
national independence" in the continental ferment.[59]   The Atlantic
Ocean, however, was a most fortunate barrier and defense against
foreign threats.   This sense of security thus based did not, however,
prevent Adams from becoming a most learned student of European
affairs.   Although he spoke of the European balance, he never concluded that it had any deep significance for the United States.

The architect of the Monroe Doctrine, therefore, never did conceive of that Doctrine as having more significance than as an American doctrine; he did not look upon the Doctrine as the symbol of an
identity of interest between Great Britain and the United States in a
balance of power in Europe.   He might tacitly accept British support
of American policy in the Western Hemisphere, but he did not believe in an American policy of support for the British in preserving a
balance of power in Europe.   He was, for example, comforted by the
assurance of continuing peace of the continent for the year 1811 based
upon the success of the Russians in avoiding being drawn in against
Napoleon, although Britain ardently sought Russian participation as a
condition leading to a re-establishment of the balance disturbed by

[56] To William Eustis, Berlin, June 22, 1809, *ibid.*, p. 320.   To John Pope, St.
Petersburg, September 10, 1810, *ibid.*, p. 502.   His neutral stand would not have
precluded an agreement wtih England, "consistent with our right and our
honor," for then, he thought, the United States could defend her commerce
against all others on the ocean.   To Thomas Boylston Adams, St. Petersburg,
April 21, 1810, *ibid.*, pp. 423–424.

[57] To the Secretary of State (Robert Smith), St. Petersburg, May 19, 1810,
ibid., p. 439.

[58] To John Adams, Berlin, January 31, 1798, *ibid.*, II, 251.

[59] To Hugh Nelson, Department of State, Washington D. C., April 28, 1823,
ibid., VII, 370.

the French.[60]   Fear might be contained in his observation that Europe was moving toward consolidation,[61] but, on the other hand, he expressed a wish that the colossal power of France might have been acquired and consolidated wisely.[62]

Although recognizing Britain's interest in the preservation of the balance, Adams indicated little fear of Russian domination of the continent following Napoleon's defeat.[63]   He agreed that the war between France and Russia, which began in 1812, had been fought for the dominion of the European continent; [64] he seemed not disquieted by the prospect of Russia's gaining the opportunity to exercise such dominion, showing no unfavorable reaction to Admiral Koutouzof's remark, *"Monsieur, la Russie bien gouvernée, est faite pour commander à l'Europe."* [65]   Although it was important for the Russians to use their new military power wisely, there was no doubt that they would become the arbiters of Europe,[66] and he saw little reason to question Russian wisdom and moderation.[67]   During the hundred days following Napoleon's return from Elba, Adams did not express fear of the re-establishment of a universal monarchy, but suggested that a counterpoise to Britain (the real *bête noir* in his mind) might result.[68]   The new domination of events by Britain made the restoration of general peace in Europe a threat to the security of the United States.[69]   The commercial monopolistic tendencies of Britain were a real threat.   Adams reminded the American Minister to Russia that this country's first commercial treaty, based on "just and magnanimous" principles, had been made with an absolute monarchy,

[60] To the Secretary of State (James Monroe), St. Petersburg, July 13, 1811, *Writings*, IV, 140–141.

[61] To Thomas Boylston Adams, February 14, 1801, *ibid.*, II, 500–501.

[62] To Thomas Boylston Adams, St. Petersburg, January 24, 1814, *ibid.*, V, 10–11.

[63] *Memoirs*, October 30, 1820, V, 194.

[64] To John Adams, St. Petersburg, November 5, 1812, *Proceedings of the American Antiquarian Society*, New Series, XXIII (April 9, 1913–October 15, 1913), p. 125.

[65] *Memoirs*, December 3, 1812, II, 425–426.

[66] To the Secretary of State (James Monroe), St. Petersburg, February 2, 1813, *Writings*, IV, 430.

[67] To Abigail Adams, St. Petersburg, April 7, 1813, *ibid.*, IV, 467.   *Memoirs*, April 10, 1813, II, 458.

[68] To John Adams, Paris, April 24, 1815, *ibid.*, V, 309.

[69] To Joseph Hall, Boston House, Ealing, near London, September 9, 1815, *ibid.*, p. 376.

France [70]—more explicitly, the United States could do business with Alexander, the titan now dominating the continent itself. But Adams felt a deep suspicion that the mistress of the seas would not be easy to handle. Anglophobia combined with a relative freedom from moral concern for intra-European affairs, the hallmarks of typical American isolationism, were the bases of Adams's isolationism. He, like many of his isolationist successors, saw only vaguely the historic strategic role that Britain had played and was playing in her relations with the continent. But one may find more reason for this incomplete understanding on the part of Adams, in view of his era, than later isolationists.

ADAMS AND WAR

The strategic role Britain played vis-a-vis the continent entailed periodical British involvement in continental and world wars. A component of Adams's attitude toward Europe was his belief that that continent suffered from a chronic malady of political and social maladjustment producing conflict. He had, therefore, an articulated aversion for war. Although, as Clark affirms,[71] it was probably true that Adams was no pacifist, it is impossible to be dogmatic concerning his attitude toward war. The picture is contradictory—his nationalism and temperament influenced him in the direction of belligerence; his profound sense of a moral imperative, impregnated with Christianity, moved him toward an aversion for war.

It has been claimed that John Quincy Adams as Secretary of State "planned a series of treaties to abolish war." [72] In the record there is no evidence to substantiate this claim, although, as Clark points out, "he [Adams] was one of the authors of perhaps the only permanently successful disarmament treaty which the world has known—that for disarming the Canadian border." [73] Beyond that, it is true, he was a declared foe of "private war" and privateering, "the plunder of private property, the pillage of all the regular rewards of honest industry and laudable enterprise, upon the mere pretence of a national contest,

[70] To George Washington Campbell, State Department, Washington, D. C., June 28, 1818, *ibid.*, VI, 368.
[71] Clark, *op. cit.*, p. 8.
[72] Anon., "The Adams Family," *Quarterly Review*, 237 (April, 1922), p. 299.
[73] Clark, *op. cit.*, p. 8. National Archives, Records of the Department of State, *Diplomatic Instructions,* All Countries, IX, 112.

[for] to the eye of reason and justice, . . . [it could] appear in no other light than that of highway robbery." [74] This attitude revealed his alliance with the main line tradition in American political thinking that considered a major task of government to be protection of property.

The attack of privateersmen and the foreign navies upon American property on the high seas had been the major cause of involvement in Europe's wars. Adams therefore supported as one of his major projects as Secretary of State, a negotiation, particularly with Britain, to accomplish a change in doctrine concerning neutral and maritime rights. [75] Not asking Britain to disavow her past acts, working for the future rather than the past, he proposed a convention for the abolition of "private war upon the sea," for recognition of the principle that the property of an enemy upon the sea should be just as safe as upon land, and for agreement that unarmed merchant vessels be allowed during war to proceed on their way unmolested. The public vengeance, in other words, should not be worked upon private individuals. [76] The principles of justice, humanity, and Christianity demanded, in particular, that free or neutral ships should make free goods and that neutral goods should be safe in enemy ships. [77] Adams thus projected a convention to abolish "private war upon the Sea, . . . an improvement entirely congenial to that of the final and total abolition of the Slave trade," congenial to the Holy Alliance, but offered first to Great Britain as the power most able to support it and benefit from it. [78] Enthusiastically he proclaimed that, should the convention be accepted, it would become a system of perpetual peace between the two countries, Britain and the United States, later to be extended to others. [79] On the ground of this claim only may it be said that he proposed a series of treaties to abolish war *per se,* although he clearly believed that the solutions that he offered came near to the root causes of war.

Some of Adams's pronouncements revealed a deep moral aversion

[74] I "Marcellus," *Writings,* I, 138.
[75] National Archives, Records of the Department of State, *Diplomatic Instructions,* All Countries, X, 72–74.
[76] *Ibid.,* X, 75.
[77] *Ibid.,* X, 78.
[78] *Ibid.,* X, 80: The proposed treaty is to be found in *ibid.,* X, 81–89.
[79] *Ibid.,* X, 98.

for war, although, as will be revealed below, that moral aversion was not unqualified. He wrote of the American colonists as "untutored in the disgraceful science of human butchery." [80] Later in Silesia he took occasion to write, "The trade of human butchery, I am told, is now about to commence again." [81] From St. Petersburg he sent forth a series of letters expatiating upon the senselessness of war. Thence also he wrote that he looked about him and saw everywhere the awful scourge of war. Peace was the "natural state of all nations, with respect to one another"; [82] an inevitable course in the "gospel dispensation" was the abolition of war. [83] It would not come about for many years to come, but true adherence to the Christian faith would mark this result. [84] War and slavery, associated institutions, should both be abolished. [85] These two had been the most "effective instruments for converting the bounties of the Creator to the race of man into a curse. . . ." [86] Hobbes was in great error in holding that government and despotism were synonymous and war the natural state of man. [87] Adams recognized that before permanent peace could be achieved the hearts of men would have to be reformed. [88] The attachment of the people to government was more important to its stability than military force. [89] The assumption was, then, that with a change in the hearts of men war in the international sphere as a coercive instrument and harsh government could both be removed.

There were many concrete examples in Adams's career of a pacifistic position. At the beginning of the wars precipitated by the French Revolution he frequently asserted the importance of a peaceful course. Prior to the War of 1812, he wrote that peace should be preserved, that war could only be injurious to both sides. [90] The day he signed the

[80] Adams, *July 4th Oration, 1793,* p. 13.

[81] Adams, *Letters on Silesia,* p. 250.

[82] II "Marcellus," *Writings,* I, 140.

[83] Letter to the Rev. J. Edwards, Quincy, July 13, 1837, quoted in Henry Adams, *Degradation of the Democratic Dogma,* pp. 29–30.

[84] National Archives, Records of the Department of State, *Diplomatic Instructions,* X, 69.

[85] Adams, *Newburyport Oration, 1837,* pp. 56–57.

[86] Lovejoy, *Memoir of the Rev. Elijah P. Lovejoy,* introduction by John Quincy Adams, p. 8.

[87] Adams, *Argument in United States v. Cinque* [15 Peters 518], p. 88.

[88] To Alexander Hill Everett, London, December 6, 1815, *Writings,* V, 437.

[89] To William Vans Murray, January 27, 1801, *ibid.,* II, 495.

[90] *Memoirs,* September 10, 1812, II, 403.

Peace of Ghent he proclaimed the happiest day of his life.   The treaty was his contribution to the restoration of peace to the world.[91]   From Britain he proclaimed his special duty to be the preaching of peace.[92] Much later in his life as the danger of war with Britain, precipitated by the slave party, seemed imminent he was vigorous in defense of peace.[93]   He would not go to war even should England take Cuba.[94] Words, he cautioned, should not be used in the legislature tending to arouse passions that might lead to war.[95]

There are, conversely, numerous instances of great bellicosity in Adams's reaction to events.   Noting his own father's decision as President to treat with France by means of a new commission, he expressed hope that a negative vote in the Senate would counteract any halting of preparations for war, for thus there might be created a firmer basis for negotiations.[96]   Upon hearing of the British burning of Washington he fulminated that the Americans should emulate the Russians following Napoleon's burning of Moscow.[97]   This response was, of course, completely natural for an American at the time.   At Ghent, in a calmer moment, it was significant that he should write that the desire of the United States for peace was one of the obstacles to the securing of peace, whereas the true course should have been a determination to defend herself to the last extremity.[98]   He belligerently retorted to Clay that it was for the British to decide how much they wanted peace.[99]   With Bayard he sought a firmer basis for terminating negotiations and continuing the war, should it be necessary.[100] Even in his more pacific old age he was confident that, should war with Britain come, the issue would be as successful as in the two previous instances.

This belligerence was accompanied by an attention to the necessity for psychological and physical preparation for war.   As his country's

[91] To Louisa Catherine Adams, Ghent, December 30, 1814, *Writings*, V, 256.
[92] To John Adams, Ealing, May 29, 1816, *ibid.*, VI, 38.
[93] *Congressional Globe*, 26th Cong., 1st sess., April 9, 1840, p. 312.   *Ibid.*, 27th Cong., 1st sess., September 4, 1841, p. 428.   *Ibid.*, 27th Cong., 2nd sess., April 14, 1842, pp. 423–429.
[94] *Ibid.*, 28th Cong., 1st sess., December 27, 1843, pp. 78–79.
[95] *Ibid.*, March 5, 1844, p. 353.
[96] To Rufus King, Berlin, April 15, 1799, *Writings*, II, 409–410.
[97] To Louisa Catherine Adams, Ghent, October 14, 1814, *ibid.*, V, 160.
[98] To Abigail Adams, Ghent, October 25, 1814, *ibid.*, V, 166.
[99] *Memoirs*, November 10, 1814, III, 68.
[100] *Ibid.*, December 13, 1814, p. 114.

involvement in the Napoleonic wars seemed to increase, he recorded his belief that Americans must "become a warlike people." [101]   During the negotiations at Ghent he concluded that he could not imagine a future state of the world in which the United States would not be "a great naval and military power." [102]   Unpreparedness had been America's tragedy during the War of 1812.   War being an ever-present evil, minds "not besotted by the spirit of faction" should see to it that none was begun "without a fair prospect of attaining its objects. . . ." [103]   The vicissitudes and dangers of the world required the strengthening of the government and military preparedness.   A nation could not slumber, at the very least it must prepare for war to have peace.[104]

Likewise, in strange contrast with the pacific side of his thinking were the instances of theoretical justification of war in his writings. Self-preservation was, in his mind, "an obligation paramount to every other law" governing political bodies.[105]   Particularly his own age he saw filled with "warlike passions and propensities." [106]   Admitting the inevitability of the War of 1812, he stated that the "effect of war upon our national character and institutions would probably be great and . . . [he hoped] favorable." [107]   This reference to "national character" was particularly important, for he was suggesting that war as such might exert a beneficial therapeutic influence upon the national psyche.   In a letter of a few months later, Adams observed that it was perhaps an advantage that the war had come when it did, since the courage of a soldier, although Gibbons had termed it "the cheapest quality of human nature," could fail a nation at critical junctures "without the aid of use, discipline, and example." [108]   The

[101] To William Vans Murray, [Berlin], July 22, 1798, *Writings*, II, 343.

[102] To William Harris Crawford, Ghent, September 14, 1814, *ibid.*, V, 140–141.

[103] To Alexander Hill Everett, Ealing near London, March 16, 1816, *ibid.*, V, 537.

[104] *Register of Debates*, 22nd Cong., 1st sess., III, appendix, p. 86.

[105] To the Secretary of State (Edmund Randolph), No. 5, The Hague, November 7, 1794, *Writings*, I, 221.

[106] To Henry Middleton, State Department, Washington, D. C., July 5, 1820, *ibid.*, VII, 48.

[107] To William Plumer, St. Petersburg, May 13, 1812, *ibid.*, IV, 329.

[108] John Quincy Adams, "Letter to John Adams, St. Petersburg, November 5, 1812," *Proceedings of the American Antiquarian Society*, New Series, XXIII (April 9–October 15, 1913), p. 124.

"enervation and languor" of continuing peace might tragically weaken the martial spirit, and such weakening particularly would have been tragic since war was inevitable.[109]   An even more direct statement in the same vein proceeds as follows:

There are great and glorious qualities in the human character, which as they can unfold themselves only in times of difficulty and danger, seem to make war from time to time a necessary evil among men.   A nation long at Peace seldom fails to become degraded.   Symptoms of this species of Corruption were very visible in our Country.   God grant that in suffering the unavoidable calamities, we may recover in all their vigour the energies of war! [110]

Invaluable skills would derive from war experience. The War of 1812 had, therefore, been an advantage from an enlarged point of view, at the least it had "raised our national character in the eyes of all Europe." [111]   In his old age, he came perhaps even closer to a justification of war on a moral basis, probably influenced by a growing conviction that slavery, America's tragic blight, could be exorcised only by the catharsis of war. He wrote: "Philosophically speaking, I believed that war was not a corrupter, but rather a purifier of the moral character of man, that peace was the period of corruption to the human race." [112]

ADAMS AND IMPERIALISM

We must not make the mistake of assuming that Adams created a system of values and social theories that was complete in all sectors. With respect to war, it in some degree violated his moral values; on the other hand, his vigorous nationalism, inescapably looking upon war as a major means of accomplishing national goals, could occasionally justify the institution in moral terms.   Therein lies another manifestation of the conflict between the values of the theorist and the necessities of action.   Going beyond war to survey

[109] John Quincy Adams, "Letter to John Adams, St. Petersburg, November 5, 1812," *Proceedings of the American Antiquarian Society*, New Series, XXIII (April 9–October 15, 1913), p. 124.

[110] John Quincy Adams, "Letter to Abigail Adams, St. Petersburg, February 18, 1813," *Proceedings of the American Antiquarian Society*, New Series, XXIII (April 9–October 15, 1913), p. 145.

[111] John Quincy Adams, "Letter to Alexander Hill Everett, Ealing near London, March 16, 1816," *American Historical Review*, XI, No. 2 (January, 1906), pp. 103–104.

[112] *Memoirs,* March 25, 1846, XII, 255.

his views of imperialist expansion, another expression of a strong nationalism, we shall find a similar contradiction. Just as the strong nationalism of France was transformed into an expansionist imperialism under the impact of revolutionary ideology, so in Adams a strong nationalism that viewed the American Revolution as *sui generis* and creative of an American system frequently became the foundation of imperialist ambitions. To the degree that this American system was judged by Adams to comprehend sound moral values implicit in a natural order, his imperialism was rationalized on a moral basis.

A moral conflict arose, however, when he found national Administrations under the influence of the slavocracy counseling expansion. Thereupon his dubiety concerning and opposition to expansion came to the fore. The impact of the political struggle is nowhere so clear as at this point. As a "conscience" Whig he could not accept the expansion of a power, even that of his own country, under influences for which he had a deep moral aversion. In addition, of course, United States expansion under slave influence, enhancing that influence, would earn the serious opposition of political enemies for purely tactical political reasons. Adams, as one of those political enemies of the slave influence, was sufficiently astute politically to see and fight against it on this issue.

Adams, as we have noted, rejected the premises of the old colonial system. His opposition to future colonial expansion in this hemisphere was, in effect, opposition to the exclusiveness of that old system, as well as a policy directed against future European encroachments. He recognized, furthermore, that exclusiveness in the control of colonies for the benefit of the imperial power was not a function of the political ideas that were dominant in that imperial power, for he noted that "the nations most highly favoured with freedom, have not always been the most friendly to the liberty of others." [113] If Great Britain, for example, had abandoned the exclusiveness of her imperial system, in effect a limitation upon colonial liberties, her dominion in the American colonies might not have been challenged. One of the fortunate results that Adams anticipated might ensue from the tragic Napoleonic wars was the destruction of the European colonial system—a system based upon inequality rather than common and free acceptance of political

[113] Adams, *July 4th Oration, 1793,* p. 9.

ideals—and he observed with interest the vacillations of Britain with respect to the Spanish American revolutions, vacillations produced by the influence of commercial ambition on the one hand, and aversion for colonial insurrection on the other.[114]   He supported a policy that would influence the chief maritime power to prefer the success of her commercial ambitions to the realization of doctrinaire colonial principles.[115]   Adams conceived of the American Revolution and the progressing revolutions in Spanish America as demonstrations of the "decayed and rotten" nature of the principles underlying the old system.[116]   The American system was the antithesis of the combination of "partial rights . . . and *exclusive privileges*" that underlay the old.[117]

The exclusive system of Spain, for example, had been based upon the "iniquitous and absurd" pretense of the Bishop of Rome to the power to grant half the world for the purpose of spreading the teachings of "the most benevolent of all religions." [118]   The exclusive system of Britain, he expostulated in biting irony, seemed to be based on an assumption of right to any spot in the "habitable globe." [119]   At the most, the "tie of colonial subjection" could be deemed compatible with the "purposes of civil government . . . only when the condition of the subordinate state is from its weakness incompetent to its own protection." [120]   The American system, supporting the principle of the most-favored-nation that was incompatible with the colonial system, had recognized one of the most important principles that must underlie America's freedom "from the thraldom of colonizing monopolies and exclusions. . . ." [121]

The French revolutionary zeal, which transformed French na-

[114] To the Secretary of State (James Monroe), No. 28, London, January 22, 1816, *Writings*, V, 488–489.

[115] To the Secretary of State (James Monroe), London, October 5, 1816, *ibid.*, VI, 103.

[116] To Alexander Hill Everett, State Department, Washington, D. C., August 10, 1818, *ibid.*, VI, 422–423.

[117] National Archives, Records of the Department of State, *Diplomatic Instructions,* All Countries, IX, 301–303.

[118] To Richard C. Anderson, State Department, Washington, D. C., May 27, 1823, *Writings*, VII, 442–443.

[119] *Memoirs,* January 27, 1821, V, 252.

[120] Adams, *July 4th, 1821 Address,* p. 12.   To Edward Everett, Washington, D. C., January 31, 1822, *Writings*, VII, 200–201.

[121] Adams, "First Annual Message," *in* Richardson, *op. cit.*, II, 302.

tionalism into a proselytizing imperialist fervor, had to be distinguished from the imperialism of the old colonial system, but Adams, rejecting in some degree the principles of that revolution, was suspicious of the drive to cover "all Europe with Great Republics" under the hegemony of France. Seeing no balancing of interests in the French system, he feared—as he eventually knew rightly— the threat in it of a "Pretorian Prefect, or a Protector [memory of Cromwell] of French liberties." [122] Not only was France moving against old monarchies, but also against "Ancient Republics" in her own interest. "The terrible republic" was robbing neutrals and preventing them from defending themselves against such robbery.

Nevertheless, Adams was an expansionist-imperialist in theory and practice, although no unqualified generalization is in order. One investigator writes: "In the long public career of John Quincy Adams the achievement which appeared to him most important was his diplomacy of expansion." [123] This statement deals with Adams's motivations, difficult in themselves to describe dogmatically, and, in addition, not all the evidence bears out this contention, although much does.

However, when the opportunity arose, the expansionist sentiments were expressed. Referring to the French West Indies before the Peace of Amiens and during the early part of the great struggle between France and Great Britain, Adams wrote, "We can and must do something there. . . . The natural connection of the West Indies is with the American and not with the European continent, and such a connection as I have in my mind . . . [is] a more natural connection than that of metropolis and colony, or in other words master and servant." [124] The Union was seen in the garb of a "great and growing empire." [125] Such allusions alone might involve merely loose or general usage of language, but the purport of the following passage from a letter to his father is unmistakable: "The whole continent of North America appears to be destined by Divine Providence to be peopled by one *nation*, speaking one language, professing one

[122] To John Adams, London, September 11, 1797, *Writings*, II, 203–204.
[123] Kenneth Potter, *The Hispanic-American Policy of John Quincy Adams, 1817–1825* (unpublished Ph. D. Thesis, University of California, 1934), p. 28.
[124] To William Vans Murray, Berlin, July 14, 1798, *Writings*, II, 336.
[125] Adams, *An Address to the Members of the Massachusetts Charitable Fire Society at their Annual Meeting, May 28, 1802*, p. 23.

general system of religious and political principles, and accustomed to one general tenor of social usages and customs." [126] In other words, even the non-Anglo-Saxon portions of the continent were to come under the aegis of American political control and culture. That was the spirit of "Manifest Destiny" asserted well before Thomas Hart Benton. Although Adams agreed that the War of 1812 could not have as its object the taking of Canada, during the war he did, remarkably, write that "our means of taking the British possessions upon our continent are so ample and unquestionable that, if we do not take them, it must be owing to the worst of qualities, without which there is no independent nation, and which we must acquire at any hazard and any cost." [127] Empire was, therefore, not simply a matter of the trends implicit in a situation, but the expression of a national ethos. No strained legalism respecting the dominions and rights of Indian savages, furthermore, should be permitted to stand in the path of this relentless development. [128]

With great vigor he pressed for recognition, particularly by the British, of American title to lands on the littoral of the "South Seas." [129] He reminded the English that the United States had had a settlement at the mouth of the Columbia before the War of 1812. [130] The Secretary of State pushed for American outposts on that river. One point of agreement that he succeeded in establishing with Cushing, with whom he was in almost consistent disagreement, in the House, was with respect to American title to the land west of the Rockies: United States title was clearly better than that of Great Britain. [131] One of the major purposes of the American people, he earlier wrote, should be to teach the world to be familiar with "our proper dominion . . . [as] the continent of North America. From the time when we became an independent people it was as much a

---

[126] To John Adams, St. Petersburg, August 31, 1811, *Writings*, IV, 209.

[127] To Thomas Boylston Adams, St. Petersburg, November 24, 1812, *ibid.*, IV, 407.

[128] *Memoirs*, August 9, 1814, II, 12. Draft of an Answer to the British Commissioners by John Quincy Adams, Ghent, August 24, 1814, *Writings*, V, 98–99. *Memoirs*, September 1, 1814, II, 25. *Ibid.*, September 25, 1814, III, 41–42.

[129] *Memoirs*, January 31, 1821, V, 261. National Archives, Records of the Department of State, *Diplomatic Instructions, All Countries*, VIII, 189–190.

[130] *Memoirs*, November 24, 1817, IV, 25.

[131] *Congressional Globe*, 25th Cong., 2nd sess., p. 381.

law of nature that this should become our pretension as that the Mississippi should flow to the sea." [132] Hearing of newly discovered islands in the Pacific he proposed the sending of a frigate and the establishment of settlements, with the particular purpose of getting ahead of the British.[133] After the independence of Spain's colonies had been established, Adams wrote with foreboding that the United States might be called upon to take a more active part: "Floating, undigested purposes of this great American Confederation [a great confederation to embrace the hemisphere], have been for some time fermenting in the imagination of many speculative statesmen, nor is the idea to be disdainfully rejected because its magnitude may appal the understanding of politicians accustomed to the more minute, but more complicated machinery of a contracted political standard." [134] There was but a little doubt in Adams's mind that the United States would eventually be the nucleus of such a general American confederation. He did not unequivocally accept the idea, but he endorsed the enlarged view that could entertain such ideas, a view such as that revealed in his inaugural address:

Since that period [the time of the making of the Constitution] a population of four millions has multiplied to twelve. A territory bounded by the Mississippi has been admitted to the Union in numbers nearly equal to those of the first Confederation. Treaties of peace, amity, and commerce have been concluded with the principal dominions of the earth. The people of other nations, inhabitants of regions acquired not by conquest, but by compact, have been united with us in the participation of our rights and duties, of our burdens and blessings. The forest has fallen by the ax of our woodsmen; the soil has been made to turn by the tillage of our farmers; our commerce has whitened every ocean. The dominion of man over physical nature has been extended by the invention of our artists. Liberty and law have marched hand in hand. All the purposes of human association have been accomplished as effectively as under any other government on the globe, and at a cost little exceeding in a whole generation the expenditure of other nations in a single year.[135]

---

[132] *Memoirs*, November 16, 1819, IV, 438–439.

[133] To the President (James Monroe), Washington, D. C., August 26, 1820, *Writings*, VII, 67.

[134] National Archives, Records of the Department of State, *Diplomatic Instructions*, All Countries, IX, 301.

[135] Adams, "Inaugural Address," *in* Richardson, *op. cit.*, II, 295.

From this type of welling nationalism derived the spirit of imperialism.

This expansive spirit of nationalism forced Adams to conclude that the law of nature governing "geographical, commercial, moral, and political relations" made inevitable the eventual inclusion of Cuba in the Union.[136] He anticipated that within fifty years annexation to the United States would be necessary. The same spirit caused Adams to consider with interest the proposal of the San Salvador congress that that province be included in the North American Union. In Adams's opinion the fathers of the Constitution had contrived "a new form of government for an extensive empire, which nothing under the canopy of heaven, but the basest degeneracy of their posterity . . . [could] prevent from becoming the greatest and the most formidable that the world ever saw." [137] This government was based upon those principles "of justice, transcending the bounds of space and time, surrounding the globe, and binding upon the conscience of every living soul upon its face." [138] Adams advised Americans to take pleasure in the growth of their empire and the fact that so many lands, such as the Caribbean islands, Texas, Panama, were seeking admission to the Union.[139] Mexico, having demonstrated its incapacity for self-government, "must be invaded and conquered by our People." [140] By the very nature of things, the "great, republican, democratic, confederated republic . . . [must] gather under the shadow of its wings, in its

---

[136] National Archives, Records of the Department of State, *Diplomatic Instructions*, All Countries, IX, 187. To Hugh Nelson, State Department, Washington, D. C., April 28, 1823, *Writings*, VII, 372–381.

[137] Adams, *The Lives of James Madison and James Monroe*, p. 208.

[138] Report No. 93, House of Representatives, 27th Cong., 3rd sess., *China and Sandwich Islands* [To accompany bills H. R. No.s 720 and 721], January 24, 1843, p. 2. Mr. Adams, from the Committee on Foreign Affairs, made the report: Adams made this point as a basis for his opinion that the Chinese isolationist position, then being forcibly modified by British arms, could not be justified on the grounds of the size of China's territory and the extent of her population. Imperial pretensions could be justified only if they were an expression of valid principles.

[139] Adams, *Newburyport Oration, 1837*, pp. 46–47.

[140] Letter to Timothy Pitkin, Washington, D. C., April 22, 1837, Tatum, *op. cit.*, pp. 387–388: In the same letter he expressed great fear that this expansion would have an unfavorable effect upon American principles. Thus a dilemma is produced. The excellence of its principles justified the United States' expansion, yet expansion threatened the decay of those principles. A sort of Adamsian dialectic!

appointed time, perhaps the whole continents of North and South America," [141] as well as "the archipelago of islands separating it from the Southern continent. . . ." [142]

On the basis of the above, Adams's imperialistic spirit appears unquestionable, yet the picture must be painted in a variety of colors. Blacks and whites will not convey the whole truth. A final impression of Adams as an undoubting nationalist-imperialist would be an approach to the truth, but faulty in significant details. We have already noted that he thought America's principles justified her expansion. On the other hand, throughout his career Adams expressed opinions indicating that he had doubts about the effect of expansion, and, what is more, doubts concerning the permission to expand granted by these principles. Answering a query of the Swedish Minister as to whether the United States would desire to buy St. Bartholomew in the West Indies, he asserted that it was "contrary to the political system of the United States to wish for the possession of colonies. . . ." [143] He added that he doubted if she would accept a West Indian island as a gift.

Adams further suggested that one of the greatest dangers to the Union was its size. [144] He opposed Cuban annexation, proposed by emissaries from that island [145] and supported by Calhoun and Jefferson, and informed the Russian Minister that the United States had no ambition to annex it. [146] He criticized the Colonization Society for smuggling "in upon us a system of establishing Colonies beyond [the] sea. . . ." [147] The long history of his opposition to the annexation of Texas and the war against Mexico must further qualify the generalization of his imperialism. During the very period wherein Adams was producing imperialist pronouncements he was recording the risks America was running and the dangers

[141] Adams, *The New England Confederacy of MDCXLIII*, p. 22.

[142] *Memoirs*, February 14, 1846, XII, 247.

[143] To the Secretary of State (Timothy Pickering), Berlin, December 24, 1798, *Writings*, II, 381–382. Of course, in this reference to "colonies" he may have meant the component parts of the old colonial system.

[144] *Memoirs*, April 13, 1820, V, 68. Adams, *The Lives of James Madison and James Monroe*, p. 43.

[145] *Memoirs*, September 27, 1822, VI, 70.

[146] *Ibid.*, May 19, 1825, VII, 9–10: The Secretary of State, of course, would face the necessity of expressing opinions not entertained by the private citizen, John Quincy Adams.

[147] *Ibid.*, April 29, 1819, IV, 354.

she was courting in succumbing to the "prospects and temptations to aggrandizement." [148]   Adams was complex, obviously not a man to be categorized easily nor generalized about on the basis of his assertions on a single occasion.   An analysis of his views of national expansion serves further to illustrate this most important fact.

[148] Adams, *The New England Confederacy of MDCXLIII*, p. 6.   *Memoirs*, April, 8, 1844, XII, 6.

PART SEVEN

Conclusion

19

A Summing Up

As life draws towards its close it loses value philosophically every day; but physically becomes more precious. For all that is past, gratitude is the only sentiment that should fill my soul, as the future should be allotted to humble hope, to firm reliance, and to resignation.

MEMOIRS, *April 30, 1827*

John Quincy Adams's social and political philosophy, which has been discussed in the preceding chapters, derived in great measure from the eighteenth-century thinkers,[1] in particular John Locke, but it constituted, as well, a special synthesis of old ideas. The creative product must generally be more synthesis of the old than entirely new substance; the creative faculty is as much the seeing of new metaphysical combinations, containing old elements, as it is the projecting of entirely new ideas into the view of men. Creators would be most rare in the history of man—they would, in fact, be a diminishing, if not an extinct breed—should only those who had produced an entirely novel idea be so classifiable. For practical purposes, an infinite range of ideas is not available to man through which man can express his views of the world. Adams was under obligation not only to Locke and his whole associated tradition of the eighteenth century, but through Locke he was also obligated to the "long tradition of medieval political thought, back to St. Thomas, in which the reality of moral restraints on power, the responsibility of rulers to the communities which they ruled, and

[1] Henry Adams, *The Education of Henry Adams* (New York: The Modern Library, 1931), p. 11.

the subordination of government to law were axiomatic." [2]   In his combinations of the Lockean position with an important emphasis upon the strong, positive role to be played by government in a program of internal improvements; his combination of a strong nationalism based upon a sense of national moral rectitude with an insistence upon self-restraint, equality, and a recognition of moral laws in the relations of nations; his combination of a constantly reiterated subscription to a natural law concept with an empirical and skeptical view in the realm of science Adams was unique among public figures of his day in the United States.   That his social and political thinking had no greater impact upon his era and, particularly, his country is to be explained by the unsystematic presentation of his ideas in a wide range and variety of materials, the unsympathetic reaction of his contemporaries to his austere and wry personality, and the unpreparedness of the citizens of his day to accept his ideological synthesis, some components of which were anachronistic and others premature.

The Lockean quality of Adams's thinking is immediately apparent when judged against the background of a summation of Locke's thought.   Like Locke, Adams vigorously rejected Hobbes's affirmation of political absolutism and was under no philosophical compulsion, as was Hobbes, to get back to basic principles to resolve the conflict between essential scientific empiricism and natural law concepts.   No more than Locke did Adams compose a formula to accommodate his concepts of government as intrinsic in social organization and, at the same time, as derived from the community and based upon popular consent.   The same conflict existed between his view of the ends of society, which had implicit within them a general human purpose, and his view of the end of man, who, according to the egoistical natural law concept to which Adams subscribed, possessed basic individual rights to be safeguarded by government at all costs.   The basic individual right of man in private property, the keystone of the system of rights, was as inherent in Adams's thinking as Locke's.

Adams, too, saw questions of right and wrong, as determined by reference to standards inherent in nature, although the rules of

[2] George H. Sabine, *A History of Political Theory* (New York: Henry Holt, 1937), p. 523.

common sense were, subconsciously, as important in governing decisions in these matters. Both thinkers derived the rules of men from a superior moral order; these rules could not create right, which must be protected at all costs by the institutions and rules established by men. Adams was, equally with Locke, ineffective in demonstrating by empirical methods that the individual has innate human rights, a task no doubt impossible for any philosopher. Adams's devotion to toleration and indifference to orthodoxy and doctrinaire views in theological matters was as strong as Locke's. This liberal conception in both men, in addition to the other points of similarity, was a natural reflection of the class interests that they both espoused.

Both propounded a theory of social compact founded upon consent, yet for both that consent could be given by tacit agreement. Perhaps Adams saw more clearly that the social compact was creative of government than did Locke from whose writings it is not clear whether government or society was created by the compact. But even to Adams the compact could be, in one instance, an historical compact such as the constitution of Massachusetts, or in another, a vague agreement of the British people lost in the mists of prehistory whereby they determined to protect their rights. Significantly both men, although more conservative than radical, were champions of dispensations established by political revolutions, although the revolutions differed in some degree as to purpose. Both placed the power of the community in a majority of the members of that community, although Adams was more careful to place limits upon the power of a majority to modify human rights than was Locke. This restriction of majority power was natural for the American since he had developed in a community accustomed to charters, limiting documents, Privy Council review of colonial acts, and, after 1787, written constitutions and judicial review. Yet even Adams, in the manner of Locke, came close to contradiction in placing the supreme constituent power of the community in the legislature while insisting that a residual power remained in the people to overthrow a despotic government. Neither man saw a conflict between assigning a supreme power to a legislative body and at the same time describing this power as nonarbitrary. Both men tended to try to link a supreme community will to a power inherent in government as long as it performed its duties.

In further demonstration of affinity in tradition: whereas Locke's theory of a vested right of historical organs of government to their places in the hierarchy of government, a carry-over from earlier times, culminated in a British Whig theory of a balance among King, Lords, and Commons, in Adams's theory the concept of a balancing of interests was more full-grown and explicit involving acceptance of a separation of powers plus a balance based upon bicameralism in the legislature. Adams defended this concept in discussion with Bentham with respect to an American political order. There was a carry-over, even more close, from Locke's rejection of the right of a just conqueror to attack the liberty and property rights of a conquered people to Adams's rejection of an American right to govern the people of Louisiana without their consent, even though the United States had gained the territory by a constitutional use of the treaty power. Both men were the champions of diversity of interests, and in attempting to comprehend disparate forces they produced systems that could be the sources of inspiration to men of contradictory ambition and purpose. Adams was therefore in the tradition of Locke, especially as he attempted to combine empiricism with a rationalist system. In his empiricism he portended the America of the future, particularly that technically competent, extractive America, fabulously efficient in exploiting the earth's riches. However, Adams would have safeguarded those riches as a treasure to be passed on to a posterity, a treasure improved and increased in a fashion that, unfortunately, his profligate posterity has neglected.

Adams's intellectual background was larger than the Lockean tradition alone, however, for he was under an obligation created by the tender ministrations of highly cultivated parents and a congenial environment to the whole Hellenic-Roman-Christian intellectual heritage of Western Europe. Linguistic facility brought him into close contact with the national facets of that general cultural heritage, and his deep devotion to the great literary figures of the English-speaking world, particularly Shakespeare, was not seriously impaired by the political cleavages that divided that world, cleavages that were accentuated by Adams's Anglophobia.

Going beyond the British to the larger heritage, we may not to any significant degree base assertions on direct references to men. But similarities and parallels of idea and thought may be noted that suggest common inspirations or accent the organic ideological relationships among different thinkers within western civilization. Adams's debt to Locke has been indicated, although some areas of divergence have been suggested. In one such area, at least, Adams appears more related to Rousseau than to Locke. That was with respect to his ardent nationalism and its derivative theory of internal improvements, in expressing which Adams was more closely related to Rousseau and more nearly in the tradition of the "romantic cult of the group," than in the tradition of the empirical British philosopher. Adams's rhetoric on the subject of the American national character and its future has an unmistakable implication. When it is considered in association with his assertions concerning a community "mind" and his faith in internal improvements, the relationship of ideas is even clearer. Adams saw internal improvements as the product of a great cooperative national effort that would bind the nation together with roads and canals, as the common effort of an expanded industry, and as a collective determination to guard the national heritage of natural resources. The community was a significant presence to Adams as the comprehension of a general welfare or purpose of which Rousseau rather than Locke was the inspiration.

Neither Adams nor Rousseau may be considered particularly democratic in his thinking except in the degree to which they stressed the component of equality and asserted the necessity of an ill-defined kind of consent to government. At this point, of course, they parted company. Adams, the practical politician, could not subscribe to the Rousseauan concept of unanimity and direct democracy plausible only for the city-state. Nor would Adams ever have been capable of describing any deviation of the individual from the community will or general will as an individual aberration in which the individual is perversely refusing to see that the general will naturally reflects his own. Adams's acquaintance with the political battle was too vivid in his experience to permit that.

In the living of his political experience Adams demonstrated his position relative to his contemporaries in the United States. His stand with respect to the Jeffersonian tradition has been discussed in Chapter XIV. Never thoroughly associated with that tradition, he was, for example, at variance with the young Calhoun, the Jeffersonian, and in conflict with Calhoun the great creative political theorist of the slavocracy. All factors worked to dissociate Adams from the South Carolinian as the latter continued along a blind alley in search of theoretical justifications of a lost cause. Calhoun thus demonstrated how potent minds may be thoroughly misled by earnest desires and by becoming entirely enmeshed in the perspectives of their own group and their own causes. Adams, the empiricist in science and the devotee of a rationalist equalitarianism, could least of all serve a democratic idea based upon a concept of social hierarchy. Adams, the romantic nationalist, could develop no loyalty to a community smaller than the entire nation, or to a state of the Union acting through the agency of a "concurrent majority," especially since a state, the geographical area of application of the "concurrent majority," was to Adams in large measure the artificial creation of the nation. Moreover, Calhoun's theory served a special social interest that Adams abhorred and against the excesses and expansion of which he thought the general government must be the main defense.

Let us turn to another main-line development of Adams's day, the liberal tradition that grew out of the radical utilitarianism of Bentham. Although Adams could dramatize in florid rhetoric the end of government as the serving of the wants of man, he rejected most of the components of the theory of the radical English thinker. This rejection was graphically illustrated in his report of his conversation with Bentham, for Adams took issue with his interlocutor on all points. Even the demand for happiness could not prevail over principle for Adams. His whole life was a tale of backbreaking travail in the service of principle. Adams criticized Blackstone for finding an absolute sovereignty in the state, whereas Bentham criticized Blackstone for placing a contractual circumscription upon the power of government. Whichever interpreted Blackstone correctly, Adams and Bentham were in conflict upon this point of legal limits upon power. And the source of conflict was the natural law, which Bentham abjured and to which Adams subscribed. The eighteenth-century tradition of which Adams was a part was distinct from that of Bentham.

As to where Adams should be placed, both the eclecticism of his thinking and the lack of organized exposition of his thought require that he be put in a category largely his own. Had he been primarily a theorist, the conclusion would have been different. Adams was the political man of action; theory was incidental to the necessities of his career, even though his loyalty to principle was extraordinary. He was in significant relation with a great many theorists, but there were areas of disagreement with all.

John Quincy Adams, mistreated by history through a peculiar conjunction of circumstances that placed his main service at the end of one era and made him unsympathetic with the era that followed, should be revived in the respect of his countrymen. This generation, at least, may overlook his bitterness, austerity, and unfriendliness, and go beyond to discover his qualities of true greatness of mind, heart, and action. An unqualified paean of praise would be incongruous; a forthright statement of his true qualities, the good and the bad, will serve him best, and, perhaps, be what he himself would prefer. It is the hope of the author that this latter purpose has been accomplished, in part, by the above study.

Bibliography

I

MONOGRAPHS AND BOOKS

The Conduct of John Quincy Adams considered in His Relations, political and moral, towards the Federal Party, containing a letter from John Quincy Adams to the Federalists of the United States, Philadelphia, August 20, 1828. Originally printed in the New York *Evening Post.* Pamphlet #4 in 50394. O. U Y 6 at the Library Co. of Philadelphia, Ridgway Library.

Correspondence between John Quincy Adams Esquire, President of the United States, and Several Citizens of Massachusetts concerning the Charge of a Design to Dissolve the Union, alleged to have existed in that State (Boston: Press of the Boston *Daily Advertiser,* 1829). 80 pp.

Plain Matters of Fact, Undenied and Undeniable (Richmond, 1828) from the Richmond *Enquirer.* 51 pp.

Token of a Nation's Sorrow. Addresses in the Congress of the United States (Washington: J. and G. S. Gideon, 1848). 32 pp.

The Treaty of Ghent and the Fisheries, or the Diplomatic Talents of John Quincy Adams Candidly Examined (Boston: J. H. A. Frost, 1824). 27 pp.

Adams, Charles Francis, ed., *Memoirs of John Quincy Adams,* comprising portions of his diary from 1795 to 1848 (Philadelphia: J. B. Lippincott, 1874–1877). 12 vols.

Adams, Henry, *The Degradation of the Democratic Dogma* (New York: Macmillan, 1919). 317 pp.

———, *The Education of Henry Adams* (New York: The Modern Library, 1931). 517 pp.

Adams, James Truslow, *The Adams Family* (Boston: Little, Brown, 1930). 364 pp.

Adams, John Quincy, *Address to the Norfolk County Temperance Society at Their Meeting at Quincy, September 29, 1842* (Boston: Russell and Cutler, 1842). 24 pp.

————, *An Address Delivered July 4, 1821, Washington, D. C.* (Cambridge: Hilliard and Metcalf, 1821). 31 pp.

————, *An Address to the Members of the Massachusetts Charitable Fire Society at their Annual Meeting, May 28, 1802* (Boston: Russell and Cutler, 1802). 25 pp.

————, *Argument before the Supreme Court in the Case of the United States, Appellants, v. Cinque, and others Africans* [15 Peters 518] . . . (New York: S. W. Benedict, 1841). 135 pp.

————, *Dermott MacMorrogh* (Boston: Carter, Hendee and Co., 1832). 108 pp.

————, *A Discourse on Education,* delivered at Braintree, Thursday, October 24, 1839 (Boston: Perkins and Marvin, 1840). 36 pp.

————, *The Duplicate Letters, the Fisheries and the Mississippi.* Documents relating to transactions at the negotiation of Ghent. Collected and pub. by John Quincy Adams (Washington, D. C.: Davis and Force, 1822). 256 pp.

————, *Eulogy on Lafayette,* delivered before both Houses of Congress on the 31st of December, 1834 (New York: Craighead and Allen, 1835). 28 pp.

————, *The Jubilee of the Constitution, a Discourse Delivered at the Request of the New York Historical Society, in the City of New York on Tuesday, the 30th of April 1839; being the Fiftieth Anniversary of the Inauguration of George Washington as President of the United States, on Thursday, the 30th of April, 1789* (New York: Samuel Colman, 1839). 136 pp.

————, *Lectures on Rhetoric and Oratory* (Cambridge: Hilliard and Metcalf, 1810). 2 vols.

————, *Letter Read at the Recent Celebration of West India Emancipation in Bangor (Me.),* Quincy, July 4, 1843. 8 pp.

————, "Letter to Andrew Stevenson, Speaker of the House of Representatives, July 11, 1832," *Daily National Intelligencer,* July 12, 1832.

————, "Letter to the Citizens of the United States, whose Petitions, Memorials and Remonstrances, have been entrusted to me, to be presented to the House of Representatives of the United States, at the third session of the 25th Congress," Quincy, May 21, 1839, Letter II, Boston *Courier,* June 6, 1839.

————, *Letters and Addresses on Freemasonry* (Dayton, Ohio: United Brethren Publishing House, 1875). 332 pp.

————, *Letters on Silesia* (London: J. Budd, 1804). 387 pp.

————, *Letters to Edward Livingston, Grand High Priest of the General Grand Royal Arch Chapter of the United States, and Late Secretary of State of the Said States* (Boston: Connecticut Antimasonic Tract Association, 1834). 56 pp.

Adams, John Quincy, *Life in a New England Town: 1787, 1788; Diary of John Quincy Adams* (Boston: Little, Brown, 1903). 204 pp.

———, *The Lives of James Madison and James Monroe* (Boston: Phillips, Sampson and Co., 1850). 432 pp.

———, *The New England Confederacy of MDCXLIII, a discourse delivered before the Massachusetts Historical Society at Boston on the 29th of May, 1843* (Boston: C. C. Little and J. Brown, 1843). 47 pp.

———, *An Oration Addressed to the Citizens of the Town of Quincy on the Fourth of July, 1831* (Boston: Richardson, Lord & Holbrook, 1831). 40 pp.

———, *An Oration Delivered at Plymouth, December 22, 1802, at the Anniversary Commemoration of the First Landing of Our Ancestors at that Place* (Boston: Richardson, Lord & Holbrook, 1831). 40 pp.

———, *An Oration, Delivered before the Cincinnati Astronomical Society on the Occasion of Laying the Corner Stone of an Astronomical Observatory* (Cincinnati: Shepard and Co., 1843). 72 pp.

———, *An Oration Delivered before the Inhabitants of the Town of Newburyport at their request, on the Sixty-first Anniversary of the Declaration of Independence, July 4, 1837* (Newburyport: Charles Whipple, 1837). 68 pp.

———, *An Oration Pronounced July 4, 1793 at the Request of the Inhabitants of the Town of Boston* (Boston: Benjamin Edes and Son, 1793). 21 pp.

———, *An Oration Spoken at the Request of the ΦBK Society at Cambridge, September 5th 1788* (typed copy of the address presented to the Massachusetts Historical Society by Worthington C. Ford).

———, *Parties in the United States* (New York: Greenberg, 1941). 136 pp.

———, *Poems of Religion and Society* (Auburn and Buffalo: Miller, Orton and Mulligan, 1848). 116 pp.

———, *The Social Compact, Exemplified in the Constitution of the Commonwealth of Massachusetts; with Remarks on the Theories of Divine Right of Hobbes and of Filmer, and the Counter Theories of Sidney, Locke, Montesquieu, and Rousseau, concerning the Origin and Nature of Government,* a lecture delivered before the Franklin Lyceum at Providence, R. I., November 25, 1842 (Providence: Knowles and Vose, 1842). 32 pp.

———, *Two Lectures on the Bequest of James Smithson to the United States of America, for the Increase and Diffusion of Knowledge among Men,* Lecture I, before the Mechanic Apprentices Library Association, November 14, 1839 (Boston, 1839), newspaper cutting located in Harvard University Library.

Bobbé, Dorothie, *Mr. and Mrs. John Quincy Adams* (New York: Minton, Balch, 1930). 310 pp.

Bowers, Claude G., *The Party Battles of the Jackson Period* (Boston and New York: Houghton Mifflin, 1922). 506 pp.

Brown, Everett Somerville, ed., *The Missouri Compromises and Presidential Politics, 1820–1825.* From the Letters of William Plumer, Junior, Representative from New Hampshire (St. Louis: Missouri Historical Society, 1926). 155 pp.

Clark, Bennett Champ, *John Quincy Adams* (Boston: Little, Brown, 1932). 437 pp.

Coleman, William, *Remarks and Criticisms on the Hon. John Quincy Adams's Letter to the Hon. Harrison Gray Otis* (Boston: Joshua Cushing, 1808). 62 pp.

Counts, George S., *The Prospects of American Democracy* (New York: John Day, 1938). 370 pp.

Cox, Samuel Hanson, *Interviews, Memorable and Useful,* from diary and memory reproduced (New York: Harper & brothers, 1855). 325 pp.

Cronin, John William, and Wise, W. Harvey, *A Bibliography of John Adams and John Quincy Adams* (Washington, D. C.: Riverford Publishing Company, 1935). 78 pp.

Dumond, Dwight Lowell, *A History of the United States* (New York: Henry Holt and Company, 1942). 882 pp.

Everett, Edward, *A Eulogy on the Life and Character of John Quincy Adams* (Boston: Dutton and Wentworth, 1848). 71 pp.

Ford, Worthington C., *John Quincy Adams, His Connection with the Monroe Doctrine (1823)* and with Charles Francis Adams, *Emancipation under Martial Law (1819–1842)* [Reprinted from the Proceedings of the Massachusetts Historical Society for January, 1902]. (Cambridge: J. Wilson and Son, 1902). 113 pp.

Ford, Worthington C., ed., *The Writings of John Quincy Adams* (New York: Macmillan, 1913–1917). 7 vols.

Jacobson, J. Mark, *The Development of American Political Thought* (New York: The Century Co., 1932). 723 pp.

Lovejoy, Joseph C. and Owen, *Memoir of the Rev. Elijah P. Lovejoy,* with an introduction by John Quincy Adams (New York: John S. Taylor, 1838). 382 pp.

MacIver, Robert M., *The Web of Government* (New York: Macmillan, 1947). 498 pp.

Morse, John Torrey, Jr., *John Quincy Adams* (Boston, New York: Houghton, Mifflin, 1883). 315 pp.

Nevins, Allan, *Ordeal of the Union* (New York: Charles Scribner's Sons, 1947). 2 vols.

Nevins, Allan, ed., *The Diary of John Quincy Adams, 1794–1845* (New York: Longmans, Green, 1919). 575 pp.

Parrington, Vernon Louis, *Main Currents in American Thought* (New York: Harcourt, Brace, 1930). 3 vols.

Potter, Kenneth, *The Hispanic-American Policy of John Quincy Adams, 1817–1825* (unpublished Ph.D. thesis, University of California, 1934). 355 numbered leaves.

Quincy, Josiah, *Memoir of the Life of John Quincy Adams* (Boston: Crosby, Nichols, Lee, 1860). 429 pp.

Richardson, James D., ed., *A Compilation of the Messages and Papers of the Presidents, 1789–1897* (Published by Authority of Congress, 1900). Vol. II.

Sabine, George H., *A History of Political Theory* (New York: Henry Holt, 1937). 797 pp.

Schlesinger, Arthur M., Jr., *The Age of Jackson* (Boston: Little, Brown, 1943). 577 pp.

Seward, William Henry, *Life and Public Services of John Quincy Adams, Sixth President of the United States* (New York and Auburn: Miller, Orton, and Mulligan, 1856). 355 pp.

II

PERIODICALS

"The Adams Family," *Quarterly Review*, 237 (April, 1922), 298–312.

Adams, John Quincy, "Letter to Abigail Adams, Revol, May 12, 1814," *Proceedings of the American Antiquarian Society*, New Series, 23 (April 9, 1913–October 15, 1913), 168–169.

———, "Letter to Abigail Adams, St. Petersburg, October 24, 1812," *Proceedings of the American Antiquarian Society*, New Series, 23 (April 9, 1913–October 15, 1913), 123.

———, "Letter to John Adams, St. Petersburg, November 5, 1812," *Proceedings of the American Antiquarian Society*, New Series, 23 (April 9, 1913–October 15, 1913), 123–125.

———, "Letter to Abigail Adams, St. Petersburg, February 18, 1813," *Proceedings of the American Antiquarian Society*, New Series, 23 (April 9–October 15, 1913), 143–145.

———, "Letter to Abigail Adams, St. Petersburg, January 17, 1814," *Proceedings of the American Antiquarian Society*, New Series, 23 (April 9–October 15, 1913), 163–165.

———, "Letters of John Quincy Adams to Alexander Hill Everett," *American Historical Review*, 11, No. 2 (January, 1906), 88–116.

———, "Letters to Thomas Boylston Adams . . . ," *Proceedings of the Massachusetts Historical Society*, Second Series, X, 1895, 1896 (Boston, 1896), 374–392.

———, "Speech delivered at North-Bridgewater, on Wednesday, November 6th, 1844," Boston *Courier*, November 11, 1844.

Griswold, A. Whitney, "The Agrarian Democracy of Thomas Jefferson,"

The American Political Science Review, XLI (August, 1946), 657–681.

Tatum, Edward H., ed., "Ten Unpublished Letters of John Quincy Adams, 1796–1837," *The Huntington Library Quarterly,* IV, No. 3 (April, 1941), 369–385.

Wickwar, W. Hardy, "Foundations of American Conservatism," *The American Political Science Review,* XLI (December, 1947), 1105–1117.

III

OFFICIAL AND GOVERNMENT PUBLICATIONS

National Archives, Record Group No. 59, General Records of the Department of State, Vol. 2, Series, *Consular Instructions,* Vol. 2.

National Archives, Records of the Department of State, *Diplomatic Instructions,* All Countries, Vols. 8–10.

State Department, *Notes to Foreign Legations,* Vols. 2–3.

U. S. Congress, *Annals of Congress,* 8th Cong., 1st sess., to 10th Cong., 1st sess.

———, *Congressional Globe,* 23rd Cong., 1st sess., to 30th Cong., 1st sess.

———, *Register of Debates,* 22nd Cong., 1st sess., to 24th Cong., 2nd sess.

———, House, Committee on Foreign Affairs. *China and Sandwich Islands,* 27th Cong., 3rd sess., H. Rept. 93 (1843). 3 pp.

———, House, *Report of the Secretary of State upon Weights and Measures,* 16th Cong., 2nd sess., H. Doc. 109 (Washington, 1821). 245 pp.

———, House, *Report from Select Committee on the Message of the President relating to the Bequest of James Smithson,* 26th Cong., 1st sess., H. Rept. 277. 155 pp.

———, House, 25th Cong., 3rd sess., H. Doc. 11, Executive. 18 pp.

Index

Abolition, 123
academic freedom, 169
Adams, Abigail, 6, 7
Adams, Brooks, 4, 49, 59, 108, 171
Adams, John, 7, 186
Adams, John Quincy
  ability, 60
  ambition, 57
  ambition for Presidency, 238
  appointment as Minister Resident to
    The Netherlands, 11
  appointment as minister to Prussia,
    12
  appointment as minister to Russia, 18
  appointment as minister to the Court
    of St. James, 27
  appointment as Secretary of State,
    29
  attitude toward mankind, 84
  bar, admittance to, 10
  career as member of House of Repre-
    sentatives, 40
  commencement speech of, 9
  as a "conscience" Whig, 270
  as a constitutionalist, 222
  death, 45
  economic forces, grasp of, 116
  economy, attitude toward, 31
  empiricism, 332
  father of (see John Adams), 7, 10,
    186
  Federalism, 240
  general welfare, 148
  human sympathy, 55
  as interpreter of European affairs,
    19
  Locke, indebtedness to, 97-98, 327-
    30
  Memoirs of, 7, 59
  mother of (see Abigail Adams), 6, 7
  parents of, 6

  personality, 31, 52, 54; as a legisla-
    tor, 54
  philosophy of, 4, 5, 327
  as political theorist, 265
  as Puritan, 10, 100
  puritanism, 66
  republicanism, 66
  as scientist, 4
  sense of duty, 61, 63
  sense of rectitude, 51
  Supreme Court, offer of appointment
    by Madison, 21
Adams, Henry, 108
Adams, Thomas Boylston, 12
Adams, William, 23
Age of Reason, 260
agrarian democracy, 263, 265
agrarian interests, 103, 115
agriculture, 110, 117
Alexander I (Emperor of Russia), 19,
  133, 281
Alien and Sedition Laws, 164
American government, 205, 209
American Philosophical Society, 82
American Revolution, 7, 97, 101, 141,
  154, 196, 209, 211, 318
American system, 79, 134, 166, 193,
  308
Amistad case, 168
Amsterdam, 8
Anglo-Saxons, 123
Annals of Congress, 5
Anti-Federalist Party, 261
Antimasonic Party, 44, 45, 58, 269
Antimasons, 269
Aquinas, St. Thomas, 327
aristocracy, 9, 104, 108, 109, 170, 171
Articles of Confederation, 214, 215
Atherton resolution, 154
authority
  paternal, 160

balance, 106
balance of power, 17; European, 307, 309
balance of powers, 222
Bancroft, George, 34
Bank of the United States, 43, 120, 220, 267
Bayard, James A., 22
bellicosity, Adams's, 314
Bentham, Jeremy, 108, 143, 234, 330, 332
Benton, Senator Thomas Hart, 50, 151, 320
bicameralism, 202, 234
Biddle, Nicholas, 43
Bill of Rights, 164, 168
Blackstone, Sir William, 156
books, 114
Bourbons, 26
Boylston Professorship of Rhetoric and Belles Lettres, 18
Braintree, Massachusetts, 7
British Commonwealth, 141
brotherly love, 75, 77
Burke, Edmund, 90
Burr, Aaron, 39

Calhoun, John C., 36, 332
Canning, Stratford, 282
Castlereagh, Lord, 28
change, 84, 129, 135
Chase, Samuel, impeachment and trial of, 17
Chesapeake, 15, 17
Christianity, 75, 279
Christian nations, community of, 78
Christian principles as the source of constitutional law, 76
Cincinnati, Adams's visit, 45
Cincinnati Astronomical Society, 45
civil liberties, 164
civil liberty
  religious basis of, 169
civil society, 89
civil war and slavery, 126, 127
Clark, Bennett Champ, 4
classes, 104, 105, 107
Clay, Henry, 23, 239
"clear and present danger" test, 164
coalition, 183
colonial system, 317
colonies, 323
Colonization Society, 323
Columbia, 152

commerce, 117
commercial relations
  "liberal" principles of, 276
common sense, rules of, 328-329
community, 331
community consensus, 194
community of nations, 78
confederacy, 222
Congress, 175, 248
  executive papers, power to call for, 236
  investigating committees, power of, 251
  quality of, 249
Congressional Globe, 5
Congressional power in the United States, 288
Congress of Vienna
  Adams's views of results of, 33
consent, 95, 178
Constant, Benjamin, 20
constituent power, 157
Constitution, 99, 112, 143, 147, 149, 164, 177, 199, 210, 214, 215, 216, 217, 219, 221, 227, 229, 230, 231
  amending power, 229
  broad construction by Adams, 226
  commerce power, 228
  emancipate slaves, power to, 228
  implied powers, 225
  recognition, power of, 244
Constitution
  States' rightists, 226
  strict constructionists, 226
  as superior law, 224, 231, 248
  tariffs, 227
  taxation, power of, 227
  war, power to declare, 243
constitutional change, 156
Constitutional Convention, 9, 10
constitutions, 107, 130, 192
  nature of, 194
  safeguards, 161
  written, 193, 223
Continental System, 284
conventions, 185
Crawford, William, 32, 39, 238
Cuba, 300

Dana, Francis, 8
"deal," charges of, between Clay and Adams, 239
Declaration of Independence, 77, 91, 97, 101, 118, 125, 212, 213, 214, 216

delegation of power, 165
demagogy, 259
democracy, 91, 111, 113, 171, 172, 173, 176, 182
de Neuville, Hyde, 36
Denmark, 8
despotism, 313
de Staël, Madame, 20
diplomacy, 282, 286
diplomacy, art of, 29
diplomat, 29
diplomatic correspondence, index for, 286
diplomatic posts, Adams's views of, 285
distribution of power, 165
Duncan, Alexander, 175
"Duplicate Letters," 239
duty, 72

economy, 144
education, 66, 144, 145
  scientific, 66
Edwards, Ninion, 151
elections, 170, 179, 242
electioneering, 174, 242
emancipation, 229
Emancipation Proclamation, 229
Embargo, 18
Embargo (Jefferson's), 117, 153, 182, 219
empire, 320
empiricism, 73, 330
equalitarianism, 332
equality, 76, 159
Erving, George William, 30
  letter of instruction to, 30
Everett, Edward, 6
evolutionary change, 131
Executive (United States), 188
executive, 187, 197, 198, 199
"executive government," 199
executive leadership, 249, 288
executive power, 199
  in the United States, 288

faction, 185
faith, 81
family compact, 94
Federal Government, 102
federalism, 170, 204, 254
Federal Jacobinism, 257
Federalist Party, 14, 15, 16, 99, 182, 183, 188, 219, 257

charges of treasonable projects, 258
federative power, 243
feudalism, 210
Filmer, Sir Robert, 196
fishing rights of New England, 24
foreign policy, control of, 199
Franklin, Benjamin, 8
France, 161, 295
Frederick the Great, 66
freedom, 163
freedom of the press, 167
freedom to exchange ideas, 169
Freemasonry, 258, 269
free trade, 119
French Revolution, 12, 17, 106, 132, 135, 156, 159, 198, 209, 296

"gag" rule, 42
Gallatin, Albert, 22
Gambier, Lord, 23
general welfare, 166, 331
Germany, 8
Ghent
  Adams member of United States peace commission, 22
  peace, negotiations of, 24
  Peace of, 314
Gibbon, Edward, 75
God, 68, 75
Goulbourn, Henry, 23
government, 74, 89, 139, 191
  balance in, 205
  definition of, 140
  despotical, 223
  mixed systems, 170
  origins of, 135, 140
  power of, 155, 198
  purpose of, 142
  purpose and function of, 4
  right of, 155
  scope of, 155
government planning, 146
Great Britain, 8, 311
  Anglophobia (of Adams), 20, 24, 28, 292, 293, 311
  commercial rivalry, 119
  constitution, 194
  foreign policy leading to War of 1812, 20
  Monroe Doctrine, relation to, 299
  Parliament, 211
  sea power of, 24, 28
Grotius, Hugo, 280

habeas corpus, 168
The Hague, 11
Harvard University, 6, 9, 18, 267
Henshaw, David, 53
Hill, Isaac, 174
Hobbes, Thomas, 93, 313, 328
Holland, 11, 163, 197
Holmes, Oliver Wendell, 165
Holy Alliance, 33-34, 285, 304
Hoover, Herbert, 139
House of Representatives, 251
    Adams asked if he will stand for
      election, 39
human nature, 82
human perfectibility, 77, 128
Hume, David, 74, 163

immortality, 75
imperialism, 317, 319
implied powers, 147
Indians, 121-22
internal improvements, 74, 77, 101,
    116, 126, 128-29, 146, 148, 149, 150,
    151, 152, 154, 161, 166, 220, 227,
    263
    aesthetic component, 147
international law, 72, 275, 278, 279
Irish Catholics, 78
isolationism, 307, 308

Jackson Administration, 39
    French crisis, 43
Jackson, Andrew, 30, 32, 35, 39, 139,
    150, 170, 266
    charges of a "deal" between Adams
      and Clay, 38, 266
Jacobinism, 159
Jacobins, 133
Jay, John, 8
Jefferson Administration, 12, 13, 18
Jefferson, Thomas, 8, 30, 220, 242, 261,
    264
Jesuits, 160
Jesus Christ, 75
Jews, 122
Johnson, Louisa Catherine (Mrs. John
    Quincy Adams), 12
judicial review, 231
judiciary, 203, 231, 252, 253
    as "coordinate branch," 253
    appointments to, 253
justice, 190, 191

"Kinderhook Democracy," 175
King, Rufus, 260
Koutouzof, Admiral, 310

Lafayette, 26, 135
law of nations, 276
legislation, 74
legislative power, 249
legislative process, 176
legislature, 187
    power to insist upon transmission of
      executive papers, 201
    tyranny of, 202
legitimacy, 178
Leopard, 15, 17
"Letter to Andrew Stevenson . . .
    July 11, 1832," 227
Leyden, University of, 8
liberal arts, 80
liberty, 83, 159, 163, 165, 170, 190
Locke, John, 89, 93, 327
Louis XVIII, 26
Louisiana, 16, 96, 156, 186

MacMorrogh, Dermott, 74
Madison, James, 18
majority, 160
manufacturing, 116, 117, 153
manufacturing interests, 103, 151
Marshall, John, 259
Massachusetts, Senate of, 13
Mayflower Compact, 93
Mazzei, 13
merit system, 188
Middleton, Henry, 33
militarism, 218
military power, 161, 246
Mill, John Stuart, 8
minority rights, 160
Mississippi, rights to navigation of, 24-
    25
Missouri Compromise, 126, 217
"the mob," 83
monarchy, 108, 180, 195, 196, 218, 246
money, 114
Monroe Doctrine, 34, 299, 300, 304,
    309
Monroe, James, 19, 32
Montesquieu, Charles, Baron de, 280
moral law, 156
moral order, 329
moral system, 191
most-favored-nation principle, 307

Napoleon I, 20, 27, 159, 196
nation
  as a moral entity, 217
  as a "moral person," 275, 276
national character, 213
national debt, 151
national ethos, 320
nationalism, 23, 25, 98, 144, 255, 317, 332
  romantic quality, 332
National Republican Party, 44, 268
natural law, 66, 67, 190, 278
  departures from, 68
natural reason, 190
natural right, 72
nature, state of, 194
naval academy, 247
naval power, 258
navy, 14, 28, 118, 153, 247
Negroes, 123
Nelson, Hugh, 30
neutrality, 21, 119, 301, 302, 308, 309
neutral zone, proposal of, between the United States and Canada, 25
New England, 163
Nicaraguan canal, 152
Non-importation Act, 186
nullification, 99, 220

obedience, 95
oligarchy, 170, 171

Paine, Thomas, 20, 108, 132, 156, 172, 260
Paris, 8
Parsons, Theophilus, 9, 66, 257
parties, 15, 71, 73, 91, 182, 184, 190, 264
  caucuses, 240
  conventions, 240
party discipline, 187
paternal authority, 94
peace, 316
Peter the Great, 152
Pensacola, Andrew Jackson's taking of, 35
petition, right of, 41, 41-42
petitions, 115
Pichegru, General, 11
Pickering, Judge John, 16
Pickering, Timothy, 13, 16
planting aristocracy, 263
planter class, 104

Plato, 141
Plumer, William, 99
Plymouth Colony, 93
politics, 40, 62, 256
popular consent, 202
popular interests, 106
popular sovereignty, 140, 143, 155
population, heterogeneity, 222
poverty, 101
power, 144
Presidency, 179, 237, 248
  Adams's views, 240, 242, 244
  contest for, during Monroe's second term, 36
President
  appointing power, recess, 235
  censorial power of, 245
  foreign affairs, power in, 235
  power to control funds for foreign missions, 288
press, 167
Prevost, J. B., 283
principle, 71
private property, 70, 105, 110, 111, 112, 113
progress, 73
property
  natural rights in, 166
property rights, 111
protective tariff, 228
Prussia, Adams's observation of, 22
public good, 82
public lands, 151
public opinion, 172, 178
Puritanism, 6

Quadruple Alliance, 285

race, 88, 121, 123
reason, 69, 81
recognition, power of, 200
Reformation, 78, 95
The Register of Debates, 5
religion, 68, 70
religious liberty, 79
religious test, 74
Report on Manufactures, 38
Report on Weights and Measures, 81
representation, 180, 181, 202
republic, 153
"Republican Hemisphere," 291
republicanism, 180, 195
Republican Party, 261

republican spirit, 134
retribution, 75, 191
revolution, 90, 96, 97, 131, 133
    American type, 135
    and despotism, 133
Revolutionary Era, 156
Rhett, Robert Barnwell, 175
right, 144
rights, 178
right of petition, 176
rights, prescriptive, 108, 110
Rights of Man, 132
Rio del Norte, 32
Roman Catholic Church, 78
Romanzoff, Count, 19
Roosevelt, Franklin D., 139
Rousseau, Jean Jacques, 90, 95, 131, 172, 331
Rush-Bagot Agreement (1818), 27
Russell, Jonathan, 23, 239
Russia, 297

Sabine River, 32
St. Petersburg, 8
Scandinavia, 11
Schlesinger, Arthur M., Jr., 256
science, 63, 73, 80
sea power, 24, 28
Secretaryship of State, 57
sectionalism, 214
self-defense, 190
Seminole War, 267
Senate, United States, 13
    confirmation of subordinate officials, 245
    interests representing, 250
    treaties, alterations of, 289
separation of powers, 234, 236, 248
Siéyès, Abbé, 192
Silesia, 12
slaveholding class, 126
slavery, 41, 56, 120, 121, 123, 124, 160, 165, 220
    and the Constitution, 125
slave trade, 154
Smith, Senator John, expulsion case, 51
Smithson, James, 81, 148
Smithsonian fund, 52
Smyth, General Alexander, 32
social change, 88, 128
social cohesion (see social solidarity), 100
social compact, 89, 92, 93, 142, 329
social contract, 89, 92, 93, 142

social obligation attached to wealth, 112
social order, 88
social solidarity, 90, 100
social stability, 135
social unity, 100
society, 89
Socrates, 72
South Carolina Convention, 255
sovereignty, 156, 158, 178
"spoils" system, 188
standing army, 246
state, 139
state sovereignty, 214
States' rights, 254
status quo ante bellum, 24
statute law, 223
suffrage, 129
    tax and property qualifications, 95
Sweden, 8

tariff, 42
tenure bills, 245
Texas, annexation of, 42
Thompson, Waddy, 32
treaties, 278
treaty-making power, 68
Treaty with Spain (February 22, 1819), 36
truth, 73
Tuyl, Baron, 34, 304
tyranny, 193

unicameralism, 202, 233
Union, 14, 102, 213, 216, 219, 220
unitary government, 205
United States, 67
    expansion of, 317
    government of, 84, 233, 308
        balance of powers, 233
        separation of powers, 233
        treaty power, 224, 225
        tripartite arrangement, 237
    military and naval power of, 315
    as nucleus of a general American system, 321
    population of, 25
United States *v.* Cinque, 63
"universal monarchy," 307
urban population, 115
urban society, 101
usages, 278
uti possed itis, 24

Van Buren, Martin, 39, 174
  views on John Quincy Adams, 64
Vattel, 280

Walsh, Robert Jr., 37
war, 311, 315
  abolition of, 311
  aversion for (Adams's), 312
  power to declare, 200
war experience, value of, 316

Washington, D. C., burning of, 314
Washington, George, 132, 145
Webster, Daniel, 150, 245, 253
Weed, Thurlow, 185
Wellesley, Marquis of, 24
West Point, 81, 145
Whig Party, 44, 270
Wickwar, W. Hardy, 223, 230, 231
working class, 101, 113, 115
World of Nations, 275